MW01166358

DYNAMICAL HIERARCHICAL CONTROL

DYNAMICAL HIERARCHICAL CONTROL

MADAN G. SINGH
Professor of Control Engineering
UMIST, Manchester, England

REVISED EDITION

1980

NORTH-HOLLAND PUBLISHING COMPANY
AMSTERDAM • NEW YORK • OXFORD

ISBN: 0 444 85488 6

First edition 1977
Revised edition 1980

Published by
North-Holland Publishing Company,
Amsterdam, New York, Oxford

Sole distributors for the U.S.A. and Canada:
Elsevier North-Holland, Inc.
52 Vanderbilt Avenue
New York, N.Y. 10017

Library of Congress Cataloging in Publication Data

Singh, Madan G
Dynamical hierarchical control.

Bibliography: p.
1. Automatic control. 2. Control theory.
I. Title.
TJ213.S4744 629.8'312 77-22543

PRINTED IN THE NETHERLANDS

To Anne-Marie

P R E F A C E

Although Large Systems Theory has been actively studied for over a decade with pioneering work by Mesarovic, Macko, Lasdon, Lefkowitz, Pearson, Takahara, Titli, Tamura and others, the theory at least for large interconnected dynamical systems has been largely inaccessible to the Engineers concerned with the design of hierarchies for the solution of practical problems. There are two main reasons for this, the first being the somewhat abstract nature of earlier works whilst the second is the fact that the work is described in papers which are relatively scattered in the literature. In this book an attempt is made to bring together the practically applicable techniques which can be used for synthesising hierarchical structures for the control and optimisation of large interconnected dynamical systems. The book is aimed at a wide audience ranging from practising Engineers to Graduate Students in Systems Engineering.

The bulk of the book provides a set of design techniques for synthesising hierarchical structures but before starting with the mathematical treatment, Chapter I deals with a number of fundamental questions ; what are hierarchies ? how do they arise "naturally" in certain systems and is it desirable to generate them to solve problems of control and optimisation for large dynamical systems ? The rest of the book is divided into 4 parts each consisting of one or two chapters. In Part I the techniques for hierarchical optimisation yielding open loop control are developed for both linear and non-linear systems. Some of these techniques are extended in Part II to provide closed loop control.

Whilst Part I and II deal with methods which yield optimal control, in Part III, some suboptimal methods are considered which utilise the structural peculiarities of certain systems to provide near optimal control. The ideas are illustrated on many practical problems including a detailed study of a hot steel rolling mill. Finally, in Part IV, the practical case of systems subject to stochastic disturbances is considered.

To emphasise the practical utility of the methods developed in the book, simulation studies are described of the application of the methods to practical problems taken from diverse fields ranging from Traffic Control Systems and Environmental Systems to more traditional Engineering Systems.

In the main text, it is assumed that the reader is reasonably familiar with standard single level functional optimisation techniques such as dynamic programming and Pontryagin's Maximum Principle as well as the Theory of Lagrange Duality, although in the appendices, a brief overview of these techniques is given for the sake of completeness.

Madan G. SINGH

Toulouse, December, 1976

PREFACE TO THE REVISED EDITION

Since the first publication of this monograph on the optimisation and control of Large Scale Systems using hierarchical techniques, there has been a resurgence of interest in the subject. A number of new results have been obtained. The main new results are in two different areas. The first are in the area of optimisation techniques for non-linear systems. Here, the field has reached sufficient maturity for the author to attempt a real unification of the concepts and results. Thus, major modifications have been made to chapter 3 to provide a coherent and easy to read review of the subject. The convergence proofs have also been unified and these are now put into the new appendices 3 and 4. Thus the thread of the main argument can be pursued more easily.

The second area where a number of new results have been obtained is on hierarchical estimation and control. Thus chapter 8 has beeen slightly modified and a new chapter 9 has been included to describe this work on the optimal multi-level filter,stochastic optimal control and on the dual problems of estimation and control. Thus, in all, a third of the book has been modified and considerably enlarged to bring it upto date.

The author is grateful to a number of his former students and colleagues whose work contributed to this revised volume. In particular, the author is grateful to Dr. M.F. Hassan of the University of Cairo in Egypt and Professor A. Titli of the LAAS-CNRS in Toulouse, France for a fruitful collaboration.

Finally, the author is grateful to Mrs. Tongue, Mrs. Butterworth, Mrs. Waterworth, Miss Brown and Miss McLeod for their willing secretarial help which made this new edition at all possible.

Madan G. Singh
Manchester, 1980.

CONTENTS

CHAPTER 1

INTRODUCTION

In this monograph we describe the "state of the art" of hierarchical control for large scale interconnected dynamical systems. To provide a basis for the discussion of the synthesis procedures for generating hierarchical structures which forms the bulk of this book, we examine in this chapter a number of fundamental questions : What are hierarchical structures ? Why are they so common ? Are there any specific reasons why they are more (or less) desirable than other structures ? Can such structures be generated artificially for solving problems of optimisation and control in large scale systems and is it advantageous to do so ? Although the discussion in this chapter is somewhat heuristic, it is tacitly assumed in subsequent chapters that hierarchical structures are indeed useful structures to synthesise and the book attempts to provide concrete synthesis procedures in the context of practical problems in the fields of Transportation Systems, Environmental Systems and more traditional Engineering Systems.

1. WHAT IS A HIERARCHY ?

We are all familiar with hierarchies since they pervade so much of our daily lives. But what characterises them ? The simplest possible hierarchy has two levels as shown in Fig. 1. Such a hierarchy could arise for example in an office where the first level consists of the staff members doing their own particular jobs and the supervisor (or coordinator) ensuring that the work load on each staff member is acceptable and that the overall objective of the office is fulfilled according to a suitable schedule. This schedule itself is determined through an

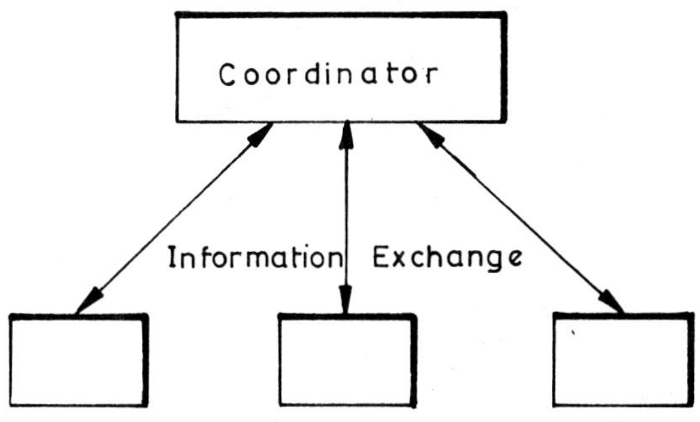

Fig. 1. : A typical two level hierarchy

iterative information exchange in which the coordinator defines a target for each staff member taking into account the interactions with the others whilst the staff member lets him know whether he can fulfil the target or not. If he cannot, the supervisor suggests an improved target taking into account those of the other workers and this process continues until an acceptable target is achieved for each of the staff members and which also fulfils the target of the office. It should be noted that whereas the higher level is interested in a longer term fulfilling of targets, the lower level is concerned with the more day to day running of the office.

Having described in a very rudimentary form a particularly simple hierarchy, let us now try to see if there are any fundamental properties which this hierarchy possesses and which it perhaps has in common with other hierarchies. The following properties might be proposed :

1. Hierarchies consist of decision making units arranged in a pyramid where at each level, a number of such units operate in parallel. Fig. 2 shows the pyramid structure.

2. Hierarchical structures exist in systems which have an overall goal and the goals of all the decision makers who constitute the hierarchy are in harmony.

3. There is an iterative information exchange between the decision making units on the various levels of the hierarchy with a precedence for the information going down which is treated as a command by the lower levels which try to obey it if they possibly can.

4. The time horizon of interest increases as one goes up the hierarchy.

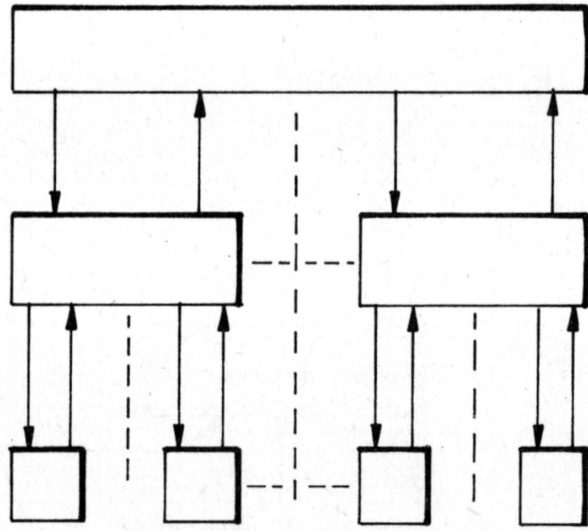

Fig. 2 : A Pyramid Structure

If we go back to our simple office hierarchy, it is clear that these properties are fundamental to it ; it has a pyramid structure (Fig. 1), an overall goal (efficiency perhaps), iterative information exchange (between staff and supervisor) and increasing time horizon of interest as one goes up the hierarchy.

Bearing these properties in mind, let us move on from our simple two level hierarchy to a more complex one : a general production process as shown in Fig. 3. Consider a company producing one industrial product. The objective of the system is perhaps the maximisation of profit or the production of a high quality product or the welfare of the workers or the welfare of the managers or some combination of these factors. Let us start at the top of the production hierarchy. This level (Top Management) decides overall policy by examining market forecasts and defining an appropriate production schedule to meet the forecasted demand.

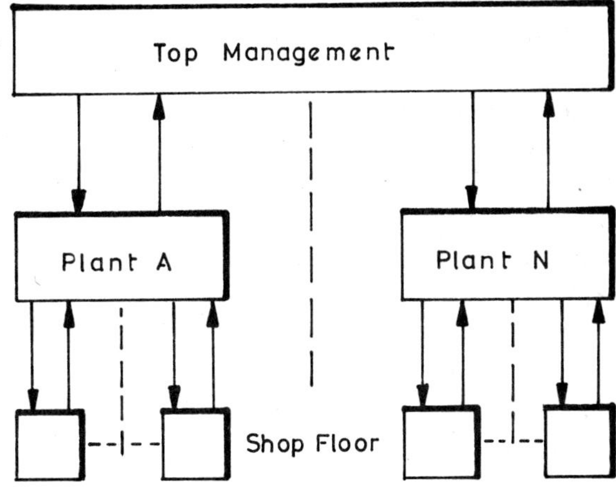

Fig. 3 : A Production Hierarchy

The top level schedule is thus a fairly coarse one since it merely fixes output targets. The next stage is to find out if, given the resources allocated by the Top Management, it is possible actually to satisfy these targets. This is clearly an iterative process where the managers of the various plants which actually produce the product (level II) receive information about their individual plants' inputs and send back estimates as to whether they can satisfy their part of the schedule. This information exchange is iterative since the individual plant managers are each concerned with their own plant only and it is the job of the Top Management to coordinate the flow between the various plants. Top Management does this by sending down orders for each plant and the plant manager indicates if the plant can carry them out or not given its own constraints. If it cannot do so, the plant manager tells Top Management the degree of imbalance between what it can achieve and what is required of it. This information is received from each plant, collated together and used to modify the orders so as to reduce successively the imbalance for each of the plant managers.* Note that although the Top Management has a long time horizon (say a year), the plant managers operate on a much more day to day basis since unknown disturbances can affect their schedules and require further iterative exchanges between this level and a level below it which is actually concerned with the fulfilling of the local managements' targets. It is possible to go down in this way to the shop floor where the actual production takes place.

---

* It should be noted that we are considering somewhat idealised hierarchies where there is no real conflict between the goals of the subsystems and the overall systems goal, i.e. they operate as a team. It is true that in real human hierarchies conflicts often do arise in which case much of the analysis of this book would have to be reconsidered. It would be interesting to analyse these real life situations by using a combination of game theoretic concepts to take into account the conflict in goals and team theoretic for the overall system. However, such a study is outside the scope of the present work.

If we go back to the four properties which characterised our simple hierarchy, we can see that these are also to be found in this much more complex example. However, there is one very important difference between our office hierarchy and the production process just defined ; in our first example, it was not absolutely clear why there should be a hierarchy since the job of the supervisor could have been performed by communication amongst the staff members. As the number of staff members increases however, communication between them becomes much more difficult and less efficient,and it is when the system reaches a certain size that a coordinator becomes essential (i.e. a hierarchy arises) if efficiency is to be maintained. This leads us on to the next question :

2. WHY DO HIERARCHIES EXIST ?

The hierarchies with which most people are familiar are found primarily in socioeconomic systems. In order to try to understand the circumstances under which they arise, let us consider the case of five people shipwrecked on a desert island. Is a hierarchy likely to emerge here[≠] ? If we assume that the goal of the five men is to ensure that the maximum number among them survive, then we have a common goal which is of course one of the requirements for the existence of a hierarchy. If we then go on to the organisation of the five, however, it may well be useful for them to operate in a decentralised way, in parallel with each other[*], but it is not necessarily desirable that one of them should do nothing but coordinate the other four. Thus here, although we could envisage a decentralised structure, the actual control could just as well be carried out if they worked as a team with each member either using some fixed strategy or communicating with all the other members. To understand what we mean by a fixed strategy, suppose that man 1 has been given the job of fishing. The team knows that they can consume n fish per day and that fish left over at the end of the day will go bad. So his fixed strategy could be to stop when n fish have been caught. Similar fixed strategies could be generated for the other men. If a sufficiently good fixed strategy could be developed, there is no reason why the whole system should not be able to operate as a team even if the number of people became much larger. Except in very special cases, however, successful fixed strategies are very difficult to generate in real life situations and communication with other members of the group generally becomes necessary. Here we come to the nub of the matter. As the number of decision makers becomes large, it becomes progressively more inefficient to transmit information between them for coordination and it becomes necessary to have a specialist coordination function, i.e. if our number of survivors became say 100, it might be much more efficient for m of them to perform the various tasks necessary for survival in parallel and the remaining (100-m) of them to coordinate their activities as opposed to all one hundred of them communicating with each other all the time. Thus the main reason why hierarchies arise is that decentralised systems having a particular goal are much too complex for one decision maker to control and it is too inefficient for parallel decision makers to communicate their interactions to each other.

Summing up these ideas, the reason why hierarchies arise are :

(a) The system having a definite goal is too complex for one decision maker to comprehend let alone control since decision makers have limited information handling capacities

---

* Since time flows sequentially, it is possible for them to do many more jobs in a given period of time if they do them in parallel.

≠ The author is grateful to Prof. Murray WONHAM of the University of Toronto for posing this problem.

(b) Since time flows sequentially, it is possible to perform more tasks in a given period of time if the jobs are done in parallel and this leads to parallel decision making by decentralised controllers.

(c) Decentralised decision makers need to coordinate their activities to satisfy the overall goal and it is more efficient to have a specialist coordination function and a hierarchy than constant communication* between all the decision makers since it increases the burden on each decision maker.

Now, in social systems, hierarchies have arisen as a response perhaps to the complexity of the decision making process in the decentralised situation and it would appear that they do serve a useful purpose in that the specialist coordination function leads to efficiency in the fulfilling of the goal at least in situations where the goal is clearly defined and genuinely shared by all members of the hierarchy. But can this idea be extended to systems other than in the socio-economic class where hierarchies have historically arisen. In other words, since most systems in Engineering, Environment, Ecology, etc. can be decomposed into a collection of interconnected subsystems, each of which, given the low price of mini-computers, can be controlled by a local decision maker (computer), is it possible to generate hierarchies for such systems ? In the rest of the book we attempt to answer this question by developing precise synthesis procedures for artificially generating hierarchies. In the rest of this chapter, on the other hand we consider the computational aspect of the problem of optimisation and control of large systems and examine whether it is advantageous to solve such problems by generating hierarchies.

3. THE NEED FOR HIERARCHICAL CONTROL AND OPTIMISATION OF LARGE DYNAMICAL SYSTEMS

Most large dynamical systems consist of interconnected subsystems. The general class of systems which will be considered in the rest of this monograph is shown in Fig. 4. This figure shows an idealised version of a system comprising many subsystems. For complex industrial processes, for example, the boxes in the figure could represent unit processes. The overall system has various interconnections between the subsystems. The interconnections shown here are not meant to describe any particular system but rather a fairly general class of industrial or other processes which transform a set of input or raw material streams to outputs or finished products.

Each subsystem has its own state, control and output vectors and the overall system's state and control vectors are defined combinations of these. Such a structure is quite general and can be used to describe most industrial and other processes. For example, in urban road traffic networks, the individual subsystems could be junctions with their own controls (traffic lights) and state vectors (queues on junction approaches). In steel rolling, the subsystems could be individual rolling stands, the local controls being the individual screw downs and the states being the thickness, temperature and certain metallurgical properties.

In the design and operation of the class of systems described above, few would dispute the need for at least approximate optimisation since it can lead to substantial economic savings. In the design stage, the objective is to determine

---

* It is possible to show (cf. Cole and Sage [1]) that under fairly mild conditions (e.g. existence of partially nested information structure in the hierarchy) the hierarchical organisation uses a minimal number of information channels (i.e. any additional channels are redundant). It has certainly a very much smaller number of channels than would be required in the team communication situation.

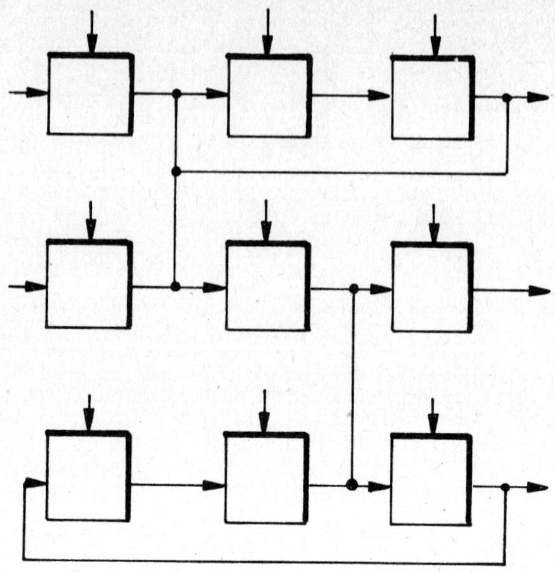

Fig. 4 : An Interconnected Dynamical System

a range of steady state operating conditions for the various subsystems. This can be done by extremising a suitable objective function subject to equality and inequality constraints. Because of the static nature of the design problem, the constraints are algebraic and the vast array of mathematical programming techniques can be brought to bear on the problem. If the number of variables is large, as is often the case for complex systems, there may be some computational difficulties because of the limited storage on digital computers and the solution process may be particularly time consuming. However, this problem can be tackled by multilevel static optimisation techniques, Lasdon [2] , Varaiya [3] , particularly since the existence of defined interconnected subsystems often leads to sparse matrices in the overall system description. This effectively takes care of the limited storage problem and since the analysis is off line, the excessive computation time is not a major problem as computer time is relatively cheap and with the advances in computer technology, it is getting cheaper every year.

A more difficult area of application of optimisation techniques for such large interconnected systems is in the operational or dynamic phase. The need for dynamic optimisation arises because the system state may differ from the desired precomputed steady state conditions. The fluctuations in the state may occur due to variations in the inputs, unwanted disturbances and plant parameter variations, etc. It may therefore be necessary to vary the control signals online in order to bring the state vector back to the desired precomputed levels. Substantial economic savings may be possible if the system is brought back to the desired levels in an "optimal" manner. Similarly it would be useful if the system states could be moved "optimally" from one set of steady state levels to another. Such a situation often arises when the output specification of the finished product is changed or the plant breaks down and has to be restarted. Here optimisation implies, as usual, the extremisation of a suitable functional of the state and control trajectories subject to constraints like system dynamics as well as hard inequality constraints on states and controls.

The optimisation of dynamical systems with large dimensional state vectors is possible, in principle, using well established methods such as Dynamic Programming [4] and Pontryagin's Maximum Principle [5], but increase in the number of variables introduces problems, in particular those which Bellman has termed "the curse of dimensionality". For a linear quadratic problem the dynamic optimisation of even a twenty variable system consumes much of the capacity of a medium sized computer, and for non-linear problems or linear problems with constraints 5-10 variables may be too many. For large scale industrial systems of practical interest , urban traffic networks or environmental systems, the number of variables may be so large that the amount of computation necessary for optimisation is prohibitive and all attempts at tackling the problem directly are subject to considerable difficulties. It is this "curse of dimensionality" that makes the direct on-line optimal control of large systems computationally unrealisable. In addition, since the state of the system changes continuously, there may be little time available for on-line dynamic optimisation.

The amount of computation necessary for dynamic optimisation increases very rapidly with the increase in the number of state variables. Even for the "linear quadratic" problem, the computational requirements increase cubically with system order. Since computers, like the human decision makers of the first part of this chapter, have limited information handling capacities,one is forced to consider decentralised optimisation. This is particularly so since (a) minicomputers are getting cheaper so that it will soon be possible to have individual minicomputers controlling the subsystems which exist in most systems and (b) each of the subsystems in an interconnected dynamical system is of considerably lower order than the overall system considered in an integrated way.

Thus we envisage a hierarchy of computers for the optimisation process where a number of computers (decision makers) operate in parallel solving the optimisation problem of each of the subsystems independently, and a higher level computer coordinates the local optimal solutions in an iterative fashion in order to achieve the overall optimum. Such a hierarchy bears close similarity to the human hierarchies considered in the beginning of this chapter and has arisen for similar reasons, i.e. the inability of any one computer to cope with the problem, leading to decentralisation and the complexity of the problem forcing one to use a specialist coordination function.

Aside from making the solution of large scale dynamical optimisation problems at all feasible, the hierarchical structure can also lead to actual computational savings if the hierarchical solution is considered as an alternative to the centralised solution (assuming now that the centralised solution is possible which for large systems is of course seldom true). These savings arise because the local computers have to solve only a low order problem thus providing an economy in computer storage. Also, if the lower level's computation is done in parallel and the number of iterations required for convergence to the optimum is not too large, there may well be a saving in computation time. In certain cases, there may be a saving in computation time even if the hierarchical solution is obtained using a single computer as opposed to a hierarchy of mini-computers. To see this, consider the simple "linear quadratic" problem. It is known that the computation time requirements for the solution of this problem vary cubically with system order. Let the overall system be of order n and let each of the N subsystems be of order n_i, i.e.

$$n = \sum_{i=1}^{N} n_i$$

Then the overall system's computation time requirements are n^3 and for the hierarchical solution, they are

$$m \left(\sum_{i=1}^{N} n_i^3 + k \right) = p$$

where m is the number of iterations to convergence, and k is the computation time of the coordinator. Hierarchical optimisation is able to yield computational savings on even a single computer if

$$n^3 > p$$

Methods developed in subsequent chapters will show that m and k are often small and since n_i corresponds to the order of the subsystem, $n \gg n_i$ so that

$$\sum_{i=1}^{N} n_i^3 \ll n^3$$

thus often leading to savings in computation time. In case one is able to use a system of mini-computers in parallel, the hierarchical solution only takes $m(n_i^{*3} + k)$ where n_i^* is the maximum subsystem order and this leads to further savings in computation time.

To sum up, it is quite plausible that hierarchical optimisation may yield computational savings in both storage and computer time thus making it attractive even for systems which are not large enough to preclude optimisation using one central computer.

Computational advantage, however, is not the only attraction of hierarchical structures in optimal control of large scale systems. There are advantages also in the installation, operation and modification of systems where hierarchical structures are used for the integrated optimisation and control. These advantages are :

(a) The system has a very flexible configuration ;

(b) It has high reliability since it is easy to add parallel redundant subsystems ;

(c) The cost of implementing the system is lower since

1. The software is simpler than for the integrated case ;
2. The same standard components can be used in many places ;

(d) The capacity of the system can be increased easily. This is important since large scale systems are usually built piecemeal and with the present approach , it is possible to ensure near optimal performance from the plant at any stage of operation.

Having discussed what hierarchies are, why they arise and the reasons why it may be useful to synthesise them for the control and optimisation of large interconnected dynamical systems,we devote the rest of this book to the development of procedures for the synthesis of such stuctures. The procedures developed are demonstrated on concrete examples taken from the fields of Transportation,Engineering and the Environment.The treatment is divided into four main parts each consisting of one or two chapters.In part I we deal with the problem of Open Loop Hierarchical Control. This is a classical problem which has been extensively treated by Mesarovic [6] , Pearson[7] , Lasdon[2] ,Sage [8] etc.We shed some new light on it, however by examining it in the context of solving practical problems.We develop algorithms for both linear and non-linear systems.The latter class of systems has not been adequately treated in the literature and we provide one of the first methods of solving such problems and unlike the methods proposed in the literature where little indication is given of their possible convergence, we give a precise convergence condition. We also develop a new, more practical approach to the control of non-linear systems. This uses the concept of a linear model which incorporates desired physical response characteristics and the non-linear system is made to follow this linear model. We also show ways of simplifying the solution of non-linear problems by hierarchical optimisation. For the "linear quadratic" problem, we describe all the currently available algorithms. We also provide definite guidelines on which ones are most suitable for solving large scale systems problems by showing simulation studies of realistic examples where they are compared. We develop all the algorithms in a practical context and demonstrate them on real life cases taken from the field of Traffic Systems and from the environmental field. The work described in this part is mainly drawn from the author's own work described in [13-25] as well as from works of Titli [9] , Sage [8] , Pearson [7] , Tamura [10, 11,] Takahara [12] , Mesarovic et al. [6] , etc.

Part II deals with the more practical problem of Closed Loop control for large scale systems. This problem has hardly been touched in the literature. We develop algorithms for both discrete time and continuous time closed loop control for the linear-quadratic problem [26, 29, 30, 31] as well as feedback control for non-linear systems [27] . For the linear-quadratic case, our examples are taken from the field of river pollution control [26] whilst for the non-linear case, they are taken from the power systems field [28] .

Whilst Part I and II deal with the optimal control problem for large scale systems, in Part III we direct our attention to a special structure which is very common in large scale systems and for which good suboptimal control can be generated. The structure is the one which arises when the subsystems are connected serially. We develop algorithms [32, 14] and demonstrate them on examples taken from river pollution control [13] and hot steel rolling [33] . The work described here is taken mainly from [13, 32, 33, 14] .

Finally, in Part IV we deal with the stochastic case. Here we describe optimal and suboptimal solutions of the filter problem and the parameter estimation problem for large scale systems.

We are now in a position to start with Part I, i.e. the development of synthesis procedures for Open Loop Control of large interconnected dynamical systems.

P A R T I

OPEN LOOP HIERARCHICAL CONTROL

In this first part of the book we begin our study of the problem of synthesising hierarchical structures for the control and optimisation of dynamical systems (which could be physical, social, economic, etc.) by examining those structures which yield open-loop control. These were the structures which were first studied by Pearson[7] , Mesarovic et al. [6] and they continue to be of great interest in the open literature. The kind of problem that is tackled is the following :

> Assume we have a dynamical system (for example a chemical plant or a national economy, etc.) which usually operates in some steady state. At some point in time it receives an unknown disturbance which takes the system from the given steady state to some other state which is known (possibly through measurement). The problem is to find a control which brings the system back to the steady state operating conditions in a finite period of time whilst minimising a suitable functional of the states and controls of the system.

We assume implicitly that the reader is familiar with standard functional optimisation techniques like the Maximum Principle, although we do give a brief overview of these techniques in the appendices for the sake of completeness.

We divide our treatment of the problem into two chapteurs : Chapter II where the system can be described by linear differential or difference equations and the cost function to be minimised is a quadratic function of the states and controls, and Chapter III where the system can only be described by non-linear differential or difference equations. In both cases, we describe the practically applicable methods that have been developed and illustrate them on concrete examples taken from the fields of Water Pollution, Traffic Control and other Engineering Systems.

CHAPTER II

OPEN-LOOP HIERARCHICAL CONTROL FOR "LINEAR-QUADRATIC" PROBLEMS

1. INTRODUCTION

In this chapter we study the problem of synthesising hierarchical structures for large interconnected dynamical systems where the system can be described by linear differential or difference equations and the cost function which defines the overall goal of the hierarchy is a quadratic function of the states and controls.

There are essentially two classes of synthesis procedures for solving the "linear-quadratic" problems treated in this chapter, i.e., the Infeasible and Feasible approaches. In the Infeasible methods, the system constraints are not satisfied at every iteration of the information exchange between the levels of the hierarchy, but are only satisfied at the optimum. In the Feasible approach, the constraints are satisfied at each iteration but in spite of the fact that one can terminate the iterative procedure at any point and still obtain a valid control, the approach is not very practical since it applies to a very limited class of problems*. Since in this book we are interested in practical, generally applicable methods, we will not discuss this approach here. The interested reader is referred to the excellent exposition by Pearson [7] .

The infeasible class of problems were first formulated in a precise form by Pearson [7] who interpreted the previous work of Mesarovic [6] , Lasdon [2] in the context of dynamical systems. In the first part of this chapter we interpret the work of Pearson and use his algorithms to solve problems of practical interest. In the case of discrete time systems, Lasdon's original work was extended by Tamura [34] who developed an elegant three level algorithm and who also obtained a solution for the significant practical case of systems with multiple delays in the states and controls as well as hard inequality constraints [10] . These algorithms are also described. The various approaches are demonstrated on significant examples taken from the fields of Traffic Control and River Pollution Control. An evaluation of the relative merits of some of the methods is also given.

2. PROBLEM FORMULATION

It is assumed that the overall system is a collection of N interconnected subsystems as shown in Fig. 1. For the ith subsystem,, $\underline{x}_i$ is an n_i dimensional state vector, $\underline{u}_i$ is an m_i dimensional control vector and $\underline{z}_i$ is an r_i dimensional vector of inputs which come in from the other subsystems. The subystem dynamics are assumed to be linear and could be represented by the following state space equations :

---

* The feasible approach only applies to the class of systems where there are at least as many controls as interaction variables.

$$\underline{\dot{x}}_i(t) = A_i\underline{x}_i(t) + B_i\underline{u}_i(t) + C_i\underline{z}_i(t) \tag{1}$$

with $\underline{x}_i(0) = \underline{x}_{i0}$

It is assumed that the vector of inputs $\underline{z}_i$ is a linear combination of the states of the N subsystems, i.e.

$$\underline{z}_i = \sum_{j=1}^{N} L_{ij}\,\underline{x}_j \tag{2}$$

In equation (2), note that we do not exclude the possibility of having i = j which represents simple feedback around the subsystem.

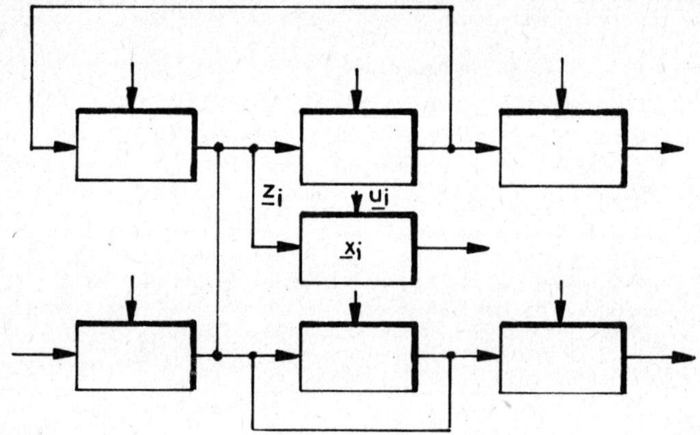

Fig. 1 : An Interconnected Dynamical System

It is desired to choose the controls $\underline{u}_1,\ldots,\underline{u}_N$ in order to minimise a cost function of the following kind ;

$$J = \sum_{i=1}^{N}\left(\frac{1}{2}\|\underline{x}_i(T)\|^2_{Q_i} + \int_0^T \frac{1}{2}\left[\|\underline{x}_i(t)\|^2_{Q_i} + \|\underline{u}_i\|^2_{R_i} + \|\underline{z}_i\|^2_{S_i}\right]dt\right) \tag{3}$$

subject to the constraints (1) and (2) where Q_i are positive semidefinite matrices and R_i, S_i are positive definite. $\|\underline{c}\|^2_L = \underline{c}^T L\underline{c}$.

If the interconnection relationship (2) is substituted back into equation (1) it is possible to obtain a standard overall description of the form

$$\underline{\dot{x}} = A\underline{x} + B\underline{u}$$

where $\underline{x} = \begin{bmatrix} \underline{x}_1 \\ \underline{x}_2 \\ \cdot \\ \cdot \\ \cdot \\ \underline{x}_N \end{bmatrix}$; $\underline{u} = \begin{bmatrix} \underline{u}_1 \\ \underline{u}_2 \\ \cdot \\ \cdot \\ \cdot \\ \underline{u}_N \end{bmatrix}$; A, B are full matrices

In the overall case it is difficult to interpret the physical significance of the quadratic term $\|\underline{z}_i\|^2_{S_i}$ since it can always be combined into the term $\|\underline{x}\|^2_Q$ in the case of the overall system. It is necessary to use this term, however, to avoid singularities as we shall discuss at the end of this section. The present formulation is taken from Pearson [7] who introduced this term but in section 9 we show that it is often possible to avoid using it [19, 20] . We begin our analysis with the "Goal Coordination" or "Interaction Balance" approach of Mesarovic [6] as specialised for "linear-quadratic" problems by Pearson [7].

2.1. The Goal Coordination Approach

The basis of the approach is that it is possible to convert the original minimisation problem into a simpler maximisation problem and then solve this problem using a two level iterative calculation structure of the kind envisaged in Chapter I. To do this, define a dual function $\phi(\underline{\lambda})$ where

$$\phi(\underline{\lambda}) = \min_{\underline{x},\,\underline{u},\,\underline{z}} \left\{ L(\underline{x}, \underline{u}, \underline{z}, \underline{\lambda}) \text{ subject to equation (1)} \right\} \tag{5}$$

where

$$L(\underline{x},\underline{u},\underline{z},\underline{\lambda}) = \sum_{i=1}^{N} \left\{ \frac{1}{2} \|\underline{x}_i(T)\|^2_{Q_i} + \int_0^T \left(\frac{1}{2} \|\underline{x}_i\|^2_{Q_i} + \frac{1}{2}\|\underline{u}_i\|^2_{R_i} + \frac{1}{2}\|\underline{z}_i\|^2_{S_i} + \underline{\lambda}^T (\underline{z}_i - \sum_{j=1}^{N} L_{ij}\, \underline{x}_j)\right) dt \right\} \tag{6}$$

where $\underline{\lambda}$ is an r dimensional vector of Lagrange multipliers. Here $L(\underline{x},\underline{u},\underline{z},\underline{\lambda})$ is the Lagrangian which has been formed in order to convert the original constrained optimisation problem into an unconstrained one. This has been done via the introduction of the Lagrange multipliers $\underline{\lambda}$, which are chosen in order to force satisfaction of the equality constraints (2). Now, as we discuss in the appendices, the theorem of strong Lagrange Duality [35] asserts that for cases like the one considered here where all the constraints are convex

$$\max_{\underline{\lambda}} \phi(\underline{\lambda}) = \min_{\underline{u}} J \tag{7}$$

i.e. an equivalent way of solving the problem of minimising J in equation (3) subject to the linear equality constraints given by equations (1) and (2) is to maximise the dual function $\phi(\underline{\lambda})$ w.r.t. $\underline{\lambda}$. This can be done within a two level structure of the type considered in Chapter I since from equation (6) for given $\underline{\lambda} = \underline{\lambda}^*$

$$L(\underline{x},\underline{u},\underline{z},\underline{\lambda}^*) = \sum_{i=1}^{N} \left\{ \frac{1}{2} \| \underline{x}_i(T)\|^2_{Q_i} + \int_0^T \left(\frac{1}{2} \|\underline{x}_i\|^2_{Q_i} + \frac{1}{2} \|\underline{u}_i\|^2_{R_i} + \frac{1}{2} \|\underline{z}_i\|^2_{S_i} + \underline{\lambda}_i^{*T} \underline{z}_i - \sum_{j=1}^{N} \underline{\lambda}_j^{*T} L_{ji}\, \underline{x}_i \right) dt \right\} = \sum_{i=1}^{N} L_i \tag{8}$$

i.e. the Lagrangian L is additively separable and can be decomposed into N independent sub Lagrangians, one for each subsystem. Thus for given $\underline{\lambda} = \underline{\lambda}^*$, which is treated as a known trajectory, it is possible to minimise the sub Lagrangian

$$L_i = \frac{1}{2}\|\underline{x}_i(T)\|^2_{Q_i} + \int_0^T \left(\frac{1}{2}\|\underline{x}_i\|^2_{Q_i} + \frac{1}{2}\|\underline{u}_i\|^2_{R_i} + \frac{1}{2}\|\underline{z}_i\|^2_{S_i} + \right.$$

$$\left. + \underline{\lambda}^{*T}_i \underline{z}_i - \sum_{j=1}^{N} \underline{\lambda}^{*T}_j L_{ji}\underline{x}_i\right)dt \tag{8a}$$

independently for the N subsystems where each subsystem's minimisation is subject to that subsystem's dynamical constraints given by equation (1). This enables us to obtain $\phi(\underline{\lambda}^*)$ in equation (5) and the $\phi(\underline{\lambda}^*)$ can be improved successively by an iterative exchange of information with a second level which improves $\phi(\underline{\lambda}^*)$ using the N independent first level minimisations. The actual mechanism for the improvement of $\phi(\underline{\lambda}^*)$ in order to maximise it relies on the fact that it is possible to write a simple expression for the gradient of $\phi(\underline{\lambda}^*)$ in terms of the solutions of the first level minimisations. In fact, the gradient is given by the error in the interconnection relationship, i.e.

$$\nabla\phi(\underline{\lambda})\Big|_{\lambda=\lambda^*} = \underline{z}_i - \sum_{j=1}^{N} L_{ij}\underline{x}_j = \underline{e}_i \qquad i = 1,2,\ldots, N \tag{9}$$

It is thus possible to envisage a two level hierarchical algorithm as shown in Fig. 2 where on level 1 for given $\underline{\lambda} = \underline{\lambda}^*$, supplied by the second level, L_i is minimised subject to the subsystem dynamic constraints and the resulting $\underline{x}_i$, $\underline{u}_i$ are sent back to level 2. At level 2, these vectors are collated and substituted into equation (9) to form the interconnection error

$$\underline{e} = \begin{bmatrix} \underline{e}_1 \\ \underline{e}_2 \\ \cdot \\ \cdot \\ \cdot \\ \underline{e}_N \end{bmatrix}$$

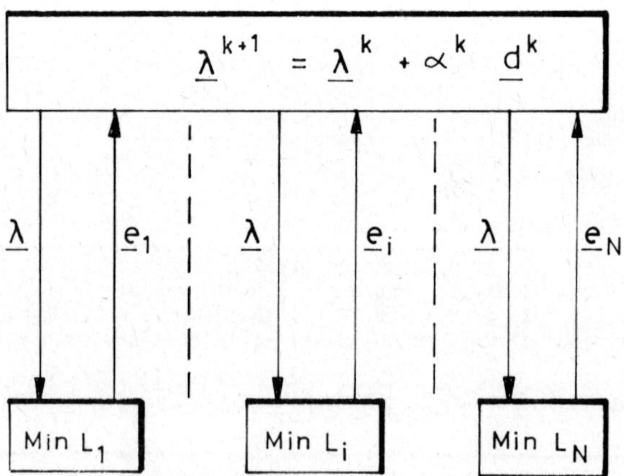

Fig. 2 : The two level Goal Coordination structure

This error vector is used in a gradient procedure to produce a new $\underline{\lambda}^*$. For example, from iteration k to k + 1

$$\underline{\lambda}^{*k+1}(t) = \underline{\lambda}^{*k}(t) + \alpha^k \underline{d}^k(t) \qquad (0 \leqslant t \leqslant T) \tag{10}$$

where α is the step length and $\underline{d}^k$ is the search direction. If the steepest ascent method is used then $\underline{d}^k(t) = \underline{e}^k(t)$ $(0 \leqslant t \leqslant T)$. On the other hand, if the conjugate gradient method is used then

$$\underline{d}^{k+1}(t) = \underline{e}^{k+1}(t) + \beta^{k+1} \underline{d}^k \quad ; \quad 0 \leqslant t \leqslant T \tag{11}$$

where

$$\beta^{k+1} = \int_0^T (\underline{e}^{k+1^T} \underline{e}^{k+1}) dt \Big/ \int_0^T (\underline{e}^{k^T} \underline{e}^k)\, dt$$

$$\text{with } \underline{d}^0 = \underline{e}^0 .$$

The overall optimum is achieved when $\underline{e}(t)$ $(0 \leqslant t \leqslant T)$ is sufficiently close to zero*.

2.2. Remarks

The above mentioned method is called the Goal Coordination Method since coordination of the subproblems is performed via the Lagrange Multipliers which enter into each subsystem cost function. Mesarovic et al [6] call it the Interaction Balance Approach since at the optimum the interactions balance, i.e. $\underline{z}_i = \sum_{j=1}^{N} L_{ij} \underline{x}_j$. The algorithm is very elegant and has been tested by Pearson on a 12th order example [7] . Its mains strengths are :

(a) It is possible to tackle large scale "linear-quadratic" problems with this approach since the computer storage requirements are no longer prohibitive. If parallel processors are used for the first level computation, truly large problems can be solved.

(b) It is possible at least in principle, to include inequality constraints on the states and controls of the subsystems since only low order subproblems are solved.

(c) It is possible to show that the two level controller will converge uniformly to the optimal solution [38] .

Against the above advantages, the method has certain drawbacks and these are perhaps the principal reason why the method has not, at least in this form, been extensively used to solve practical large scale problems. The main disadvantages of the method are :

(a) Although the second level algorithm is attractive in principle since the gradient is easy to calculate, the choice of the step length causes some problems since one can either use a constant one or attempt to find an α at each iteration which gives the biggest increase in $\phi(\underline{\lambda})$. In the former cases no α is in general suitable for the whole of the convergence process since a large one may be desirable in the beginning when we are quite far from the optimum whilst

---

* In principle one cannot be sure that the maximum of a function has been achieved merely because the gradient is zero. However, we know (cf. appendix 2) that (a) the dual function to be maximised is concave thus having a unique maximum and (b) the gradient algorithm ensures that we approach this maximum at each iteration since we only go in that direction of the gradient which increases $\phi(\underline{\lambda})$. Thus in this case if the error becomes zero,we have indeed solved the original problem

a much smaller one may be most appropriate nearer the optimum. If a one dimensional search is made for the best α, a lot of additional computation is required since it will be necessary to solve the lower level problem a number of times to obtain the best step length. Given that one requires to do all this at each iteration and since the whole convergence process may require many iterations, the overall calculation although yielding substantial savings in computer storage (since only low order problems are solved) is unlikely to yield a saving in computation time if a single computer is used to perform the calculations of the two levels sequentially. However, this may not be a real drawback since in future applications it is quite likely that parallel mini-computers will be used at the first level thus improving the computation time.

(b) The large computation time on a single computer of the present approach could perhaps be reduced if one was willing to accept good suboptimal control by terminating the iterations before the optimum was reached. However, this is not possible because the method, like all the other infeasible methods that we shall consider, does not give a practical control except at the optimum since it is only at this point that all the system and interconnection constraints are satisfied. Thus using an intermediate control could blow up the plant !

(c) Another disadvantage of the approach is that the inclusion of the term $\frac{1}{2}\|\underline{z}_i\|^2_{S_i}$ in the cost function does not correspond to a realistic physical situation and has been added in purely to ensure that singular solutions do not arise at the first level. To see how such solutions arise in large scale problems, consider the lower level minimisation problem for the ith subsystem. The problem is to minimise L_i in equation (8a) subject to equation (1). Write the Hamiltonian of the subsystem as

$$H_i = \frac{1}{2}\|\underline{x}_i\|^2_{Q_i} + \frac{1}{2}\|\underline{u}_i\|^2_{R_i} + \frac{1}{2}\|\underline{z}_i\|^2_{S_i} + \underline{\lambda}_i^{*T}\underline{z}_i - \sum_{j=1}^{N}\underline{\lambda}_j^{*T} L_{ji}\underline{x}_i + \underline{p}_i^T(A_i\underline{x}_i + B_i\underline{u}_i + C_i\underline{z}_i) \tag{12}$$

The singular solution arises if $\frac{1}{2}\|\underline{z}_i\|^2_{S_i}$ does not exist because it is necessary to minimise L_i w.r.t. $\underline{x}_i,\underline{u}_i,\underline{z}_i$ and the latter minimisation involves setting $\frac{\partial H_i}{\partial \underline{z}_i} = \underline{0}$ which in this case becomes

$$\underline{z}_i = - S_i^{-1}\left[C_i^T\underline{p}_i + \underline{\lambda}_i^*\right] \tag{13}$$

but which would be singular if no quadratic term in $\underline{z}_i$ existed in the Hamiltonian. But since the dynamics of the system are linear and the interconnection relationship is also linear, the quadratic term in $\underline{z}_i$ can only come from the cost function J. Thus it is necessary to include the quadratic term in $\underline{z}_i$ in the cost function to avoid singularities in the lower level solutions.

Now, although singular solutions are perfectly valid solutions to optimisation problems, they are certainly undesirable in our iterative hierarchical scheme since they complicate the lower level calculation enormously whilst one of the main justifications of hierarchical optimisation is the ease of calculation achieved by decentralisation. Thus although the Goal Coordination method is attractive since its convergence is assured and it is thus able to solve large scale problems, it has not been extensively used for the two main reasons that the second level calculation gets complicated because of the need for finding a good step length which necessitates multiple solutions of the first level problems during a single iteration and the need to introduce terms which are not physically meaningful in order to avoid singularities. Nevertheless, the method is significant because of its conceptual simplicity and for this reason we next demonstrate the application of the approach on the relatively large example of a 12th order system where the overall system is decomposed into four subsystems.

This example was first treated by Pearson [7] and is sufficiently large to give one a "feel" for the computational approach whilst not being so excessively large that it cannot be solved by standard single level techniques. In a subsequent section of this chapter we will solve the same problem using the interaction prediction approach thus providing a numerical comparison between these two main approaches to hierarchical optimisation.

3. THE APPLICATION OF THE GOAL COORDINATION APPROACH TO THE 12th ORDER EXAMPLE

The overall system consists of four subsystems as shown in Fig. 3. Each subsystem is of order three. Here we use Pearson's [7] values for the parameters where available and reasonable values for the ones he does not give. Pearson felt that one could represent a counter current flow process such as a distillation column or a heat exchanger by a suitable use of such a configuration. The dynamic behaviour of the system can be described by :

Subsystem 1 :

$$\begin{aligned} \dot{x}_1 &= x_2 \\ \dot{x}_2 &= x_3 \\ \dot{x}_3 &= a_{31}x_1 + a_{32}x_2 + a_{33}x_3 + u_1 + z_1 \end{aligned} \tag{14}$$

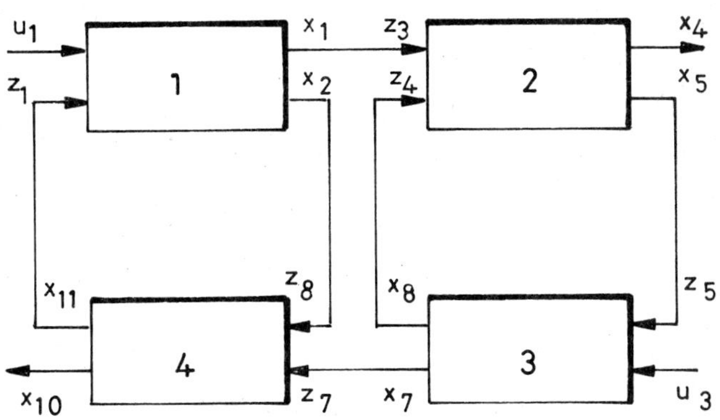

Fig. 3 : The 12th Order counter-current example of Pearson

The outputs $\underline{y}$ are given by

$$\begin{bmatrix} y_1 \\ y_2 \end{bmatrix} = \begin{bmatrix} 1 & 0 & 0 \\ 0 & 1 & 0 \end{bmatrix} \begin{bmatrix} x_1 \\ x_2 \\ x_3 \end{bmatrix}$$

The interaction inputs are given by $z_1 = x_{11}$ where as shown in Fig. 3, x_{11} is a state of subsystem 4.

Subsystem 2 :

$$\begin{aligned} \dot{x}_4 &= x_5 \\ \dot{x}_5 &= x_6 \\ \dot{x}_6 &= a_{64}x_4 + a_{65}x_5 + a_{66}x_6 + z_3 + z_4 \end{aligned} \tag{15}$$

$$\begin{bmatrix} y_3 \\ y_4 \end{bmatrix} = \begin{bmatrix} 1 & 0 & 0 \\ 0 & 1 & 0 \end{bmatrix} \begin{bmatrix} x_4 \\ x_5 \\ x_6 \end{bmatrix}$$

$z_3 = x_1 \quad , \quad z_4 = x_8$

Subsystem 3 :

$$\begin{aligned} \dot{x}_7 &= x_8 \\ \dot{x}_8 &= x_9 \\ \dot{x}_9 &= a_{97}x_7 + a_{98}x_8 + a_{99}x_9 + u_3 + z_5 \end{aligned} \tag{16}$$

with

$$\begin{bmatrix} y_5 \\ y_6 \end{bmatrix} = \begin{bmatrix} 1 & 0 & 0 \\ 0 & 1 & 0 \end{bmatrix} \begin{bmatrix} x_7 \\ x_8 \\ x_9 \end{bmatrix}$$

and $z_5 = x_5$

Subsystem 4 :

$$\begin{aligned} \dot{x}_{10} &= x_{11} \\ \dot{x}_{11} &= x_{12} \\ \dot{x}_{12} &= a_{12,10}\, x_{10} + a_{12,11} + a_{12,12}\, x_{12} + z_7 + z_8 \end{aligned} \tag{17}$$

with

$$\begin{bmatrix} y_7 \\ y_8 \end{bmatrix} = \begin{bmatrix} 1 & 0 & 0 \\ 0 & 1 & 0 \end{bmatrix} \begin{bmatrix} x_{10} \\ x_{11} \\ x_{12} \end{bmatrix}$$

Since no values were given by Pearson [7] for the 'a's, these were chosen to be

$$a_{31} = -1, \quad a_{32} = -2, \quad a_{33} = -3 \quad , \quad a_{64} = -2, \quad a_{65} = -3$$
$$a_{66} = -1, \quad a_{97} = -3, \quad a_{98} = -2, \quad a_{99} = -1, \quad a_{12,10} = -1$$
$$a_{12,11} = -2, \quad a_{12,12} = -3$$

Here N = 4 in the cost function of equation (3). The system weighting matrices were chosen to be block diagonal with

$$Q_{ii} = \begin{bmatrix} 1 & 0 & 0 \\ 0 & 1 & 0 \\ 0 & 0 & 0 \end{bmatrix} \quad ; \quad i = 1,2,3,4$$

and the control weighting matrices were taken to be $[1]$. The interconnection weighting matrices were taken to be $S_{ii} = I_2$, the second order identity matrix, for subsystem 2, 4 and $[1]$ for subystem 1, 3.

Simulation results

The lower level problem is to minimise L_i for each of the four subsystems subject respectively to the dynamic constraints given by equations (14-17) given a Lagrange multiplier trajectory $\underline{\lambda} = \underline{\lambda}^*$ where $\underline{\lambda}$ and $\underline{\lambda}^*$ are of order 6 (since there are six interconnection constraints). The period of optimisation here is from zero to 10, with the time discretisation being in steps of 0.1. These lower level problems were solved sequentially (in the order of : Min (L_1, L_2, L_3, L_4) on the IBM 370/165 digital computer at the Laboratoire d'Automatique et d'Analyse des Systèmes (LAAS) at Toulouse by integrating for each subsystem a third order matrix Riccati equation and a third order vector differential equation and some simple multiplication and addition operations for the calculation of the control from these solutions.

On the second level, a conjugate gradient type of algorithm as described by equation (10, 11) was used to improve the $\underline{\lambda}^*$ trajectories. Convergence was measured by the error criterion defined by Pearson [7], i.e.

$$\text{Error} = \sum_{i=1}^{4} \int_0^{10} \left\{ \underline{z}_i - \sum_{j=1}^{4} L_{ij}\underline{x}_j \right\}^T \left\{ \underline{z}_i - \sum_{j=1}^{4} L_{ij}\underline{x}_j \right\} dt/\Delta T$$

where ΔT is the integration step length which was taken to be 0.1. Here the period of optimisation T is taken to be 10 so that 101 time points are considered. The division by ΔT in the error measure is performed to normalise the error. In this error measure when $\underline{z}_i \simeq \sum_{j=1}^{4} L_{ij}\underline{x}_j$, then the primal problem is solved, i.e. if the error approaches zero, the resulting $\underline{x}$, $\underline{u}$ are the optimal state and control trajectories.

Fig. 4 shows the decrease of this error measure at each iteration of the second level. The error stabilises around 10^{-5} because numerical inaccuracies build up around this point and this reduces the rate of convergence.

Remarks

From Fig. 4 we see that the error decreases rapidly, i.e. it takes only 6 iterations for the error to decrease to 10^{-5} thus providing a solution adequately close to the optimum of the original problem. It is instructive to compare the computational requirements of the scheme with those of the overall solution obtained using a standard single level method.

The computational requirements can be conveniently split into two parts : computation time and fast computer storage. A good measure of the computation time requirements is the number of elementary multiplication operations involved since such a measure is independent of the computer system used. Now, for linear-quadratic problems of the type considered here, the optimal solution's requirements are proportional to a cube of the system order. Thus in this case, the overall solution requires 100×12^3 elementary multiplication operations approximately since the system is of order 12 and there are 100 integration points.

The hierarchical structure requires at the lowest level approximately

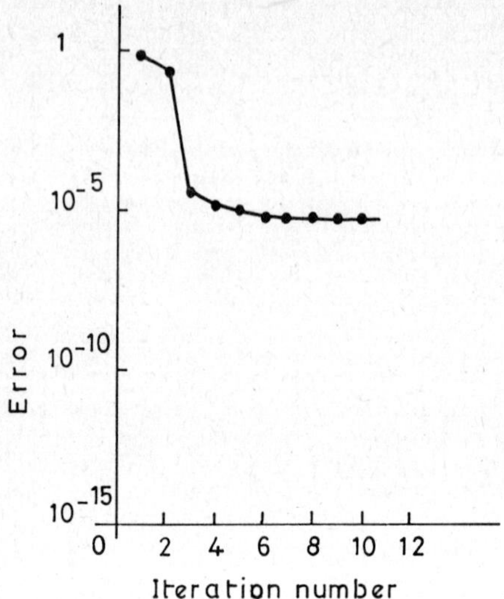

Fig. 4 : Convergence of the Goal Coordination method on Pearson's example

100 x 3^3 multiplications for each subsystem Riccati equation plus 100 x 3^2 for the vector equation. In principle, these could be done in parallel if a multiprocessor is used. On the second level it requires 6 iterations plus 3 further evaluations of the first level per iteration (since quadratic interpolation can be used for the linear search). Thus the total number of multiplication operations is 18 x 36 x 100 = 648 x 10^2. However, if the problem is solved sequentially, as was done in this case, the time for doing the multiplication operations increases by a factor of 4. Note that this time is not bigger than the global solutions time requirements for performing 1728 x 10^2 multiplication operations. Thus, even on a single processor, this relatively inefficient method has computation time requirements better than those of the global single level solution.

For the computer storage, the gains are more spectacular. The reason is that instead of having to store a 12 x 12 Ricatti matrix at each of the 100 points, it is necessary merely to store 4, 3 x 3, Ricatti matrix trajectories and 4, 3rd order vector trajectories for the first level and a 6 th order trajectory for the $\underline{\lambda}^{*S}$. However, if a single computer is being used then the trajectories for $\underline{\lambda}^{*}$ can be stored in the locations of the first level since the second level calculation is done after that of the first level. Thus there is a saving in storage of a factor of three if a single computer is used.

In studying the above example we have seen that it is possible to solve large scale system problems using the method although it is not very attractive to do so unless a multiprocessor was used at least for the case where the overall system is small enough for it to be solvable using a single level method. Of course if the system is of very high order, it will not be possible to store all the matrices required by the single level solution whilst it may well be possible to do so using the present approach. Even for relatively low order systems, an interesting modification by Tamura [34] makes the Goal Coordination approach more attractive. The basis of the modification is to convert the lower level problems from a functional to a parametric optimisation by adding an additional level to the hierarchy. In the next section we describe this three level method of Tamura.

4. THE THREE LEVEL METHOD OF TAMURA

The development in this section is done in discrete time since many problems of interest are best formulated as discrete time problems. It is more natural in any case for the Tamura method to treat the problem in discrete time since the discretisation is actually necessary for the lowest level. For the sake of completeness we shall start by describing the Goal Coordination Method for discrete dynamical systems and then formulate the modification of Tamura.

4.1. The Goal Coordination Method for Discrete Dynamical Systems

The problem is to minimise

$$J = \sum_{i=1}^{N} \left[\frac{1}{2} \|\underline{x}_i(K)\|^2_{Q_i(K)} + \sum_{k=0}^{K-1} \frac{1}{2} \left(\|\underline{x}_i(k)\|^2_{Q_i(k)} + \|\underline{z}_i(k)\|^2_{S_i(k)} + \|\underline{u}_i(k)\|^2_{R_i(k)} \right) \right] \tag{18}$$

where $\frac{1}{2}\|\underline{x}_i(K)\|^2_{Q_i(k)}$ is the cost for the terminal interval and the terms within the inner summation represent the cost over the rest of the optimisation sequence, i.e. from k =0 to K-1.

This minimisation is to be performed subject to the subsystem dynamic constraints, i.e.

$$\underline{x}_i(k+1) = A_i \underline{x}_i(k) + B_i \underline{u}_i(k) + C_i \underline{z}_i(k) \tag{19}$$

$$i = 1,2,\dots, N \quad ; k = 0, 1, 2\dots K-1 ;$$

and it is assumed that the initial state is known, i.e.

$$\underline{x}_i(0) = \underline{x}_{i0} \tag{20}$$

As in the continuous time case, $\underline{z}_i$ is the vector of interaction inputs coming in from the other subsystems, i.e.

$$\underline{z}_i(k) = \sum_{j=1}^{N} L_{ij} \underline{x}_j(k) \quad ; \quad k = 0, 1,\dots K-1 , \ i=1,2\dots,N \tag{21}$$

To solve this problem it is necessary as in the continuous time case described in the previous section to maximise a dual function $\phi(\underline{\lambda})$ w.r.t. $\underline{\lambda}$ where

$$\phi(\underline{\lambda}) = \min_{\underline{x},\underline{u},\underline{z}} L(\underline{x},\underline{u},\underline{z},\underline{\lambda}) \tag{22}$$

subject to equations (19, 20) where

$$L(\underline{x},\underline{u},\underline{z},\underline{\lambda}) = \sum_{i=1}^{N} \left\{ \frac{1}{2} \|\underline{x}_i(K)\|^2_{Q_i} + \sum_{k=0}^{K-1} \frac{1}{2} \|\underline{x}_i(k)\|^2_{Q_i} + \frac{1}{2}\|\underline{z}_i(k)\|^2_{S_i} + \frac{1}{2}\|\underline{u}_i(k)\|^2_{R_i} + \underline{\lambda}_i^T \underline{z}_i - \sum_{j=1}^{N} \underline{\lambda}_j^T L_{ji}\underline{x}_i(k) \right\} = \sum_{i=1}^{N} L_i \tag{23}$$

where

$$L_i = \frac{1}{2}\|\underline{x}_i(K)\|^2_{Q_i(K)} + \sum_{k=0}^{K-1} \frac{1}{2}\|\underline{x}_i(k)\|^2_{Q_i(k)} + \frac{1}{2}\|\underline{u}_i(k)\|^2_{R_i(k)} + \frac{1}{2}\|\underline{z}_i\|^2_{S_i}$$

$$+ \underline{\lambda}_i^T \underline{z}_i - \sum_{j=1}^{N} \underline{\lambda}_j^T L_{ji}\, \underline{x}_i(k) \tag{24}$$

Thus as in the continuous time case, it is possible to separate the problem of minimising the Lagrangian L into minimising N independent sub-Lagrangians L_i for given sequences $\underline{\lambda} = \underline{\lambda}^*$ supplied by a second level each subject to equations (19,20). The Lagrange Multiplier vector sequences can be improved at the second level by using a gradient type algorithm since

$$\nabla \phi(\underline{\lambda})\Big|_{\underline{\lambda}=\underline{\lambda}^*} = \underline{z}_i(k) - \sum_{j=1}^{N} L_{ij}\, \underline{x}_j(k) \tag{25}$$

$$i = 1,2,\ldots N \quad ; \quad k = 0,1,\ldots K-1$$

and this simple analytical expression for the gradient can be used in a steepest ascent or conjugate gradient type of algorithm as in the continuous time case. Having reformulated the Goal Coordination Method in discrete time we are now in a position to examine the modification of Tamura.

4.2. The Modification of Tamura

The basis of the approach is the observation that for a given trajectory $\underline{\lambda}^*(k)$, $k = 0,1,\ldots K-1$, the First Level problem of minimising L_i subject to the dynamic constraints given by equations (19, 20) can itself be treated by duality and decomposition. Here, instead of decomposing the Lagrangian into the sub-Lagrangians for each subsystem, the subsystem Lagrangian itself is decomposed by the index k leading at the lowest level to a parametric as opposed to a functional optimisation.

Define the dual problem of minimising L_i in equation (24) subject to equation (19) as

Maximise $M(\underline{p})$

where

$$M(\underline{p}) = \min_{\underline{x},\underline{u},\underline{z}} \Big\{ \frac{1}{2}\|\underline{x}_i(K)\|^2_{Q_i} + \sum_{k=0}^{K-1} \big(\frac{1}{2}\|\underline{x}_i(k)\|^2_{Q_i} + \frac{1}{2}\|\underline{u}_i(k)\|^2_{R_i} + \frac{1}{2}\|\underline{z}_i\|^2_{S_i}$$

$$+ \underline{p}_i(k)^T \big[A_i\underline{x}_i(k) + B_i\underline{u}_i(k) + C_i\underline{z}_i(k) - \underline{x}_i(k+1)\big] + \underline{\lambda}_i^{*T}\underline{z}_i -$$

$$\sum_{j=1}^{N} \underline{\lambda}_j^{*T} L_{ji}\,\underline{x}_i \quad \big) \Big\} \tag{26}$$

subject to the known initial state $\underline{x}_i(0) = \underline{x}_{i0}$.

To solve this dual problem numerically, it is necessary to compute the value of the dual function $M(\underline{p})$ for given $\underline{p} = \underline{p}^*$ and then to maximise $M(\underline{p})$ by some gradient technique. The gradient of $M(\underline{p})$ is given by

$$M(\underline{p})\Big|_{\underline{p}=\underline{p}^*} = -\underline{x}_i(k+1) + A_i\underline{x}_i(k) + B_i\underline{u}_i(k) + C_i\underline{z}_i(k) \tag{26a}$$

$$k = 0,1,\ldots K-1 \quad ; \quad i = 1,2,\ldots N$$

where $\underline{x}_i$, $\underline{u}_i$ are the solutions obtained after minimising L_i subject to equation

(19) for given $\underline{p} = \underline{p}^*$. The computation of $M(\underline{p})$ for a fixed $\underline{p} = \underline{p}^*$ and $\underline{\lambda} = \underline{\lambda}^*$ can be performed by minimising the function independently for each time index k as follows :

Define the Hamiltonian of the ith subsystem by

$$H_i(\underline{x}_i(k),\underline{u}_i(k),\underline{z}_i(k),k) = \frac{1}{2}\|\underline{x}_i(k)\|^2_{Q_i} + \frac{1}{2}\|\underline{u}_i(k)\|^2_{R_i} + \frac{1}{2}\|\underline{z}_i\|^2_{S_i} + \underline{\lambda}_i^{*T}\underline{z}_i$$

$$- \sum_{j=1}^{N} \underline{\lambda}_j^{*T} L_{ji}\underline{x}_i + \underline{p}_i^{*T}(k)\left[A_i\underline{x}_i(k) + B_i\underline{u}_i(k) + C_i\underline{z}_i(k)\right] \qquad (27)$$

$$k = 0,1....K-1 \quad ; \quad i = 1,2,....N$$

Then using equation (26)

$$M(\underline{p}) = \frac{1}{2}\|\underline{x}_i(K)\|^2_{Q_i(K)} - \underline{p}_i^{*T}(K-1)\,\underline{x}_i(K) + \sum_{k=0}^{K-1}(H_i(\underline{x}_i(k),\underline{u}_i(k),\underline{z}_i(k),k)$$

$$- \underline{p}_i^*(k-1)^T\,\underline{x}_i(k))$$

where $\underline{p}(-1)$ is defined to be zero.

The minimisation problem for a fixed $\underline{p} = \underline{p}^*$ then becomes :

for k = 0

Minimise w.r.t. $\underline{u}_i(0)$, $\underline{z}_i(0)$:$\{H_i(\underline{x}_i(0), \underline{u}_i(0), \underline{z}_i(0))$ subject to $\underline{x}_i(0)=\underline{x}_{i0}\}$ .It is possible to obtain an explicit solution in this case by setting the partial derivatives of H_i w.r.t. $\underline{u}_i(0)$, $\underline{z}_i(0)$ to zero to yield

$$\underline{u}_i(0) = -R_i^{-1}B_i^T\underline{p}_i^*(0) \quad ; \quad \underline{z}_i(0) = -S_i^{-1}(C_i^T\underline{p}_i^*(0) + \underline{\lambda}_i^*(0)) \qquad (28)$$

for k = 1,2,.... K-1

Minimise $\quad H_i(\underline{x}_i(k), \underline{u}_i(k), \underline{z}_i(k),k) - \underline{p}_i^*(k-1)^T\,\underline{x}_i(k)$

w.r.t. $\quad \underline{x}_i(k)$, $\underline{u}_i(k)$, $\underline{z}_i(k)$

The explicit solution in this case is

$$\underline{x}_i(k) = -Q_i(k)^{-1}\left[A_i^T\underline{p}_i^*(k) + \underline{p}_i^*(k-1) + \sum_{j=1}^{N}\left[\underline{\lambda}_j^{*T}L_{ji}\right]^T\right]$$

$$\underline{u}_i(k) = -R_i^{-1}B_i^T\underline{p}_i^*(k) \qquad (29)$$

$$\underline{z}_i(k) = -S_i^{-1}(C_i^T\underline{p}_i^*(k) + \underline{\lambda}_i^*(k))$$

for k = K

Minimise w.r.t. $\underline{x}_i(K)$

$$\frac{1}{2}\|\underline{x}_i(K)\|^2_{Q_i(K)} - \underline{p}_i^{*T}(K-1)\,\underline{x}_i(K)$$

which gives

$$\underline{x}_i(K) = \underline{p}_i^*(K-1) \qquad (30)$$

Thus the integrated problem of minimising J in equation (18) subject to the dynamics given by equations (19-21) can be solved by a three level algorithm where on level 1 for given $\underline{\lambda}^*(k)$, $\underline{p}^*(k)$ sequences, it is merely necessary to substitute into the explicit solutions given by equations (28-30) in order to obtain the optimal $\underline{x},\underline{u},\underline{z}$, which can be used at the second level to calculate the gradient of $M(\underline{p})$ from equation (26a) and this gradient can be used to improve $\underline{p}$ in order to maximise $M(\underline{p})$. On the third level, the optimal $\underline{p}$ obtained from the second level optimisation can be used to iteratively improve $\phi(\underline{\lambda})$ in order to maximise it. The overall optimum is achieved when both $\phi(\underline{\lambda})$ and $M(\underline{p})$ go to zero. Fig. 5 shows the optimisation structure.

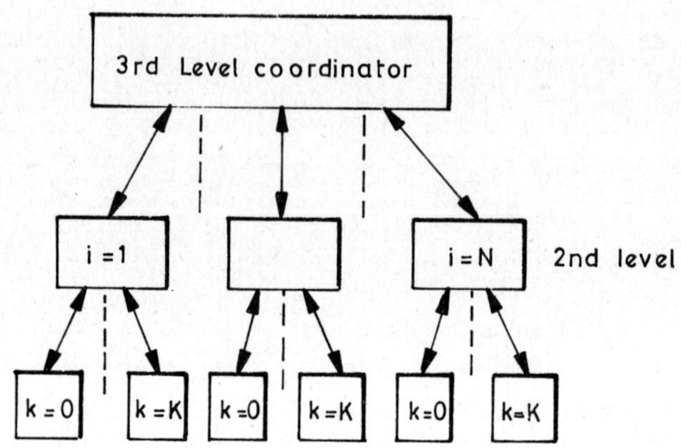

Fig. 5 : The three level method of Tamura

4.3. Remarks

1) The above method is attractive because an explicit solution is obtained at the lowest level making this level's problem trivial and ensuring that it is not necessary to solve complicated equations.

2) It is still necessary as in the standard Goal Coordination Method considered previously to introduce the term $\|\underline{z}_i\|^2_{S_i}$ in the cost function in order to avoid a singular solution.

In the next section we describe how Tamura used this concept of the three level hierarchy to produce one of the most powerful and useful algorithms in hierarchical optimisation practice, i.e. the Time Delay Algorithm [10] .

5. THE TIME DELAY ALGORITHM OF TAMURA

This algorithm solves a class of problems which are of great practical importance. The overall system has multiple pure time delays in the state and control variables. In addition, the states and controls are bounded by hard inequality constraints.

The system dynamics are assumed to be represented by a high order difference equation of the form

$$\underline{x}(k+1) = A_0\underline{x}(k) + A_1\,\underline{x}(k-1)+\ldots+A_\theta\,\underline{x}(k-\theta) + B_0\underline{u}(k) + \\ + B_1\,\underline{u}(k-1) +\ldots+ B_\theta\,\underline{u}(k-\theta) \qquad (31)$$

where A_i $(i=0,1,\dots\theta)$ are n x n matrices, $\underline{x}$ is a n x 1 vector, $\underline{u}$ is a r x 1 vector, B_i $(i = 0,1,\dots.\theta)$ are n x r matrices.

In addition it is assumed that $\underline{x}(k) = 0$; $\underline{u}(k) = 0$ for $k < 0$

and $\underline{x}(0) = \underline{x}_0$ (32)

Equation (32) can be interpreted as follows :

The system is assumed to be at some steady state operating point up to the instant $k = 0$ when it receives an unknown disturbance which takes the state of the system to a known value $\underline{x}_0$. Although the steady state operating point is assumed to be zero here, it is just as easy to consider a non zero operating point by interpreting the sequences $\underline{x}(k)$, $\underline{u}(k)$, $k > 0$ to be varying about this actual steady state.

The state can be bounded by the inequality constraints

$$\underline{x}_{Min} \leq \underline{x}(k) \leq \underline{x}_{Max} \quad , \quad k = 1,\dots K$$
$$\underline{u}_{Min} \leq \underline{u}(k) \leq \underline{u}_{Max} \quad , \quad k = 0, 1,\dots K-1 \tag{33}$$

and it is desired to minimise

$$J = \frac{1}{2} \|\underline{x}(K)\|^2_{Q(K)} + \sum_{k=0}^{K-1} \frac{1}{2} \left(\|\underline{x}(k)\|^2_{Q(k)} + \|\underline{u}(k)\|^2_{R(k)} \right) \tag{34}$$

where Q and R are assumed to be positive definite diagonal matrices.

It is very difficult to solve such a problem for large scale systems mainly because of the existence of the multiple time delays as well as the inequality constraints on the states and controls. The delays are usually eliminated in such problems by augmenting the state space by introducing additional variables for the delays (cf. Noton [39]). But this is undesirable for large scale systems since even the dimension of the problem without the augmentation of the state space is too large to enable one to solve it by standard techniques. The inequality constraints pose even more of a problem if functional optimisation techniques are used. In the Tamura method both these difficulties are circumvented if one uses the basic concept of the three level hierarchy as described in the previous section where at the lowest level a quadratic programming problem is solved.

Write the "Hamiltonian"* of the overall system as

$$H(\underline{x}(k),\underline{u}(k),\underline{p}(k),k) = \frac{1}{2} \left(\|\underline{x}(k)\|^2_{Q(k)} + \|\underline{u}(k)\|^2_{R(k)} + \sum_{j=0}^{\theta} \underline{p}(k+j)^T (A_j \underline{x}(k) + B_j \underline{u}(k)) \right) \quad ; k = 0,1,\dots, K-1 \tag{35}$$

where $\underline{p}(k)$ is defined to be zero for $k \geq K$.

For a fixed $\underline{p}^T = \underline{p}^{*T} = [\underline{p}(0)^{*T},\dots\underline{p}(K-1)^{*T}]$ it is possible to write the Lagrangian as

$$L(\underline{x},\underline{u},\underline{p}^*,k) = \frac{1}{2} \|\underline{x}(K)\|^2_{Q(K)} - \underline{p}^{*T}(K-1)\,\underline{x}(K) + \sum_{k=0}^{K-1} \left\{ H(\underline{x},\underline{u},\underline{p}^*,k) - \underline{p}^*(k-1)\,\underline{x}(k) \right\} \tag{36}$$

subject to

---

* The "Hamiltonian" here is defined for convenience and it corresponds to the conventional Hamiltonian of the discrete maximum principle[82] if $\theta = 0$, i.e. for the no delay case.

$$\underline{x}_{Min} \leqslant \underline{x}(k) \leqslant \underline{x}_{Max} \quad ; \quad k = 1,2,\ldots K$$

$$\underline{u}_{Min} \leqslant \underline{u}(k) \leqslant \underline{u}_{Max} \quad ; \quad k = 0,1,2,\ldots.K-1$$

and as in the previous sections, in order to obtain the optimal control, it is necessary to maximise w.r.t. $\underline{p}$ the minimum w.r.t. $\underline{x}$, $\underline{u}$ of the Lagrangian $L(\underline{x},\underline{u},\underline{p}^*,k)$. One of the attractions of this formulation is that the Lagrange multiplier vector $\underline{p}$ is of the same dimension as $\underline{x}$ despite the existence of the delays.

As in the three level algorithm, on examining the expression for the Lagrangian in equation (36) it follows that the Lagrangian can be decomposed into the following (K+1) independent minimisation problems for fixed $\underline{p}^*$.

i) <u>for k = 0</u>

From equation (36) using the definition of H from equation (35), the first problem is :

$$\underset{\underline{u}(0)}{\text{Min}} \; H(\underline{x}(0),\underline{u}(0),\underline{p}(0)) = \underset{\underline{u}(0)}{\text{Min}} \; \frac{1}{2}(\|\underline{x}(0)\|^2_{Q(0)} + \|\underline{u}(0)\|^2_{R(0)}) + \sum_{j=0}^{\theta} \underline{p}^{*T}(j)\,(A_j\,\underline{x}(0) + B_j\,\underline{u}(0))$$

subject to

$$\underline{x}(0) = \underline{x}_0 \;,\; \underline{u}_{Min} \leqslant \underline{u}(0) \leqslant \underline{u}_{Max}\,.$$

The solution of this parametric optimisation problem is further simplified by the fact that here R(0) has been assumed to be a diagonal matrix so that the minimisation problem reduces to a set of r independent one variable minimisations. For a single variable minimisation it is of course easy to include the inequality constraints. The explicit solution is thus given by

$$\underline{u}^*(0) = \text{Sat}_2\left[-R^{-1}(0)\sum_{j=0}^{\theta} B_j^T\,\underline{p}^*(j)\right] \tag{37}$$

where for i = 1,2,...r , the ith element of $\text{Sat}_2(\eta)$ is given by

$$\text{Sat}_2\,(\eta) = \begin{cases} u_{Max,i} & \text{if} \quad \eta_i > u_{Max,i} \\ \eta_i & \text{if} \quad u_{Min,i} \leqslant \eta_i \leqslant u_{Max,i} \\ u_{Min,i} & \text{if} \quad \eta_i < u_{Min,i} \end{cases} \tag{38}$$

The solution given in equation (37) is obtained from a trivial manipulation by setting $\partial H/\partial \underline{u}(0) = \underline{0}$ and then noting that since R is a diagonal matrix, this can be viewed as a set of r independent one variable solutions bounded by the limits.

ii) <u>for k = 1,2,...K-1</u>

Similarly, for this case the minimisation problem is :

Minimise w.r.t. $\underline{x}(k)$, $\underline{u}(k)$

$$H(\underline{x}(k),\, \underline{u}(k),\, \underline{p}^*(k),k) - \underline{p}^*(k-1)^T\,\underline{x}(k)$$

subject to

$$\underline{x}_{Min} \leqslant \underline{x}(k) \leqslant \underline{x}_{Max}$$

$$\underline{u}_{Min} \leq \underline{u}(k) \leq \underline{u}_{Max} .$$

Again since Q(k), R(k) are assumed to be diagonal matrices, this becomes a set of n + r independent one variable minimisations with the solution given by

$$\begin{aligned} \underline{x}^*(k) &= Sat_1 \left\{ -Q^{-1}(k) \left[-\underline{p}^*(k-1) + \sum_{j=0}^{\theta} A_j^T \underline{p}^*(k+j) \right] \right\} \\ \underline{u}^*(k) &= Sat_2 \left\{ -R^{-1}(k) \left[\sum_{j=0}^{\theta} B_j^T \underline{p}^*(k+j) \right] \right\} \end{aligned} \tag{39}$$

where for i = 1,2,...n, the ith element of $Sat_1(\xi)$ is

$$Sat_1(\xi) = \begin{cases} x_{Max,i} & \text{if} \quad \xi_i > x_{Max,i} \\ \xi_i & \text{if} \quad x_{Min,i} \leq \xi_i \leq x_{Max,i} \\ x_{Min,i} & \text{if} \quad \xi_i < x_{Min,i} \end{cases} \tag{40}$$

iii) <u>for k = K</u>

$$\underset{\underline{x}(K)}{\text{Minimise}} \quad \frac{1}{2} \|\underline{x}(K)\|^2_{Q(K)} - \underline{p}^{*T}(K-1)\, \underline{x}(K)$$

subject to

$$\underline{x}_{Min} \leq \underline{x}(K) \leq \underline{x}_{Max}$$

The solution is

$$\underline{x}^*(K) = Sat_1 \left[Q^{-1} \underline{p}^*(K-1) \right] . \tag{41}$$

The solutions given by equations (37-41) enable one to obtain the minimum of the Lagrangian analytically for a given $\underline{p} = \underline{p}^*$. On the second level it is necessary to improve $\underline{p}^*$ in order to maximise the dual function but this is easy to do since the gradient is given by the error in the system equation (i.e. R.H.S. of equation (31) minus $\underline{x}(k+1)$) so that a simple gradient method of the kind discussed previously could be used.

<u>Remarks</u>

The Time Delay algorithm of Tamura is virtually the only Goal Coordination type algorithm which has so far been used to solve practical problems. The main reasons for this are :

(a) There is a substantial computational saving since it is not necessary to augment the state space to account for the delays.

(b) The inequality constraints are treated in a very simple way

(c) The cost function is meaningful since no additional terms have been introduced to avoid the singular solutions which occur in the standard Goal Coordination solution.

Thus the method is able to get around most of the disadvantages of the standard Goal Coordination approach (except that it is still necessary to perform a linear search for the second level gradient algorithm). However, the most important practical advantage of the approach is that time delay systems of the kind where the Tamura algorithm can be used have in general relatively slow dynamics (because of the delays). This means that given some disturbance before the origin of time which takes the system state to some known state $\underline{x}_0$ (or a state $\underline{x}_0$ which can be obtained by suitable measurement), it may well be possible to calculate the control sequences rapidly enough before the initial state changes significantly. This is one of the few cases where open-loop control methods of the kind developed here could well be used for on-line control*. In the next section we apply the method to a significant practical problem which has slow dynamics, i.e. computer control of rush hour traffic.

6. APPLICATION OF THE TAMURA METHOD TO CONTROL RUSH HOUR TRAFFIC

Almost all cities have a rush hour period when the traffic volumes are too large for the network to be able to cope with. During such periods the cost to the community can be enormous not only in terms of high fuel consumption and decreased possible production or leisure time or under-utilisation of vast amounts of capital locked up in the delayed vehicles but also in terms of the extra wear and tear of the vehicles due to stops and starts, additional pollution of the atmosphere in our cities due to slow vehicular movement in low gears, driver frustration and resulting accidents. The advantages of optimal control of urban road traffic signals can therefore be substantial.

In this section we give a brief outline of the method of modelling oversaturated networks and then we use the Tamura algorithm to obtain the optimal control trajectories for a particularly troublesome network in London using some basic data provided by the Greater London Council. Note that time delays arise in a natural way in urban road traffic networks and these ensure that the system has a slow dynamic response.

6.1. Model [16, 17] of an oversaturated traffic network

Urban road traffic networks consist of junctions and interconnecting roads. It is possible to model the dynamic behaviour of oversaturated networks by treating the queues at junction approaches as the state variables. Consider first a simple one-way no-turn intersection as shown in Fig. 6. Let $q_i(t)$ denote the arrival rates of vehicles in the direction i. Let $i = 1$ denote the horizontal traffic direction and $i = 2$ the vertical direction. Let s_i denote the saturation flow rates of vehicles in the direction i. This is the maximum number of vehicles which can pass through the intersection per cycle, in the direction i if this direction had all the available green signal. Let C be the duration of the cycle time and l the loss time due to the amber phase. Then $C = G_1 + G_2 + l$ where G_i $i = 1, 2$, is the duration of the green in direction i. Let $\bar{g}_i(t)$ be the average departure rate (number of vehicles/C). Define the control variables $u_i(t)$ to be the percentage of green in the direction i. Then it is easy to see that [17]

$$u_i(t) = \bar{g}_i(t) \Big/ s_i(t) = G_i/C \qquad i = 1,2$$

In this formulation, the cycle time C is a known constant. The justification for this is the classical experiment of Webster [40] who showed that for C to vary 50 per cent around the optimum only increases the delays by about 10 per cent.

If the cycle time C is a constant, then it is necessary to have only one control $u = u_i$ and the other control is then $C - u_i - l$.

* Aside from the class of systems with slow dynamics, other classes of problems where such open-loop control can be used for on-line regulation are ones where the plant is restarted or the output specifications are changed, etc. giving us a well defined initial state and long enough to calculate the control before $\underline{x}_0$ changes significantly.

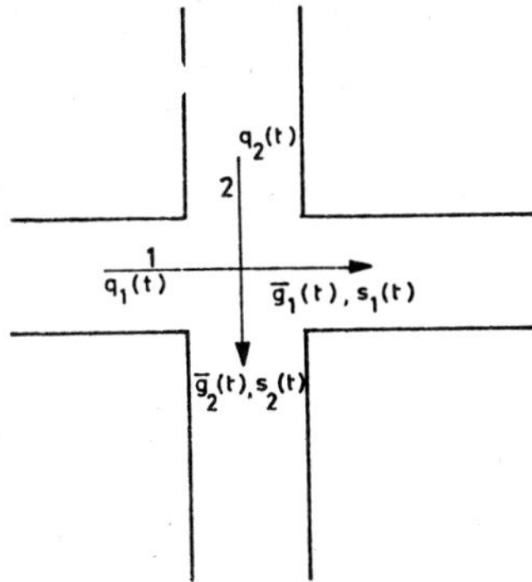

Fig. 6 : An oversaturated intersection

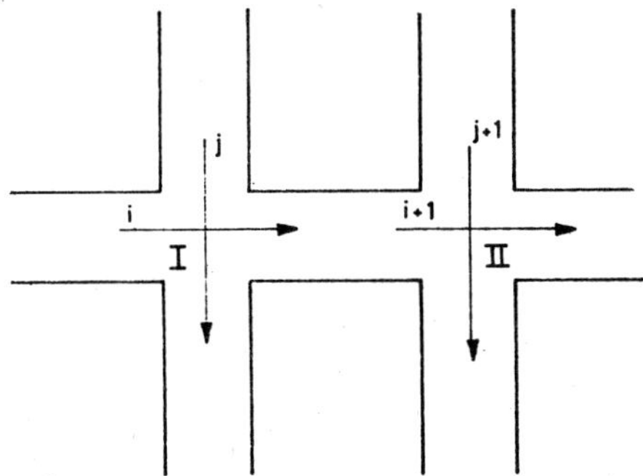

Fig. 7 : A model for the interconnecting road

The controls u must be subject to inequality constraints*

$$u_{min} \leqslant u \leqslant \text{max}$$

Now, define the state variables $x_i(t)$ as the instantaneous queue length in the direction i. Then, from one cycle to the next, the evolution of the queues can be described by

$$x_i(k+1) = x_i(k) + q_i(k) - \bar{g}_i(k) = x_i(k) + q_i(k) - s_i u_i(k)$$

Since queues exist in practice on interconnecting roads, such queues must be subject to inequality constraints of the form

$$0 \leqslant x_i(k) \leqslant x_{max,i} \ .$$

* Too short a green is wasteful. On the other hand, if the green is too long, drivers tend to believe that the traffic signals have broken down. Hence the upper constraints.

Now, since averaging over one cycle is performed and over this period the diffusion phenomenon on interconnecting roads (due to overtaking) can be ignored, it is possible to model the interconnecting roads as pure delay elements so that, for example, in Fig. 7

$$q_3(k) = s_1 u_1(k-m)$$

where u_1 is the control for junction I and s_1 is the horizontal direction saturation flow from I and m is the number of unit delays, the cycles, between the two junctions.

Extending these ideas, it is easy to see that the dynamic behaviour of networks could be described by linear vector difference equations of the form

$$\underline{x}(k+1) = A\underline{x}(k) + B_0\underline{u}(k) + B_1\underline{u}(k-1)+\ldots+B_m\underline{u}(k-m) + \underline{V} \;,$$

where A is an n x n identity matrix for a network with n queues, $\underline{x}^T=(x_1,x_2\ldots,x_n)$ are the queues , B_j (j=0,1,2,...,m) are appropriate matrices, $\underline{u}$ is a r x 1 vector of the r traffic signals and $\underline{V}$ is a vector which accounts for the external inputs which come in from outside the system.

The states and controls are of course subject to inequality constraints

$$\underline{0} \leqslant \underline{x}(k) \leqslant \underline{x}_{max},$$

$$\underline{u}_{min} \leqslant \underline{u}(k) \leqslant \underline{u}_{max}$$

6.2. Cost function

A suitable cost function for this system is

$$J = \min_{\underline{u}(k)} \sum_{k=1}^{K-1} \tfrac{1}{2}\|\underline{x}(k)\|_Q^2 + \tfrac{1}{2}\|\underline{u}(k) - \underline{u}^0\|_R^2$$

where Q and R are diagonal weighting matrices and $\underline{u}^0$ is a nominal control vector chosen a priori to maximise the utilisation of the network. Note that the term $\frac{1}{2}\|\underline{u}(k) - \underline{u}^0\|_R^2$ is not convincing from a practical point of view. It has been added in essentially to fit the present problem into the standard form. For this reason R is usually chosen so as to make $\frac{1}{2}\|\underline{u}(k) - \underline{u}^0\|_R^2$ a very small component of J.

Such a cost function minimises delays, maximises utilisation while at the same time penalising more heavily those queues which are longer.

6.3. Numerical study

The traffic network optimisation problem is in a form where Tamura's Delay Algorithm can be used directly. As an example, consider the small network in London shown in Fig. 8.

The network consists of three junctions and is a major trouble spot in the West London area. The difficulties arise because the junctions are very close, both to each other and to the neighbouring junctions, so that the storage available on the linking roads is fairly small. The state inequality constraints cannot therefore be relaxed. Based on the existing control structure, the system has the following three controls, i.e.

u_1 = fraction of the green associated with the flows 1 and 2,

u_2 = fraction of the green associated with the flows 6 and 7 and with a two-cycle delay with respect to u_1,

u_3 = fraction of the green associated with flows 10 and 12 and with a one-cycle delay with respect to u_2.

The cycle time for all the junctions is 1 min and the loss time is 6 sec. The time delays between junctions 236 and 234 in Fig. 8 is 2 min and between junctions 233 and 234, the delay is 1 min.

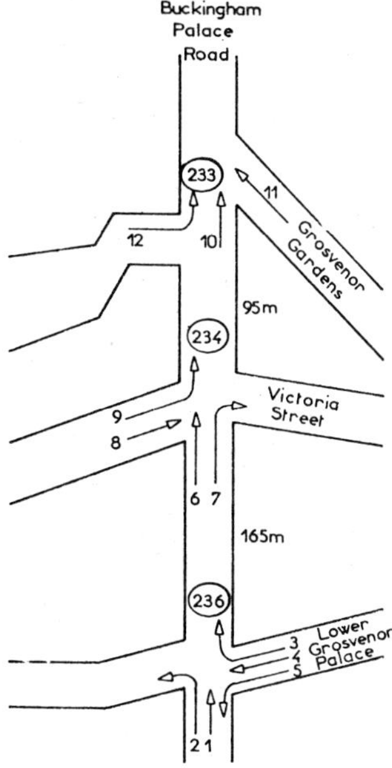

Fig. 8 : Junctions 233, 234 and 236 in the West London network

Based on saturation flows, desired values for the controls were chosen to be $u_1^0 = 0.45$, $u_2^0 = 0.30$, $u_3^0 = 0.50$. New control variables were then defined to be deviations from these values. Thus

$$\Delta u_1 = u_1 - 0.45 \quad , \quad \Delta u_2 = u_2 - 0.3 \quad , \quad \Delta u_3 = u_3 - 0.5$$

Using data on inflows into this network and saturation flows as measured between 17.00 and 18.00 hrs by the Greater London Council and provided to the author, the state equations could be written in vector matrix form as

$$\underline{x}(k+1) = I_{12}\underline{x}(k) + B\Delta\underline{u}(k) + B_1\Delta\underline{u}(k-1)+B_2\Delta\underline{u}(k-2) + \underline{V}$$

where I_{12} is the twelfth-order identity matrix and where

$$B = \begin{bmatrix} -65 & 0 & 0 \\ -25 & 0 & 0 \\ 34 & 0 & 0 \\ 31 & 0 & 0 \\ 4 & 0 & 0 \\ 0 & -64 & 0 \\ 0 & -26 & 0 \\ 0 & 132 & 0 \\ 0 & 34 & 0 \\ 0 & 0 & -96 \\ 0 & 0 & 90 \\ 0 & 0 & 25 \end{bmatrix} ;B_1 = \begin{bmatrix} 0 & 0 & 0 \\ 0 & 0 & 0 \\ 0 & 0 & 0 \\ 0 & 0 & 0 \\ 0 & 0 & 0 \\ 0 & 0 & 0 \\ 0 & 0 & 0 \\ 0 & 0 & 0 \\ 0 & 0 & 0 \\ 0 & 0 & 0 \\ 0 & 30 & 0 \\ 0 & 0 & 0 \end{bmatrix} ;\ B_2 = \begin{bmatrix} 0 & 0 & 0 \\ 0 & 0 & 0 \\ 0 & 0 & 0 \\ 0 & 0 & 0 \\ 0 & 0 & 0 \\ 42.7 & 0 & 0 \\ 18.3 & 0 & 0 \\ 0 & 0 & 0 \\ 0 & 0 & 0 \\ 0 & 0 & 0 \\ 0 & 0 & 0 \\ 0 & 0 & 0 \end{bmatrix}$$

$$\underline{v}^T = \{-21.6,\ -8.2,\ 8.4,\ 7.7,\ 9\ 2.56,\ 1.62,\ -64.2,\ -16.4,\ -8.4,\ -33.6,\ -10.5\}$$

The cost function was chosen to be

$$I = \sum_{k=0}^{3} \|\underline{x}(k)\|_Q^2 + 100\|\underline{u}(k)\|_R^2$$

where $R = I_3$ and Q is a twelfth-order diagonal matrix with the diagonal given by Q_D, where

$$Q_D = [1,\ 1,\ 1,\ 1,\ 1,\ 1.5,\ \ 1.5,\ 1,\ 1,\ 2,\ 1,\ 1].$$

Here the states x_6, x_7, x_{10} are favoured because of the limited storage on the interconnecting roads between the junctions. Note that in this cost function only 3 time steps are taken. The reason for this is that because of the high variability of traffic flow, it is not realistic to predict the inputs which come in from outside the system boundary for very much more than 3-4 minutes. The state and control constraints were chosen to be

$$0 \leqslant x_i \leqslant 40, \quad i = 1, 2, 3, 8, 9, 11, 12$$
$$0 \leqslant x_i \leqslant 80, \quad i = 4, 5,$$
$$0 \leqslant x_i \leqslant 50, \quad i = 6, 7,$$
$$0 \leqslant x_{10} \leqslant 25$$

$$-0.25 \leqslant \Delta u_1 \leqslant 0.25, \quad -0.1 \leqslant \Delta u_2 \leqslant 0.4, \quad -0.3 \leqslant \Delta u_3 \leqslant 0.2$$

For the initial conditions, a fairly loaded network was chosen with the following values :

$$x_i(0) = 30, \quad i = 1, 2, 8, 9, 11, 12$$
$$x_i(0) = 70, \quad i = 3, 4, 5,$$
$$x_i(0) = 40 \quad i = 6, 7,$$
$$x_{10} = 20$$

Note that this is a realistic problem of high dimension which is difficult to tackle without decomposition. Dynamical optimal solutions for such systems have not been obtained previously using single level techniques.

6.4. Simulation results

The optimisation problem for this oversaturated network was solved on the IBM 370/165 digital computer at Cambridge University using Tamura's Time-Delay Goal Coordination algorithm. Convergence to the optimum took place in 153 iterations which required 2.73 min to execute. The optimal primal and dual costs were

$$\text{Primal costs} = 0.284 \times 10^5,$$

$$\text{Dual cost} = 0.284 \times 10^5$$

Table 1 shows the optimal control sequence and Fig. 9 the resulting state trajectories of the system as obtained from a simulation of the system with the optimal control sequences incorporated. Note that the queues x_3, x_4, x_5 are hardly reduced.

k	1	2	3
u_1	20 %	20 %	20 %
u_2	70 %	68 %	61 %
u_3	61 %	62 %	63 %

Table 1 : Optimal control sequence for the network example

The reason for this is the high inflows q_3, q_4, q_5 compared to the corresponding saturation flows s_3, s_4, s_5, so that even though the control u_1 is such that the maximum permitted green is provided for these queues, the saturation flow is too small for the queues to be dissipated. This is the reason why the network is a trouble spot since unless a near optimal policy is implemented x_3, x_4, x_5 will build up and clog all the neighbouring junctions ; with the optimal controls calculated here on the other hand, the rest of the queues are all dissipated to low values and even the critical queues x_3, x_4, x_5 are not allowed to build up.

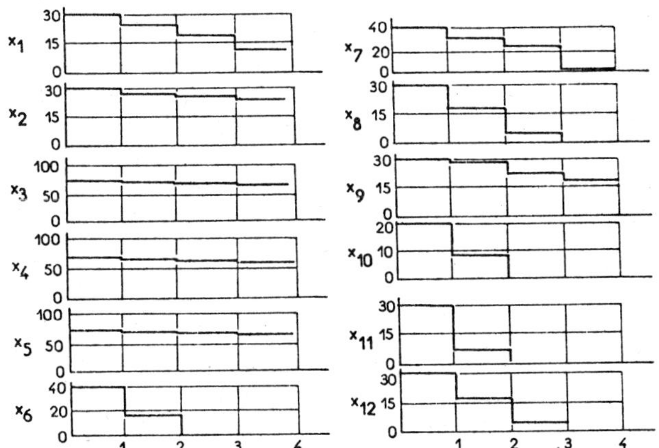

Fig. 9 : The optimal state trajectories for the London network

6.5. Remarks

We see that it is possible to solve real life problems with the Tamura approach. The approach has in fact found many other applications. For example, Tamura himself applied it to river pollution control [11] and more recently Fallside and Perry [36] have solved a Water Resource Management problem using the algorithm.

Now, although the method has been demonstrated on many simulation examples, practising Engineers are still somewhat reluctant to use it because of the open loop nature of the resulting control. We will show in part II of this book how it is possible to develop a more practical closed loop control. In the rest of this chapter, however, we continue with our discussion of practically applicable open loop hierarchical optimisation techniques.

So far we have extensively discussed the Goal Coordination approach and seen that it can solve certain problems of practical interest. However, all the methods that we have considered suffer from the disadvantage that a linear search is necessary for the second level and this requires time consuming multiple evaluations of the first level. The interaction prediction approach gets around this difficulty completely to provide a simple and computationally attractive algorithm.

7. THE INTERACTION PREDICTION APPROACH [12, 9, 8]

This approach was first formulated by Takahara [12] who also gave a convergence proof for the method. Recently Cohen et al. [37] have given a more elegant convergence proof. Since our interest is primarily in the use of the method, we shall not go through the convergence proofs. Suffice it to say that with the proof of Cohen, it is possible to ensure convergence for virtually all "linear-quadratic" problems of practical interest.

The overall system as usual consists of N linear interconnected subsystems described by

$$\dot{\underline{x}}_i = A_i\underline{x}_i + B_i\underline{u}_i + C_i\underline{z}_i \tag{42}$$

$$i = 1,2,\dots, N$$

where

$$\underline{z}_i = \sum_{j=1}^{N} L_{ij}\,\underline{x}_j \tag{43}$$

and it is desired to minimise

$$J = \sum_{i=1}^{N} \frac{1}{2}\|\underline{x}_i(t)\|^2_{Q_i(T)} + \int_0^T \left(\frac{1}{2}\|\underline{x}_i(t)\|^2_{Q_i} + \frac{1}{2}\|\underline{u}_i(t)\|^2_{R_i}\right)dt \tag{44}$$

Let us write the Lagrangian as

$$L = \sum_{i=1}^{N}\Big\{\frac{1}{2}\|\underline{x}_i(T)\|^2_{Q_i(T)} + \int_0^T \Big(\frac{1}{2}\|\underline{x}_i(t)\|^2_{Q_i(t)} + \frac{1}{2}\|\underline{u}_i(t)\|^2_{R_i(t)} +$$

$$\underline{\lambda}_i^T[\underline{z}_i - \sum_{j=1}^{N} L_{ij}\underline{x}_j] + \underline{p}_i^T[-\dot{\underline{x}}_i + A_i\underline{x}_i + B_i\underline{u}_i + C_i\underline{z}_i]\Big)dt\Big\} \tag{45}$$

where $\underline{p}_i$ is the n_i dimensional adjoint vector and $\underline{\lambda}_i$ is the r_i dimensional vector of Lagrange multipliers. Now for given $\underline{\lambda}_i = \underline{\lambda}_i^*$, $\underline{z}_i = \underline{z}_i^*$, L in equation (45) is additively separable, i.e.

$$L = \sum_{i=1}^{N} L_i = \sum_{i=1}^{N} \Big\{ \frac{1}{2} \|\underline{x}_i(T)\|^2_{Q_i(T)} + \int_0^T \Big(\frac{1}{2} \|\underline{x}_i(t)\|^2_{Q_i(t)} + \frac{1}{2} \|\underline{u}_i(t)\|^2_{R_i(t)} + \underline{\lambda}_i^{*T} \underline{z}_i^* - \sum_{j=1}^{N} \underline{\lambda}_j^{*T} L_{ji}\underline{x}_i + \underline{p}_i^T \big[-\dot{\underline{x}}_i + A_i \underline{x}_i + B_i \underline{u}_i + C_i \underline{z}_i^* \big] \Big) dt \Big\}$$

where

$$L_i = \frac{1}{2} \|\underline{x}_i(T)\|^2_{Q_i(T)} + \int_0^T \Big(\frac{1}{2} \|\underline{x}_i(t)\|^2_{Q_i} + \frac{1}{2} \|\underline{u}_i\|^2_{R_i} + \underline{\lambda}_i^{*T} \underline{z}_i^* - \sum_{j=1}^{N} \underline{\lambda}_j^{*T} L_{ji}\underline{x}_i + \underline{p}_i^T \big[A_i \underline{x}_i + B_i \underline{u}_i + C_i \underline{z}_i^* - \dot{\underline{x}}_i \big] \Big) dt \tag{46}$$

Here, unlike in the Goal Coordination case where the coordination vector was only the Lagrange multiplier vector, the coordination vector is $\left[\frac{\underline{\lambda}}{\underline{z}}\right]$. This is of higher dimension than the coordination vector for the Goal Coordination case. However, the second level algorithm is exceedingly simple and this ensures that there is no disadvantage in using this more complex coordination vector. The second level algorithm provides an improvement for the coordination vector by reinjecting the value of the vector from the previous iteration into the stationarity conditions, i.e. from iteration k to k+1

$$\begin{bmatrix} \underline{\lambda}^{*\,k+1} \\ \underline{z}^{*\,k+1} \end{bmatrix} = \begin{bmatrix} \underline{\lambda}^* (\underline{x}^k, \underline{u}^k, \underline{p}^k) \\ \underline{z}^* (\underline{x}^k, \underline{u}^k, \underline{p}^k) \end{bmatrix} \tag{47}$$

where the expression on the R.H.S. of equation (47) is obtained by setting

$$\frac{\partial L}{\partial \underline{z}_i^*} = \underline{0} \quad \text{and} \quad \frac{\partial L}{\partial \underline{\lambda}_i^*} = \underline{0}$$

i.e. $$\underline{\lambda}_i^* = C_i^T \underline{p}_i \quad \text{and} \quad \underline{z}_i^* = \sum_{j=1}^{N} L_{ij} \underline{x}_j$$

thus making the coordination rule

$$\begin{bmatrix} \underline{\lambda}_i^* \\ \underline{z}_i^* \end{bmatrix}^{k+1} = \begin{bmatrix} C_i^T \underline{p}_i \\ \sum_{j=1}^{N} L_{ij} \underline{x}_j \end{bmatrix}^k \tag{48}$$

The method therefore involves minimising the N independent sub-Lagrangians L_i for given $\underline{\lambda}_i^*$, $\underline{z}_i^*$ and then using the resultant $\underline{p}$ and $\underline{x}$ to calculate the new prediction for $\underline{\lambda}_i^*$, $\underline{z}_i^*$ by substituting into the R.H.S. of equation (48).

7.1. Remarks

The above method is attractive for many reasons. For example :

(a) The second level algorithm is very simple. It is not necessary to do the inefficient linear search as in the Goal Cordination method.

(b) The problem formulation is more meaningful since we do not have to include a quadratic term in $\underline{z}$ to avoid singularities as in the Goal Coordination approach.

(c) Experience [18] shows that the method has extremely fast convergence.

This method was originally formulated by Takahara [12] and Titli (who calls it the Mixed Method [9]). Recently, Sage [8] used a direct extension of the approach to the non-linear case. For a comparative discussion of these extensions cf. Singh et al. [14] .

It is worthwhile to make a comparison of this approach with the Goal Coordination approach numerically. We will use the 12th order example of Section 3 as the vehicle for our numerical comparison. It should be noted that whilst it was necessary to include a quadratic term in $\underline{z}$ in the cost function for the Goal Coordination method, this is not strictly necessary for the prediction approach. However, to make the comparison meaningful we have included such a term thus making the cost function identical to the one used in Section 3.

8. A COMPARISON OF THE GOAL COORDINATION AND PREDICTION PRINCIPLE METHODS

8.1. Computational Load :

The computational requirements of the two methods can be split into the storage requirements and the computation time requirements.

8.1.1. Storage

Both methods require roughly the same storage at the first level since they are both solving a very similar problem. On the second level, the Goal Coordination method requires the following amount of storage :

If the conjugate gradient method is used, it is necessary to store both the current and the previous error trajectories. Thus if the interaction error vector is of order r and there are α discrete points in the integration interval (i.e. $T/\Delta T = \alpha$) then it is necessary to store $(1 + 3r)\alpha$ variables for each iteration. If the steepest ascent method is used, it is necessary to store only $(1 + 2r)\alpha$ variables. Now, since the second levels computation is performed sequentially with the first, it is possible to use some common storage locations for the two. Usually, the second level's storage of $(1 + 2r)\alpha$ or $(1 + 3r)\alpha$ is smaller than that of the first level in which case the total storage requirements are the same as those of level one plus $r\alpha$ for the previous error trajectory. This is roughly true also for the prediction approach so that the storage requirements of the two methods are quite comparable.

8.2. Computation Time

For the computation time requirements, again the first level's computation being very similar requires roughly the same amount of time. On the second level, however, the Goal Coordination method requires repeated evaluations of the lower level solutions (3 if a quadratic fit is done or 4 if a cubic fit is done) to compute the step length. Thus if the lower level calculation requires β elementary multiplication operations then the second level requires approximately 3β for calculating the step length plus some simple updating to get the new Lagrange multiplier trajectory whilst the prediction approach only requires simple updating plus β for the first level. Thus the Goal Coordination method requires 2β more multiplications than the prediction principle. This would not be too serious if the method had substantially faster convergence characteristics. We next compare the convergence of the two methods on our 12th order example.

8.3. Convergence Characteristics

Consider again the 12th order counter current example first treated in Section 3. This problem was solved using the prediction principle on the IBM 370/165 digital computer at the LAAS in Toulouse. Fig. 10 shows the convergence of the error measure, i.e. of the quantity

$$\text{Error} = \sum_{i=1}^{6} \int_{0}^{10} \left[z_i - \sum_{j=1}^{4} L_{ij}\, x_j\right]^T \left[z_i - \sum_{j=1}^{4} L_{ij} x_j\right] dt/0.1$$

with each iteration. We see that the error converges to 10^{-5} in only 3 second level iterations.

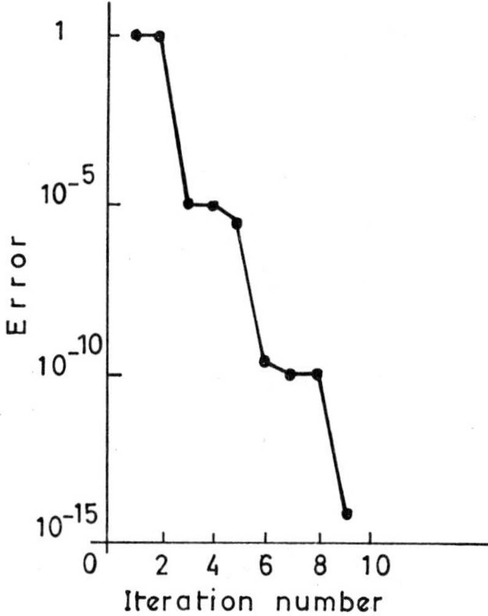

Fig. 10 : Convergence using the prediction approach on Pearson's 12th order example

Thus the interaction prediction approach appears to provide vastly faster convergence. The present comparison was made with the Goal Coordination method using the conjugate gradient algorithm at the second level. Its convergence is of course much slower if a simple gradient method is used although the calculation is a little simpler. Thus the interaction prediction approach would appear to require decreased computation time but similar storage to the Coordination method.

It would be interesting to compare the storage and computation time of the prediction principle and the global single level solution for this example. The latter for this 12th order example requires approximately $12^3 \times 10^2$

elementary multiplication operations and a storage of a 12 x 12 matrix trajectory at 100 points. The prediction principle requires on the other hand $(4x3^3 + 4x3^2)$ $3x10^2$ = 43200 multiplications compared to the 172800 required for the global solution. Thus, for this example, the hierarchical solution requires only 25 % of the computation of the global solution even though the hierarchical solution was obtained sequentially using one computer. Its storage requirements are only $4x3^2 + 4x3 + 24 = 72$ at a hundred points, i.e. about 50 % of the Global Solutions.

Thus, at least for the example treated, the interaction prediction approach appears to be much more attractive than either the Goal Coordination approach or the global solution . However, the prediction approach (as well as the Goal Coordination approach) has been helped by the fact that the decomposition chosen is quite a favourable one. One would expect the approach to give similar computational advantages provided the overall system consisted of a large number of low order subsystems. In other words we would not expect to get such results if the overall system is split into two subsystems of order 6 and 6 but would if the system is split into 6 subsystems of order 2. The main reason for this is that the computational load as measured by the number of multiplication operations increases cubically with system order so that it is desirable to have low order subsystems since the cubes of small numbers are much smaller than the cubes of large numbers.

In the next section we demonstrate the interaction prediction approach on a more practical example taken from the field of environmental systems, i.e. River Pollution Control.

9. RIVER POLLUTION CONTROL

In recent years there has been much interest in regulating the levels of pollution in rivers [11, 41-43] . A good measure of the "quality" of a stream can be obtained from two main factors, (a) the instream biochemical oxygen demand (B.O.D.)* and (b) the Dissolved Oxygen (D.O.) in the stream. If the D.O. falls below certain levels or the B.O.D. rises above certain levels, fish die. In industrial societies, rivers are used as dumps for sewage except that the sewage is treated at sewage stations prior to discharge into the stream. Sewage works in general operate a fixed level of treatment which would be determined by the level of B.O.D. in the sewage which can be safely absorbed in the stream. However, the ecological balance of the river is often disturbed by unknown perturbations and it becomes necessary to vary the B.O.D. content of the sewage (by increasing or decreasing the treatment levels) in order to bring the river quality back to the desired values. It is the problem of on-line regulation of sewage discharge B.O.D. from multiple sewage works on a polluted river that we treat in this Section.

9.1. The Model

If a reach of a river is defined as a stretch of a river of some convenient length which receives one major controlled effluent discharge from a sewage treatment facility then Beck [41] has developed a second order state space equation which describes the B.O.D.-D.O. relationship at some average point in the reach. Each reach is thought of as an ideal stirred tank reactor, as shown in Fig. 11 so that the parameters and variables are uniform throughout the reach and the output concentrations of B.O.D. and D.O. are equal to those in the reach.

---

* The Biochemical Oxygen Demand (B.O.D.) is a measure of the rate of absorption of oxygen by decomposing organic matter.

Then, from mass balance considerations, the following equations can be written

$$\text{B.O.D.}\quad \dot{z}_i = -K_{1i}\, z_i + \frac{Q_{i-1}}{V_i}\, z_{i-1} - \frac{Q_i+Q_E}{V_i} + \frac{m_i Q_E}{V_i}$$

$$\text{D.O.}\quad \dot{q}_i = K_{2i}\,(q_i^s - q_i) - \frac{Q_{i-1}}{V_i}\, q_{i-1} - \frac{Q_i+Q_E}{V_i}\, q_i - K_{1i} z_i - \frac{\eta_i}{V_i} \qquad (49)$$

where the symbols mean :

V_i is the volume of water in reach i in million gallons ,
Q_E is the flow rate of the effluent in reach i in million gallons/day ;
z_i, z_{i-1} are the concentrations of B.O.D. in reaches i and i-1 in mg/litre
q_i, q_{i-1} are the concentrations of D.O. in reaches i and i-1 in mg/litre
K_{1i} is the B.O.D. decay rate $(\text{day})^{-1}$ in reach i ;
K_{2i} is the D.O. reaeration rate $(\text{day})^{-1}$ in reach i ;
Q_i, Q_{i-1} are the stream flow rates in reaches i and i-1 in million gallons/day
q_i^s is the D.O. saturation level for the ith reach (mg/litre) ;
$\frac{\eta_i}{V_i}$ is the removal of D.O. due to bottom sludge requirements (mg/litre $(\text{day})^{-1}$);
m_i is the concentration of B.O.D. in the effluent in mg/litre.

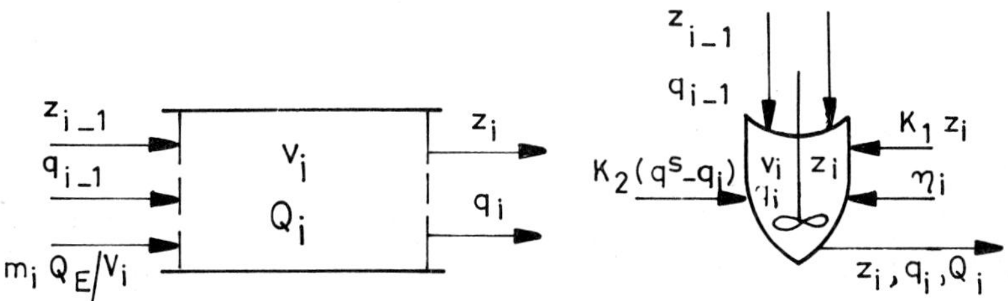

Fig. 11 : An ideal stirred tank reactor model for a reach of a river

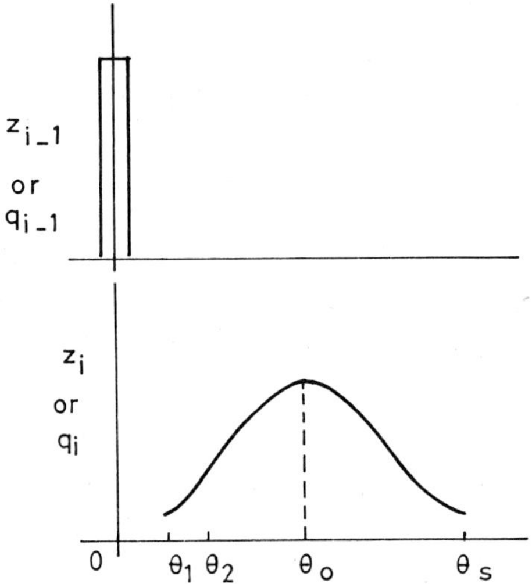

Fig. 11 a : The distributed delay phenomenon

Beck [41] found that for a section of the river Cam near Cambridge in England, the following values for the coefficients in equation (49) were appropriate :

$$k_{1i} = 0.32 \text{ day}^{-1} \quad , \quad K_{2i} = 0.2 \text{ day}^{-1} \; ,$$

$$\frac{\eta_i}{V_i} = 0.1 \text{ mg/litre day}^{-1} \quad , \quad q_i{}^s = 10 \text{ mg/litre,}$$

$$\frac{Q_E}{V} = 0.1 \qquad \frac{Q}{V} = 0.9$$

Thus, for the ith reach, equation (49) could be rewritten as :

$$\frac{d}{dt}\begin{bmatrix} z_i \\ q_i \end{bmatrix} = \begin{bmatrix} -1.32 & 0 \\ -0.32 & -1.2 \end{bmatrix}\begin{bmatrix} z_i \\ q_i \end{bmatrix} + \begin{bmatrix} 0.1 \\ 0 \end{bmatrix} m_i + \begin{bmatrix} 0.9\, z_{i-1} \\ 0.9\, q_{i-1} + 1.9 \end{bmatrix} \tag{50}$$

9.2. Steady State Considerations

Before considering the control problem, it is necessary to define the "desired" values of the controlled variables which any controller should try to maintain. These "desired" values should clearly be consistent with the dynamics of the system since otherwise it will not be possible for the controller to attain them. Appropriate desired values are therefore the steady state values of the system.

In the steady state $\frac{d}{dt}\begin{bmatrix} z \\ q \end{bmatrix} \rightarrow 0$. From equation (50) therefore, if z_0^*, z_1^*, z_2^*, z_3^*, q_0^*, q_1^*, q_2^*, q_3^*, m_1^*, m_2^*, m_3^* are the desired values in reaches 0, 1, 2, 3 then

$$\begin{aligned} - 1.32\, z_i^* + 0.9\, z_{i-1}^* + 0.1\, m_i^* = 0 \\ - 0.32\, z_i^* - 1.2\, q_i^* + 0.9\, q_{i-1}^* + 1.9 = 0 \end{aligned} \tag{51}$$

Let it be assumed that the reach 0 is always very 'clean' so that $z^* = 0$ mg/litre, $q_0^* = 10$ mg/litre. Let the desired values of D.O. in reaches 1, 2 and 3 be 8 mg/litre, 6 mg/litre and 4.69 mg/litre respectively. Then from equation (51), $z_1^* = 4.06$, $z_2^* = 5.94$, $z_3^* = 5.237$, $m_1^* = 53.5$, $m_2^* = 41.9$, $m^*_3 = 15.91$. Table 1 gives the "desired" values of z^*, q^*, m^* for the three reaches and these are the values which will be used in the control studies in the following sections.

Reach	Desired B.O.D. mg/l	Desired D.O. mg/l	Resulting Effluent Discharge mg/l
0	0	10	0
1	4.06	8	53.5
2	5.94	6	41.9
3	5.237	4.69	15.91

Table 1

9.3. Multiple Effluent Inputs

Beck's model [41] is based on a single reach of the river Cam which has only one effluent input. The interesting problem, however, is the one with multiple inputs. Since no additional data is available, we assume that there exists a system of many reaches each one of which has the properties of Beck's model.

The most realistic description of such a stream with multiple polluters was given by Tamura [11] who assumed that each reach was separated from the next by a distributed delay. This model is able to account for the dispersion of pollutants which actually occurs in rivers. In this model, for $j = 1,2,\dots,s$, a fraction a_j of B.O.D. and D.O. in the (i-1) th reach at time $(t-\theta_j)$ arrives in the ith reach at time t, i.e. the transport delays are distributed in time between θ_1 and θ_s. Thus in equation (52), z_{i-1}, q_{i-1} are given by

$$\begin{aligned} z_{i-1}(t) &= \sum_{j=1}^{s} a_j\, z_{i-1}(t-\theta_j) \\ q_{i-1}(t) &= \sum_{j=1}^{s} a_j\, q_{i-1}(t-\theta_j) \end{aligned} \tag{52}$$

$$\sum_{j=1}^{m} a_j = 1 \;;\; \text{mean of } \theta_j = \theta_0 \;;\; \theta_1 < \theta_2 < \dots \theta_s .$$

Fig. 11a shows the distributed delay phenomenon whereby B.O.D. (or D.O.) is discharged at time t=0 in the $(i-1)^{th}$ reach and fractions a_j arrive at $t = \tau_j$, $j = 1,2,\dots,s$ in the ith reach. Thus, it is possible to write the state equations for a 3 reach system with distributed delays as :

$$\dot{z}_1 = -1.32\, z_1 + 0.1\Delta m_1 + 0.9\, z_0 + 5.35 \tag{53}$$

$$\dot{q}_1 = -0.32\, z_1 - 1.2\, q_1 + 0.9\, q_0 + 1.9 \tag{54}$$

$$\dot{z}_2 = 0.9 \sum_{j=1}^{s} a_j z_1(t-\tau_j) - 1.32\, z_2 + 0.1\Delta m_2 + 4.19 \tag{55}$$

$$\dot{q}_2 = 0.9 \sum_{j=1}^{s} a_j q_1(t-\tau_j) - 1.32\, z_2 - 1.29\, q_2 + 1.9 \tag{56}$$

$$\dot{z}_3 = 0.9 \sum_{j=1}^{s} a_j z_2(t-\tau_j) - 1.32\, z_3 + 0.1\Delta m_3 + 1.591 \tag{57}$$

$$\dot{q}_3 = 0.9 \sum_{j=1}^{s} a_j q_2(t-\tau_j) - 0.32\, z_3 - 1.29\, q_3 + 1.9 \tag{58}$$

where $\Delta m = m - m^*$

Tamura gives the following values for s, τ, a etc. for each of the distributed delays :

$$s = 3,\; \tau_1 = 0,\; \tau_2 = \tfrac{1}{2}\text{ day},\; \tau_3 = 1\text{ day},\; z_0 = 0,\; q_0 = 10$$

$$a_1 = 0.15,\; a_2 = 0.7,\; a_3 = 0.15$$

The system as described by equations (53-58) is nominally of infinite dimension in the state space. It is possible to obtain a good finite dimensional approximation by expanding the delayed terms in a Taylor series and taking the first two terms. For example, consider equation (55) which can be rewritten as :

$$\dot{z}_2 = 0.9\,[0.15\, z_1(t) + 0.7\, z_1(t-0.5) + 0.15\, z_1(t-1)] - 1.32\, z_2 + 0.1\, m_2 + 4.19$$

Here we have 2 delays so it is necessary to introduce four additional states. Let these be given by z_4, z_5, z_6, z_7.
Let $z_4(t) = z_1(t-0.5)$; then $z_4(s) = z_1(s)\,e^{-0.5s}$.
Now

$$z_1(s)\,e^{-0.5s} = z_1(s)\left[1 + 0.5s + \frac{0.25}{2}s^2 + \ldots\right]^{-1}$$

Taking only the first three terms :

$$z_1(t) = z_4(t) + 0.5\,\dot{z}_4 + 0.125\,\ddot{z}_4(t)$$

let $\qquad \dot{z}_4 = z_5 \qquad$ (59)

then $\qquad \dot{z}_5 = 8\,z_1 - 8\,z_4 - 4\,z_5 \qquad$ (60)

Similarly for the other delay we let

$$z_1(t-1) = z_6$$

then $\qquad \dot{z}_6 = z_7 \qquad$ (61)

$$\dot{z}_7 = 2\,z_1 - 2\,z_6 - 2\,z_7 \qquad (62)$$

Thus we can rewrite equation (55) as

$$\dot{z}_2 = 0.135\,z_1 + 0.63\,z_4 + 0.135\,z_6 - 1.32\,z_2 + 0.1\,m_2 + 4.19 \qquad (63)$$

Similarly we can introduce four additional variables each for the delays in equations (56), (57), (58). This makes the overall system of order 22.

9.4. Hierarchical solution using the prediction principle

Having described the dynamics of this 22nd order system, we are now in a position to examine the application of the prediction principle to this problem. In order to do so, let us decompose our system into three subsystems where subsystem 1 consists of equations (53-54), subsystem 2 consists of equations (55), (56) which ultimately yields 10 equations once the approximation to the delay is defined and subsystem 3 consists of equations (57), (58) which again gives us a 10th order system once the delays are approximated by a second order Taylor series. Thus our system is decomposed into three parts respectively of order 2, 10 and 10. Clearly many other decompositions are possible but the present one is the most convenient since it retains the subsystem structure. Other decompositions which consider for example 8, 7, 7 variables are almost certainly more efficient computationally but with such decompositions one does loose one's feel for the problem since the decomposition does not have a clear physical meaning. In any case, we are most concerned with the methodology since it will be possible to use the interaction prediction approach for systems with many more reaches and as the number of reaches increases, such a decomposition becomes computationally more attractive.

Let us assume that the problem is to minimise a cost function of the form

$$J = \int_0^8 \Big[2(z_1-z_1^*)^2 + (q_1-q_1^*)^2 + 2(z_2-z_2^*)^2 + (q_2-q_2^*)^2 + 2(z_3-z_3^*)^2 + (q_3-q_3^*)^2 + (m_1-m_1^*)^2 + (m_2-m_2^*)^2 + (m_3-m_3^*)^2\Big]\,dt \qquad (64)$$

Minimising such a cost function ensures that if before time zero an unknown disturbance takes the system state to some value $\underline{x}_0$ where $\underline{x}_0$ is a 22nd order vector then it will be possible to bring the system back to the steady state values of z_1^*, q_1^*, z_2^*, q_2^*, z_3^*, q_3^* and the controls back to the steady state controls m_1^*, m_2^*, m_3^* whilst ensuring that there are no unacceptably large deviations from the steady state B.O.D., D.O. or controls. Note that both positive and negative deviations are penalised. In the case of the control, this is meaningful since the treatment process is biological and it costs money to change the control in either direction. For the B.O.D. and D.O. such a penalty is not meaningful since we really want to ensure that B.O.D. does not exceed some value and D.O. is always greater than some value. It is nevertheless possible to interpret the quadratic form as follows : let us assume that there is some band $(z_1^* \pm z_1^{**})$ and $q_1^* \pm q_1^{**})$ $(i = 1,2,3)$ within which we should like our B.O.D.s and D.O.s to lie. Then the quadratic forms will ensure that this is so provided adequate weights are used in the cost function. We have found after extensive experimentation that the weights given in equation (64) are adequate.

9.5. Simulation Results

The problem of minimising J in equation (64) subject to the system dynamics given in equations (53-58) was solved using a hierarchical interaction prediction principle structure on the IBM 370/165 digital computer at the LAAS, Toulouse. The initial conditions for the B.O.D.s and D.O.s were taken to be :

$$z_1(0) = 10 \text{ mg/1} , \quad z_2(0) = 5.94 \text{ mg/1}, \quad z_3(0) = 5.237 \text{ mg/1},$$

$$q_1(0) = 7 \text{ mg/1} , \quad q_2(0) = 6 \text{ mg/1}, \quad q_3(0) = 4.69 \text{ mg/1}$$

Such an initial condition implies that before t = 0, some disturbance affected reach one to make it very polluted whilst reaches 2 and 3 were in their desired steady state.

Convergence to the optimum took place in 11 2nd level iterations. Figs. 12, 13 show the resulting state trajectories. These figures show how the effect of the pollution load is gradually attenuated down the river. Note that the results are quite realistic with the distributed delay since the reaches downstream are only gradually affected as the pollutants are dispersed.

9.6. Remarks

In this Section we have demonstrated the applicability of the prediction principle approach by solving a realistic large scale systems problem. We see that even for this very large system, convergence of the two level algorithm is very rapid even though our integration interval is very long. This rapid convergence property as well as the ease of programming makes this one of the most powerful approaches to hierarchical optimisation. In the next Chapter we will show how the method can be modified in order to apply it to the difficult nonlinear case. Here we continue our discussion of the main hierarchical optimisation method which enables one to avoid in certain important cases the singularities which arise.

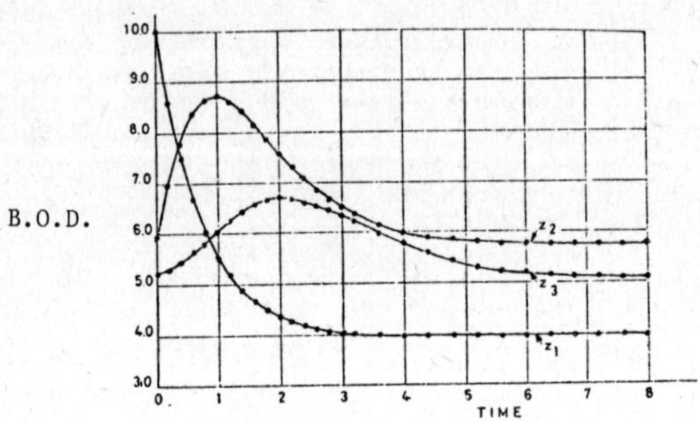

<u>Fig. 12</u> : Optimal B.O.D. trajectories for the 3 reaches

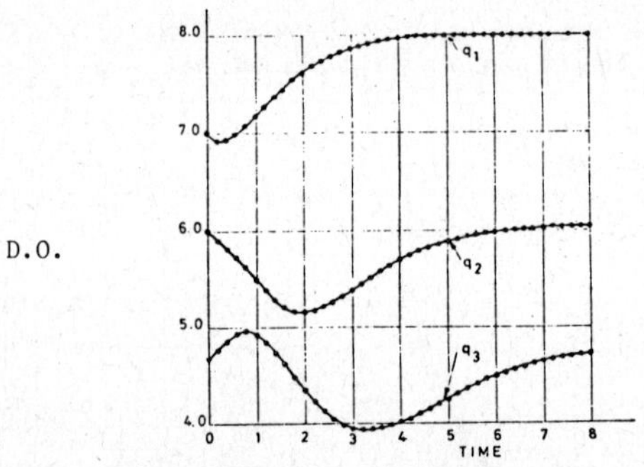

<u>Fig. 13</u> : Optimal D.O. trajectories for the 3 reaches

10. AN IMPROVEMENT TO THE GOAL COORDINATION METHOD

The first way of avoiding singularities in the Goal Coordination method was proposed by Bauman [44] who suggested squaring the interconnection constraints Consider for example the system

$$\dot{x}_1 = x_2 \tag{65}$$

$$\dot{x}_2 = u - x_2 \tag{66}$$

and it is desired to minimise

$$J = \frac{1}{2} \int_0^1 (x_1^2 + x_2^2 + u^2)\, dt \tag{67}$$

Since the only coupling between the equations is through equation (65), it is possible to define an interconnection relationship of the form

$$z = x_2 \tag{68}$$

Then the Hamiltonian can be written as

$$H = \left[\frac{1}{2} x_1^2 - \mu z + \lambda_1 z\right] + \left[\frac{1}{2}(x_2^2 + u^2) + \mu x_2 + \lambda_2 (u - x_2)\right] \tag{69}$$

But in this Hamiltonian, z enters linearly (as it must since no quadratic term has been included in the cost function as we discussed at the end of Section 2) so that its minimisation leads to a singular solution.

Bauman [44] suggested squaring the interconnection relationship to $x_2^2 - z^2 = 0$ to avoid singularity and then solved the problem using the Goal Coordination approach. However, this made convergence extremely slow. Moreover, for some initial conditions, the solution converged to $x_2 = -z$ (this, as Bauman points out, is much like extraneous roots introduced by squaring to solve algebraic equations).

10.1. Reformulation of the decomposition to avoid singular problems [19]

Another approach to avoiding singularities in a number of cases whilst at the same time avoiding the disadvantages of the approach of Bauman is to substitute for the interconnection vector $\underline{z}$ into the quadratic term for the state $\underline{x}$. The justification for this is that at the optimum, the Goal Coordination solution ensures that the interconnection relationship is satisfied so that we have solved the original problem whilst during the iterative process we have at the same time avoided the singular solutions at the first level.

To see this in more detail, consider the minimisation of J where

$$J = \int_{t_0}^{t_f} \left(\frac{1}{2} \|\underline{x}(t)\|_Q^2 + \frac{1}{2} \|\underline{u}(t)\|_R^2\right) dt \tag{70}$$

where as usual $\underline{x}$ is a $\sum_{i=1}^{N} n_i \times 1$ dimensional state vector consisting of N n_i dimensional sub-state vectors, $\underline{u}$ is a $\sum_{i=1}^{N} m_i \times 1$ dimensional control vector, Q, R are respectively $\sum_{i=1}^{N} n_i \times \sum_{i=1}^{N} n_i$ and $\sum_{i=1}^{N} m_i \times \sum_{i=1}^{N} m_i$ dimensional block diagonal matrices.

It is desired to minimise J in equation (70) subject to the system dynamics

$$\dot{\underline{x}} = A\underline{x} + B\underline{u} + \underline{z} \tag{71}$$

where A is a $\sum_{i=1}^{N} n_i \times \sum_{i=1}^{N} n_i$ dimensional block diagonal matrix and $\underline{z}$ is a $\sum_{i=1}^{N} r_i$ dimensional vector of interaction inputs from other subsystems. B is an $\sum_{i=1}^{N} n_i \times \sum_{i=1}^{N} m_i$ dimensional block diagonal matrix. The interaction input $\underline{z}$ is given by

$$\underline{z} = M\,\underline{x} \tag{72}$$

where M^{-1} is assumed to exist.

In order to solve this problem by the Goal Coordination approach, it is necessary to find the maximum w.r.t. $\underline{\lambda}$ of the minimum w.r.t. $\underline{x},\underline{u},\underline{z}$ of the Lagrangian L where

$$L = \int_{t_0}^{t_f} \left(\tfrac{1}{2}(\|\underline{x}\|_Q^2 + \|\underline{u}\|_R^2) + \underline{\lambda}^T[\underline{z} - M\underline{x}] + \underline{p}^T[\dot{\underline{x}} - A\underline{x} - B\underline{u} - \underline{z}]\right) dt \tag{73}$$

However, on setting $\frac{\partial L}{\partial z} = \underline{0}$ singularities arise. Now, since at the optimum $\underline{z} = M\underline{x}$, substitute $\underline{x} = M^{-1}\underline{z}$ in the quadratic term. Then, in order to minimise L w.r.t. $\underline{x},\underline{u},\underline{z}$ for given $\underline{\lambda}$, the Hamiltonian can be written as

$$H = \tfrac{1}{2}\|M^{-1}\underline{z}\|_Q^2 + \tfrac{1}{2}\|\underline{u}\|_R^2 + \underline{\lambda}^T\underline{z} - \underline{\lambda}^T M\underline{x} + \underline{p}^T\left[A\underline{x} + B\underline{u} + \underline{z}\right]$$

This yields

$$\underline{z} = -\,M\,Q^{-1}\,(\underline{\lambda} + \underline{p})$$

$$\underline{u} = -\,R^{-1}\,B^T\,\underline{p}$$

and the resulting optimal state equation is

$$\dot{\underline{x}} = A\underline{x} - BR^{-1}B^T\underline{p} - MQ^{-1}(\underline{\lambda} + \underline{p}) \tag{74}$$

$$\underline{x}(t_0) = \underline{x}_0$$

with the costate equation

$$\dot{\underline{p}} = -\,M^T\underline{\lambda} + A^T\underline{p} \;;\; \underline{p}(t_f) = \underline{0} \tag{75}$$

Note that since equation (74) does not have a term in $\underline{x}$, this equation can be integrated directly and the resulting $\underline{p}$ can be substituted in (75) to yield the optimum $\underline{x}$. This simplifies the computations considerably. Note also that because A, B, Q, R are block diagonal, equations (74), (75) can be solved independently subsystem by subsystem provided $\|M^{-1}\underline{z}\|_Q^2$ remains separable in $\underline{z}$.

10.2. Remarks

The above approach ensures that the subproblems are not singular, thus eliminating one of the main disadvantages of the standard Goal Coordination solution. However, it is necessary that M^{-1} exist and $\| M^{-1} \underline{z} \|_Q^2$ be separable and these restrictions limit the number of cases where the improved Goal Coordination method could be used. However, there are still a number of interesting problems where the approach works. We next illustrate the approach on Bauman's example.

10.3. Numerical example

Consider again Bauman's example which was formulated in the beginning of Section 10. The Hamiltonian of equation (71) can be rewritten as

$$H = \left\{ \frac{1}{2}(z^2 + x_1^2) + \lambda_1 z - \mu z \right\} + \left\{ \frac{1}{2} u^2 - \lambda_2 x_2 + \lambda_2 u + \mu x_2 \right\}$$

In this case, the subproblems become

Subproblem 1

$$\frac{\partial H}{\partial x_1} = -\dot{\lambda}_1 = x_1$$

$$\frac{\partial H}{\partial z} = 0 \text{ or } z + \lambda_1 - \mu = 0$$

$$\dot{x}_1 = z$$

Let $x_1(0) = 2$; also $\lambda_1(T) = 0$

Subproblem 2

$$\frac{\partial H}{\partial x_2} = -\dot{\lambda}_1 = -\lambda_2 + \mu$$

$$\frac{\partial H}{\partial u} = 0 \quad \text{or} \quad u = -\lambda_2$$

$$\dot{x}_2 = -x_2 + u \quad ; \quad \lambda_2(T) = 0$$

Let $x_2(0) = 2$

Second level : It is necessary to ensure that

$$z - x_2 = 0$$

Simulation Results

This problem was solved on the IBM 370/165 digital computer at the LAAS, Toulouse. On the second level, a simple gradient algorithm was used. For T=1, $\Delta T = 0.1$, convergence to the optimum took place in 11 second level iterations, yielding the true solution as opposed to the false solution found by Bauman using his modified approach. This solution is given in Fig. 14 .

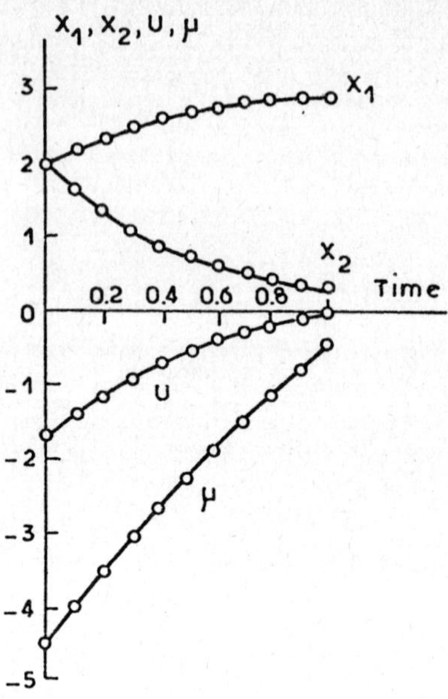

Fig. 14 : Optimal trajectories for Bauman's linear example

11. DISCUSSION

In this Chapter we have examined most of the currently available methods for the practical optimisation of large interconnected dynamical systems and we are now in a position to answer the problem facing an Engineer with a large scale system to optimise, i.e. which method is most appropriate in which situation. We have essentially examined two general classes of method, i.e. those based on the interaction balance principle and those based on the prediction principle. The Goal Coordination class of methods is particularly attractive when the system to be optimised has delays, is in discrete time and it is necessary to include hard upper and lower bounds on the states and controls. In this case Tamura's Time-Delay Algorithm is by far the best of these methods. This method can of course also be used if there are no delays and/or the system is in continuous time. The no delay case does not affect the use of the method although it gives smaller computational savings since one of the main sources of the savings is that the coordination variables are of the same order as the system despite the existence of the delays. The continuous time system can usually be suitably discretised. Recently Fallside and Perry [36] solved a water resource problem which was originally in continuous time by discretisation and application of the Tamura algorithm even though there were no delays in the system. They felt the approach was useful because of the necessity of including hard inequality constraints in the system description. One disadvantage of using the approach where the system is in continuous time is that it is computationally prohibitive to use fine discretisation.

The method can also be attractive if the system of interest belongs to the class defined in Section 10 since there, singularity problems can be avoided on the first level.

For other cases, it is much more attractive to use the interaction prediction approach. The main reasons for this are : (a) the computational effort is more modest as we discussed in Section 8 since the method appears to have faster convergence, at least on all the examples that have so far been tested (b) it is much easier to program the method since it is necessary merely to integrate a Riccati type equation and a linear vector differential equation for each subsystem at the first level and perform a simple updating at the second. The ease of programming the second level algorithms is one of the main advantages of the prediction method (c) it is not necessary to modify the problem to a form which is not physically meaningful to avoid singular solutions at the first level as in the case of the standard Goal Coordination approach.

We have discussed in this Chapter the most useful hierarchical optimisation methods for "linear quadratic" problems and given some guidelines as to which method is more appropriate for which class of problems. However, "linear quadratic" problems, 'though interesting, cannot be used to describe all systems. There are many systems where it is not adequate to use a linearisation about some operating point or trajectory and we are forced to consider the non-linear situation as such. In the next Chapter we examine the problem of solving non-linear dynamic optimisation problems using a hierarchical structure.

CHAPTER III

HIERARCHICAL OPTIMISATION FOR NON-LINEAR DYNAMICAL SYSTEMS

In this chapter we examine the possibility of calculating optimal control for large scale systems which consist of non-linear dynamical subsystems using the hierarchical structures considered in the previous chapter. Unfortunately, the non-linear systems problem is exceedingly complex and it is not possible to extend the methods of the previous chapter directly to this case. The main difficulty is that whilst both the Goal Coordination and Prediction Principle approaches could ensure that the necessary conditions for optimality are satified, no globally sufficient conditions are available for the non-linear case. This difficulty did not arise for the linear-quadratic class of problems treated in the previous chapter since for such problems, satisfying the necessary conditions automatically meant that the sufficient conditions were satisfied. In the Goal Coordination method for non-linear systems, the lack of globally sufficient optimality conditions manifests itself through the existence of a possible duality gap, i.e. a gap between the primal problem minimum and the dual problem maximum. More precisely, this arises because the Theorem of Strong Lagrange Duality [35] which was used to convert the original minimisation problem into a simpler maximisation problem in Chapter II, is not applicable here since the Theorem requires that the constraints be convex whilst the non-linear constraints which represent the dynamics cannot be convex.

In certain cases, for non-linear problems as well, the necessary conditions for optimality will also be sufficient. In that case we would be able to obtain the correct solution and this solution would in fact be globally optimal since the dual function that we are maximising is concave. Although we would not know a priori for any particular problem if a duality gap will arise, the approach is well worth investigating for those problems where it works. We begin our analysis in this chapter by examining the Goal Coordination approach for non-linear systems and applying it to a sliding mass system as well as to a system of two coupled synchronous machines.

1. THE GOAL COORDINATION METHOD FOR NON-LINEAR SYSTEMS

The method is a direct extension of the approach developed in Chapter II to the non-linear case although all the previous workers in this area, for example Bauman [44] , Smith and Sage [8] etc. considered the non-linear case first with the "linear-quadratic" problem being treated as a special class of problems. However, although it is never stated explicitly, all these authors implicitly use the Theorem of Strong Duality which, as Geoffrion [35] shows, does not apply if the constraints are not convex and again Whittle [45] has shown that non-linear equality constraints are not convex. Thus, basically the necessary conditions are satisfied but not the sufficient conditions so the method may or may not yield the correct solution.

The problem is to minimise

$$J=\sum_{i=1}^{N}\left\{\pi_i(\underline{x}_i(t_f)) + \int_{t_0}^{t_f} f_i(\underline{x}_i(t),\ \underline{u}_i(t),\ \underline{z}_i(t))\ dt\right\} \tag{1}$$

where $\pi_i(\underline{x}_i(t_f))$ is the terminal cost for the ith subsystem, $f_i(\underline{x}_i(t),\underline{u}_i(t),\underline{z}_i(t))$ is the cost at time t for the ith subsystem where $i = 1,2,\ldots,N$. The above functional J is to be minimised subject to the constraints which define the subsystem dynamics, i.e.

$$\dot{\underline{x}}_i(t) = \underline{g}_i\ (\underline{x}_i(t),\ \underline{u}_i(t),\ \underline{z}_i(t)) \tag{2}$$

$$t_0 \leqslant t \leqslant t_f$$

$$\underline{x}_i\ (t_0) = \underline{x}_{i0}$$

$$i = 1,2,\ldots,\ N$$

where $\underline{z}_i(t)$ is the ith subsystem's interaction input vector. Also

$$\begin{matrix} \underline{G}_i^*\ (\underline{x}_i(t),\ \underline{z}_j(t)) \leqslant \underline{0} & i = 1,\ldots,\ N \\ t_0 \leqslant t \leqslant t_f & j = 1,\ldots,\ N \end{matrix} \tag{3}$$

Such a structure is clearly very general and in actual fact there will be very few systems indeed where it is necessary to use a non-linear relationship of the kind defined in equation (3). Most commonly, the relationship will be linear.

In the Goal Coordination method, we consider another problem which is obtained by maximising the dual function $\phi\ (\underline{\lambda})$ w.r.t. $\underline{\lambda}\ (t)$ $(t_0 \leqslant t \leqslant t_f)$ where

$$\phi(\underline{\lambda}) = \underset{\underline{x},\underline{u},\underline{z}}{\text{Min}} \left\{L\ (\underline{x},\underline{u},\underline{z},\underline{\lambda})\ \text{subject to equation (2)}\right\} \tag{4}$$

where $\underline{x} = \begin{bmatrix} \underline{x}_1 \\ \cdot \\ \cdot \\ \cdot \\ \underline{x}_N \end{bmatrix}$ $\underline{u} = \begin{bmatrix} \underline{u}_1 \\ \cdot \\ \cdot \\ \cdot \\ \underline{u}_N \end{bmatrix}$ $\underline{z} = \begin{bmatrix} \underline{z}_1 \\ \cdot \\ \cdot \\ \cdot \\ \underline{z}_N \end{bmatrix}$

Also $\underline{\lambda} = \begin{bmatrix} \underline{\lambda}_1 \\ \cdot \\ \cdot \\ \cdot \\ \underline{\lambda}_N \end{bmatrix}$ where $\underline{\lambda}$ is a vector of Lagrange multipliers which arise in the definition of the Lagrangian in equation (4)

i.e.

$$L(\underline{x},\underline{u},\underline{z},\underline{\lambda}) = \sum_{i=1}^{N}\left\{\pi_i(\underline{x}_i(t_f)) + \int_{t_0}^{t_f} f_i(\underline{x}_i,\underline{u}_i,\underline{z}_i,t)\ dt + \int_{t_0}^{t_f} \underline{\lambda}^T\ \underline{G}_i^*\ (\underline{x}_i,\underline{z}_j,t)\ dt\right\}$$

$$j = 1,2,\ldots,N \tag{5}$$

Let us rewrite the Lagrangian as

$$L = \sum_{i=1}^{N} L_i = \sum_{i=1}^{N} \Big\{ \pi_i(\underline{x}_i(t_f) + \int_{t_0}^{t_f} [f_i(\underline{x}_i,\underline{u}_i,\underline{z}_i,t) + \underline{\lambda}^T \underline{G}_i(\underline{x}_i,\underline{z}_i,t)] \, dt \Big\} \tag{6}$$

where $$L_i = \pi_i(\underline{x}_i(t_f) + \int_{t_0}^{t_f} [f_i(\underline{x}_i,\underline{u}_i,\underline{z}_i,t) + \underline{\lambda}^T \underline{G}_i(\underline{x}_i,\underline{z}_i,t)] \, dt \tag{7}$$

and where $\underline{\lambda}^T \underline{G}_i^{*}(\underline{x}_j,\underline{z}_j,t)$ has been refactored into the form $\underline{\lambda}^T \underline{G}_i(\underline{x}_i,\underline{z}_i,t)$, i.e. into a form separable in the index i.

Now in certain cases

$$\underset{\underline{u}_i}{\text{Min}}\, J = \underset{\underline{\lambda}}{\text{Max}}\, \phi(\underline{\lambda}) \qquad i = 1,\ldots,N \tag{8}$$

and if equation (8) is valid, then an alternative way of optimising J is to maximise $\phi(\underline{\lambda})$.

Thus consider a two level optimisation structure where on level 1, for given $\underline{\lambda}$, the following N independent minimisation problems are solved, i.e.

$$\underset{\underline{x}_i,\underline{u}_i,\underline{z}_i}{\text{Min}} \quad L_i = \Big\{ \pi_i(\underline{x}_i(t_f)) + \int_{t_0}^{t_f} [f_i(\underline{x}_i,\underline{u}_i,\underline{z}_i,t) + \underline{\lambda}^T \underline{G}_i(\underline{x}_i,\underline{z}_i,t)] \, dt \Big\} \tag{9}$$

subject to $$\dot{\underline{x}}_i = \underline{g}_i(\underline{x}_i, \underline{u}_i, \underline{z}_i, t) \qquad t_0 \leqslant t \leqslant t_f$$
$$\underline{x}_i(t_0) = \underline{x}_{i0} \tag{10}$$

and on level 2, the $\underline{\lambda}$ trajectory is improved in order to maximise $\phi(\underline{\lambda})$. This can be done using say the steepest ascent method, i.e. from iteration j to j+1

$$\underline{\lambda}(t)^{j+1} = \underline{\lambda}(t)^j + \alpha^j \underline{d}^j(t) \qquad t_0 \leqslant t \leqslant t_f \tag{11}$$

where $$\underline{d} = \nabla \phi(\underline{\lambda})\Big|_{\underline{\lambda}=\underline{\lambda}^*} = \sum_{i=1}^{N} \underline{G}(\underline{x}_i^*, \underline{z}_i^*) \tag{12}$$

where $\nabla\phi(\underline{\lambda})$ is the gradient of $\phi(\underline{\lambda})$ for a fixed $\underline{\lambda} = \underline{\lambda}^*$ trajectory, $\underline{x}_i^*$, $\underline{z}_i^*$ are the values of $\underline{x}_i$, $\underline{z}_i$ which minimise L_i in equation (9) whilst using $\underline{\lambda} = \underline{\lambda}^*$, $\alpha^j > 0$ is the step length and $\underline{d}^j$ is the steepest ascent search direction. At the optimum $\underline{d}^j \rightarrow 0$ and the appropriate Lagrange multiplier trajectory is the optimum one.

1.1. Discussion

The whole argument hinges on the validity of the assertion Max $\phi(\underline{\lambda})$=Min J and this may in fact not be valid since $\underline{G}_i$, $\underline{g}_i$ need to be linear for the constraints to be convex and the convexity of the constraints is necessary to prove the assertion [35] . This means that for any particular problem, equation (8) may not be valid so that maximising $\phi(\underline{\lambda})$ on the R.H.S. of the equation using the hierarchical structure of Fig. 1 may not give the optimal control. Unfortunately, at the present time, we cannot say a priori for any given problem if there will be a difference between the values on the L.H.S. and R.H.S. of equation (8) (called a duality gap). Nevertheless, the method has an intrinsic simplicity which makes it attractive. Another attraction of the approach is that the dual function is still concave for this non-linear case. For a proof see Lasdon [2]. This ensures that if the duality assertion is valid, the optimum obtained is the Global Optimum. This is clearly a very useful property for non-linear systems since none of even the single level methods guarantee this.

We will now look at some examples where the method does work. The first of these is a classical one which was originally treated by Bauman [44] and the second is of two coupled synchronous machines. It should be noted that the Goal Coordination method for the non-linear case suffers from the same difficulty of possible singular solutions as for the linear case, at the first level, if the interconnection relationship is linear which it usually is. However, it is often possible to get around this difficulty using the modification outlined in Section 10 of Chapter 2 and we do this for the first example.

2. EXAMPLE 1 : A SLIDING MASS SYSTEM

Fig. 2 shows the sliding mass system. Bauman [44] gives the state equations as

$$\begin{aligned} \dot{y}_1 &= y_2 \\ \dot{y}_2 &= m - y_2^2 \operatorname{sgn} y_2 \end{aligned} \tag{13}$$

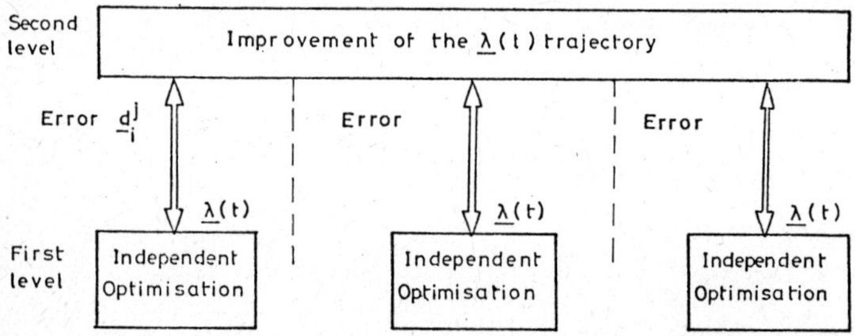

Fig. 1 : The two level structure of the controller

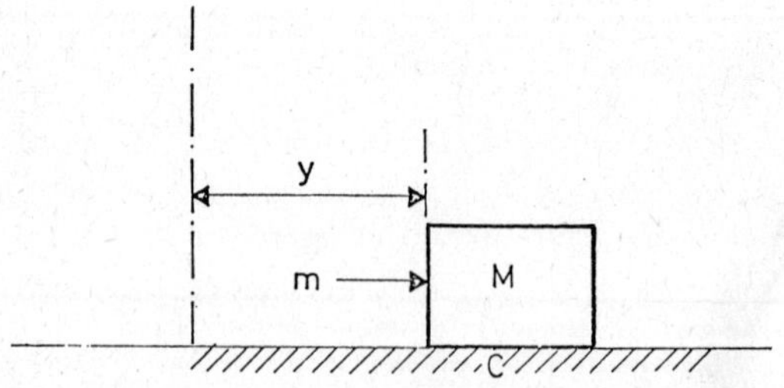

Fig. 2 : The sliding mass system

where $$\operatorname{sgn} y_2 = \begin{cases} +1 & \text{if } y_2 > 0 \\ -1 & \text{if } y_2 < 0 \end{cases}$$

and it is necessary to minimise

$$J = \int_0^T \frac{1}{2}(y_1^2 + y_2^2 + m^2)\,dt \qquad (14)$$

where m is the control. Define a coupling relationship of the kind

$$y_2 = x \qquad (15)$$

Then equations (13) can be rewritten as

$$\dot{y}_1 = x$$
$$\dot{y}_2 = m - y_2^2 \operatorname{sgn} y_2$$

The Hamiltonian of the overall system becomes

$$H = \frac{1}{2}y_1^2 + \frac{1}{2}y_2^2 + \frac{1}{2}m^2 + \lambda(-y_2+x) + p_1 x + p_2(m - y_2^2 \operatorname{sgn} y_2)$$
$$= \left\{\frac{1}{2}y_1^2 + \lambda x + p_1 x\right\} + \left\{\frac{1}{2}y_2^2 + \frac{1}{2}m^2 + p_2(m-y_2^2 \operatorname{sgn} y_2) - \lambda y_2\right\}$$
$$= H_1 + H_2 \quad \text{where } H_1 = \frac{1}{2}y_1^2 + \lambda x + p_1 x \text{ and } H_2 = \frac{1}{2}y_2^2 + \frac{1}{2}m^2 +$$
$$p_2(m - y_2^2 \operatorname{sgn} y_2) - \lambda y_2 \qquad (16)$$

and to solve the problem using the Goal Coordination method, it is merely necessary to minimise H_1 and H_2 independently w.r.t. y_1, x and y_2,m respectively on level 1 and to use a gradient coordinator to force x to equal y_2 eventually. Unfortunately, on setting $\partial H_1/\partial x = 0$, we obtain a singular solution. Such singular solutions arise less often for non-linear problems than for the "linear-quadratic" case discussed in Chapter 2. The reason for this is that certain non-linear interconnection relationships on differentiating enable us to calculate $\underline{z}$ explicity. However, if the coupling is through the states of the system, which is often the case, it is necessary to use the method outlined in Section 10 of Chapter 2, if it is applicable, to bypass the singular solution. For this problem, Bauman tried to get around the singularity problem by squaring the coupling constraints, i.e. he set

$$y_2^2 = x^2$$

2.1. The modification of Bauman [44]

If we substitute this new coupling relationship, our Hamiltonian is modified to

$$H = \frac{1}{2}y_1^2 + \frac{1}{2}y_2^2 + \frac{1}{2}m^2 + \lambda(-y_2^2 + x^2) + p_1 x + p_2(m - y_2^2 \operatorname{sgn} y_2)$$
$$= \left\{\frac{1}{2}y_1^2 + \lambda x^2 + p_1 x\right\} + \left\{\frac{1}{2}y_2^2 + \frac{1}{2}m^2 - \lambda y_2^2 + p_2(m - y_2^2 \operatorname{sgn} y_2)\right\} \qquad (17)$$

and the two subproblems now become :

Subproblem 1 : Minimise w.r.t. y_1, x : $\frac{1}{2} y_1^2 + \lambda x^2 + p_1 x$ for given λ

and Subproblem 2 : Minimise w.r.t. y_2, m : $\left\{ \frac{1}{2} y_2^2 + \frac{1}{2} m^2 - \lambda_2 y_2^2 + p_2 (m - y_2^2 \operatorname{sgn} y_2) \right\}$ for given λ.

The quadratic term in x in subproblem 1 bypasses the singularity problem.

This modified problem was solved on the IBM 370/165 computer at the LAAS in Toulouse using a gradient coordinator at the second level, i.e. where from iteration k to k+1

$$\lambda^{k+1} = \lambda^k - K\,(x^2 - y_2^2)^k \tag{18}$$

The parameter values used were :

$$y_1(0) = 2 \quad , \quad y_2(0) = -2 \quad , \quad T = 1$$

Convergence to the optimum took place in 53 second level iterations which took 27.32 seconds to perform. At the maximum value of the dual function, the trajectories were substituted into the overall cost function and they yielded the same value for the cost J as the maximum value obtained for $\phi(\lambda)$ thus verifying that we had indeed been able to obtain the optimal control. Fig. 3 shows these trajectories. We next consider the modification by Titli et al. [20] .

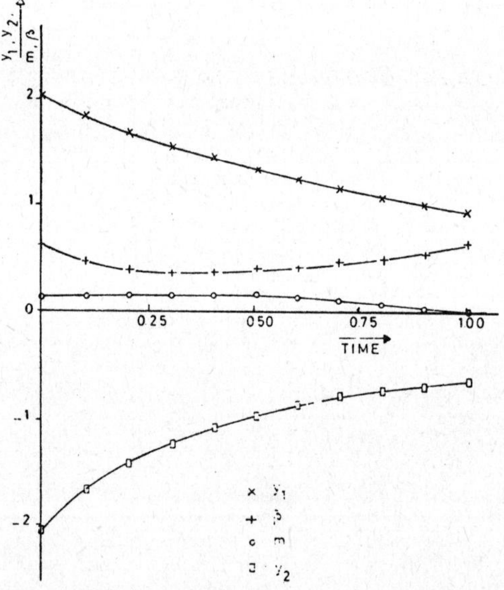

Fig. 3 : The optimal trajectories for the sliding mass system

2.2. The modification of Titli et al.[20]

We can use the same idea as in the method given in Section 10 of Chapter 2 for linear systems to avoid singularity problems. The idea is that since at the optimum, the coupling constraints will be satisfied, we are justified in using these constraints in the Hamiltonian to modify it to a more amenable form. In this case, for example, let us rewrite the Hamiltonian as

$$H = \left\{ \frac{1}{2} y_1^2 + \frac{1}{2} x^2 + \lambda x + p_1 x \right\} + \left[\left\{ \frac{1}{2} m^2 - \lambda y_2 \right\} + p_2 (m - y_2^2 \text{ sgn } y_2) \right] \quad (19)$$

i.e. we have replaced the y_2^2 term in the overall cost function by x^2 by using the coupling relationship and then put this term into subproblem 1. This again avoids the singular solution at level 1.

This modified problem was also solved on the IBM 370/165 computer at the LAAS in Toulouse using a gradient coordinator of the form.

$$\lambda^{k+1} = \lambda^k + K (y_2 - x)^k \quad (20)$$

on the second level and a simple independent minimisation of the 2 terms in the brackets in equation (19) for given λ at the first. Convergence to the optimum took place in 7 second level iterations which took 3.79 seconds to perform.

2.3. Remark

We have seen that direct coupling through the state variables for non-linear systems can lead to singular problems at the first level and that for many cases they can be satisfactorily resolved. In fact, the resolution using the approach is very efficient as seen by the vast computational saving compared to the approach of Bauman.

We have also seen that even though the assertion Max $\phi(\lambda)$ = Min J does not always apply to non-linear problems, there are important cases where it does apply. We next consider a fairly practical non-linear problem, i.e. the control of two coupled synchronous machines where the approach also gives us an optimal control using a Goal Coordination type of calculation structure. This problem is the highest order non-linear problem that has so far been solved using a hierarchical method.

3. EXAMPLE 2 : CONTROL OF TWO COUPLED SYNCHRONOUS MACHINES

The problem is to control the excitation voltages of two coupled synchronous machines optimally. A model for a single machine is given by Mukhopadhayay [46] which is of order 3. In this case, for the two machines, the model has 6 coupled non-linear differential equations given by

$$\dot{y}_1 = y_2$$

$$\dot{y}_2 = B_1 - A_1 y_2 - A_2 y_3 \sin y_1 - \frac{B_2}{2} \sin 2 y_1$$

$$\dot{y}_3 = u_1 - C_1 y_3 + C_2 \cos y_1$$

$$\dot{y}_4 = y_5$$

$$\dot{y}_5 = B_4 - A_4 y_5 - A_5 y_6 \sin y_4 - \frac{B_5}{2} \sin 2 y_4$$

$$\dot{y}_6 = u_2 - C_4 y_6 - C_5 \cos y_4$$

where $y_1, y_2, \ldots, y_6$ are the six state variables and u_1, u_2 are the two controls. The parameters are given by [46]

$$A_1 = A_4 = 0.2703, \quad A_2 = 12.012, \quad A_5 = 14.4144$$

$$B_1 = B_4 = 39.1892, \quad B_2 = -48.048, \quad B_5 = -57.6576$$

$$C_1 = C_4 = 0.3222, \quad C_2 = 1.9, \quad C_5 = 2.28$$

and the system comprises two subsystems coupled by $y_1 = y_4 = x$.

It is desired to minimise J where

$$J = \int_0^2 \tfrac{1}{2} \left[\| \underline{y} - \underline{y}_p \|_Q^2 + \| \underline{u} - \underline{u}_p \|_R^2 \right] dt$$

where $\underline{y}_p^T = \left[0.7461 \quad 0 \quad 7.7438 \quad 0.7461 \quad 0 \quad 7.7438 \right]$

$$\underline{u}_p^T = \left[1.1 \qquad 1.1 \right]$$

are desired steady state values.

$R = I_2$ the second order identity matrix and Q is a diagonal matrix with the diagonal given by Q_D where

$$Q_D = \left[20 \quad 20 \quad 2 \quad 20 \quad 20 \quad 2 \right]$$

Note that here again it is necessary to use the modification of the previous section. Using the modification, the problem was solved on the IBM 370/165 computer at the LAAS in Toulouse using a simple gradient coordinator at the second level. The initial condition used was

$$\underline{y}^T(0) = \left[0.7347 \quad -0.2151 \quad 7.7443 \quad 0.7347 \quad -0.2151 \quad 6.9483 \right]$$

and the optimum was reached in 10 second level iterations. At this point the primal and dual costs were found to be identical, i.e.

$$J = \emptyset = 1.1658$$

In another test, the initial conditions were changed to

$$y^T(0) = \left[1 \quad 0.1 \quad 10 \quad 1 \quad 0.1 \quad 8.69 \right]$$

The problem was resolved in 10 second level iterations giving in this case

$$J = \emptyset = 78.5048$$

3.1. Remarks

In this Section we have obtained the solution of a practical problem using the Goal Coordination method. There are many other cases where the method works (cf. Smith and Sage [8]). However, there are still others were it does not but one is not able to know this prior to simulation. This is obviously a serious drawback for the practical optimisation of large scale systems since for such systems even the simulation is costly.

Aside from the Goal coordination approach, there now exists a substantial number of hierarchical algorithms for the dynamic optimisation of non-linear systems [22,24,83-85,93,94,96-98,102]. We next unify this body of literature. In doing so we rely heavily on the thesis of Hassan [94] and on [102]. We begin by considering a generalisation to the non-linear case of the method of Takahara that we considered in the previous chapter.

4. THE GENERALISATION OF TAKAHARA'S ALGORITHM FOR NON-LINEAR SYSTEMS

As we have seen, Takahara [12] suggested a reinjection type coordination algorithm for systems comprising linear interconnected dynamical subsystems. We will see how we could extend this to the non-linear case. For ease of exposition, we limit ourselves to non-linear dynamics and quadratic cost functions, the extension to the more general case being straightforward.

The general idea of the approach is to write the criterion functional to be minimised in the form of a seperable quadratic part and a non-seperable part and the non-linear dynamic equations of the large scale system in the form of a linear (stationary or non-stationary) part which is seperable by blocks (corresponding perhaps to subsystems) and another part which contains the non-linearities and interaction terms. A higher level could fix the non-seperable part in the criterion function and non-linear part in the dynamic equations by specifying certain variables. This would lead to a set of simple low order dynamic optimisation problems which could be solved in parallel. The higher level could successively approximate the specified variables to their optimal values.

4.1 Formulation of the problem

Consider the following problem:

$$\min_{\underline{x},\underline{u}} J = \tfrac{1}{2}\,||\underline{x}(T)||^2_{S_1} + \tfrac{1}{2}\int_0^T (||\underline{x}||^2_{Q_1} + ||\underline{u}||^2_{R_1})dt \tag{21}$$

s.t.

$$\dot{\underline{x}} = f(\underline{x},\underline{u},\underline{t}) \tag{22}$$

where $\underline{x} \in R^n$ state vector; $\underline{u} \in R^m$ control vector;

$Q_1, S_1 \geq 0$; $R > 0$ (J has a non-seperable form)

$\underline{f} : R^n \times R^m \rightarrow R^n$

The above problem is equivalent to the following

$$\min_{\underline{x},\underline{u},\underline{u}} \quad J = \tfrac{1}{2}\,||\underline{x}(T)||^2_S + \tfrac{1}{2}\,||\underline{x}^0(T)||^2_{S_2} + \tfrac{1}{2}\int_0^T \{||\underline{x}||^2_Q + ||\underline{u}||^2_R + ||\underline{x}^0||^2_{Q_2} + ||\underline{u}^0||^2_{R_2} + \tfrac{1}{2}\,||\underline{u}-\underline{u}^0||^2_H\}dt \tag{23}$$

s.t.

$$\left.\begin{aligned} &\dot{\underline{x}} = A\underline{x} + B\underline{u} + \underline{D}(\underline{x}^0,\underline{u}^0,t); \quad \underline{x}(0) = \underline{x}_0 \\ &\underline{x} = \underline{x}^0 \\ &\underline{u} = \underline{u}^0 \end{aligned}\right] \tag{24}$$

where $\underline{D}(\underline{x}^0,\underline{u}^0,t) = \underline{f}(\underline{x}^0,\underline{u}^0,t) - A\underline{x}^0$ (25)

$$Q_1 = Q+Q_2,\ R_1 = R+R_2;\ \ S_1 = S+S_2$$

A, B are block-diagonal stationary or non-stationary matrices with N blocks corresponding to N-subsystems, and which we shall assume, for the moment, don't change during the iterations. Q,R,S, and H are block diagonal matrices with blocks:

$$S_i,Q_i \geqslant 0;\ \ R_i > 0;\ \ H_i \geqslant 0;\ \ i = 1 \text{ to } N$$

Writing the Hamiltonian of this problem we obtain

$$\mathcal{H} = \tfrac{1}{2}\,||\underline{x}||^2_Q + \tfrac{1}{2}\,||\underline{x}^0||^2_{Q_2} + \tfrac{1}{2}\,||\underline{u}||^2_R + \tfrac{1}{2}\,||\underline{u}^0||^2_{R_2} + \tfrac{1}{2}\,||\underline{u}-\underline{u}^0||^2_H$$

$$+ \underline{\lambda}^T\left[A\underline{x} + B\underline{u} + \underline{D}(\underline{x}^0,\underline{u}^0,t\right] + \underline{\pi}^T(\underline{x}-\underline{x}^0) + \underline{\beta}^T(\underline{u}-\underline{u}^0) \tag{26}$$

where $\underline{\lambda} \in R^n$; the adjoint vector; $\pi \in R^n$; $\beta \in R^m$ are Lagrange multipliers. The necessary conditions of optimality are:

$$\frac{\partial\mathcal{H}}{\partial\pi} = \underline{0};\quad \frac{\partial\mathcal{H}}{\partial\beta} = \underline{0};\quad \frac{\partial\mathcal{H}}{\partial\underline{x}^0} = \underline{0};\quad \frac{\partial\mathcal{H}}{\partial\underline{u}^0} = \underline{0};\quad \frac{\partial\mathcal{H}}{\partial\underline{u}} = \underline{0};\quad \frac{\partial\mathcal{H}}{\partial\lambda} = \dot{x}$$

$\frac{\partial\mathcal{H}}{\partial\underline{x}} = \dot{\lambda}$; which gives:

$$\underline{x} = \underline{x}^0 \tag{27}$$

$$\underline{u} = \underline{u}^0$$

$$= R^{*-1}B^T\underline{\lambda} + R^{*-1}\,H\underline{u}^0 - R^{*-1}\,\underline{\beta} \tag{28}$$

where $R^* = R+H$

$$\underline{\pi} = Q_2\underline{x}^0\left[\left.\frac{\partial\underline{f}^T}{\partial x}\right|_{\substack{\underline{x}=\underline{x}^0\\ \underline{u}=\underline{u}^0}} - A^T\right]\underline{\lambda} \tag{29}$$

$$\underline{\beta} = (R_2+H)\,\underline{u}^0 - H\left[-R^{*-1}B^T\underline{\lambda} + B^{*-1}H\underline{u}^0 - R^{*-1}\underline{\beta}\right]$$

$$+ \left[\left.\frac{\partial\underline{f}^T}{\partial u}\right|_{\substack{\underline{x}=\underline{x}^0\\ \underline{u}=\underline{u}^0}} - B^T\right]\underline{\lambda} \tag{30}$$

$$\underline{u} = R^{*-1}B^T\underline{\lambda} + R^{*-1}H\underline{u}^0 - R^{*-1}\underline{\beta} \tag{31}$$

$$\dot{\underline{x}} = A\underline{x} + BR^{*-1}\left[-B^T\underline{\lambda} + H\underline{u}^0 - \underline{\beta}\right] + \underline{D}(\underline{x}^0,\underline{u}^0,t) \tag{32}$$

with $\underline{x}(0) = \underline{x}0$

$$\dot{\underline{\lambda}}^0 = -A^T\underline{\lambda} - Q\underline{x} - \underline{\pi} \tag{33}$$

with $\underline{\lambda}(T) = S\ \underline{x}(T) + S_2\underline{x}^0(T)$

We therefore propose the following algorithm:

1. The second level provides an initial guess of the trajectories $\underline{x}^0, \underline{u}^0, \underline{\pi}, \underline{\beta}$ and we put k=1 (where k is the iteration index).

2. Since Q,R,S,H,A & B are all block diagonal and since $\underline{x}^0, \underline{u}^0, \underline{\pi}, \underline{\beta}$ are fixed by the second level, the equation (31) to (33) are seperable. Thus at the first level each subsystem solves independently the equations:

$$\underline{u}_i = -R_i^{*-1} B_i^T \underline{\lambda}_i + R_i^{*-1} H_i \underline{u}_i - R_i^{*-1} \underline{\beta}_i \tag{34}$$

$$\dot{\underline{x}}_i = A_i \underline{x}_i + B_i R_i^{*-1} \left[-B_i^T \underline{\lambda}_i + H_i \underline{u}_i^0 - \beta_i \right] + \underline{D}_i(\underline{x}^0, \underline{u}^0, t) \tag{35}$$

with $\underline{x}_i(0) = \underline{x}_{i0}$

$$\dot{\underline{\lambda}}_i = -A_i^T \lambda_i - Q_i \underline{x}_i - \underline{\pi}_i \tag{36}$$

with $\underline{\lambda}_i(T) = S_i \underline{x}_i(T) + \sum_{j=1}^{N} S_{2_{ij}} \underline{x}_j^0(T)$

$i = 1$ to N.

3. The 2nd level predicts the trajectories $\underline{x}^0, \underline{u}^0, \underline{\pi}, \underline{\beta}$ from the equations (27) to (30) using the values of $\underline{x}, \underline{u}, \underline{\lambda}$ calculated at the 1st level and we put k = k+1. If

$$\int_0^T \| \underline{\alpha}^{k+1} - \underline{\alpha}^k \|^2 \, dt \leq \varepsilon \; ; \quad \underline{\alpha}^{k^T} = \left[\underline{x}^{Ok^T}, \pi^{k^T}, \underline{u}^{Ok^T}, \beta^{k^T} \right]$$

, where ε is a small fixed apriori constant, is satisfied, we record the trajectories, otherwise we go to step (2).

Figure 4 represents the exchange of information between the two levels characterising this method.

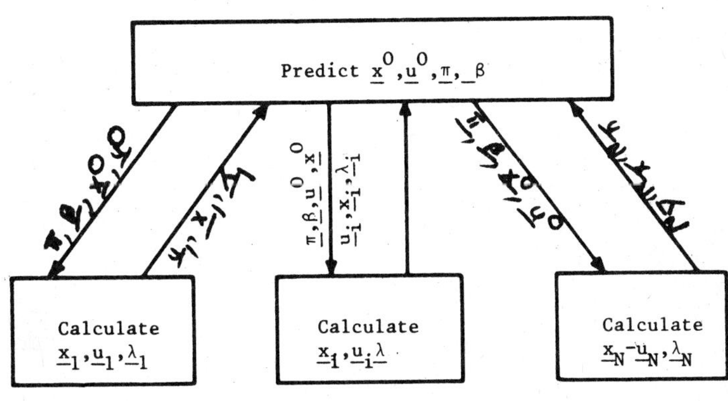

Fig. 4 :

The advantage of this method is that at the first level we solve simple linear problems with quadratic cost without iteration and at the higher level we predict new values for $\underline{x}^0, \underline{u}^0, \underline{\beta}, \underline{\pi}$.

The convergence of this method is established from the following two theorems for which a proof is given in the appendix 3.

Theorem 1

Assume that there exists an optimal solution for this problem given by $\hat{\underline{x}}, \hat{\underline{u}}$. Let us define the matrix Γ_2 as follows:

$$\Gamma_2 = \begin{bmatrix} R^{*-1}H & -R^{*-1} \\ H+R_2-HR^{*-1}H & HR^{*-1} \end{bmatrix}$$

Then if

(a) $\mu_1 < 1$ where $\mu_1 = \sup\{||Q_2||, ||\Gamma_2||\}$

(b) The components of $\underline{f}$ are continuous bounded functions of $\underline{x}$ and $\underline{u}$.

(c) The components of $\underline{f}$ are continuously differentiable functions w.r.t. $\underline{x}$ and $\underline{u}$ and their derivatives are bounded w.r.t. $\underline{x}$ and $\underline{u}$.

Then, there exists an open interval of time such that for all the final values of times that are inside this interval the algorithm converges to the optimal solution.

Theorem 2

Assume that there exists an optimal solution for the problem given by $\hat{\underline{x}}, \hat{\underline{u}}$. Let the matrix Γ_2 be defined as in theorem (1). Then if

(a) $\mu_1 < 1$ where $\mu_1 = \sup\{||Q_2||, ||\Gamma_2||\}$

(b) the components of the vector $\underline{f}$ are continuous functions of $\underline{x}$ and $\underline{u}$ and their values cannot take infinite values except if $\underline{x}$ and/or $\underline{u}$ is infinite.

(c) the components of $\underline{f}$ are continuously differentiable functions w.r.t. $\underline{x}$ and $\underline{u}$ and their derivatives cannot take infinite values if $\underline{x}$ and/or $\underline{u}$ is infinity.

(d) $\underline{x}^{01}, \underline{u}^{01}, \underline{\pi}^1, \underline{\beta}^1$ are chosen in the neighbourhood of the optimal solution $\hat{\underline{x}}, \hat{\underline{u}}, \hat{\underline{\pi}}, \hat{\underline{\beta}}$.

Then there exists an open interval of time $\tau < 0$, which depends on the initial choice of the vectors $\underline{x}^{01}, \underline{u}^{01}, \underline{\beta}^1, \underline{\pi}^1$, such that for $T < \tau$ all the points obtained from the successive iterations rest in a compact domain containing the optimal solution and this ensures the convergences of the algorithm to the optimal solution.

The proof of convergence for these two theorems is given in the appendix 3.

4.2 Discussion

1. The block diagonal matrices A and and B in equation (24) can be chosen as follows:

(a) Assume that the equilibrium point of the system is given by $\underline{x}^*$, and $\underline{u}^*$, i.e. $\underline{f}(\underline{x},\underline{u},t) = \underline{0}$ for $\underline{x} = \underline{x}^*$, $\underline{u} = \underline{u}^*$. Thus the blocks of A_i and B_i of the matrices A and B corresponding to the $\underline{ith}$ subsystem are given by:

$$A_i = \left[\frac{\partial \underline{f}_i^T}{\partial \underline{x}_i} \Bigg|_{\substack{\underline{x}=\underline{x}^* \\ \underline{u}=\underline{u}^*}} \right]^T ; \quad B_i = \left[\frac{\partial \underline{f}_i^T}{\partial \underline{u}_i} \Bigg|_{\substack{\underline{x}=\underline{x}^* \\ \underline{u}=\underline{u}^*}} \right]^T$$

In this case, the matrix Riccati equation P_i; $i = 1,\ldots N$ are needed to be solved once and only once in order to solve the linear subproblems with quadratic cost at the first level.

(b) Another possibility for the choice of the matrices A and B is as follows

Assume that $\underline{x}^{0k}$ and $\underline{u}^{0k}$ are the predicted trajectories given by the 2nd level at the $\underline{kth}$ iteration. Then we can change the matrices A_i^k and B_i^k as given below

$$A_i^k = \left[\frac{\partial \underline{f}_i^T}{\partial \underline{x}_i} \Bigg|_{\substack{\underline{x}=\underline{x}^{0k} \\ \underline{u}=\underline{u}^{0k}}} \right]^T ; \quad B_i = \left[\frac{\partial \underline{f}_i^T}{\partial \underline{u}_i} \Bigg|_{\substack{\underline{x}=\underline{x}^{0k} \\ \underline{u}=\underline{u}^{0k}}} \right]^T$$

In this case we have

i) if $\underline{f}$, $\frac{\partial \underline{f}^T}{\partial \underline{x}}$, $\frac{\partial \underline{f}^T}{\partial \underline{u}}$ satisfy the conditions given by theorem (2), then the open interval of time in which the algorithm converges depends on the initial choice of $\underline{x}^0$, $\underline{u}^0$, $\underline{\pi}^0$, $\underline{\beta}^0$. In other words, for a given horizon of optimization, the convergence of the algorithm depends on $\underline{x}^0$, $\underline{u}^0$, $\underline{\pi}^0$, $\underline{\beta}^0$.

ii) The matrix Riccati equations P_i ; $i = 1$ to N have to be solved for each iteration of the 2nd level in order to solve the linear-quadratic subproblems at the first level.

iii) If the algorithm converges the convergence will be quadratic as in the quasilinearization method.

2. Since the open interval of time in which the algorithm converges depends on the initial guess of the trajectories $\underline{x}^0$, $\underline{u}^0$, $\underline{\pi}^0$, $\underline{\beta}^0$ as well as the matrices Q and R, then the algorithm can be modified in two different ways

I) a) To begin with we choose the horizon of optimization to be sufficiently small and then we apply the algorithm until it converges

b) The horizon of optimisation will be increased by ΔT, and we use the trajectories obtained from step (a) above as an initial guess and then apply the algorithm.

c) We continue the procedure till the desired horizon of optimisation is achieved.

II) a) We start the algorithm with the matrix R^* sufficiently large and the matrix Q^{**} sufficiently small, then the algorithm will be applied until it converges.

b) The matrix R^* will be decreased by ΔR and the matrix Q^{**} will be increased by ΔQ; then we apply the algorithm using the trajectories obtained in (a) as an initial guess.

c) We continue the process of decreasing R^* and increasing Q^{**} till we arrive at their original values.

We note that in the above two approaches the values of ΔT, ΔR and ΔQ can vary during the iterations.

To compare this method with that of the quasilinearisation method from the storage requirements point of view, we shall give in the next section the number of trajectories to be stored for each method as a measure of the storage requirements.

4.3 Comparison between this method and that of quasilinearization from the storage requirements point of view

Here, we shall use the number of trajectories that have to be stored for each method as a measure for the storage requirements. For this purpose, we assume the following

i) n is the dimension of the state vector

ii) N is the number of subsystems

iii) $\frac{n}{N}$ is the dimension of the state vector for each subsystem

iv) m is the dimension of the control vector

v) we use a monoprocessor system.

I. For the generalised Takahara method

We have to store in the memory the following trajectories

1. $\left[\frac{n}{2N}\left(\frac{n}{N}+1\right)\right]N$ trajectories for Riccati matrices

2. n trajectories for the vector $\underline{\xi}$

3. n+m trajectories for the vector $\underline{x}$ and $\underline{u}$

4. 2n + 2m trajectories for $\underline{x}^0$, $\underline{\beta}$, $\underline{u}^0$, $\underline{\pi}$ at the kth iteration

5. m trajectories for $\underline{\beta}$ at the $(k+1)^{\underline{th}}$ iteration ($\underline{\pi}^{k+1}$ can be stored in the place of $\underline{\xi}$).

II. For the quasilinearization method [96]

We need to store

1. 2n trajectories for the initial guess of $\underline{x}$ and $\underline{\lambda}$.

2. $2n^2$ trajectories for the homogeneous solution of $\underline{x}$ and $\underline{\lambda}$.

3. 2n trajectories for the particular solution of $\underline{x}$ and $\underline{\lambda}$

4. m trajectories for the solution of $\underline{u}$

To illustrate the method, we next solve an example of the control of a synchronous machine. For the purpose of verification of the theorems, the example will be solved for different values of T, $\underline{x}(0)$, R, Q and for each trial, we shall give the necessary time of calculation to arrive at the final convergence.

4.4 Example (Regulation of a Synchronous Machine)

The model of a synchronous generator connected to an infinite bus-bar and which receives at a given instant a perturbation equivalent to a step change in power is given by Mukhopadyay [46] as

$$\begin{aligned} \dot{y}_1 &= y_2 \\ \dot{y}_2 &= B_1 - A_1 y_2 - A_2 y_3 \sin y_1 - \frac{B_2}{z} \sin 2y_1 \\ \dot{y}_3 &= u' - c_1 y_3 + c_2 \cos y_1 \end{aligned} \tag{37}$$

where y_1 represents the angular position of the rotor, y_2 the variation in the speed, y_3 the variation in the flux, u' the variation in the control. A_1, A_2, B_1, B_2, C_1 and C_2 are the constants that characterise the machine and the bus-bar and are given by

$$A_1 = 0.27 \; ; \quad B_1 = 38.18 \; ; \quad C_1 = 0.32 \; ; \quad A_2 = 12.01, \; B_2 = 48.04$$

$$C_2 = 1.9$$

The optimisation problem consists of

$$\min_{y,u'} \; J = \tfrac{1}{2} \int_0^T \Big[G_1 (y_1 - y_{1p})^2 + G_2 (y_2 - y_{2p}) + G_3 (y_3 - y_{3p}^2$$

$$+ R (u' - u_p)^2 \Big] dt \tag{38}$$

s.t. (37)

where $\underline{y}_p^T = [0.7461 \quad 0 \quad 7.7438] \; ; \quad u_p = 1$

In this example A_i^* and B_1^* are chosen as follows

$$A_i^* = \left[\frac{\partial \underline{f}_i^T}{\partial \underline{y}_i} \Bigg|_{\substack{\underline{y}=\underline{y}_p \\ \underline{u}=\underline{u}_p}} \right]^T \; ; \quad B_i^* = \left[\frac{\partial \underline{f}_i^T}{\partial u_i} \Bigg|_{\substack{\underline{y}=\underline{y}_p \\ \underline{u}=\underline{u}_p}} \right]^T$$

let $\underline{x} = \underline{y} - \underline{y}_p$; $u = u' - u_p$; the system (3-1) can be written as follows

$$\dot{\underline{x}} = A^* \underline{x} + B^* \underline{u} + |\underline{f}(\underline{y}, \underline{u}_p, t) - A^* \underline{x}|$$

$$B^{*T} = [0 \quad 0 \quad 1]$$

We shall decompose this problem into two problems, the 1st consisting of the states x_1 and x_2 while, the second consisting of x_3. However, by this decomposition, only the 2nd subsystem will have a control u while the first one will not have one and thus the inversion of the matrix R will be impossible.

To overcome this, we shall define a "pseudo" control variable, for the 1st sub-system as follows

$$\frac{d}{dt}\begin{bmatrix} \underline{x}_1 \\ x_3 \end{bmatrix} = \begin{bmatrix} A_1^* & 0 \\ 0 & A_2^* \end{bmatrix}\begin{bmatrix} \underline{x}_1 \\ x_3 \end{bmatrix} + \begin{bmatrix} B_1^* & 0 \\ 0 & B_2^* \end{bmatrix}\begin{bmatrix} u_1 \\ u_2 \end{bmatrix} + \left\{ \underline{f}(\underline{y},t) - A^*\underline{x} \right\} \tag{39}$$

$$\text{where } A_1^* = \left.\begin{bmatrix} \frac{\partial f_1}{\partial y_1} & \frac{\partial f_1}{\partial y_2} \\ \frac{\partial f_2}{\partial y_2} & \frac{\partial f_2}{\partial y_2} \end{bmatrix}\right|_{\substack{\underline{y}=\underline{y}_p \\ u=u_p}} = \begin{bmatrix} 0 & 1 \\ -64.5348 & -0.2713 \end{bmatrix}$$

$$A_2^* = \left.\frac{\partial f_3}{\partial y_3}\right|_{\substack{\underline{y}=\underline{y}_p \\ u=u_p}} = 0.3222$$

$$B_1^{*T} = [0 \quad 0] \; ; \; B_2^* = 1$$

Putting $\underline{x}=\underline{x}^0$ for the term $\{\underline{f}(\underline{y},t) - A^*\underline{x}\}$ in equation (39), the problem can be decomposed at the 1st level into the following sub-problems

Sub-problem (1) : given $\underline{x}=\underline{x}^0$

$$\min_{\underline{x}_1,\, u_1} J_1 = \tfrac{1}{2}\int_0^T (||\underline{x}_1||^2_{Q_1} + R_1u_1^2)dt \tag{40}$$

$$\text{s.t.} \quad \dot{\underline{x}}_1 = A_1^*\underline{x}_1 + B_1^*u_1 + D_1(\underline{x}^0,t) \tag{41}$$

$$\text{where } \underline{D}_1(\underline{x}^0,t) = \begin{bmatrix} f_1(y_p + \underline{x}^0,t) - \sum_{i=1}^{2} a_{1i}^* x_i^0 \\ f_2(y_p + \underline{x}^0,t) - \sum_{i=1}^{2} a_{2i}^* x_i^0 \end{bmatrix} \tag{42}$$

Sub-problem (2) ; again given that $\underline{x}=\underline{x}^0$

$$\min_{x_3,u_2} J_2 = \tfrac{1}{2}\int_0^T (Q_2\, x_3^2 + R_2u_2^2)dt \tag{43}$$

$$\text{s.t.} \quad \dot{x}_3 = -0.3222\, x_3 + u_2 + \{f_3(y_p + x^0,\, u_p,\, t) - a_{33}^*\, x_3^0\} \tag{44}$$

Writing the necessary conditions of optimality we get:

At the first level we solve the following equations:

$$\dot{P}_i = P_i A_i^* - A_i^{*T} P_i + P_i B_i^* R_i^{-1} B_i^{*T} P_i - Q_i \tag{45}$$

with $P_i(T) = [0]$

$$\dot{\xi}_i = (-A_i^{*T} + P_i B_i^* R_i^{-1})\ \underline{\xi}_i - \underline{D}_i - \underline{\pi}_i \tag{46}$$

with $\underline{\xi}_i(T) = \underline{0}$ and $\underline{\pi}_i$ the Lagrange multiplier corresponding to the constraint $\underline{x}=\underline{x}0$.

$$\underline{u}_i = -R_i^{-1}\ B_i^{*T}\ [P_i \underline{x}_i + \xi_i] \tag{47}$$

$$\dot{\underline{x}}_i = A_i^* \underline{x}_i - B_i^* R_i^{-1} B_i^{*T} P_i \underline{x}_i - B_i^* R_i^{-1} B_i^{*T} \xi_i + \underline{D}_i \tag{48}$$

While at the 2nd level we have to solve

$$\underline{x}^{0k+1} = \underline{x}^k \tag{49}$$

$$\underline{\pi}^{k+1} = \left[\frac{\partial \underline{D}^T}{\partial x^0} \bigg|_{\underline{x}^0 = \underline{x}^0 t} \right] \underline{\lambda}^k \tag{50}$$

where $\underline{\lambda} = P\underline{x} + \xi$ is the adjoint vector

since $\underline{D} = \underline{f}(\underline{x}^0, t) - \underline{A}^* \underline{x}^0$

$$\therefore\ \underline{\pi}^{k+1} = A^{*T} \underline{\lambda}^k + \left[\frac{\partial \underline{f}^T}{\partial x^0} \bigg|_{\underline{x}^0 = x^{0k}} \right] \underline{\lambda}^k$$

with
$$\frac{\partial \underline{f}^T}{\partial \underline{x}^0} = \begin{bmatrix} 0 & A_2 x_2^0 \cos x_1^0 + B_2 \cos 2x_1^0 & C_2 \sin x_1^0 \\ -1 & A_1 & 0 \\ 0 & A_2 \sin x_1^0 & C_1 \end{bmatrix}$$

<u>Results and comments</u>

This problem was solved on the IBM 370/165 computer for different values of $\underline{x}(0)$, T, Q, R. Table 1 gives the different values of x(0), T, Q and R used as well as the necessary time of calculation for each trial. The test for convergence was chosen as follows

$$\sum_{i=1}^{3} \int_0^T (x_i^{0k+1} - x_i^{0k})^2 dt < 10^{-4}$$

and
$$\sum_{i=1}^{3} \int_0^T (\pi_i^{k+1} - \pi_i^k)^2 dt < 10^{-4}$$

The initial guess is chosen to be: $\underline{x}^{01} = \underline{o}$, $\underline{\pi}^1 = \underline{0}$.

From the results of this example, we note that

1. The algorithm converges more rapidly if R_0 is sufficiently large, Q and T sufficiently small and the initial choice of $\underline{x}^{01}$, $\underline{\pi}^{1}$ is in the neighbourhood of the optimal solution. (This is indicated by the values of $\underline{x}(0)$. Thus if $\underline{x}(0)$ is small, the initial guess of $\underline{x}^{01}$, $\underline{\pi}^{1}$ which we have chosen is in the neighbourhood of the optimal solution.

2. The algorithm diverges if

i) For the same values of $\underline{x}(0)$, Q, T the matrix R is not sufficiently large.

ii) For the same values of Q, T, R the initial perturbation $\underline{x}(0)$ is sufficiently large (which means that the initial guess of $\underline{x}^{01}$ and $\underline{\pi}^{1}$ is far from the optimal solution).

iii) For the same values of $\underline{x}(0)$ the horizon of optimization is sufficiently large, the matrix Q is not sufficiently small and the matrix R is not sufficiently large.

Also we tried to solve the problem with

$$\underline{y}0^T = [0.5 \; - \; 0.4 \;\; 8.0] \; ; \quad Q = \text{diag}\,[16.75 \;\; 16.75 \;\; 11.75]$$

$$R = \text{diag}\,[8 \;\; 8] \text{ and } T = 2 \text{ sec.}$$

but the algorithm diverged. However, to arrive at the convergence of the algorithm for these values of $\underline{x}(0)$, Q, R, T the algorithm can be initialised with R_1 sufficiently large and Q_1 sufficiently small such that the algorithm converges. Then each time we can decrease the matrix R_1 by $\Delta R = 0.20$ and increase the matrix Q_1 by $\Delta Q = 0.25$ until we get the convergence of the algorithm for the desired values of R, Q, T, $\underline{x}(0)$.

Figures 5 to 8 represent the optimal trajectories of x_1, x_2, x_3, and u respectively. The numbers in the curves correspond to the following

Curve (1) the solution obtained for

$$\underline{y}_0^T = [0.5 \;\; -0.4 \;\; 8.0] \; ; \quad Q = \text{diag}\,[11 \;\; 11 \;\; 5], \; R = 4 \; ; \quad T = 2 \text{ sec}$$

Curve (2) the solution of the free system, i.e. the control u_s is constant and equal to 1.1.

Finally, to compare this method with the quasilinearization one, the problem is solved for

$$\underline{y}_0^T = [0.7347 \;\; -0.2151 \;\; 7.7450] \; ; \quad R = 100 \; ; \quad Q = \text{diag}\,[1 \;\; 1 \;\; 0.1]$$

and $T = 2$ sec.

by the quasilinearization method. The optimal solution is obtained at the end of 15 sec in comparison with 6.26 sec with the method developed here.

Hence we can conclude that: if the physical problem is well adapted to this method, the time of calculation necessary to solve the problem is less than that required by the quasilinearization method even if the sub-problems are solved sequentially on a monoprocessor. In addition to this, we have the following two advantages

a) the possibility of using a multiprocessor system

b) the storage requirements is less than that of the quasilinearization method.

On the other hand, one can see that this method is sensitive to the values

TABLE (1)

	The initial conditions $\underline{y}^T(t_o)$			Q	R	T	Time of calculation
1	0.735	-0.215	7.745	diag [1 1 0.1]	diag [100 100]	2 sec.	6.26 sec.
2	0.5	-0.4	8.0	diag [1 1 0.1]	diag [100 100]	2 sec.	7.15 sec.
3	0.5	-0.4	8.0	diag [1 1 0.1]	diag [10 10]	2 sec.	13.49 sec.
4	0.5	-0.4	8.0	diag [10 10 5]	diag [15 15]	2 sec.	19.63 sec.
5	0.5	-0.4	8.0	diag [15 15 10]	diag [15 15]	2 sec.	26.48 sec.
6	0.5	-0.4	8.0	diag [10 10 5]	diag [15 15]	3 sec.	58.98 sec.
7	0.5	-0.4	8.0	diag [10 10 5]	diag [15 15]	4 sec.	divergence
8	0.5	-0.4	8.0	diag [10 10 5]	diag [25 25]	4 sec.	81.59 sec.
9	0.5	-0.5	8.0	diag [10 10 15]	diag [15 15]	6 sec.	divergence
10	0.5	-0.5	8.0	diag [1 1 0.1]	diag [100 100]	6 sec.	31.26 sec.
11	-0.5	1.4	10.	diag [15 15 10]	diag [15 15]	2 sec.	divergence
12	-0.5	1.4	10.	diag [15 15 10]	diag [40 40]	2 sec.	54.81 sec.
13	-0.5	1.4	10.	diag [15 15 10]	diag [50 50]	2 sec.	36.89 sec.

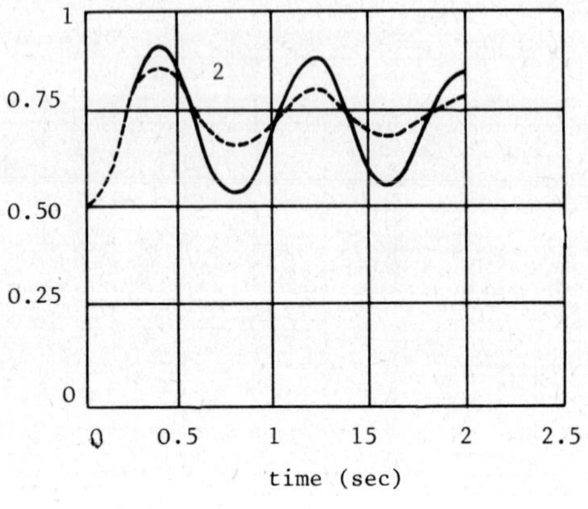

Figure (5)

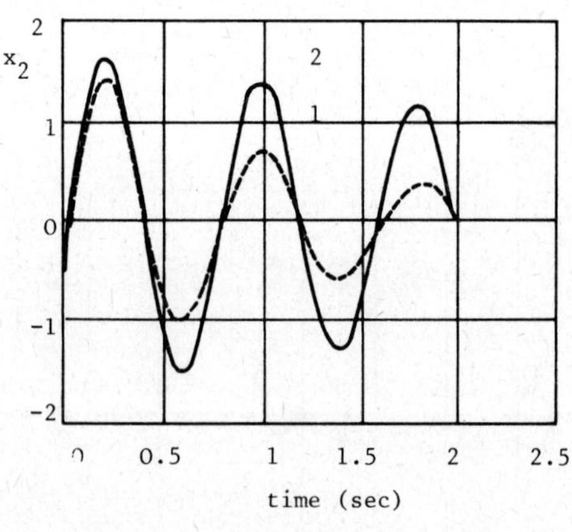

Figure (6)

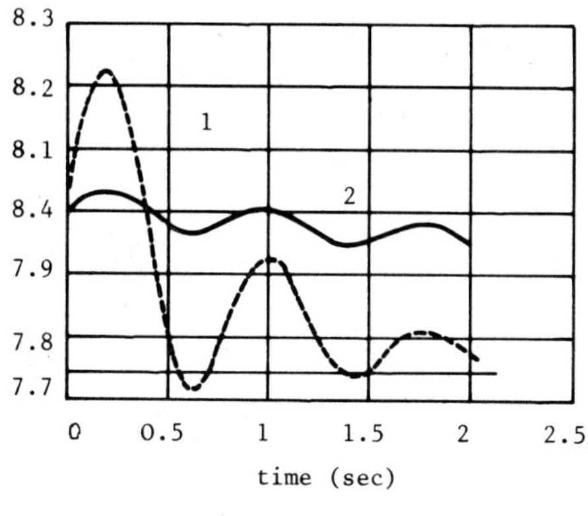

Figure (7)

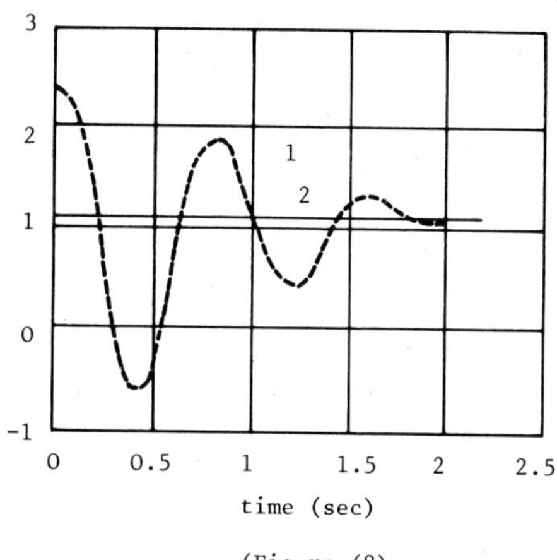

(Figure (8)

of the matrices Q and R, the initial guess of $\underline{x}^0$, $\underline{u}^0$, $\underline{\pi}$ and $\underline{\beta}$ as well as to the horizon of optimization T.

However, these limitations can be found in all the methods, for example, the quasilinearization method is also sensitive to the initial guess of the state vector as well as the adjoint vector [87].

4.5 Conclusion

In these two sections we examined in detail an important algorithm for the optimization of non-linear systems using a decomposition-coordination technique which is oriented towards the successive approximation methods and in which we used the prediction or relaxation principle.

Three essential conclusions arise from this study

1. There exists an interval of time in which the algorithm converges towards the optimal solution and which depends on the weighting matrices Q and R as well as on the initial guess of the coordinating variables. Although it is possible to increase the no. of cases for which the algorithm converges this is limited by the necessary time of calculation.

2. The algorithm only satisfies the set of equations of the global system at the end of the iterations. Therefore, one has to wait till the convergence of the algorithm before applying the control law to the system. Thus, this method is an off-line method of calculation. Naturally, for systems with slow dynamics w.r.t. the necessary time of calculations, one can investigate the applicability of this algorithm on-line.

3. This algorithm is well adapted to the utilisation of multiprocessor system. Also, it allows a reduction of the storage requirements even if the problem is solved on a single processor. Finally, for problems inside the domain of applicability of this algorithm, there is a reduction in the computational time at least for the example we have treated.

5. OPTIMIZATION OF NON-LINEAR SYSTEMS BY A TWO LEVEL COSTATE PREDICTION METHOD [97, 47]

In this approach, the second level predicts all the vectors generating the non-linearities in the system as well as the costate vector. Thus, we pass from non-linear systems to linear time varying or invariant systems at the first level. By solving the primal problem and without the use of the strong duality theorem of Lagrange, we avoid the difficulty of the existence of a duality gap between the primal and dual problems. At the first level, we have to integrate the state equation with the given initial conditions while at the second level we predict the states and controls generating the non-linearities in the system as well as the vectors of the Lagrange multipliers and integrate the costate vector with known final conditions. Thus we avoid the solution of the matrix Riccati equation at the first level and hence one can expect a saving in the calculations required

5.1 Formulation of the problem

Consider the following problem

$$\min_{\underline{x},\underline{u}} J = \tfrac{1}{2}\,||\underline{x}(T)||^2_{S_i} \int_0^T (||\underline{x}||^2_{Q_1} + ||\underline{u}||^2_{R_1})dt \tag{51}$$

s.t. $\quad \dot{\underline{x}} = \underline{f}(\underline{x},\underline{u},t)$ (52)

where: $\quad \underline{x}\epsilon R^n,\ \underline{u}\epsilon R^m,\ \underline{f}\ ;\ \ R^n \times R^m \rightarrow R^n\ ;\ \ Q_1, S_1 \geqslant 0\ ;\ \ R_i \quad 0$

This problem can be written in the form

$$\min_{\underline{x},\underline{x}^0,\underline{u},\underline{u}^0} \quad J = \tfrac{1}{2}\ ||\underline{x}(T)||^2_S + \tfrac{1}{2}\ ||\underline{x}^0(T)||^2_{S_2} + \tfrac{1}{2}\int_0^T \{||\underline{x}||^2_Q + ||\underline{x}^0||^2_{Q_2}$$

$$+ ||\underline{u}||^2_R + ||\underline{u}^0||^2_{R_2}\}dt$$

s.t.
$$\dot{\underline{x}} = A\underline{x} + B\underline{u} + \left[\underline{f}(\underline{x}^0,\underline{u}^0,t) - A\underline{x}^0 - B\underline{u}^0\right]$$

$$\underline{x}^0 = \underline{x}$$

$$\underline{u}^0 = \underline{u}$$

where A, B, Q, R and S are block diagonal matrices with N blocks corresponding to N subsystems, A and B are assumed to be stationary for the moment; $R_i > 0$, Q_i and $S_i \geqslant 0$.

By writing the Hamiltonian of this problem one can get the following 1st order necessary conditions for optimality

$$\underline{u} = -R^{-1}B^T\underline{\lambda} - R^{-1}\underline{\beta} \tag{53}$$

$$\dot{\underline{x}} = A\underline{x} + BR^{-1}\left[-B^T\underline{\lambda} - \underline{\beta}\right] + \underline{D}(\underline{x}^0,\underline{u}^o,t) \tag{54}$$

with $\quad \underline{x}(0) = \underline{x}_0$

where $\quad \underline{D}(\underline{x}^0,\underline{u}^0,t) = f(\underline{x}^0,\underline{u}^0,t) - A\underline{x}^0 - B\underline{u}^0$ (55)

$$\dot{\underline{\lambda}} = -A^T\underline{\lambda} - \underline{\Pi} - Q\underline{x} \tag{56}$$

with $\quad \underline{\lambda}(T) = S_2\underline{x}^0(T) + S\underline{x}(\tau)$

$$\underline{x}^0 = \underline{x} \tag{57}$$

$$\underline{u}^0 = \underline{u} \tag{58}$$

$$\dot{\underline{\lambda}} = Q_2\underline{x}^0 + \left[\left.\frac{\partial \underline{f}^T}{\partial \underline{x}}\right|_{\substack{\underline{x}=\underline{x}^0 \\ \underline{u}=\underline{u}^0}} - A^T\right]\underline{\lambda} \tag{59}$$

$$\underline{\beta} = R_2\underline{u}^0 + \left[\left.\frac{\partial \underline{f}^T}{\partial \underline{u}}\right|_{\substack{\underline{x}=\underline{x}^0 \\ \underline{u}=\underline{u}^0}} - B^T \right] \underline{\lambda} \qquad (60)$$

where $\underline{\Pi}$ and $\underline{\beta}$ are the Lagrange multipliers corresponding to the equality constraints $\underline{x}^0=\underline{x}$ and $\underline{u}^0=\underline{u}$.

Based on these equations, we propose the following algorithm:

1. The upper level provides an initial guess of the vectors $\underline{x}^0$, $\underline{u}^0$, $\underline{\beta}$, $\underline{\lambda}$ and we put k = 1 (where k is the iteration index).

2. At the first level, each subsystem solves the equations (53) and (54) for the trajectories $\underline{x}^k$ and $\underline{u}^k$ and sends the results to the 2nd level.

3. The 2nd level calculates first the vector $\underline{\Pi}^{k+1}$, then it solves the equation (56) to get $\underline{\lambda}^{k+1}$ and hence calculates $\underline{\beta}^{k+1}$ and finally the trajectories $\underline{x}^{0k+1}$, $\underline{u}^{0k+1}$ from the equation (60), (57) and (58) respectively.

If: $$\int_0^T ||\boldsymbol{\lambda}^{k+1} - \boldsymbol{\lambda}^k||^2 \, dt \leq \varepsilon \; ; \quad \boldsymbol{\lambda}^{k^T} = \left[\underline{u}^{0k^T}, \underline{\beta}^{k^T}, \underline{x}^{0k^T}, \underline{\lambda}^{k^T}\right]$$

where ε is a small number chosen apriori, we stop the iterations and record the optimal solution. If not we go to step (2).

Fig. 9 represents the transfer of informations between the two levels achieved by this method.

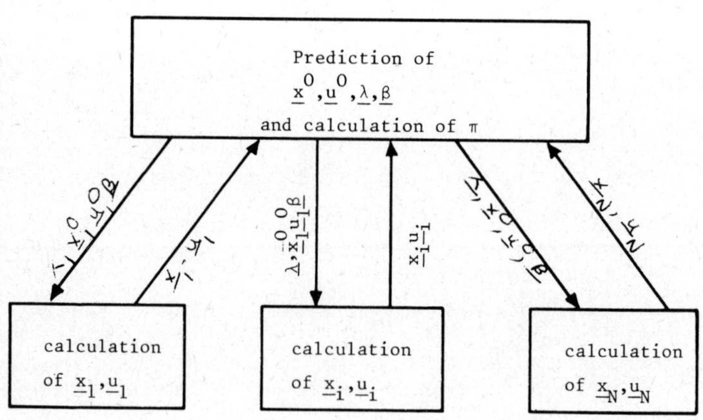

Fig. 9

The study of the convergence of this method is presented in appendix 4 on the basis of the following two theorems

Theorem 1

Assuming that the problem has an optimal solution given by $\hat{\underline{x}},\hat{\underline{u}}$ let us define the matrix Γ as follows

$$\Gamma = \begin{bmatrix} R^{-1} & -R^{-1}B^T \end{bmatrix}$$

Then if

a) $\mu_1 < 1$ where $\mu_1 = \sup\{||\Gamma||,||R_2||\}$

b) the components of $\underline{f}$ are continuous bounded functions of $\underline{x}$ and $\underline{u}$

c) the components of $\underline{f}$ are continuously differentiable functions w.r.t. $\underline{x}$ and $\underline{u}$ and their derivatives are bounded functions of $\underline{x}$ and $\underline{u}$. Then

there exists an open interval of time such that for all values of the final time taken in this interval the algorithm converges to the optimal solution.

Theorem 2

Assuming that the problem has an optimal solution given by $\hat{\underline{x}}$ and $\hat{\underline{u}}$ let the matrix Γ be defined as in theorem 1. Then if

a) $\mu_1 < 1$ where $\mu_1 = \sup\{||\Gamma||,||R_2||\}$

b) the components of $\underline{f}$ are continuous functions of $\underline{x}$ and $\underline{u}$ and cannot take infinite values except if $\underline{x}$ and/or $\underline{u}$ are infinite

c) the components of $\underline{f}$ are continuously differentiable functions w.r.t. $\underline{x}$ and $\underline{u}$ and their derivatives cannot take infinite values except if $\underline{x}$ and/or $\underline{u}$ are infinite

d) $\underline{x}^{01},\underline{u}^{01},\underline{\beta}^{1},\underline{\lambda}^{1}$ are chosen in the neighbourhood of the optimal solution $\hat{\underline{x}},\hat{\underline{u}},\hat{\underline{\beta}},\hat{\underline{\lambda}}$.

then there exists an open interval of time $\tau > 0$, depending on the initial choice of $\underline{x}^{01},\underline{u}^{01},\underline{\beta}^{1},\underline{\lambda}^{1}$ such that for $T < \tau$ all the points of the successive iterations remain in a compact domain which contains the optimal solution and this ensures the convergence of the algorithm to the optimal solution.

5.2 Applications

In this section, we shall apply the discrete version of this algorithm to two examples. The first one is that treated by Mahmoud et al [97] while the second one is that of the control of a synchronous machine given by Jamshidi [99] for which we shall apply the algorithm for different values of k_f, $\underline{x}(k0)$, Q,R. Finally and for the purpose of comparison, we shall apply this algorithm on the example of the synchronous machine treated in Part I of this paper.

5.3 Example (1)

The problem is given by

$$\min J = \sum_{k=0}^{50} 0.05x_1^2(k) + 0.05\, x_2^2(k) + 0.1\, u_1^2(k) + 0.05\, u_2^2(k)$$

s.t.

$$\left.\begin{aligned} x_1(k+1) &= 0.9\, x_1(k) + 0.1\, x_2(k) + 0.1\, u_1(k) \\ x_2(k+1) &= 0.9\, x_1(k) + 0.1\, x_2(k) - 0.1\, x_2^2(k) + 0.1\, u_2(k) \end{aligned}\right\}$$

with $x_1(0) = 10.0$; $x_2(0) = 4.5$

By fixing the non-linearities and decomposing the system into two subsystems we get the following optimization problem.

min (3.1)

s.t.

$$\left.\begin{aligned} x_1(k+1) &= 0.9\, x_1(k) + 0.1\, x_2^*(k) + 0.1\, u_1(k) \\ x_2(k+1) &= 0.2\, x_1^*(k) + (0.1 - 0.1\, x_2^*(k)\, x_2(k) + 0.1\, u_2(k) \end{aligned}\right\}$$

$$x_1^*(k) = x_1(k)$$

$$x_2^*(k) = x_2(k)$$

Results and remarks

This problem was solved on the IBM 370/165 computer. The convergence took place after 1.63 sec. The test for the end of the convergence was chosen to be:

$$\sum_{i=1}^{2} \sum_{k=0}^{50} \left[x_i^{L+1}(k) - x_i^L(k)\right]^2 < 10^{-3}$$

$$\sum_{i=1}^{2} \sum_{k=0}^{50} \left[\lambda_i^{L+1}(k) - \lambda_i^L(k)\right]^2 < 10^{-3}$$

where L is the iteration index and $\underline{\lambda}$ is the adjoint vector.

Figs. 10 to 13 represent the optimal solution which corresponds to a value for $J = 30.9765$.

Comparing this result with that obtained by Mahmoud et al [97] we found that they get a value of $J = 57.2$.

This difference may be explained by the fact that using a coordination method based on the duality theorem for a non-linear problem (with equality constraints) a duality gap may exist [100].

5.4 Example (2)

In this example we apply the algorithm to the problem of optimization of the synchronous machine [6th order model] given by Jamshidi [99]. The problem is

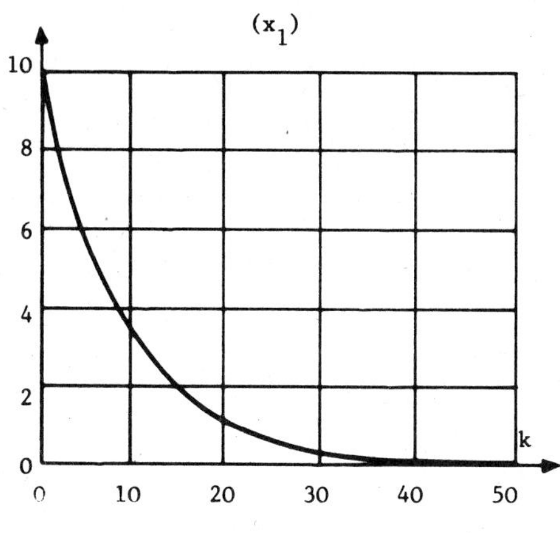

Figure (10)

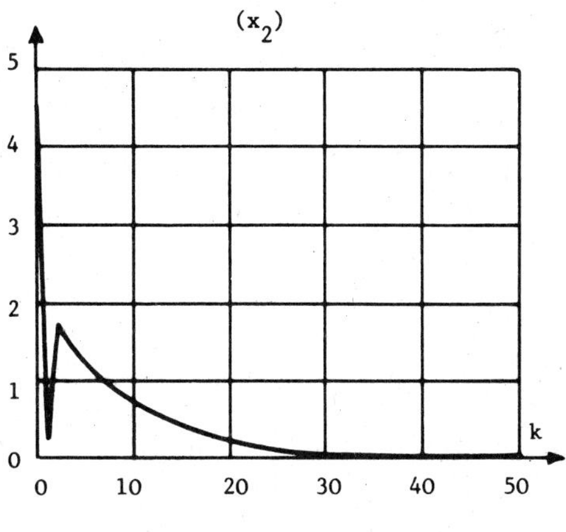

Figure (11)

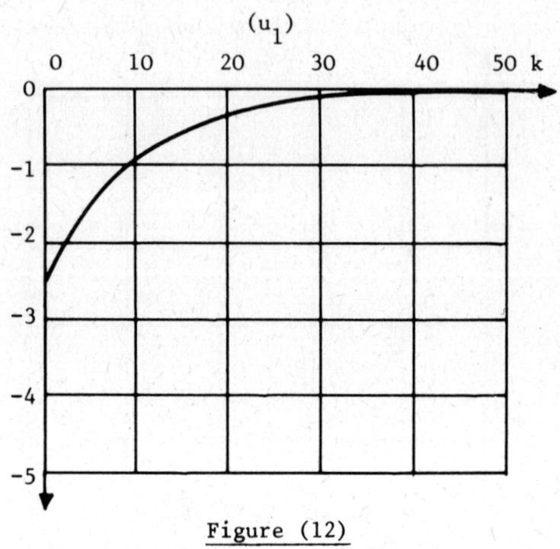

Figure (12)

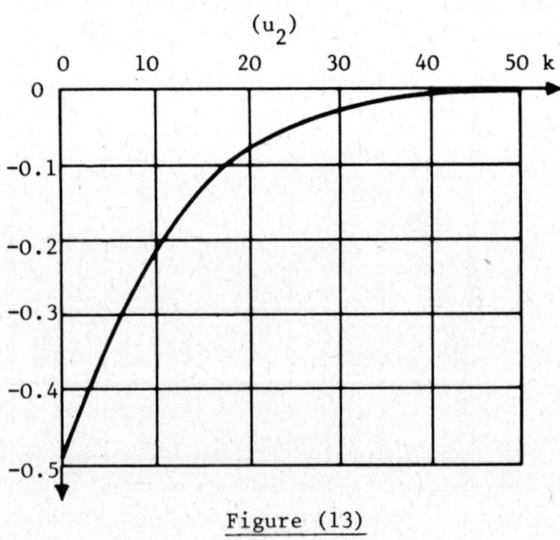

Figure (13)

as follows

$$\min J = \tfrac{1}{2}\int_0^T \Big[Q_{11}(x_1 - x_{f1})^2 + Q_{33}(x_3 - x_{fs})^2 + R_{11}(u_1 - u_{f1})^2 + R_{22}(u_2 - u_{f2})$$
$$R_{22}(u_2 - u_{f2})^2\Big]dt$$

s.t.

$$\left.\begin{aligned}
\dot{x}_1 &= x_2 \\
\dot{x}_2 &= C_1x_2 - C_2x_3\sin x_1 - 0.5\ C_3 \sin 2x_1 + \frac{x_5}{M} \\
\dot{x}_3 &= x_6 - C_4x_3 + C_5 \cos x_1
\end{aligned}\right\}$$

$$\dot{x}_4 = K_1u_1 + K_2x_2 - K_3x_4$$

$$\dot{x}_5 = K_4x_4 - K_5x_5$$

$$\dot{x}_6 = K_6u_2 - K_7x_6$$

where $C_1 = 2.165$ $C_2 = 13.957$ $C_3 = 55.565$ $C_4 = 1.02$ $C_5 = 4.0491$

$K_1 = 9.4425$ $K_2 = 1.019$ $K_3 = 5.0$ $K_4 = 2.04$ $K_5 = 2.04$

$K_6 = 1.5$ $K_7 = 0.5$ $x_{f1} = 0$ $x_{f3} = 3.969$ $u_{f1} = u_{f2} = 0$

Discretising the problem in time and taking $\Delta T = \frac{T}{N-1}$ we get

$$\min J = \frac{\Delta T}{2}\sum_{k=1}^{N}\Big|Q_{11}(x_1(k) - x_{f1})^2 + Q_{33}(x_3(k) - x_{f3})^2 + R_{11}(u_1(k) - u_{f1})^2$$
$$+ R_{22}(u_2(k) - u_{f2})^2\Big|$$

s.t.

$$\left.\begin{aligned}
x_1(k+1) &= x_1(k) + \Delta T\ x_2(k) \\
x_2(k+2) &= (1 - \Delta T\ C_1)\ x_2(k) - \Delta T\ C_2\ x_3(k)\ \sin x_1(k) \\
&\quad -0.5\ \Delta T\ C_3\ \sin 2\ x_1(k) + \frac{\Delta T}{M}\ x_5(k) \\
x_3(k+1) &= (1 - \Delta T\ C_4)\ x_3(k) + \Delta T\ x_6(k) + \Delta T\ C_5\ \cos x_1(k) \\
x_4(k+1) &= (1 - \Delta T\ K_3)\ x_4(k) + K_2\ \Delta T\ x_2(k) + \Delta T\ K_1\ u_1(k) \\
x_5(k+1) &= (1 - \Delta T\ K_5)\ x_5(k) + \Delta T\ K_4\ x_4(k)
\end{aligned}\right\}$$

$$x_6(k+1) = (1 - \Delta T\ K_2)\ x_6(k) + \Delta T\ K_6\ u_2(k)$$

By fixing the non-linearities and decomposing the problem into 6 subproblems we finally get min J

$$\text{s.t.} \quad \left.\begin{aligned} x_1(k+1) &= x_1(k) + \Delta T\, x_2^*(k) \\ x_2(k+1) &= (1 - \Delta T\, C_1)\, x_2(k) - \Delta T\, C_2\, x_3^*(k) \sin x_1^*(k) - \\ &\quad 0.5\ T\, C_3 \sin 2\, x_1^*(k) + \frac{\Delta T}{M} x_5^*(k) \\ x_3(k+1) &= (1 - \Delta T\, C_4)\, x_5(k) + \Delta T\, x_6^*(k) + \Delta T\, C_5\, C_j\, x_1^*(k) \\ x_4(k+1) &= (1 - \Delta T\, K_3)\, x_4(k) + K_2\, \Delta T\, x_2^*(k) + \Delta T\, K_1\, u_1(k) \\ x_5(k+1) &= (1 - \Delta T\, K_5)\, x_5(k) + \Delta T\, K_4\, x_4^*(k) \\ x_6(k+1) &= (1 - \Delta T\, K_7)\, x_6(k) + \Delta T\, K_6\, u_2(k) \end{aligned}\right\}$$

$$x_i^*(k) = x_i(k) \qquad i=1,2,\ldots 6$$

Results and discussion

This problem was solved for different values of $\underline{x}(1)$, N, Q and R. Table (2) gives the chosen values for these variables and the necessary computational time to get the convergence.

The test at the end of the convergence was chosen to be

$$\sum_{i=1}^{6} \sum_{k=1}^{N} (x_i^{0L+1}(k) - x_i^{0L}(k))^2 < 10^{-4}$$

$$\sum_{i=1}^{6} \sum_{k=1}^{N} (\lambda_i^{L+1}(k) - \lambda_i^{L}(k))^2 < 10^{-4}$$

with the initial guess given by

$$x_1^{01}(k) = 0\ ;\quad x_2^{01}(k) = 0,\ x_3^{01}(k1 = 3.969,\ x_4^{01}(k) = 0,\ x_5^{01}(k) = 0$$

$$x_6^{01}(k) = 0\ ;\quad \underline{\lambda}(k) =)\quad k = 1,2,\ldots N$$

Figs. 14 to 21 represent the trajectories of the state variables $x_i(k)$; $i=1,2,\ldots 6$ and controls $u_i(k)$; $i=1,2$ respectively for the 16th trial for which J = 0.3319.

From these results we note that

1. for fixed values of $\underline{x}(1)$ and N the algorithm converges more rapidly if R is large and Q small.

2. On the other hand for fixed values of $\underline{x}(1)$ and N if R is not sufficiently large and Q not sufficiently small, the algorithm converges

3. For the same values of $\underline{x}(1)$, Q, R, the algorithm converges more rapidly if N is small.

4. If N, Q, R are fixed, the algorithm converges more rapidly if the initial choice of $\underline{x}^0$ and $\underline{\lambda}$ are in the neighbourhood of the optimal solution. (In other words, the algorithm converges more rapidly if $\underline{x}(1)$ if smaller.)

TABLE (2)

	Initial conditions $\underline{x}(1)$						Q_{11}	Q_{44}	R_{11}	R_{22}	N with $\Delta T = 0.025$	Time of calculation
1	0.7105	0	4.2	0.8	0.8	0.5	4	4	1.0	1.0	161	2.33 sec.
2	0.7105	0	4.2	0.8	0.8	0.5	100	100	1.0	1.0	161	2.82 sec.
3	0.7105	0	4.2	0.8	0.8	0.5	100	100	0.1	0.1	161	3.62 sec.
4	0.7105	0	4.2	0.8	0.8	0.5	120	120	0.1	0.1	161	4.12 sec.
5	0.7105	0	4.2	0.8	0.8	0.5	100	100	0.05	0.05	161	4.48 sec.
6	0.7105	0	4.2	0.8	0.8	0.5	150	150	0.1	0.1	161	osc.
7	0.7105	0	4.2	0.8	0.8	0.5	100	100	0.01	0.01	161	diverg.
8	0.7105	0	4.2	0.8	0.8	0.5	100	100	0.1	0.1	201	5.48 sec.
9	0.7105	0	4.2	0.8	0.8	0.5	100	100	0.1	0.1	241	7.52 sec.
10	0.4105	0.1	3.5	0.2	-0.3	0.3	120	120	0.1	0.1	161	3.85 sec.
11	0.4105	0.1	3.5	0.2	-0.3	0.3	50	50	0.1	0.1	161	2.95 sec.
12	0.4105	0.1	3.5	0.2	-0.3	0.3	50	50	0.1	0.1	241	6.04 sec.
13	0.4105	0.1	3.5	0.2	-0.3	0.3	10	10	0.01	0.01	241	7.32 sec.
14	0.4105	0.1	3.5	0.2	-0.3	0.3	50	50	0.05	0.05	241	7.39 sec.
15	0.4105	0.1	3.5	0.2	-0.3	0.3	10	10	0.1	0.1	241	4.3 sec.
16	0.4105	0.1	3.5	0.2	-0.3	0.3	4	4	0.01	0.01	241	5.65 sec.
17	0.4105	0.1	3.5	0.2	-0.3	0.3	4	4	0.005	0.005	241	6.78 sec.

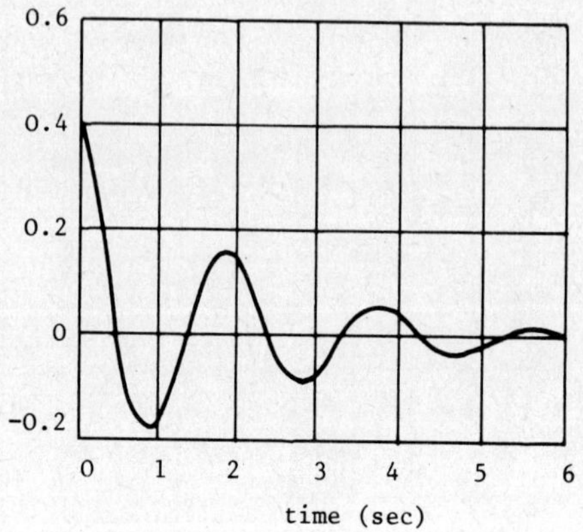

Figure (14)

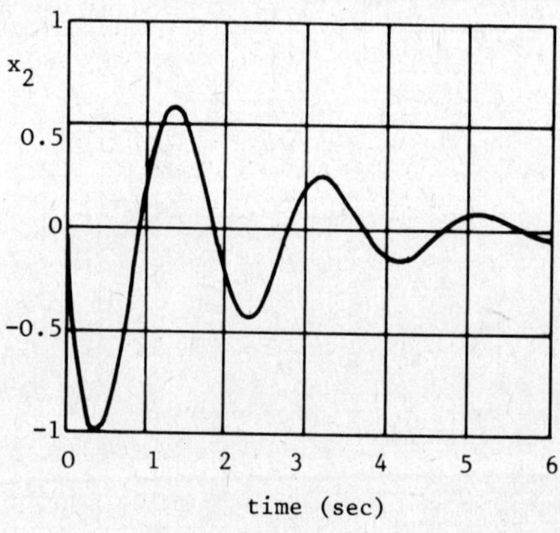

Figure (15)

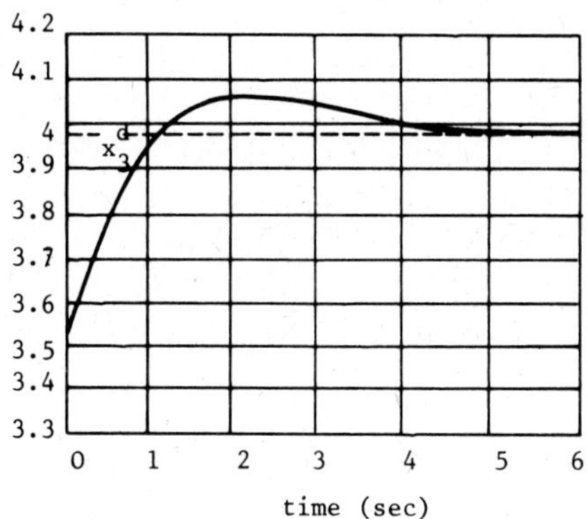

Figure (16)

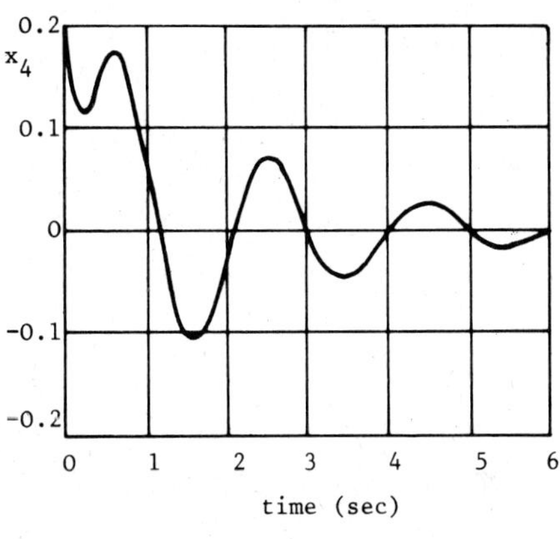

Figure (17)

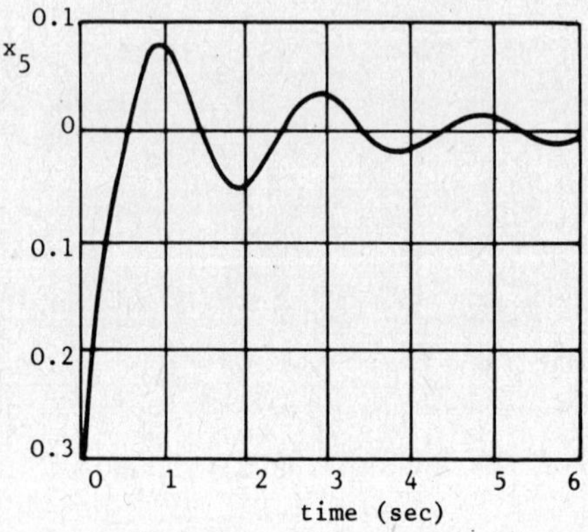

Figure (18)

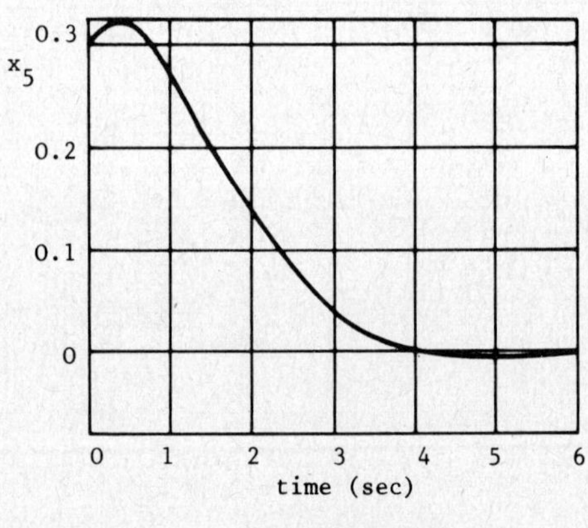

Figure (19)

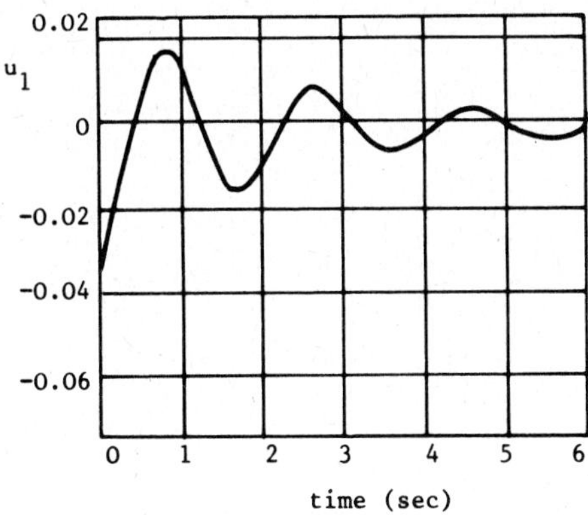

Figure (20)

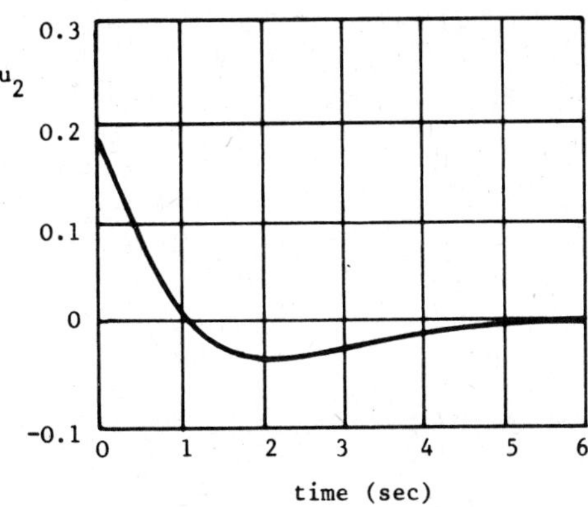

Figure (21)

5.5 Example (3)

To compare this method with that developed earlier in this chapter, we applied this algorithm to the example of the synchronous machine treated earlier. We got the following results

1. For $\underline{Y}_0^T = [0.7347 \ - 0.2151 \ \ 7.7450]$, R = 100,

   Q = diag [1.0 1.0 0.1]; T = 2 sec. The convergence was obtained after 2.23 secs

2. For $\underline{Y}_0^T = [-0.5 \ \ 1.4 \ \ 1.0]$; Q = diag [15 15 10]

   R = 50, T = 2 sec. the algorithm oscillated.

Thus, we note that

1. This algorithm is more sensitive than the previous method to the initial guess of the trajectories.

2. If the problem is well adapted to this method, the convergence is more rapid than both that of the method developed in Part I and the classical quasilinearisation technique.

6. OPTIMIZATION OF NON-LINEAR SYSTEMS USING A THREE LEVEL ALGORITHM [98,101]

In this section we develop a three level algorithm of the same class as that developed in section 5. The only difference is that we add a third level which solves the equations of the costate vector. Thus, we again avoid the solution of the $TPBV_p$ at the same level and this also makes the problem of the convergence at each level much easier and we hope that it reduces the necessary time to get the final convergence. The algorithm uses at the third level the prediction principle of Takahara [12] and at the second level the method of the coordination of the adjoint vector developed previously.

6.1 Problem Formulation

For this algorithm we consider the same problem as given in section 5.1. Rewriting the necessary conditions of optimality we have

$$\underline{u} = -R^{-1}B^T\underline{\lambda} \ -R^{-1}\underline{\beta} \tag{61a}$$

$$\dot{\underline{x}} = A\underline{x} + BR^{-1}\left[-B^T\underline{\lambda} - \underline{\beta}\right] + \underline{D}(\underline{x}^0,\underline{u}^0,t) \tag{61b}$$

with $\underline{x}(0) = \underline{x}_0$

where $\underline{D}(x^0,\underline{u}^0,t) = \underline{f}(\underline{x}^0,\underline{u}^0,t) - A\underline{x}^0 - B\underline{u}^0$

$$\dot{\underline{\lambda}} = A^T\underline{\lambda} - \underline{\pi} - Q\underline{x} \tag{63}$$

with $\underline{\lambda}(T) = S_2\underline{x}^0(T) + S\,\underline{x}(T)$

$\underline{x}^0 = \underline{x}$

$$\underline{u}^0 = \underline{u} \tag{64}$$

$$\underline{\Pi} = Q_2\underline{x}^0 + \left[\frac{\partial \underline{f}^T}{\partial \underline{x}} \Bigg|_{\substack{\underline{x}=\underline{x}^0 \\ \underline{u}=\underline{u}^0}} - A^T \right] \underline{\lambda} \tag{65}$$

$$\underline{\beta} = R_2\underline{u}^0 + \left[\frac{\partial \underline{f}^T}{\partial u} \Bigg|_{\substack{\underline{u}=\underline{u}^0 \\ \underline{x}=\underline{x}^0}} - B^T \right] \underline{\lambda} \tag{62b}$$

Substituting from 4.1.7 in 4.1.4 we get

$$\dot{\underline{\lambda}} = - \left[\frac{\partial \underline{f}^T}{\partial \underline{x}} \Bigg|_{\substack{\underline{x}=\underline{x}^0 \\ \underline{u}=\underline{u}^0}} \right] \underline{\lambda} - Q_2\underline{x}^0 - Q\underline{x} \tag{62a}$$

Hence, we propose the following algorithm

1. The 3rd level provides an initial guess of the trajectories $\underline{x}^0, \underline{u}^0$ and sends them to the 1st and 2nd level (we put k=1 where k is the iteration index).

2. The 2nd level gives an initial guess to the vectors $\underline{\lambda}(t)$ and $\underline{p}(t)$. We put the iteration index L=0 and we transfer this information to the 1st level.

3. At the 1st level, each subsystem calculates the control vector $u_i^{kL}(t)$ as well as the state vector $\underline{x}_i^{kL}(t)$, i=1 to N from equations (61 a,b) and communicates the results to the 2nd and 3rd levels.

4. At the 2nd level we integrate equation 62a for $\underline{\lambda}(t)$ with the given final conditions, put L=L+1. Then we calculated $\underline{\beta}^{k(L+1)}(t)$ using the results $\underline{\lambda}^{k(L+1)}(t)$. If

$$\int_0^T ||\underline{x}^{0k+1} - \underline{x}^{0k}||^2 \, dt \leq \varepsilon_x$$

and

$$\int_0^T ||\underline{u}^{0k+1} - \underline{u}^{0k}||^2 \, dt \leq \varepsilon_u$$

(where ε_x and ε_u are chosen apriori) are satisfied simultaneously, $\underline{x}(t)$ and $\underline{u}(t)$ are the optimal trajectories of the problem. If not we put L=1 at the second level, use the same trajectories of $\underline{\lambda}$ and $\underline{\beta}$ obtained at the final iteration and go to step 3.

Fig. 22 gives the transfer of information between the three levels in this algorithm.

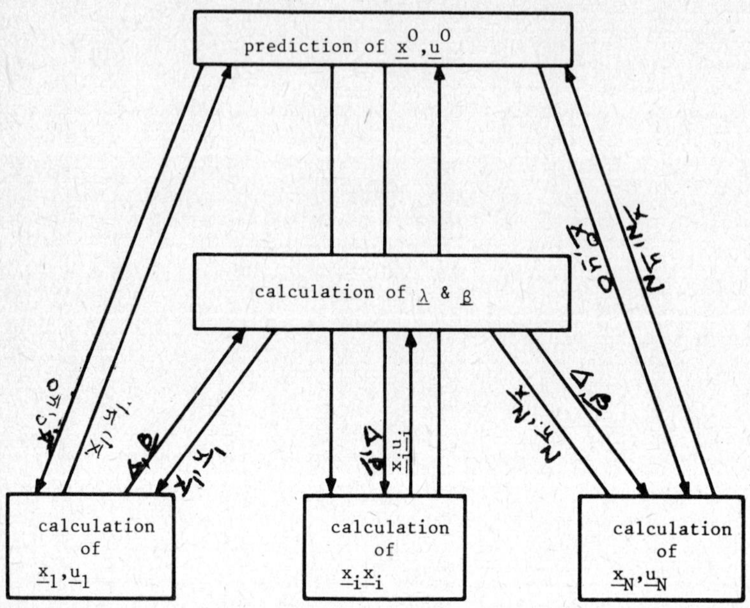

Fig. 22

Remarks

1. With this algorithm we avoid the solution of the TPBVP at the same level.

2. At each level we integrate simple vector equations and not a matrix equation.

3. By dividing the job between the 2nd and 3rd levels one can expect that the convergence of each level is more rapid. This may explain the reduction in the computation time that we have obtained at least for the example we have treated.

The convergence of this algorithm can be obtained from the method developed in section 4 and that developed in section 5. In other words, the convergence of the first two levels can be obtained from theorems (1) and (2) developed in appendix 3 while the convergence of the group |first and second level| on the one hand and the 3rd level on the other can be obtained from theorems (1) and (2) developed in appendix 4.

6.2 Application

To compare the different methods developed in this paper and in section 4 this algorithm was applied to the example of the synchronous machine with $\underline{Y}_0 = [0.7347 \; -0.2151 \; 7.7450]$; R = 1000, Q = diag $[1 \quad 1 \quad 0.1]$ and T = 2.0 sec. The convergence was obtained ater 1.67 sec. in comparison with 6.26 seconds with the method developed in section 4, 2.23 seconds with the algorithm developed in section 5 and 15 seconds with the quasilinearisation technique. Also, as in the method developed in section 5 the algorithm oscillates with $Y_0 = [-0.5 \quad 1.4 \quad 10]$; Q = diag $[15 \quad 15 \quad 10]$, R = 50 which indicates that this algorithm is also sensitive to the initial choice.

6.3 Comparison between the different methods from the point of view of storage requirements

To give an idea about the storage requirements for each algorithm we shall give, in this section, the number of trajectories that must be stored in the memory for each method. For this reason, and for the purpose of simplicity we shall assume that

i) n is the dimension of the state variables

ii) N is the number of subsystems

iii) $\frac{n}{N}$ is the dimension of the state vector for each subsystem

iv) m is the dimension of the control vector

v) We use a single processor system.

I. Takahara's generalized method for non-linear systems (cf. section 4)

In this method we have to store the following

1. $\left[\frac{n}{2N}\left(\frac{n}{N}+1\right)\right]N$ trajectories for the matrix Riccati equation

2. $[n]$ trajectories for the vector $\underline{\xi}$

3. n+m trajectories for $\underline{x}$ and $\underline{u}$.

4. 2n+2m trajectories for $\underline{x}^0, \underline{\beta}, \underline{u}^0, \pi$ at the kth iteration

5. m trajectories for $\underline{\beta}$ at the $(k+1)^{th}$ iteration ($\underline{\pi}^{k+1}$ can be stored in the place of $\underline{\xi}$).

II. Prediction of the adjoint vector and the non-linearities

Here, we have to store the following trajectories

1. 2n+2m trajectories for $\underline{\lambda}, \underline{x}^0, \underline{u}^0, \underline{\beta}$ at the kth iteration

2. n+m trajectories for $\underline{\lambda}, \underline{\beta}$ at the $(k+1)^{th}$ iteration

3. n+m trajectories for $\underline{x}$ and $\underline{u}$.

III. The three level method

1. 2(n+m) trajectories for $\underline{\lambda}, \underline{x}^0, \underline{u}^0, \underline{\beta}$ at the kth iteration

2. n trajectories for $\underline{\lambda}$ at the $k(L+1)^{th}$ iteration

3. n+m trajectories for $\underline{x}, \underline{u}$.

IV. Quasilinearisation [87]

1. 2n trajectories for the initial guess of $\underline{x}, \underline{\lambda}$

2. $2n^2$ trajectories for the homogeneous solution of $\underline{x}, \underline{\lambda}$

3. 2n trajectories for the solution of $\underline{u}$.

6.4 Conclusion

In this chapter we have developed two algorithms for the optimisation of non-linear systems by means of hierarchical calculation and which are oriented towards the class of successive approximation techniques. Again, we used the prediction principle in the development of these algorithms and thus avoided the existence of the duality gap between the primal and dual problem which occurs when using the strong duality theorem of Lagrange [100].

From our study of these algorithms we have three essential conclusions, i.e.

1. For each algorithm there exists an open interval of time in which the algorithm converges to the optimal solution and which depends on the matrices Q and R as well as the initial guess of the coordinating variables.

2. These algorithms don't satisfy the set of equations of the global system except at the end of the iterations.

3. They are well adapted to the use of multiprocessor systems.

In addition, from our comparison between the different methods developed in this chapter and the quasilinearization method we found that the three level algorithm has minimum storage requirements and is the most rapid one at least for the example we have treated. However, it is necessary to study in a detailed quantitative manner the convergence of each algorithm to get a clear idea about the necessary computational time for each method.

7. THE HIERARCHICAL MODEL FOLLOWING CONTROLLER [24, 25]

The problem is to provide a control for a large non-linear plant described by

$$\dot{\underline{x}} = \underline{f}\ (\underline{x},\ t) + B\ \underline{u}_1\ (t) \tag{66}$$

where as usual $\underline{x}$ is an n dimensional state vector $\underline{u}_1$ is an m dimensional control vector, $\underline{f}$ is a non-linear function in C^2. This model describes a system which is linear in the controls. This is an important class of systems.

Now, Control Engineers are most familiar with linear systems and are usually able to define their design objectives in terms of the locations of the pole and zeros, etc. In the present approach we will control our non-linear plant described by equation (66) by forcing it to track the output of a linear plant which has desirable poles and zeros and which thus incorporates realistic design objectives over the fixed horizon of interest 0 - T.

Let us assume that the 'Engineering' design objectives for the plant could be incorporated in the state $\underline{x}_m$ of a linear model whose dynamics are defined by

$$\dot{\underline{x}}_m = A\ \underline{x}_m + B\ \underline{u}_2 \tag{67}$$

where A is the model matrix whose poles have desirable locations, $\underline{x}$ and $\underline{x}_m$ are assumed to be of the same dimension.

Let us define an error $\underline{e}$ between the actual state $\underline{x}$ of the non-linear plant and the desired state $\underline{x}_m$ that the plant should follow, i.e.

let $$\underline{e} = \underline{x} - \underline{x}_m \tag{68}$$

Then $$\dot{\underline{e}} = A\ \underline{e} + B\ \underline{u} + \underline{f}(\underline{x},t) - A\underline{x}$$

or $$\dot{\underline{e}} = A\ \underline{e} + B\ \underline{u} + \underline{\gamma}\,(\underline{x},t) \tag{69}$$

where $$\underline{\gamma}\,(\underline{x},t) = \underline{f}\ (\underline{x},t) - A\ \underline{x} \quad \text{and} \quad \underline{u} = \underline{u}_1 - \underline{u}_2\ . \tag{70}$$

Now, we want to force our non-linear plant's state $\underline{x}$ to track the desired state $\underline{x}_m$ but at the same time we do not want to use excessive control effort. To do this, let us define a cost function of the form

$$J = \int_0^T \left(\tfrac{1}{2}\,\|\underline{e}\|_Q^2 + \tfrac{1}{2}\,\|\underline{u}\|_R^2\right) dt \tag{71}$$

where Q is a block diagonal positive semi-definite matrix and R is a block diagonal positive definite matrix. Let us assume that there are N blocks Q_i, R_i $(i = 1,2,\ldots, N)$ in Q and R. Then J in equation (71) can be rewritten as

$$J = \sum_{i=1}^{N} \int_0^T \tfrac{1}{2}\left(\|\underline{e}_i\|_{Q_i}^2 + \|\underline{u}_i\|_{R_i}^2\right) dt \tag{72}$$

and it is desired to minimise this J subject to the system dynamics (69). Now, it is possible to decompose (69) itself into the form

$$\dot{\underline{e}}_i = A_i\ \underline{e}_i + B_i\ \underline{u}_i + C_i\ \underline{z}_i + \underline{\gamma}_i \tag{73}$$

where $$\underline{z}_i = \sum_{j=1}^{N} L_{ij} \underline{e}_j \tag{74}$$

If γ_i was linear, it would have been possible to solve this problem by duality theory using the Goal Coordination method. However, with the non-linear equality constraint, this method may yield a solution of the dual problem which is different from that of the primal problem,i.e. a duality gap may arise. To avoid this, it will be necessary to use one of the methods described in previous sections which use the prediction principle. Here we will use the penalty function/prediction approach of Hassan and Singh [47] . To do this, define a vector $\underline{e}^*$ of dimension n such that the problem is modified to :

$$J^1 = \sum_{i=1}^{N} \frac{1}{2} \int_0^T \left[\| \underline{e}_i \|^2_{Q_i} + \| \underline{u}_i \|^2_{R_i} + \| \underline{e}_i - \underline{e}_i^* \|^2_{S_i} \right] dt \tag{75}$$

where S_i is a positive definite matrix. J^1 in (75) is to be minimised subject to

$$\dot{\underline{e}}_i = A_i \underline{e}_i + B_i \underline{u}_i + C_i \underline{z}_i^* + \underline{\gamma}_i^* \tag{76}$$

where $$\underline{z}_i^* = \sum_{j=1}^{N} L_{ij} \underline{e}_j^* \tag{77}$$

$$\begin{aligned} \underline{\gamma}_i^* &= \underline{f}_i (\underline{x}_i, t) - A_i \underline{x}_i \\ &= \underline{f}_i (\underline{e}_i^* + \underline{x}_m, t) - A_i \underline{e}_i^* - A_i \underline{x}_m . \end{aligned} \tag{78}$$

Note that if an $\underline{e}^*$ could be found such that $\underline{e} = \underline{e}^*$, then this modified problem becomes identical to the problem of minimising J in (72) subject to (73) and (74). To ensure this, write the Hamiltonian as≠

$$H = \sum_{i=1}^{N} \frac{1}{2} \| \underline{e}_i \|^2_{Q_i} + \frac{1}{2} \| \underline{u}_i \|^2_{R_i} + \frac{1}{2} \| \underline{e}_i - \underline{e}_i^* \|^2_{S_i}$$

$$+ \underline{\lambda}_i^T \left[A_i \underline{e}_i + B_i \underline{u}_i + C_i \underline{z}_i^* + \underline{\gamma}_i^* \right] + \underline{p}_i^T (\underline{e}_i - \underline{e}_i^*) \tag{79}$$

where $\underline{\lambda}_i$ is the adjoint variable for the ith subsystem and $\underline{p}_i$ is a multiplier for the equality constraint

$$\underline{e}_i = \underline{e}_i^* \tag{80}$$

which must be satisfied at the optimum.

Now the Hamiltonian in equation (79) is additively separable and this leads to a two level algorithm where on the first level a "linear quadratic" problem is solved independently for the N subsystems and at the second level $\underline{e}^*$ and $\underline{p}_i$ are improved using the prediction principle, i.e. from iteration k to k + 1

$$\begin{bmatrix} \underline{e}^{*k+1} \\ \underline{p}^{k+1} \end{bmatrix} = \begin{bmatrix} \underline{e}^* (\underline{e}^k, \underline{u}^k, \underline{e}^{*k}, \underline{p}^k) \\ \underline{p} (\underline{e}^k, \underline{u}^k, \underline{e}^{*k}, \underline{p}^k) \end{bmatrix} \tag{81}$$

≠ Since the problem is linear in $\underline{u}$, it is not necessary to add a penalty for $\underline{u}$.

where the function on the R.H.S. is calculated by using the conditions

$$\frac{\partial H}{\partial \underline{e}^*} = \underline{0} \quad \text{and} \quad \frac{\partial H}{\partial \underline{p}} = \underline{0}$$

Remarks

We have shown in a previous Section that such an algorithm will converge uniformly to the optimum. The overall approach is attractive here because

(a) the non-linear problem has been converted into a linear-quadratic problem so that it is not necessary to solve a difficult two point boundary value problem

(b) the design is more practical since it is possible to include "Engineering" considerations in a natural way

(c) experience shows that the two level algorithm is quite efficient

This algorithm has been tested on a number of examples where good results have been obtained. We next describe the application to one of these examples which has been considered by other methods in previous sections, i.e. that of synchronous machine excitation.

8. THE APPLICATION OF THE HIERARCHICAL MODEL FOLLOWER TO SYNCHRONOUS MACHINE EXCITATION

8.1. The System Model

A model for a single machine connected by a transmission line to an infinite bus bar was given as before by Mukhopadhayay [46] to be

$$\begin{aligned} \dot{y}_1 &= y_2 \\ \dot{y}_2 &= B_1 - A_1 y_2 - A_2 y_3 \sin y_1 - \frac{B_2}{2} \sin 2 y_1 \\ \dot{y}_3 &= u - c_1 y_3 + c_2 \cos y_1 \end{aligned} \qquad (83)$$

where we recall that y_1 is the rotor angle (radians)
y_2 is the speed deviation ($\frac{d}{dt}$ y_1 in rad/s)
y_3 is the field flux linkage

and control u is the voltage applied to the field windings of the synchronous machine and is assumed to be available for optimal manipulation. Mukhopadhayay [46] gives desired values for this system to be

$$y_1^* = 0.7461 \text{ radians} \quad ; \quad y_2^* = 0 \text{ rad/s}$$
$$y_3^* = 7.7438 \quad ; \quad u^* = 1.1$$

where in the steady state $y_i \rightarrow y_i^*$ $i = 1, 2, 3$ and $u \rightarrow u^*$. Also
$A_1 = 0.27$, $A_2 = 12.01$, $B_1 = 39.18$, $B_2 = -48.04$, $C_1 = 0.32$, $C_2 = 1.9$

8.2. The Linear Model

It is desired that the system should come back to the given steady state values of y_i^* i = 1,2,3 and u "rapidly". A suitable linear model which incorporates this objective and which has been constructed from steady state considerations could be written as

$$\dot{\underline{y}}_m = A_m \underline{y}_m + B u_m \tag{84}$$

where

$$A_m = \begin{bmatrix} 0 & 1.0 & 0 \\ -64.535 & -0.2703 & -8.1535 \\ -1.28968 & 0.0 & -0.3222 \end{bmatrix} \qquad B = \begin{bmatrix} 0 \\ 0 \\ 1 \end{bmatrix}$$

It is desired that the model should follow the plant.

8.3. Application to the problem

The algorithm of Section 7 was applied to solve the synchronous machine excitation problem using the non-linear machine model given by equations (83) and the linear model given by equation (84). The error dynamics equation could be written as

$$\dot{\underline{e}} = A\,\underline{e} + B\,\underline{u} + \underline{\gamma} \tag{85}$$

with $\underline{\gamma} = \underline{f}(\underline{x}, t) - A\,\underline{x}$

with $A = A_m$ given by equation (84), $\underline{B}^T = (0 \quad 0 \quad 1)$ and $\underline{f}$ being the R.H.S. of equation (83).

The error dynamic equation (85) can be split into two subsystems given by

$$\frac{d}{dt}\begin{bmatrix} e_1 \\ e_2 \end{bmatrix} = \begin{bmatrix} 0 & 1 \\ -64.535 & -0.2703 \end{bmatrix}\begin{bmatrix} e_1 \\ e_2 \end{bmatrix} + \begin{bmatrix} \gamma_1^* \\ \gamma_2^* \end{bmatrix} + \begin{bmatrix} 0 \\ -8.1535 \end{bmatrix} e_3^* \tag{86}$$

and

$$\frac{d}{dt} e_3 = -0.3222\, e_3 + u + \gamma_3^* - 1.28968\, e_1^* \tag{87}$$

where

$$\gamma_1^* = 0 \;;\quad \gamma_2^* = B_1 - A_1 (y_{m_2} - e_2^*) - A_2 (y_{m_3} - e_3^*)$$

$$\sin (y_{m_1} - e_2^*) - \frac{B_2}{2} \sin 2(y_{m_2} - e_1^*)$$

$$-\left[-64.535(y_{m_1} - e_1^*) - 0.2703\,(y_{m_2} - e_2^*) - 8.1535(y_{m_3} - e_3^*)\right]$$

and

$$\gamma_3^* = 1.1 - C_1 (y_{m_3} - e_3^*) + C_2 \cos (y_{m_1} - e_1^*) - \Big[-1.28968\,(y_{m_1} - e_1^*)$$

$$- 0.3222\,(y_{m_3} - e_3^*)\Big]$$

The cost function was chosen to be

$$J = \sum_{i+1}^{2} J_i = \sum_{i=1}^{2} \frac{1}{2} \int_0^{12} (\underline{e}_i^T Q_i \underline{e}_i + \underline{u}_i^T R_i \underline{u}_i + \underline{p}_i^T(\underline{e}_i - \underline{e}_i^*)$$
$$+ (\underline{e}_i - \underline{e}_i^*)^T S (\underline{e}_i - \underline{e}_i^*)) \, dt$$

where

$$Q_1 = \begin{bmatrix} 1 & 0 \\ 0 & 1 \end{bmatrix} \quad Q_2 = 1 \; , \quad R_2 = 1 \quad S_1 = \begin{bmatrix} 1 & 0 \\ 0 & 1 \end{bmatrix} \quad S_2 = 1$$

First level problems

For given e_i^* , p_i , $i = 1,2,3$ it is necessary to minimise J_1 and J_2 independently subject respectively to equations (86) and (87). This can be done by solving a Riccati type equation.

Second level

The second level algorithm here becomes from iteration j to j + 1

$$\underline{e}^{*j+1} = \underline{e}^j$$

and

$$\underline{p}^{j+1} = \left[- S(\underline{e} - \underline{e}^*) - A^T \underline{\lambda} + D^T \underline{\lambda} - \frac{\partial \underline{f}^T}{\partial \underline{e}^*} \underline{\lambda} \right]^j$$

where

$$D = \begin{bmatrix} 0 & 0 & -1.28968 \\ 0 & 0 & 0.0 \\ 0 & -3.1535 & 0 \end{bmatrix}$$

and $\dfrac{\partial \underline{f}^T}{\partial \underline{e}^*} =$

$$\begin{bmatrix} 0 & A_2(y_{m_3} - e_3^*) \cos(y_{m_1} - e_1^*) + P_2 \cos 2(y_{m_1} - e_1^*) & C_2 \sin(y_{m_1} - e_1^*) \\ -1 & A_1 & 0 \\ 0 & A_2 \sin(y_{m_1} - e^*_1) & C_1 \end{bmatrix}$$

Simulation results

The above two level algorithm was programmed on the IBM 370/165 digital computer at LAAS. The system was started from the initial conditions $y_1(0)=0.5$, $y_2(0) = -0.4$, $y_3(0) = 8$. The model states were taken to be the same at time 0. Note that these are very far from the desired steady state.

Convergence took place in 54 iterations of the second level and at this point

$$\begin{bmatrix} \sqrt{\int_0^{12} (\underline{e}^{*j+1} - \underline{e}^{*j})^2 \, dt} \\ \sqrt{\int_0^{12} (\underline{p}^{j+1} - \underline{p}^{j})^2 \, dt} \end{bmatrix} < \begin{bmatrix} 10^{-5} \\ 10^{-5} \end{bmatrix}.$$

Figs. 23, 24, 25 show the 3 states $\underline{y}$ and $\underline{y}_m$. Note that the model follows the plant quite closely. Fig. 26 shows the control and it is seen that it gets back to the steady state quite rapidly. Figs. 27, 28, 29 show the error function $\underline{e}$ on a very exaggerated scale. It is seen that the error eventually does become very small. The reason why the error e_3 is slightly larger than e_1 and e_2 is that the state y_3 has a large value for the steady state and larger deviations from it.

As a comparison for the calculation time, some results were availabe to the author for an optimal solution of the problem using a similar quadratic cost function over the period 0-12 where the problem was solved by quasilinearisation. There, the global solution required 59.72 seconds to compute compared to 26.01 seconds for the hierarchical solution. The reason for this large computational saving is that the present method merely requires a second order and a scalar Riccati equation to be solved at the first level compared to an iterative quasi-linearisation solution of a 3rd order problem for the overall system.

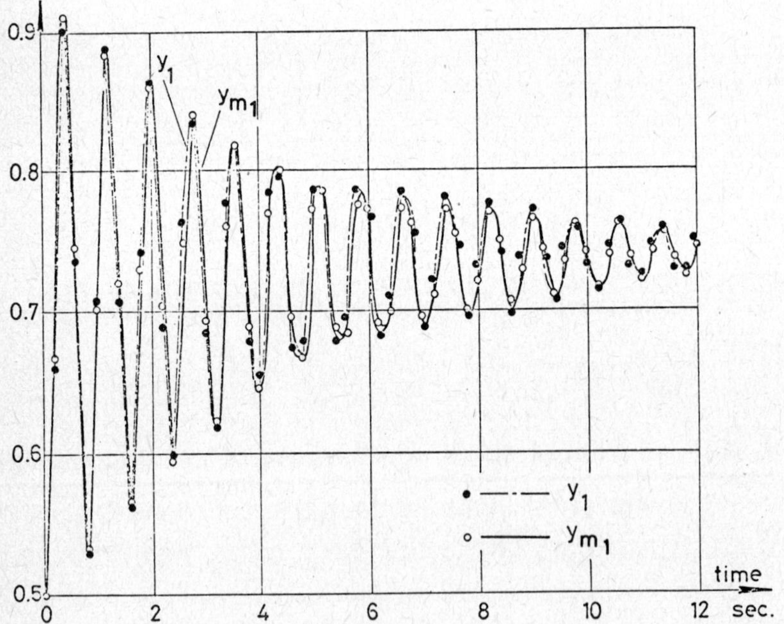

Figure 23

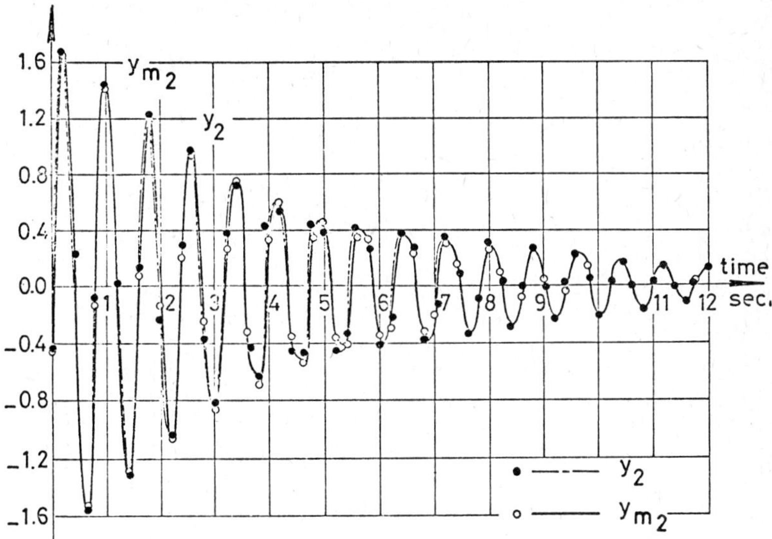

Figure 24

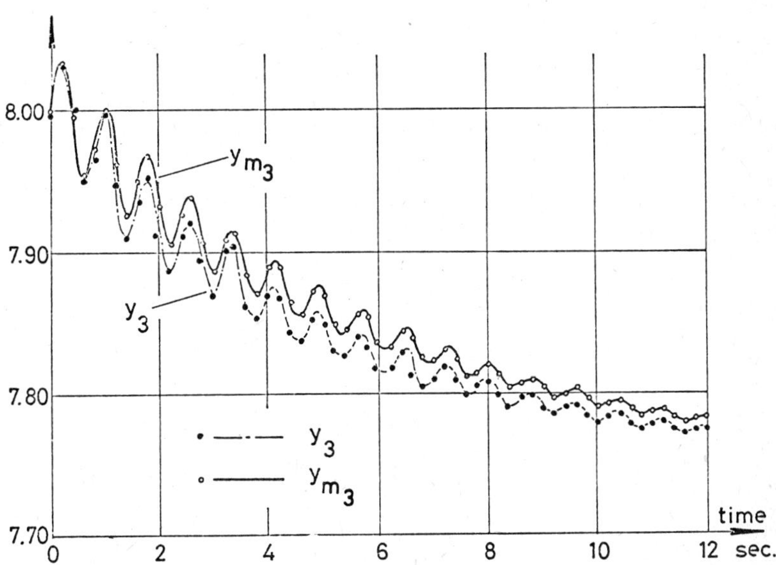

Figure 25

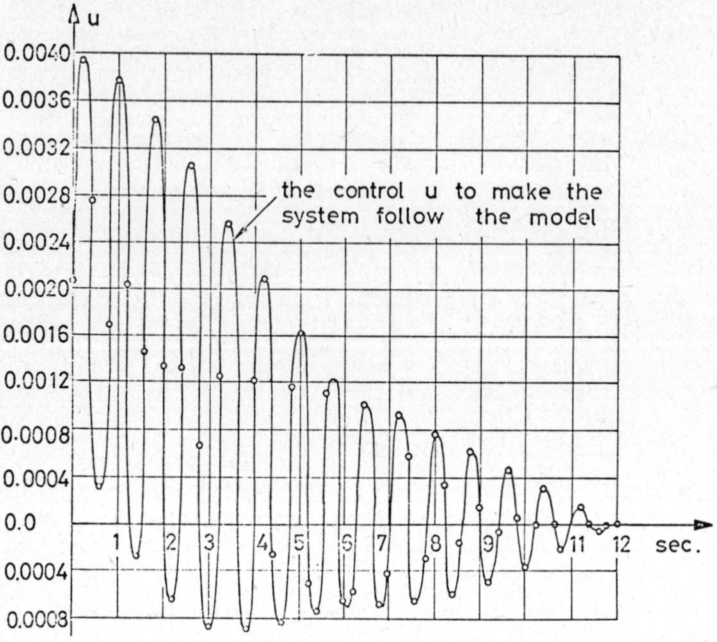

Figure 26

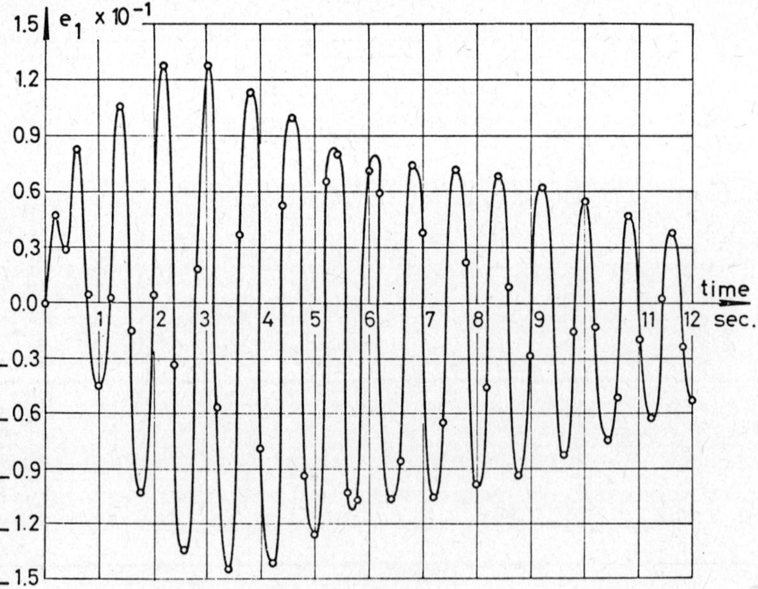

Figure 27

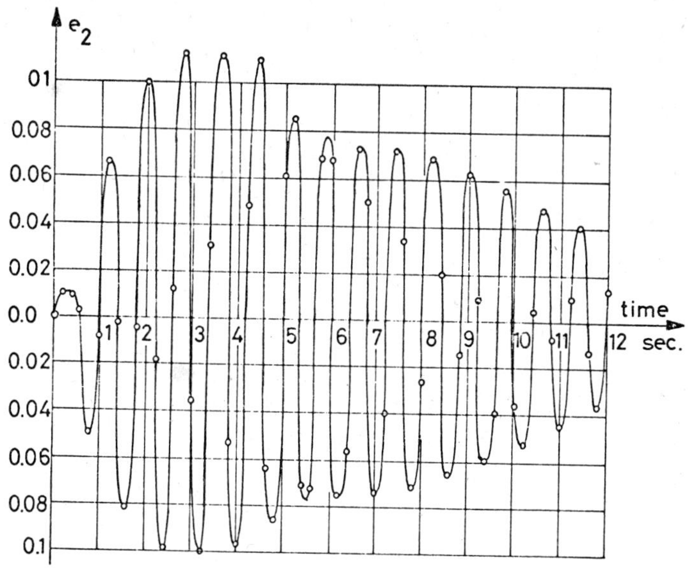

Figure 28

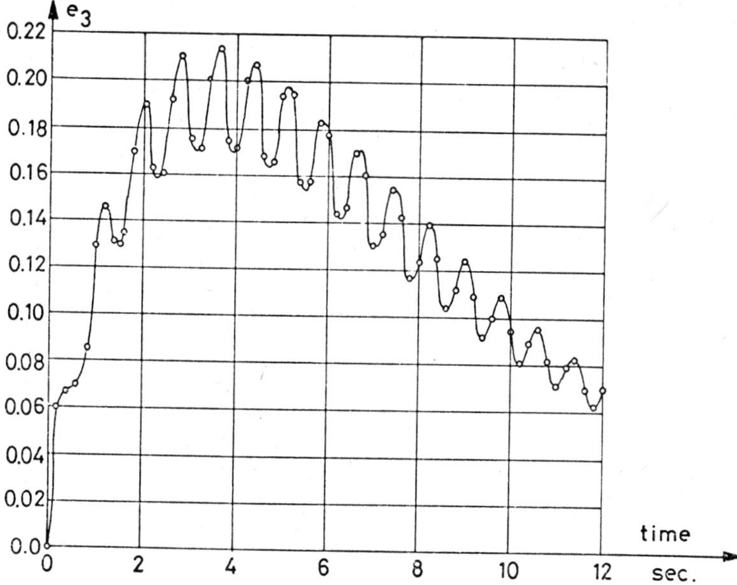

Figure 29

We have so far considered a number of approaches to the practical optimisation of non-linear systems. The prediction approaches are useful because we can always obtain convergence and experience shows that the convergence is quite rapid. This rapidity of convergence means that although we might only obtain a local optimum, we can attempt to find a better local optimum if desired, by starting again from different initial guesses of the coordination variables. With the Goal Coordination approach, on the other hand, if no duality gap arises, we will obtain the global optimum. This is clearly a very desirable property of such methods and for this reason a number of attempts have been made recently to modify the procedures in order to avoid the duality gap for certain special cases.

9. EXTENSIONS OF DUAL COORDINATION [51, 52]

9.1. The Approach of Javdan

The first extension arises from the fact that whilst inequality constraints can be convex, equality constraints must be linear for dual coordination to work. However, equality constraints can be identical to appropriate inequality constraints if all the constraints are binding. To make these notions more precise consider the problem

$$\begin{aligned} &\text{Min} \quad f(\underline{x}) \\ &\text{s.t.} \quad \underline{g}(\underline{x}) \in \emptyset \\ &\qquad \underline{x} \in X \end{aligned} \tag{88}$$

where f is a convex function, X a convex set and $\emptyset$ takes the form of either $\emptyset = \{0\}$ or $\emptyset = \{\underline{a} : \underline{a} \leqslant \underline{0}\}$; $\underline{a} \in R^m$.

The dual problem is

$$\underset{\underline{\lambda} \geq 0}{\text{Max}} \quad \underset{\underline{x} \in X}{\text{Min}} \left\{ f(x) + \underline{\lambda}^T \underline{g}(x) \right\} \tag{89}$$

For the case of $\emptyset = \{\underline{a} : \underline{a} \leqslant 0\}$, (89) and (88) have the same solutions provided that $\underline{g}$ is a vector of convex functions, whilst if $\emptyset = \{\underline{0}\}$, the two problems can be guaranteed to have the same solution only if $\underline{g}$ is linear (cf. Whittle [45] p. 62). Thus, if the optimisation problem has inequality constraints instead of equality constraints we can handle the more general convex constraints. One way of ensuring the solution of problems with equality constraints where $\underline{g}(\underline{x})$ are general convex functions is to make all the inequality constraints binding at the optimum. Consider thus the modified problem of equations (88)

$$\begin{aligned} &\text{Min} \quad f(\underline{x}) + \underline{k}^T \underline{g}(\underline{x}) \\ &\text{s.t.} \quad \underline{g}(\underline{x}) \leqslant \underline{0} \\ &\qquad \underline{x} \in X \end{aligned} \tag{90}$$

where $\underline{k} \in R^m$

Then if a $\underline{k}$ could be found which makes all the constraints $\underline{g}(\underline{x}) \leqslant \underline{0}$ binding at the optimum, we have a problem for which dual coordination works. This result is of course also true for discrete dynamical systems.

Although for general convex $\underline{g}$, it may not be easy to find a $\underline{k}$ which makes all the inequality constraints active at the optimum, Javdan [51] has shown that for certain quadratic constraints, such a $\underline{k}$ can be found relatively easily. The class of quadratic problems of interest is the one where each part of the second order non-linearity appears only once in the equality constraints. More precisely, the discrete dynamical control problem is

$$\text{Min} \sum_{\ell=1}^{m} (\|\underline{x}(\ell)\|^2_{A(\ell)} + \underline{b}^T(\ell)\,\underline{x}(\ell) \quad + C \tag{91}$$

$$\text{s.t.} \sum_{i=1}^{m} \left\{ \|\underline{x}(i)\|^2_{R_j(i)} + \underline{p}_j^T(i)\,\underline{x}(i) \right\} + q_j = 0 \tag{92}$$

$j = 1,2,\ldots, m$; $\underline{x} \in X$ where A, R are diagonal matrices.

Then the modified primal problem for

$$\underline{k} = (k_1,\ldots, k_m)^T \tag{93}$$

can be written as

$$\text{Min} \sum_{\ell=1}^{m} \left\{ \|\underline{x}(\ell)\|^2_{A(\ell)} + \underline{b}^T x + C + \right.$$

$$\left. \sum_{j=1}^{m} k_j \left\{ \sum_{i=1}^{m} \|\underline{x}(i)\|^2_{R_j} \right\} + \underline{p}_j^T \underline{x} + q \right\} \tag{94}$$

$$\text{s.t.} \sum_{=1}^{m} \left\{ \|\underline{x}(i)\|^2_{R_j(i)} + \underline{p}_j^T \underline{x} + q^j \right\} \leqslant 0 \tag{95}$$

$j = 1,\ldots, m$

$x \in X$

Javdan [51] has shown that if $R_j(i) = \delta_{ij}$, S_j, where S_j is a positive definite matrix of dimension (x $(R_j(j)$, C $(R_j(j)))$ then an activating index vector $\underline{k}$ can be found which, whilst keeping the modified objective function convex forces the solution of the modified problem to a point in the X-space where all the m non-linear constraints are binding. The element k_i of the activating index vector is given by the smallest number k_i for which the matrix $\{A(i) + k_i S^i\}$ is positive definite.

Javdan has applied this approach to a water resource example where quadratic equality constraints of the type defined above arise.

9.2. The approach of Simmons [52]

Another way of getting around the limitation of linear equality constraints is suggested by Simmons. This approach is applicable to more general non-linear problems than those considered by Javdan. However, it is necessary in this approach that there exist buffer stores between each of the interconnected subsystems. There are many systems where such buffer stores naturally exist as for example in certain production lines as well as in some chemical processes. The idea here is due to Whittle [45] that if instead of trying to satisfy each interconnection constraint instantaneously, we only satisfy it on average, the strong Lagrangian principle works and the resulting goal coordination solution is the best one. This average constraint satisfaction is achieved through the use of the buffer stores.

10 . COMMENTS

In this Chapter we have extensively considered the various methods which can be used for the optimisation of large scale systems which consist of non-linear dynamical subsystems. The Goal Coordination method would appear to work some of the time but it is risky to use it without extensive a priori simulation due to the possibility of a duality gap. The new prediction coordination methods would appear to work rather well and they are in the author's opinion, the best ones which can be used in general. For special cases, however, as for example for certain quadratic problems, the method of Javdan is of interest whilst for problems with buffer stores, Simmons' method could prove quite useful.

In this first part of the book we have seen that it is generally possible to use multi-level techniques for the optimisation of large scale systems. However, the resulting control is open-loop. In Part II we consider multi-level closed loop control.

PART II

HIERARCHICAL FEEDBACK CONTROL

In Part I we examined the various currently available methods for the practical optimisation of large interconnected dynamical systems which comprised linear or non-linear dynamical subsystems. However, the resulting control was open loop. There are many disadvantages to the implementation of such open loop control if it is desired to regulate the process in real time. First of all, open loop control is much too sensitive. In addition, it is not possible to correct the control as the process evolves since the control does not explicitly depend on the current state. Moreover, the control is valid for only one initial condition and it is necessary to recalculate the open loop control if the initial state changes. In this second part of the book we investigate the possibility of calculating feedback control laws which get around some of these difficulties.

We know that in general it is possible to compute feedback control laws for linear-quadratic problems in which the feedback parameters are independent of initial conditions. In Chapter IV we will develop closed loop controllers with this desirable property for large scale linear-quadratic problems within a decentralised computational structure. We will illustrate the methods on the river pollution control example of Chapter II.

At the present time, for general non-linear systems it is not possible to calculate a feedback solution for the integrated case which is independent of initial conditions. That being the case we would not expect to be able to obtain a feedback control which is not initial state dependent for the hierarchical case. Nevertheless it is possible to achieve a feedback control i.e. a control which is a function of the current state and the initial state and which can therefore be corrected as the process evolves. In addition, it is possible to derive an expression for the sensitivity of the cost function to variations in the initial state. If, from the sensitivity relationship, it appears that the closed loop control is strongly dependent on the initial conditions, it is possible to develop a two level algorithm for the on-line improvement of the control as the initial condition changes. Such an approach also largely desensitises the control to various disturbances which are manifested by a perturbation in the value of the current state. The hierarchical feedback controller for non-linear systems is developed in Chapter V and the control concepts are illustrated on both the sliding mass example and the two machine system of Chapter III.

The material for this part of the book is taken mainly from references [26,29-31,49] for the linear-quadratic case and from [27,28,48] for the non-linear case. We start our analysis of feedback control by considering once again the linear-quadratic class of problems which we first examined in Chapter II.

CHAPTER IV

HIERARCHICAL FEEDBACK CONTROL FOR LINEAR-QUADRATIC PROBLEMS

1. INTRODUCTION

In Part I we considered the optimisation problem to arise from the following kind of situation : we have some large scale system operating in a steady state when some unknown disturbance occurs at time t_0 which changes the state vector $\underline{x}$ from the given steady state value $\underline{x}_s$ to some known value $\underline{x}_0$. It is then necessary to calculate some control over the fixed period (t_f-t_0) to bring the system back to steady state $\underline{x}_s$ whilst minimising some integral function of the states and controls. In that case, it was assumed that we could perform our hierarchical calculation sufficiently rapidly and apply the control before the state had significantly changed. However, this is not a realistic situation unless the system has particularly slow dynamics (as, for example, in the case of the river) or if we know a priori precisely what the initial state value $\underline{x}_0$ will be (as for example in the case of start up or shut down of plants or change of product, etc.).In the general case, although we may be able to measure the initial state $\underline{x}_0$, it will almost certainly have changed by the time (we have calculated our control and applying the open loop control for the actual state $\underline{x}$ instead of for the initial state $\underline{x}_0$ for which the hierarchical calculation was done) could prove to be disastrous. It is therefore highly desirable to be able to calculate a feedback control which is independent of initial conditions since then we could apply the control as soon as a measurement was available. In such cases, it would also not be necessary to calculate the controls repeatedly for differing initial conditions since the same control law would be valid for all initial conditions. In this chapter we develop such control laws for the only case where such laws exist for the integrated problems,i.e. for systems comprising "linear-quadratic" subsystems.

This problem of providing on-line control using a hierarchical structure has been previously considered by a number of authors. Mesarovic [6] considered a suboptimal approach which attempted to improve the control as the process evolved and Sage [8] has used a similar suboptimal approach for the filter problem [53,54] . The actual problem of computing an optimal feedback control was first considered by Cheneveaux [30] who developed a method for calculating the parameters of the closed loop controllers for large scale systems comprising "linear-quadratic" subsystem problems. The main difficulty in using his method is that is is necessary to solve off-line the two point boundary value problem of the overall system. More recently Cohen et al. [31, 37] have examined this problem exhaustively and reached the conclusion that it is only possible to obtain a "partial" closed loop control.Thus their controllers always have an open loop part dependent upon initial conditions. In the first method developed in this chapter, we go further than the open loop algorithm of Cohen et al. and calculate a complete feedback control. The general philosophy of the present approach is different from that of Cohen et al. [37] who envisage using their algorithm on-line where each iteration gives an improved control. Here, the whole hierarchical calculation will be performed off-line and the resulting feedback gains will be implemented on-line. The resulting controller having "gains" independent of the initial conditions will bring the system back to the steady state "optimally" from any state that an unknown disturbance takes the system to. Such a scheme is ideal for on-line implementation since the actual on-line calculation is quite minimal.

2. THE INTERACTION PREDICTION APPROACH TO DECENTRALISED CONTROL

In the first part of this chapter the interaction prediction principle approach of Takahara [12], as formulated in chapter II, is used as the vehicle for the development of the closed loop decentralised control. The main reason for this is that the prediction method requires very little second level calculation as we discussed in chapter II. This is important since for all multi-level methods, the overall system variables are manipulated at the second level and for truly large systems computational difficulties could arise with other methods. Nevertheless it is easy to do a similar analysis for the other hierarchical optimisation approaches although this will not be done here except for the discrete time case where we use the Tamura method for the off-line optimisation.

The dynamic optimisation problem for an interconnected system can be written as before as :

$$\text{Minimise } J = \sum_{i=1}^{N} \int_{t_0}^{t_f} \left(\tfrac{1}{2} \|\underline{x}_i\|^2_{Q_i} + \tfrac{1}{2} \|\underline{u}_i\|^2_{R_i}\right) dt \tag{1}$$

where Q_i is positive semidefinite and R_i is positive definite.

Subject to

$$\dot{\underline{x}}_i = A_i\underline{x}_i + B_i\underline{u}_i + C_i\underline{z}_i \qquad i = 1,\dots, N \tag{2}$$

$$\underline{z}_i = \sum_{j=1}^{N} L_{ij}\,\underline{x}_j \qquad i = 1,\dots, N \tag{3}$$

Here $\underline{x}_i$ is the n_i dimensional state vector of the ith subsystem, $\underline{u}_i$ is the m_i dimensional control vector and $\underline{z}_i$ is the q_i dimensional vector of interconnections from the other subsystems. $\underline{z}_i$ is a linear combination of the states of the overall system as described by equation (3). Such a problem can be viewed in the integrated or composite sense as a large multivariable regulator but with a special structure. In order to utilise this structure to reduce the computer storage, let us write down the necessary conditions for optimality.

We will decompose the necessary conditions within a two level structure. Thus, let us write the Lagrangian as

$$L(\underline{x}_i,\underline{u}_i,\underline{\lambda},\underline{z}_i,\underline{p}_i) = \sum_{i=1}^{N} \int_{t_0}^{t_f} \Big(\tfrac{1}{2} \|\underline{x}_i\|^2_{Q_i} + \tfrac{1}{2} \|\underline{u}_i\|^2_{R_i} + \underline{\lambda}_i^T\Big[\underline{z}_i - \sum_{j=1}^{N} L_{ij}\underline{x}_j\Big] + \underline{p}_i^T\Big[-\dot{\underline{x}}_i + A_i\underline{x}_i + B_i\underline{u}_i + C_i\underline{z}_i\Big]\Big)dt \tag{4}$$

where $\underline{\lambda}$ is a $\sum_{i=1}^{N} q_i$ dimensional vector of Lagrange multipliers and $\underline{p}_i$ is an n_i dimensional vector of adjoint variables.

Now, in this linear case, convexity assures that the necessary conditions for optimaltiy are also sufficient so that by satisfying the necessary conditions we can obtain the global optimum. To satisfy the necessary conditions within a two level computational structure, let us rewrite the Lagrangian L as

$$L = \sum_{i=1}^{N} L_i = \sum_{i=1}^{N} \left\{ \int_{t_0}^{t_f} \left\{ \frac{1}{2} \|\underline{x}_i\|^2_{Q_i} + \frac{1}{2} \|\underline{u}_i\|^2_{R_i} + \underline{\lambda}_i^T \underline{z}_i \right. \right.$$

$$\left. \left. - \sum_{j=1}^{N} \underline{\lambda}_j^T L_{ji} \underline{x}_i + \underline{p}_i^T \left[-\dot{\underline{x}}_i + A_i \underline{x}_i + B_i \underline{u}_i + C_i \underline{z}_i \right] \right\} dt \right\} \tag{5}$$

From equation (5) we see that the Lagrangian L is additively separable for any given $\underline{z}_i$ and $\underline{\lambda}$ trajectory. This implies that for any given z_i, $\underline{\lambda}$ can be obtained by N independent minimisations the ith of which is L_i in equation (7). This leaves the problem of improving $\underline{z}_i$, $\underline{\lambda}$. A necessary condition for doing this is that

$$\frac{\partial L}{\partial \underline{z}_i} = \underline{0} \tag{6}$$

$$\frac{\partial L}{\partial \underline{\lambda}} = \underline{0} \tag{7}$$

which gives

$$\underline{\lambda}_i = - C_i^T \underline{p}_i \quad \text{and} \quad \underline{z}_i = \sum_{j=1}^{N} L_{ij} \underline{x}_j \tag{8}$$

The coordination rule using the interaction prediction principle is from iteration k to k + 1

$$\begin{bmatrix} \underline{\lambda}_i \\ \underline{z}_i \end{bmatrix}^{k+1} = \begin{bmatrix} - C_i^T \underline{p}_i \\ \sum_{j=1}^{N} L_{ij} \underline{x}_j \end{bmatrix}^{k} \tag{9}$$

i.e. the $\underline{x}_i$, $\underline{p}_i$ which are obtained from the independent minimisations in equation (7) are used in equation (8) to get the values of $\underline{\lambda}_i$, $\underline{z}_i$ (i = 1,..., N) which are subsequently used as the new prediction of $\underline{\lambda}_i$ and $\underline{z}_i$. The important point to note is that at the second level it is necessary to do very little work, i.e. the 2nd level only evaluates the R.H.S. of equation (9) which involves a few multiplications. The lower level also does very little work since only low order problems are solved here. Also, the convergence is extremely rapid.

2.1. Modification to give partial feedback control

Consider the lower level problem. The Hamiltonian for the ith independent subproblem can be written as :

$$H_i = \frac{1}{2} \|\underline{x}_i\|^2_{Q_i} + \frac{1}{2} \|\underline{u}_i\|^2_{R_i} + \underline{\lambda}_i^T \underline{z}_i - \sum_{j=1}^{N} \underline{\lambda}_j^T L_{ji} \underline{x}_i +$$

$$\underline{p}_i^T \left[A_i \underline{x}_i + B_i \underline{u}_i + C_i \underline{z}_i \right] \tag{10}$$

Then from the necessary conditions

$$\dot{\underline{p}}_i = - Q_i \underline{x}_i - A_i^T \underline{p}_i + \sum_{j=1}^{N} \left[\underline{\lambda}_j^T L_{ji} \right]^T \tag{11}$$

with $\underline{p}_i(t_f) = \underline{0}$ (12)

$$\underline{u}_i = - R_i^{-1} B_i^T \underline{p}_i \tag{13}$$

Let $\underline{p}_i = K_i \underline{x}_i + \underline{s}_i$ (14)

where $\underline{s}_i$ is the open loop compensation vector.

Then $\dot{\underline{p}}_i = K_i \dot{\underline{x}}_i + \dot{K}_i \underline{x}_i + \dot{\underline{s}}_i$ (15)

substituting into equation (2) gives

$$\dot{\underline{x}}_i = A_i \underline{x}_i - B_i R_i^{-1} B_i^T K_i \underline{x}_i - B_i R_i^{-1} B_i^T \underline{s}_i + C_i \underline{z}_i \tag{16}$$

using equation (15)

$$\left[\dot{K}_i + A_i^T K_i + K_i A_i - K_i B_i R_i^{-1} B_i^T K_i + Q_i \right] \underline{x}_i + \left[\dot{\underline{s}}_i + A_i^T \underline{s}_i - K_i B_i R_i^{-1} B_i^T \underline{s}_i + K_i C_i \underline{z}_i - \sum_{j=1}^{N} \left[\underline{\lambda}_j^T L_{ji} \right]^T \right] = \underline{0} \tag{17}$$

Since this equation is valid for arbitray $\underline{x}_i$

$$\dot{K}_i + K_i A_i + A_i^T K_i - K_i B_i R_i^{-1} B_i^T K_i + Q_i = 0 \tag{18}$$

with $K_i(t_f) = 0$

and $$\dot{\underline{s}}_i = \left[K_i B_i R_i^{-1} B_i^T - A_i^T \right] \underline{s}_i - K_i C_i \underline{z}_i + \sum_{j=1}^{N} \left[\underline{\lambda}_j^T L_{ji} \right]^T \tag{19}$$

with $\underline{s}_i(t_f) = \underline{0}$

and the local control $\underline{u}_i$ is given by

$$\underline{u}_i = - R_i^{-1} B_i^T K_i \underline{x}_i - R_i^{-1} B_i^T \underline{s}_i \tag{20}$$

2.2. Remarks

(i) The K_i in equation (18) is independent of the initial state $\underline{x}(0)$. Thus the N matrix Riccati equations each involving $\frac{n_i \times (n_i+1)}{2}$ non-linear differential equations can be solved independently from the given final condition $K_i(t_f) = 0$. These give a partial feedback control.It can be argued that this feedback around each subsystem does provide some degree of stabilisation against small disturbances and moreover allows one to correct the control based on the current state as opposed to the initial condition.

(ii) $\underline{s}_i$ in equation (19) is not independent of the initial state $\underline{x}_i(t_0)$. Thus the second term in equation (20) provides open loop compensation. To see this, using equation (8), at the optimum, $\underline{s}_i$ can be written as

$$\dot{\underline{s}}_i = [- A_i^T + K_i B_i R_i^{-1}] \underline{s}_i - K_i C_i \sum_{j=1}^{N} L_{ij} \underline{x}_j + \sum_{j=1}^{N} L_{ji}^T [- C_j^T K_j \underline{x}_j - C_j^T \underline{s}_j] \quad (21)$$

i.e. $\underline{s}_i$ is a function of the states of all the other subsystems, and is thus dependent on the intial state $\underline{x}(t_0)$ of the overall system.

3. THE CLOSED LOOP CONTROLLER

Let $\underline{x}$ be the overall state vector of the system, $\underline{u}$ the overall control vector, $\underline{s}$ the overall open loop part of the compensator and A, B, C, L, Q, R, K etc. the matrices for the overall system. Then we have

Theorem : The open loop compensation vector $\underline{s}$ and the state $\underline{x}$ are related by a transformation Y

i.e. $\underline{s} = Y \underline{x}$

Where Y is an n x n matrix.

Proof : Rewrite equation (21) for the integrated system as

$$\dot{\underline{s}} = [- A^T + K B R^{-1} B^T - L^T C^T] \underline{s} - (K C L + L^T C^T K) \underline{x}$$

Then

$$\underline{s}(t) = \emptyset_1(t,t_0) \underline{s}(t_0) - \int_{t_0}^{t} \emptyset_1(t,\tau) (KCL+L^T C^T K) \underline{x}(\tau) d\tau \quad (22)$$

where $\emptyset_1(t,t_0)$ is the transition matrix associated with $[-A^T+KBR^{-1} B^T-L^T C^T]$

Now consider the composite system

$$\dot{\underline{x}} = A \underline{x} + B \underline{u} \quad (23)$$

and the cost function

$$J = \int_{t_0}^{t_f} \frac{1}{2} (\|\underline{x}\|_Q^2 + \|\underline{u}\|_R^2) dt \quad (24)$$

the optimal control $\underline{u}$ is given by

$$\underline{u} = - R^{-1} B^T P \underline{x} \quad (25)$$

where P is the solution of the composite Riccati equation.

Then

$$\dot{\underline{x}} = (A - B R^{-1} B^T P) \underline{x} \quad (26)$$

or

$$\underline{x}(t) = \emptyset_2(t,t_0) \underline{x}(t_0) \quad (27)$$

where $\emptyset_2(t,t_0)$ is the transition matrix associated with the optimal composite feedback system matrix

$$(A - B R^{-1} B^T P) \quad (28)$$

substituting for $\underline{x}$ from (27) in (22),

$$\underline{s}(t) = \emptyset_1(t,t_0)\,\underline{s}(t_0) - \int_{t_0}^{t} \emptyset_1(t,\tau)\,(KCL + L^T C^T K)\emptyset_2(\tau,t_0)\,\underline{x}(t_0)d\tau \tag{29}$$

Now at $t = t_f$, $\underline{s}(t) = \underline{0}$. Substituting this in equation (29),

i.e.

$$\underline{0} = \emptyset_1(t_f,t_0)\,\underline{s}(t_0) - \int_{t_0}^{t_f} (\emptyset_1(t_f,\tau)\,(KCL + L^T C^T K)\,\emptyset_2(\tau,t_0)\,d\tau\,\underline{x}(t_0))$$

or

$$\underline{s}(t_0) = \emptyset_1(t_0,t_f) \int_{t_0}^{t_f} \emptyset_1(t_f,\tau)\,(K\,C\,L + L^T C^T K)\emptyset_2(\tau,t_0)\,d\tau\,\underline{x}(t_0) \tag{30}$$

i.e.

$$\underline{s}(t_0) = Y(t_f,t_0)\,\underline{x}(t_0) = \left[\int_{t_0}^{t_f} \emptyset_1(t_0,\tau)\,(KCL+L^T C^T K)\emptyset_2(\tau,t_0)d\tau\right]\underline{x}(t_0) \tag{31}$$

where $$Y(t_f,t) = \int_{t}^{t_f} \emptyset_1(t,\tau)\,(KCL + L^T C^T K)\,\emptyset_2(\tau,t)\,d\tau \tag{32}$$

or

$$\underline{s}(t) = Y(t_f,t)\,\underline{x}(t) \tag{33}$$

which completes the demonstration.

On examining equation (30), if $t = t_f \to \infty$ and A, B, C, Q, R are time invariant S and K are constant and then $Y(t_f,t)$ (cf. Sage [55]) becomes a constant matrix which leads to :

For the infinite time regulator $Y(t_f,t)$ is time invariant.

3.1. The regulator solution

As seen in equation (21), $\underline{s}$ provides the open loop part of the controller and the above theorem shows that $\underline{s}$ is related very simply to the overall state vector. However $\underline{s}$ is not easy to obtain directly from the above relationship since the evaluation of the Y matrix involves the calculation of the Riccati equation for the composite system and this is clearly an unattractive calculation for large systems.

However, for the infinite time regulator Y is particularly easy to compute since near $t = 0$, Y is constant whereas $\underline{x}$ and $\underline{s}$ are not. Thus if the values of $\underline{x}$ and $\underline{s}$ are recorded at the first $n = \sum_{i=1}^{N} n_i$ time points, very close to $t=t_0$, Y can be determined as follows

Form the matrix $S = [\underline{s}(t_0)\ \underline{s}(t_1) \ldots\ \underline{s}(t_n)]$ and

$X = [\underline{x}(t_0), \underline{x}(t_1) \ldots \underline{x}(t_n)]$ and then

$S = Y X$

or $Y = S X^{-1}$

This inversion of X should not pose much of a problem for even large systems since it is to be done off-line*

If it is desired to calculate the time varying γ (i.e. if the horizon must be considered finite) it is possible to do so by solving the problem n times for n different initial conditions and then forming the n x n matrices

$$S = \left[\underline{s}^1(t), \underline{s}^2(t) \ldots \underline{s}^n(t)\right]$$

$$X = \left[\underline{x}^1(t), \underline{x}^2(t) \ldots \underline{x}^n(t)\right]$$

for each integration point and determining each value of γ by the relationship

$$\gamma = S X^{-1}$$

3.2. Remarks

(1) The above method enables one to solve the large interconnected systems regulator problem within a completely decentralised calculation structure.

(2) The resulting gains are independent of the initial conditions since using equation (20) in the composite case

$$\underline{u} = -R^{-1} B^T K \underline{x} - R^{-1} B^T \underline{s} \tag{34}$$

where K is block diagonal and substituting for $\underline{s}$ from equation (33)

$$\underline{u} = -R^{-1} B^T K \underline{x} - R^{-1} B^T \gamma \underline{x} = -\left[R^{-1} B^T K + R^{-1} B^T \gamma\right] \underline{x} = -G\underline{x} \tag{35}$$

where none of the terms in the gain matrix G are dependent on $\underline{x}_0$. Thus this gain will bring the system back to the steady state optimally from any initial condition.

(3) Against the above advantages, there is the difficulty that a large amount of off-line calculation needs to be done for the finite time case. However, even here, all this off-line computation is within a decentralised structure so that its storage requirements are minimal. Also, for large systems, the case of most practical interest is the one where the period of optimisation is infinite and for this important case, the off-line computational requirements are very small.

The method also has the advantage that once the gains have been calcula-

---

* It should be noted that the approach hinges on one's ability to invert X which basically depends on the linear independence of the chosen record. In practical cases, if a large enough perturbation is given, it will be possible to obtain an invertible X. Otherwise, one can solve the problem off-line n times successively for the initial conditions

$$\underline{x}(t_0) = \begin{bmatrix} 1 \\ 0 \\ \cdot \\ \cdot \\ 0 \end{bmatrix}, \begin{bmatrix} 0 \\ 1 \\ \cdot \\ \cdot \\ 0 \end{bmatrix}, \ldots\ldots, \begin{bmatrix} 0 \\ 0 \\ \cdot \\ \cdot \\ 1 \end{bmatrix}$$

Then $\gamma = S$ and it is not necessary to invert X. This of course requires more computation but this is off-line and decentralised.

ted, the on-line calculation is minimal . It may not even be necessary to implement the controller using a digital computer - a few hardware components like amplifiers is all that is required for the infinite time case.

3.3. Example

As a very simple illustrative example, consider the minimisation of J where

$$J = \frac{1}{2} \int_0^8 (x_1^2 + 2\,x_2^2 + u_1^2 + u_2^2)\,dt$$

subject to

$$\dot{x}_1 = -\,x_1 + x_2 + u_1$$

$$\dot{x}_2 = -\,x_2 + u_2$$

This can be broken into 2 subproblems by defining the interaction variable $Z=x_2$.

Then the first level problems become

$$\text{Min } J_1 = \int_0^8 \left[\frac{1}{2}\,x_1^2 + \frac{1}{2}\,u_1^2 + \lambda Z\right]$$

subject to

$$\dot{x}_1 = -\,x_1 + Z + u_1$$

and

$$\text{Min } J_2 = \int_0^8 \left[x_2^2 + \frac{1}{2}\,u_2^2 - \lambda x_2\right]$$

subject to

$$\dot{x}_2 = -\,x_2 + u_2$$

This problem was solved on the IBM 370/165 digital computer at LAAS for initial conditions (1.5, 5). Convergence to the optimum took place in 10 second level iterations. Here the period of optimisation is long enough for it to be considered infinite and the constant partial feedback gains were found to be $K_1 = 0.4142$ and $K_2 = 0.732$ respectively. Using the values of $\underline{x}$ and $\underline{s}$ at time $t = 0, 1$, γ was evaluated by inverting a 2 x 2 matrix and multiplying with a 2 x 2 matrix to be

$$\gamma = \begin{bmatrix} -\,0.0055 & 0.1274 \\ 0.1274 & 0.0675 \end{bmatrix} = R^{-1}\,B^T\,\gamma$$

adding to

$$R^{-1}\,B^T K = \begin{bmatrix} 0.4142 & 0 \\ 0 & 0.732 \end{bmatrix}$$

gave the overall gain to be

$$G = \begin{bmatrix} 0.4087 & 0.1274 \\ 0.1274 & 0.7995 \end{bmatrix}$$

which is identical to that obtained by solving the Riccati equation for the composite system.

4. EXTENSION TO THE SERVOMECHANISM CASE

Consider now the problem

$$\text{Min } J = \sum_{i=1}^{N} \frac{1}{2} \int_{t_0}^{t_f} \left[\| \underline{x}_i - \underline{x}_i^* \|^2_{Q_i} + \| \underline{u}_i \|^2_{R_i} \right] dt \tag{36}$$

subject to

$$\dot{\underline{x}}_1 = A_i \underline{x}_i + B_i \underline{u}_i + C_i \underline{z}_i + \underline{D}_i \tag{37}$$

and

$$\underline{z}_i = \sum_{j=1}^{N} L_{ij} \underline{x}_j \tag{38}$$

Here $\underline{x}_i^*$ is a constant known desired trajectory for the ith subsystem and $\underline{D}_i$ is a vector of constant known inputs which come into the ith subsystem.

Using a similar development as in section 3, it is easy to show that the control is given by

$$\underline{u} = - R^{-1} B^T K \underline{x} - R^{-1} B^T \underline{\xi} \tag{39}$$

where R, B, K are block diagonal matrices. Similarly, it is also easy to show that

$$\underline{\xi} = T_1 \underline{x} + \underline{T}_2 \tag{40}$$

where for the infinite time case for A, B, C, $\underline{D}$ etc. time invariant , T_1 is an $\sum_{i=1}^{N} n_i \times \sum_{i=1}^{N} n_i$ constant matrix and $\underline{T}_2$ is a $\sum_{i=1}^{N} n_i$ dimensional constant vector.

Thus

$$\underline{u} = -\left[R^{-1} B^T K + R^{-1} B^T T_1\right] \underline{x} - R^{-1} B^T \underline{T}_2$$

or

$$\underline{u} = - G\underline{x} - R^{-1} B^T \underline{T}_2 \tag{41}$$

Here again, as for the regulator case, for $t_f - t_0 \to \infty$, T_1 and $\underline{T}_2$ can be obtained from the $(\sum_{i=1}^{N} n_i + 1)$ time points by inverting a $(\sum_{i=1}^{N} n_i \times \sum_{i=1}^{N} n_i)$ matrix where the points are obtained from an off-line decentralised calculation using the interaction prediction principle.

Note that for the servomechanism case, the form of the overall optimal control law for the composite system is the same as that given in equation (41)

5. EXAMPLE : RIVER POLLUTION CONTROL

As a practical example of the application of the approach, let us consider our river pollution control problem first considered in Chapter 2. We will begin by recapitulating the various river pollution models that have been suggested and then apply the approach to each model.

5.1. The River Pollution Control Models

The basic elements of the models is the dynamics of Biochemical Oxygen Demand (B.O.D.) and Dissolved Oxygen (D.O.) in the stream, as we stated in Chapter 2. For a reach which is defined as a section of the river of some convenient length having one polluter, these can be represented by the state space equations

$$\dot{\underline{x}}_i(t) = A\,\underline{x}_i(t) + B\,\underline{u}_i\,(t) + \underline{C}_i \tag{42}$$

where for the ith reach

$$\underline{x}_i = \begin{bmatrix} z_i \\ q_i \end{bmatrix}$$

where z_i is the concentration of B.O.D. in reach i (mg/l) and q_i is the concentration of D.O. in reach i. u_i is the concentration of B.O.D. in the effluent discharged into the stream.

From the River Cam model [41]

$$A = \begin{bmatrix} -1.32 & 0 \\ -0.32 & -1.2 \end{bmatrix} \qquad B = \begin{bmatrix} 0.1 \\ 0 \end{bmatrix} \qquad C_i = \begin{bmatrix} 0.9\,z_{i-1} \\ 0.9\,q_{i-1} + 1.0 \end{bmatrix}$$

In equation (42), C_i can be written in several ways to account for the different transport delays between the reaches as Tamura [11] points out.

1) No delay model

Here

$$\begin{bmatrix} z_{i-1}(t) \\ q_{i-1}(t) \end{bmatrix} = \begin{bmatrix} z_{i-1}(t) \\ q_{i-1}(t) \end{bmatrix} \tag{43}$$

2) Pure delay model

Here

$$\begin{bmatrix} z_{i-1}(t) \\ q_{i-1}(t) \end{bmatrix} \quad \begin{bmatrix} z_{i-1}(t-\theta_0) \\ q_{i-1}(t-\theta_0) \end{bmatrix} \tag{44}$$

$$\theta_0 = \frac{V_i}{Q_{i-1}} = 1$$

where V_i is the volume of water (m.gl/d) in reach i and Q_{i-1} is the volume of water which flows from the (i-1)th reach to the ith reach in one day (m.gl.) θ_0 is the pure delay.

3) Distributed delay model

$$z_{i-1}(t) = \sum_{j=1}^{m} a_j \, z_{i-1}(t - \theta_j)$$

$$q_{i-1}(t) = \sum_{j=1}^{m} a_j \, q_{i-1}(t - \theta_j) \tag{45}$$

$$\sum_{j=1}^{m} a_j = 1 \text{ ; mean of } \theta_j = \theta_0 \quad ; \quad \theta_1 < \theta_2 < \cdots < \theta_m .$$

The "no delay" model shows that the state of the (i-1)th reach affects the state of the ith reach immediately. Equations (42) and (43) give the Kendrick model [50] . The "pure delay" model assumes that there exists a pure time delay between adjacent reaches,i.e. the state of the (i-1)th reach affects the state of the (i)th reach after θ_0 days. The "distributed delay" model shows that for j =1, 2,..., m, a fraction a_j of B.O.D. and D.O. in the (i-1)th reach at time $(t-\theta_j)$ arrives in the ith reach at time t i.e. the transport delays are distributed in time between θ_1 and θ_m. Fig. 1 shows the distributed phenomenon whereby B.O.D. (or D.O.) is discharged at time t = 0 in the (i-1)th reach and fractions a_j arrive at $t = \theta_j$, j=1,..., m in the ith reach. We know that this last model is particularly realistic since it takes into account the dispersion of pollutants in the river.

5.2. The Optimisation Problem

A realistic optimisation problem for an N reach system is to minimise

$$J = \sum_{i=1}^{N} \int_0^{\infty} [(\underline{x}_i - \underline{x}_i^*)^T Q_i (\underline{x}_i - \underline{x}_i^*) + \underline{u}_i^T R_i \underline{u}_i] \, dt \tag{46}$$

where $\underline{x}_i^* = \begin{bmatrix} z_i^* \\ q_i^* \end{bmatrix}$ are the desired levels of B.O.D. and D.O. in the stream, Q_i is an appropriate 2 x 2 constant positive definite weighting matrix and R_i is a positive scalar. The period of optimisation here is taken to be long enough for the system to return to the steady state from any initial condition that an unknown disturbance may take the system to.

J in equation (46) is to be minimised subject to the system dynamics (42) and successively to the three models given by equations (43), (44) and (45) for the delays.

5.3 Feedback control for a two reach river system

5.3.1. No delay model

The "no delay" model for the Cam river of two reaches is already in the form given by equations (2) and (3). This problem was solved on the IBM 370/165 at LAAS for the initial state $z_1(0)$ = 10 mg/1, $q_1(0)$ = 7 mg/1, $z_2(0)$ = 5 mg/1, $q_2(0)$ = 7 mg/1. These initial conditions imply that the second reach is initially "clean" while the first reach suddenly receives a pollution load. The cost function was chosen to be such that

$$Q_i = \begin{bmatrix} 2 & 0 \\ 0 & 1 \end{bmatrix} \qquad i = 1, 2$$

and $\quad R_i = 1 \qquad i = 1,2$

The desired states were chosen to be consistent with the steady state of the system as $z_1^* = 4.06$ mg/1 ; $q_1^* = 8$ mg/1 ; $z_2^* = 5.94$ mg/1 , $q_2^* = 6$ mg/1, $u_1^* = 53.3$ mg/1, $u_2^* = 41.9$ mg/1.

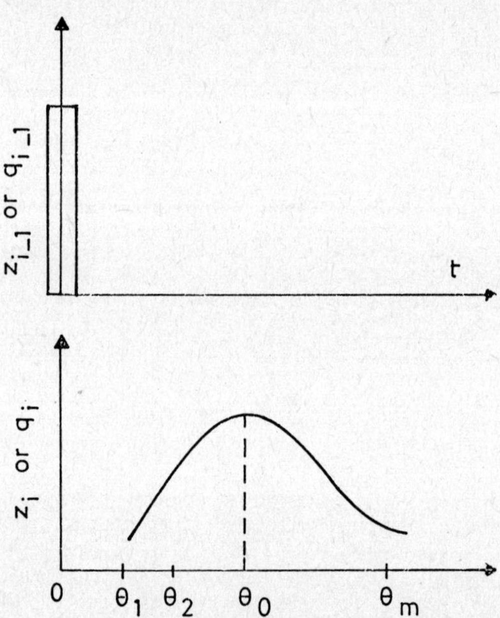

Fig. 1 : The Distributed Delay Phenomenon

The subsystem Riccati equations, etc. were integrated over a period of 8 days. This period is certainly sufficiently long for the system to reach a steady state. From the open loop control which was obtained after 6 second level iterations, the states x and u were recorded at the first 5 sampling points and from this the gain matrix G was calculated to be

$$G = \begin{bmatrix} 0.0960 & -0.0095 & 0.0270 & -0.0038 \\ 0.0270 & -0.0038 & 0.0768 & -0.0053 \end{bmatrix}$$

and $\underline{\xi}$ to be

$$\underline{\xi} = \begin{bmatrix} -.4295 \\ -.2693 \end{bmatrix}$$

and the optimal feedback control was

$$\underline{u} = G\,\underline{x} + \underline{\xi}\,.$$

These feedback parameters were found to be identical with those obtained from a globally optimal solution calculated from the overall Riccati equation. Figs. 2, 3 show the trajectories of B.O.D. and D.O. for the two reaches using the above control law and Fig. 4 the resulting control deviations $\Delta u_1, \Delta u_2$ from the steady state control of 53.3 mg/l for reach 1 and 41.9 for reach 2.

These trajectories show that the B.O.D. and D.O. are forced towards their desired values exponentially in reach 1 whereas in reach 2, they get the effect of the pollution in reach 1. The responses are not too realistic since the effect of the pollution is apparent immediately in reach 2 whereas in practice it should occur after some time.

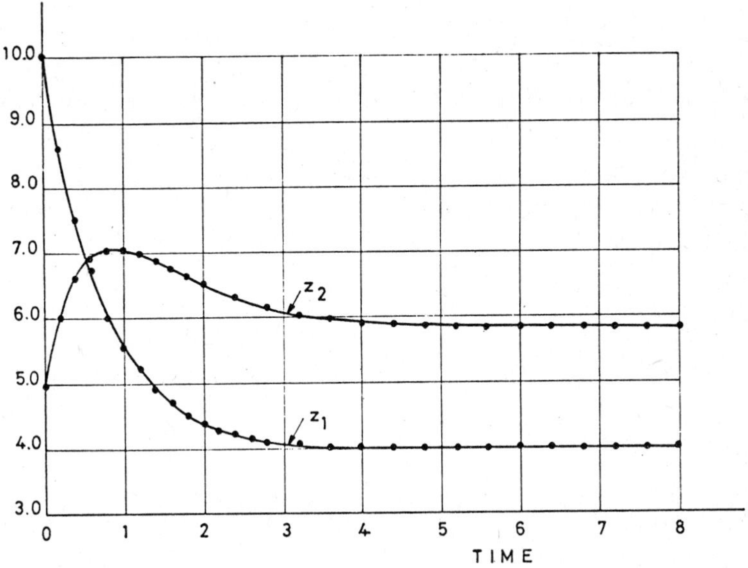

Fig. 2 : Optimal B.O.D. trajectories for the no delay model

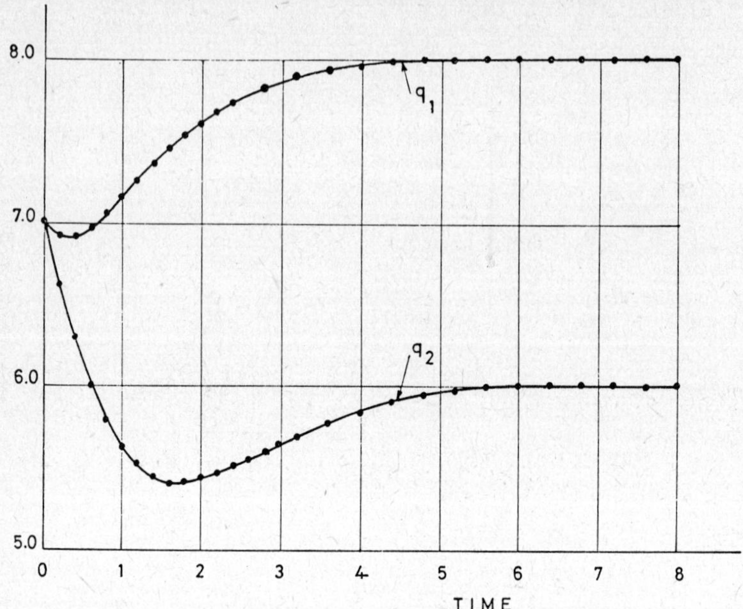

Fig. 3 : Optimal D.O. trajectories for the no-delay model

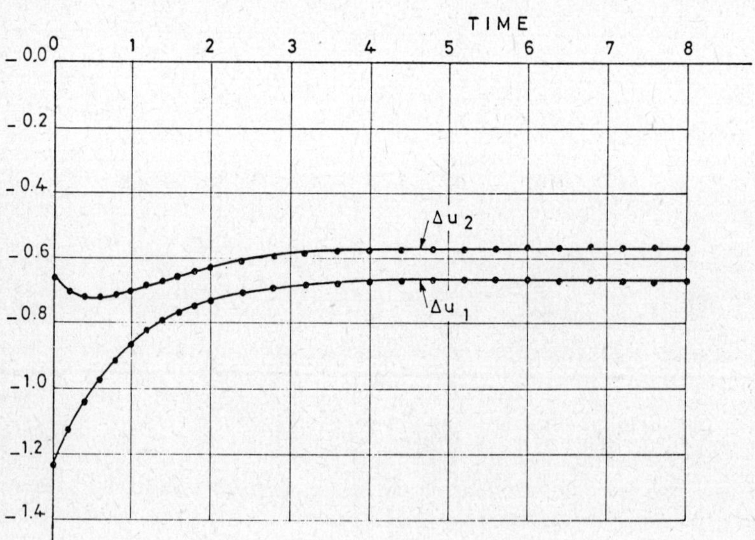

Fig. 4 : Optimal control trajectories for the no-delay model

5.3.2. Pure delay model

For the two reach pure delay model, the delays were approximated by a 2nd order Taylor series expansion, i.e. in this case the state equations were

$$\dot{z}_1 = -1.32\, z_1 + 0.1\, u_1 + 0.9\, z_0 + 5.35 \tag{47}$$

$$\dot{q}_1 = -0.32\, z_1 - 1.2\, q_1 + 0.9\, q_0 + 1.9 \tag{48}$$

$$\dot{z}_2 = 0.9\, z_1\, (t-\tau) - 1.32\, z_2 + 0.1\, u_2 + 4.19 \tag{49}$$

$$\dot{q}_2 = 0.9\, q_1\, (t-\tau) - 0.32\, z_2 - 1.2\, q_2 + 1.9 \tag{50}$$

Let $z_3(t) = z_1(t-\tau)$ then $z_3(s) = z_1\,(s)\, e^{-s\tau}$ where s is the Laplace variable.

Now $z_1\,(s)\, e^{-s\tau} = z_1(s)\left[1 + s\tau + s^2\, \frac{\tau}{2}^2 + \ldots\right]^{-1}$ taking only the first three terms

$$z_1(t) = z_3(t) + \tau \dot{z}_3(t) + \frac{\tau^2}{2}\, \ddot{z}_3(t)$$

This requires the introduction of two additional variables z_3, z_4 such that

$$\dot{z}_3 = z_4 \tag{51}$$

$$\dot{z}_4 = \frac{2}{\tau^2}\, z_1 - \frac{2}{\tau^2}\, z_3 - \frac{2}{\tau}\, z_4 \tag{52}$$

Similarly for q,

$$\dot{q}_3 = q_4 \tag{53}$$

$$\dot{q}_4 = \frac{2}{\tau^2}\, q_1 - \frac{2}{\tau^2}\, q_3 - \frac{2}{\tau}\, q_4 \tag{54}$$

Then the state equations are given by equations (47-54).

In this analysis, τ was taken to be 1/2 day .

The system was divided into two subsystems with (z_1, q_1) as the states of subsystem 1 and $(z_2, q_2, z_3, q_3, z_4, q_4)$ as the states of subsystem 2.

For the optimisation, Q_1, R_1 were the same as for the no delay case for subsystem 1. However, for subsystem 2, Q_2 and R_2 were chosen to be

$$Q_2 = \begin{bmatrix} 2 & 0 & 0 & 0 & 0 & 0 \\ 0 & 0 & 0 & 0 & 0 & 0 \\ 0 & 0 & 0 & 0 & 0 & 0 \\ 0 & 0 & 0 & 1 & 0 & 0 \\ 0 & 0 & 0 & 0 & 0 & 0 \\ 0 & 0 & 0 & 0 & 0 & 0 \end{bmatrix}$$

and $R_2 = 1$

This problem was again solved on the IBM 370/165 computer at LAAS and the resulting gain matrix G and disturbance vector $\underline{\xi}$ are given in Table 1.

These were again found to be identical with the global solution obtained by integrating the 8th order Riccati equation for the overall system. Using these gains, the system was simulated for initial conditions

$$z_1(0) = 10 \text{ mg/l} , \; z_2(0) = 5.94 \text{ mg/l}, \; q_1(0) = 7 \text{ mg/l}, \; q_2(0) = 6 \text{ mg/l}$$

Figs. 5, 6 show the B.O.D. and D.O. trajectories and Fig. 7 the corresponding control sequences. On comparing Figs. 6, 5 with Figs. 3, 2 the response of the "pure delay" model appears to be more realistic than that of the "no delay" model.

<u>The Gain G for 2 reaches with pure delay</u> :

<u>The first row</u> :

+ 0.094848156 - 0.009303570 + 0.014567137 + 0.009602249 + 0.002856791

- 0.002140164 - 0.001366377 - 0.000450552

<u>The second row</u> :

+ 0.014566869 - 0.003238410 + 0.076799244 + 0.024565300 + 0.004629463

- 0.005270749 - 0.002777129 - 0.000679225

<u>The Disturbance vector</u> $\underline{\xi}$

- 0.471007645

- 0.238365799

<u>TABLE 1</u>

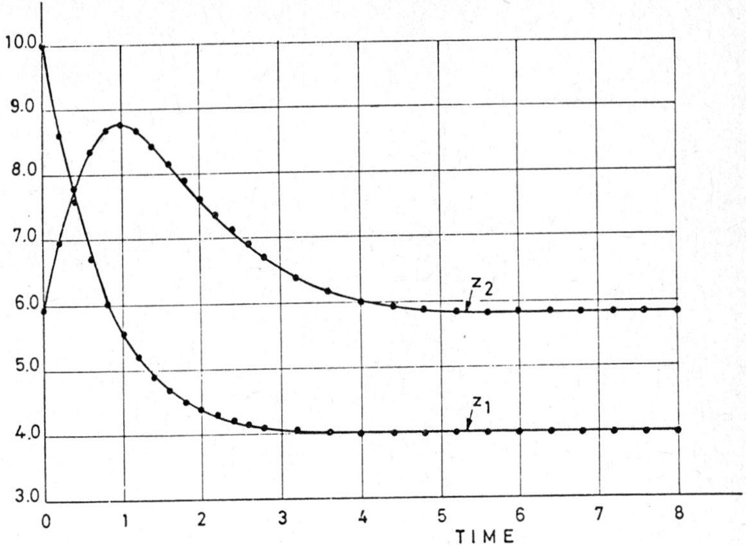

Fig. 5 : Optimal B.O.D. trajectories for the pure delay model

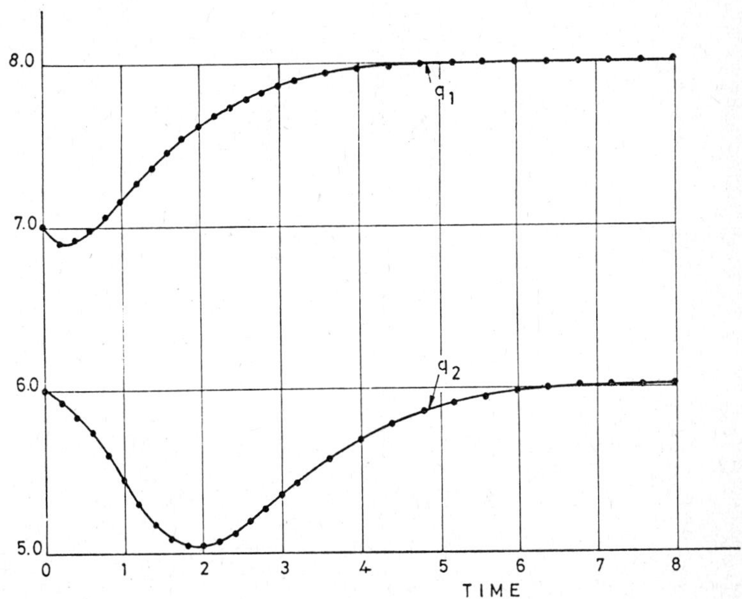

Fig. 6 : Optimal D.O. trajectories for the pure delay model

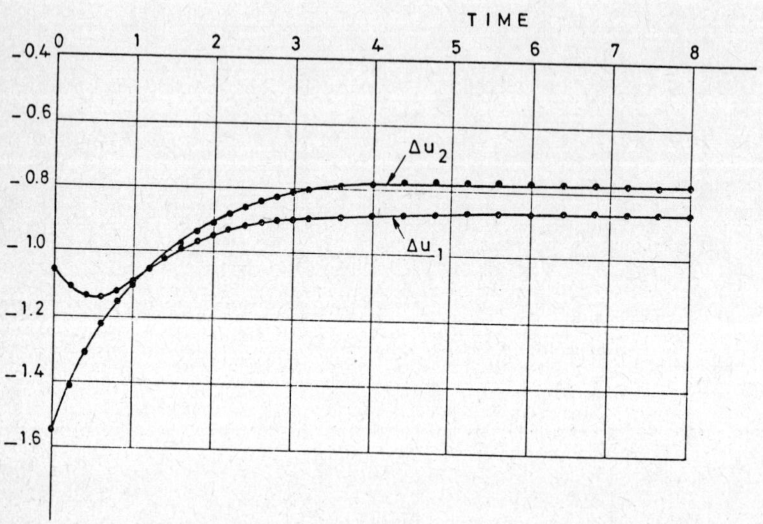

Fig. 7 : Optimal control trajectories for the pure delay model

5.3.3. Distributed delay model

In this case, the state equations for the first reach are the same as equations (47), (48) whereas for the second reach

$$\dot{z}_2 = 0.9 \sum_{i=1}^{m} a_i\, z_1(t - \tau_i) - 1.32\, z_2 + 0.1\, u_2 + 4.19 \tag{55}$$

$$\dot{q}_2 = 0.9 \sum_{i=1}^{m} a_i\, q_1(t - \tau_i) - 0.32\, z_2 - 1.2\, q_2 + 1.9$$

As in [11] , m, τ_i were chosen as :

$$m = 3,\ \tau_1 = 0,\ \tau_2 = \frac{1}{2},\ \tau_3 = 1\ ;\ z_0 = 0,\ q_0 = 10\ ;\ a_1 = 0.15,\ a_2 = 0.7,\ a_3 = 0.15$$

As for the pure delay case, it is possible to use a second order approximation for the delay and this now requires the introduction of the additional variables (z_3, q_3, z_4, q_4, z_5, q_5, z_6, q_6) (since there are two delays).

This overall 12th order system was split into two subsystems, one of order 2 and the other of order 10. Note that such a decomposition is useful in that we are able to retain the subsystem structure. However, there is little if any

The gain matrix G for 2 reaches with distributed delay

The first row :

+ 0.093525320	- 0.009112746	+ 0.015547663	+ 0.006788820	+ 0.001955301	+ 0.003402621
+ 0.001717001	- 0.002268046	- 0.001000434	- 0.000320464	- 0.000610203	- 0.000370532

The second row :

+ 0.015546888	- 0.003200263	+ 0.076798409	+ 0.017195493	+ 0.003240615	+ 0.005426496
+ 0.001640528	- 0.005270392	- 0.001943916	- 0.000475317	- 0.000784606	- 0.000327557

The disturbance vector $\underline{\xi}$

- 0.468761355

- 0.241522819

TABLE 2

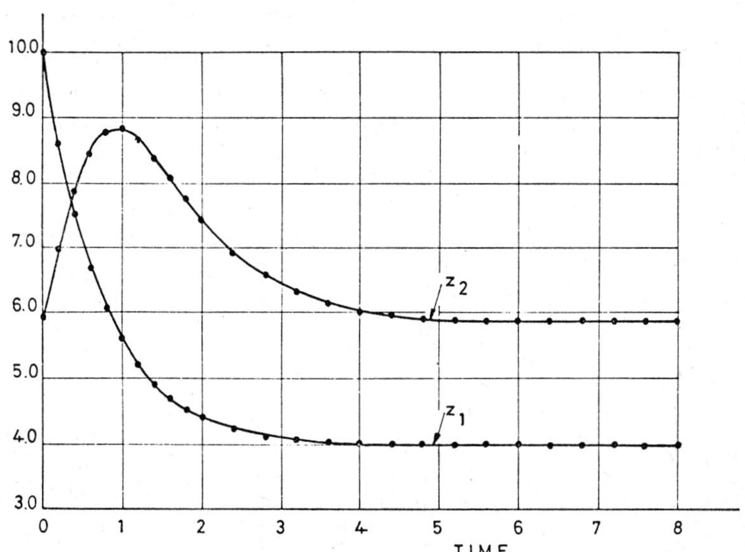

Fig. 8 : Optimal B.O.D. trajectories for distributed delay model

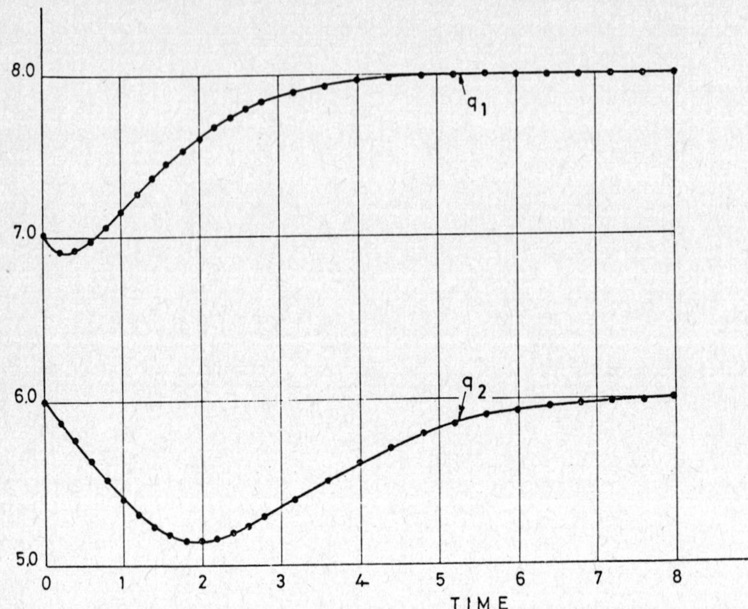

Fig. 9 : Optimal D.O. trajectories for the distributed delay model

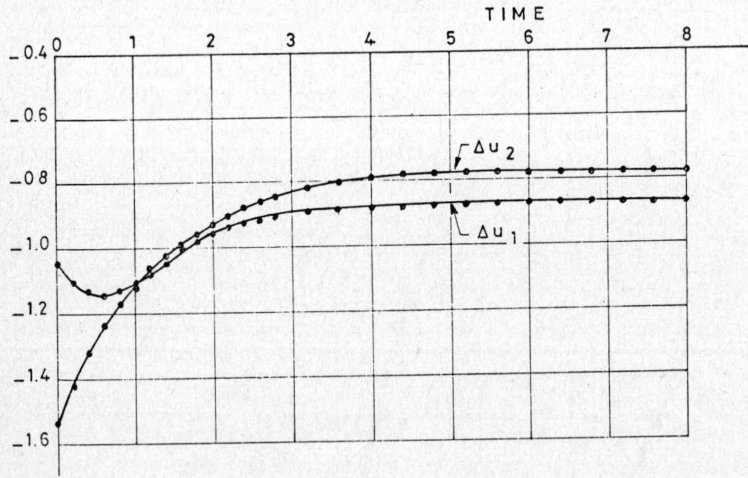

Fig. 10 : Optimal control trajectories for the distributed delay model

The gain matrix G for the 3 reaches with distributed delays

The first row :

+ 0.099062085	- 0.010958791	+ 0.022846639	+ 0.009379625	+ 0.002637625	+ 0.004595816
+ 0.002281010	- 0.004275560	- 0.001736045	- 0.000522673	- 0.000974357	- 0.000555217
+ 0.003174365	+ 0.001376390	+ 0.000480294	+ 0.000990987	+ 0.000697553	- 0.000700831
- 0.000285327	- 0.000102699	- 0.000220478	- 0.000178099		

The second row :

+ 0.022842050	- 0.005539298	+ 0.093502045	+ 0.022300422	+ 0.004415929	+ 0.007374823
+ 0.002398074	- 0.009108484	- 0.003236697	- 0.000795007	- 0.001329780	- 0.000566363
+ 0.015544653	+ 0.006787241	+ 0.001954496	+ 0.003401399	+ 0.001715660	- 0.002267599
- 0.001000464	- 0.000320613	- 0.000610054	- 0.000370383		

The third row :

+ 0.003168851	- 0.001074106	+ 0.015543908	+ 0.003468424	+ 0.000657767	+ 0.001095563
+ 0.000330418	- 0.003199846	- 0.000376218	- 0.000188380	- 0.000311464	- 0.000111490
+ 0.076797992	+ 0.017195195	+ 0.003240436	+ 0.005426317	+ 0.001640469	- 0.005270451
+ 0.003240436	+ 0.005426317	- 0.000784665	- 0.000327677	- 0.001944035	- 0.000475317

The disturbance vector ξ

- 0.588996768

- 0.410924196

- 0.112484366

TABLE 3

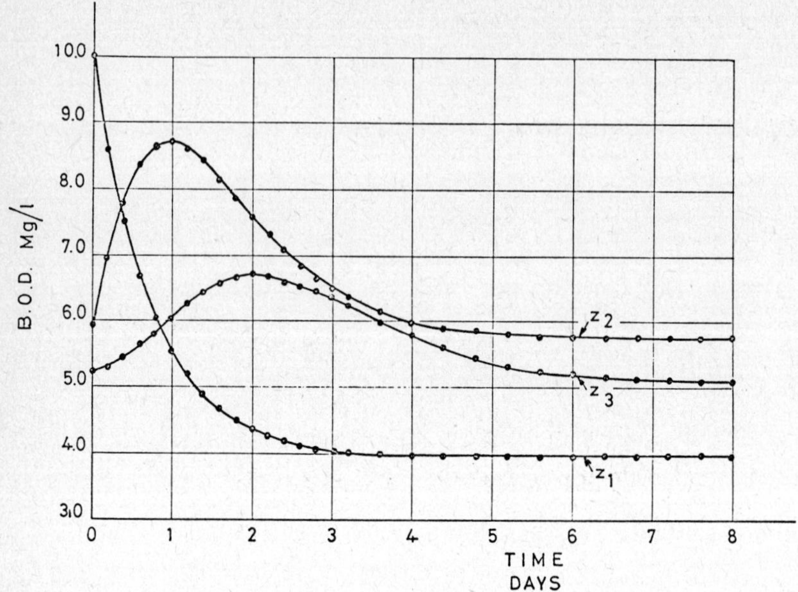

Fig. 11 : Optimal B.O.D. trajectories for the three reach distributed delay model

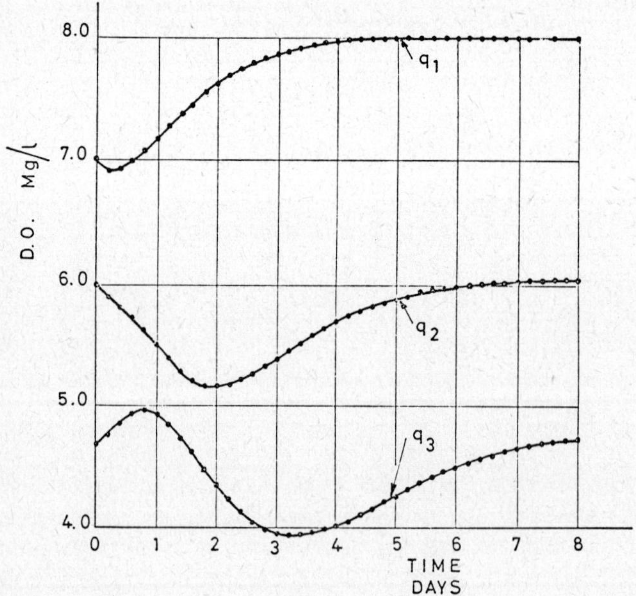

Fig. 12 : Optimal D.O. trajectories for the three reach distributed delay model

computational advantage in splitting a 12th order system into 2 subsystems of order 10 and 2. But here we are only demonstrating the methodology. As the number of subsystems increases, the decomposition becomes more computationally viable as we see in the next example where a three reach system is considered.

Using similar weighting matrices as for the no delay and pure delay cases, the gain matrix G and the vector $\underline{\xi}$ were calculated using the hierarchical approach. Table 2 gives G and $\underline{\xi}$. Using these, the system was simulated. Figs. 8, 9 give the trajectories for B.O.D. and D.O. and Fig. 10 the corresponding control trajectories for the same initial conditions as for the pure delay case. These were found to be more spread out showing the effects of the dispersion of the pollutants.

We next apply the method to the "distributed delay" model for 3 reaches.

5.4 Control of the 3 reach distributed delay model

In this case, the system is of order 22 which can be split up into 3 subsystems of order 2, 10 and 10. From a steady state analysis, the desired values for the 3rd reach are :

$$z_3^* = 5.237 \quad ; \quad q_3^* = 4.69$$

and the control for reach 3 was taken to be a deviation of the B.O.D. in the effluent discharge from 15.91 mg/1. All the other parameters were taken to be the same as for the 2 reach distributed delay model.

Results

This 3 reach 22nd order system was solved using the decentralised 3 subsystem calculation structure on the IBM 370/165 at Toulouse. For the off-line calculation, convergence took place in 11 second level iterations. From this, the control gain matrix was calculated to be as shown in Table 3. Fig. 11 and Fig. 12 show the trajectories of B.O.D. and D.O. for the 3 reaches from initial conditions

$$z_1(0) = 10 \text{ mg/1} \;,\; z_2(0) = 5.94 \text{ mg/1}, \; z_3(0) = 5.237 \text{ mg/1}$$

$$q_1(0) = 7 \text{ mg/1}, \quad q_2(0) = 6 \text{ mg/1}, \quad q_3(0) = 4.69 \text{ mg/1}$$

Physically, these imply that the 2nd and 3rd reaches are in the steady state when a large pollution load comes into reach 1. Figs. 11, 12 show the attenuation of this pollution down the river. Fig. 13 shows the control trajectory.

Remark

A method of providing optimal constant feedback control has been demonstrated for river pollution control using some data from the river Cam near Cambridge. The method is advantageous since the resulting control is closed loop and the gain matrix is constant so that a computer is not necessary for its implementation. It is also optimal for any initial condition.

Our various simulation studies on the river pollution problem have shown the efficacy of the method for river pollution control.

We next develop a feedback structure for discrete time systems but using in this case the Goal Coordination method of Tamura described in chapter 2.

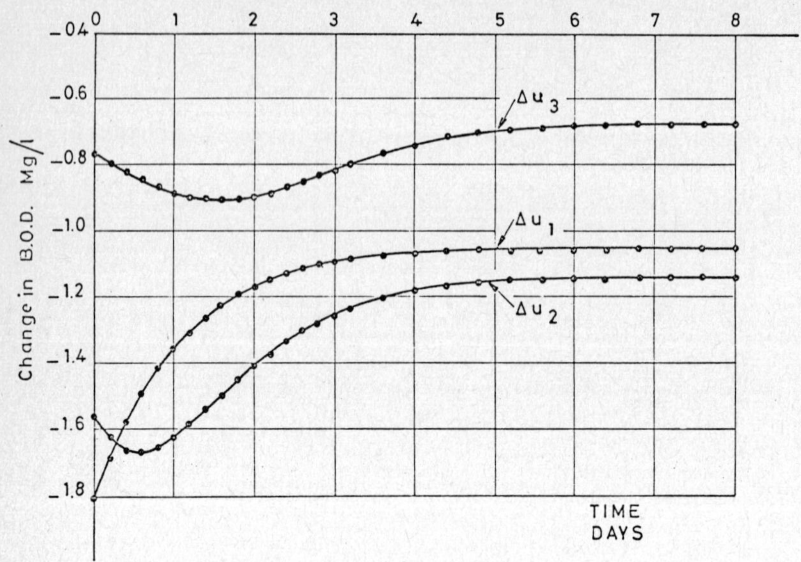

Fig. 13 : Optimal control trajectories for the 3 reach distributed delay model

Essentially we develop a method of providing a constant feedback control for the infinite stage regulator and servomechanism. The basis of the approach is to calculate the open loop control and state trajectories for a large discrete time linear quadratic problem using the goal coordination method for a period long enough for the system to reach its steady state (e.g. several time constants). Then, for a system of order n, n samples of the state and control are used for the calculation of the gain matrix. This is the only additional calculation over and above that required for open loop hierarchical optimisation, and since it is done off-line, if should not pose much problem.

In the rest of the chapter, to begin with, the goal coordination method for discrete "linear quadratic" problems is briefly recapitulated. Then the method for calculating the gains is outlined. Finally, this approach is used to calculate the gains for the two reach "no delay" river pollution control problem.

6. OPEN LOOP HIERARCHICAL OPTIMISATION BY DUALITY AND DECOMPOSITION

6.1. Problem formulation

The problem to be solved could be written as

Minimise J $(\underline{x}(k), \underline{u}(k), k)$

w.r.t. $\underline{u}(k)$

where $k = 0,1,\dots, K-1$

$$J = \frac{1}{2}\|\underline{x}(K)\|^2_Q + \frac{1}{2}\sum_{k=0}^{K-1}(\|\underline{x}(k)\|^2_Q + \|\underline{u}(k)\|^2_R) \quad (56)$$

where $\underline{x}$ is an n dimensional state vector, $\underline{u}$ is an r dimensional control vector, Q, R are respectively n x n and r x r positive definite diagonal matrices. $\|\underline{1}\|^2_E$ represents the quadratic form $\underline{1}^T E \underline{1}$, K is assumed to be "very" large.

J in equation (56) is to be minimised subject to the system dynamics.

$$\underline{x}(k+1) = A\,\underline{x}(k) + B\,\underline{u}(k) \quad (57)$$

$$\underline{x}(0) = \underline{x}_0 \quad (58)$$

where A is an n x n time invariant matrix and B is an n x r time invariant matrix.

6.2. Open loop hierarchical optimisation structure

The approach of Tamura to tackling this problem is to solve instead the dual maximisation problem since from the theorem of strong Lagrange duality, Geoffrion [35] , the solution of the two problems is equivalent at the extremum.

In order to formulate the dual problem, it is necessary to define the dual function $\emptyset(\underline{p}) = \emptyset[\underline{p}(0), \underline{p}(1), \ldots, \underline{p}(K-1)]$ which is to be maximised where $\underline{p}(k) \in E^n$ are the dual variables. The dual function $\emptyset : E^{nxK} \rightarrow R$ is given by

$$\emptyset(\underline{p}) = \underset{\underline{x},\underline{u}}{\text{Min}}\; L(\underline{x}, \underline{u}, \underline{p}) \quad (59)$$

where $L(\underline{x}, \underline{u}, \underline{p})$ is the Lagrangian function defined as

$$L(\underline{x},\underline{u},\underline{p}) = \frac{1}{2}\|\underline{x}(K)\|^2_Q + \sum_{k=0}^{K-1} \frac{1}{2}\|\underline{x}(k)\|^2_Q + \frac{1}{2}\|\underline{u}(k)\|^2_R - \underline{p}(k)^T$$
$$[\underline{x}(k+1) - A\underline{x}(k) - B\,\underline{u}(k)] \quad (60)$$

The Lagrangian can be rewritten as

$$L(\underline{x},\underline{u},\underline{p}) = \frac{1}{2}\|\underline{x}(K)\|^2_Q - \underline{p}(K-1)^T\underline{x}(K) + \sum_{k=0}^{K-1}(\frac{1}{2}\|\underline{x}(k)\|^2_Q +$$
$$\frac{1}{2}\|\underline{u}(k)\|^2_R - \underline{p}(k-1)^T\underline{x}(k) + \underline{p}(k)^T[A\underline{x}(k) + B\underline{u}(k)]) \quad (61)$$

Define the Hamiltonian function H by

$$H(\underline{x}(k), \underline{u}(k), \underline{p}(k), k) = \frac{1}{2}\|\underline{x}(k)\|^2_Q + \frac{1}{2}\|\underline{u}(k)\|^2_R +$$
$$\underline{p}(k)^T[A\,\underline{x}(k) + B\underline{u}(k)] \quad (62)$$

Then the Lagrangian function can be written using the Hamiltonian as

$$L(\underline{x},\underline{u},\underline{p}) = -\underline{p}(K-1)^T\underline{x}(K) + \frac{1}{2}\|\underline{x}(K)\|^2_Q + \sum_{k=0}^{K-1}[H(\underline{x},\underline{u},\underline{p},k)$$
$$-\underline{p}(k-1)^T\,\underline{x}(k)] \quad (63)$$

where we assume that $\underline{p}(-1) = \underline{0}$; $\underline{p}(k) = \underline{0}$ for $k \geq K$.

To evaluate the value of the dual function in equation (59) for fixed $\underline{p} = \underline{p}^* = (\underline{p}^*(0)^T, \underline{p}^*(1)^T, \ldots, \underline{p}^*(K-1)^T)^T$, it is necessary to minimise the Lagrangian function in equation (63) w.r.t. $\underline{x}$, $\underline{u}$. However, for fixed $\underline{p}$, this functional minimisation problem can be separated into K + 1 independent parametric minimisation problems.

These are given by

(i) For k = 0

$$\min_{\underline{u}(0)} H(\underline{x}(0), \underline{u}(0), \underline{p}^*(0)) = \frac{1}{2}\|\underline{x}(0)\|_Q^2 + \frac{1}{2}\|\underline{u}(0)\|_R^2 + \underline{p}^*(0)^T\left[A\underline{x}(0) + B\underline{u}(0)\right]$$

subject to $\underline{x}(0) = \underline{x}_0$.

Since R is assumed to be a positive definite diagonal matrix, this minimisation problem splits up into r independent one variable minimisation problems whose analytical solution is given by

$$\underline{u}^*(0) = -R^{-1}B^T\underline{p}^*(0) \tag{64}$$

(ii) For k = 1,2,... K-1

$$\min_{\text{w.r.t.}\underline{x}(k),\underline{u}(k)} H(\underline{x}(k), \underline{u}(k), \underline{p}^*(k), k) - \underline{p}^*(k-1)^T\underline{x}(k)$$

$$= \frac{1}{2}(\|\underline{x}(k)\|_Q^2 + \|\underline{u}(k)\|_R^2) - \underline{p}^*(k-1)^T\underline{x}(k) + $$

$$+ \underline{p}^*(k)\left[A\underline{x}(k) + B\underline{u}(k)\right].$$

Since this is a set of (n+r) independent one variable minimisation problems the solution is given by

$$\begin{aligned} \underline{x}^*(k) &= -Q^{-1}\left[-\underline{p}^*(k-1) + A^T\underline{p}^*(k)\right] \\ \underline{u}^*(k) &= -R^{-1}B^T\underline{p}^*(k) \end{aligned} \tag{65}$$

(iii) For k = K

$$\min_{\underline{x}(K)} -\underline{p}^*(K-1)\underline{x}(K) + \frac{1}{2}\|\underline{x}(K)\|_Q^2$$

The solution is

$$Q^{-1}\underline{p}^*(K-1) = \underline{x}^*(K) \tag{66}$$

Equations (64), (65) and (66) give the solutions to the first level problems and thus enable the value of the dual function $\emptyset$ to be evaluated for a fixed $\underline{p} = \underline{p}^*$. It merely remains to find a $\underline{p} = \underline{p}^{**}$ which maximises $\emptyset$. This is easy to do since the gradient of $\emptyset(\underline{p})$ at $\underline{p} = \underline{p}^*$ is given by

$$\nabla\emptyset(\underline{p})\Big|_{\underline{p}=\underline{p}^*} = -\underline{x}^*(k+1) + A\underline{x}^*(k) + B\underline{u}^*(k) \tag{67}$$

Using the value of the dual function calculated by substituting the solutions given in equations (60), (61) and (62) into the Lagrangian in equation (61) as well as the resulting gradient given in equation (67), it is possible to maximise $\emptyset(\underline{p})$ by a gradient technique such as the conjugate gradient method.

The complete algorithm is given below .

6.3. The Algorithm

Step 1 : Choose arbitrary initial values of $\underline{p}^i=(\underline{p}^i(0)^T,\underline{p}^i(1)^T\ldots\underline{p}^i(K-1)^T)^T$. Set i = 1. One could use $\underline{p}^1 = \underline{0}$ for i = 1.

Step 2 : Substitute $\underline{p} = \underline{p}^i$ in equations (64), (65) and (66) to obtain the local optimal solutions

$$\underline{x}^i = (\underline{x}^i(1)^T,\ \underline{x}^i(2)^T,\ldots,\ \underline{x}^i(K)^T)^T$$

$$\underline{u}^i = (\underline{u}^i(0)^T,\ \underline{u}^i(1)^T,\ldots,\underline{u}^i(K-1)^T)^T \tag{68}$$

Then, using equations (67), compute the n x K dimensional error vector (gradient of $\emptyset$) which comprises the error in each system equation, i.e.

$$\underline{e}(\underline{p}^i) = \nabla\,\emptyset(\underline{p})\Big|_{\underline{p}=\underline{p}^i} = \begin{bmatrix} \nabla_{\underline{p}(0)}\emptyset(\underline{p})\Big|_{\underline{p}=\underline{p}^i} \\ \nabla_{\underline{p}(1)}\emptyset(\underline{p})\Big|_{\underline{p}=\underline{p}^i} \\ \nabla_{\underline{p}(K-1)}\emptyset(\underline{p})\Big|_{\underline{p}=\underline{p}^i} \end{bmatrix} \tag{69}$$

if $\|\underline{e}(\underline{p}^i)\|^2 \leq E$ for a small positive E where $\|\underline{e}\|$ is the Euclidian norm, record $\underline{x}^i$, $\underline{u}^i$ as the optimal solutions of equation (56) subject to (57) and (58). Else.

Step 3 : Set $\underline{p}^{i+1}$ according to

$$\underline{p}^{i+1} = \underline{p}^i + \alpha_i\,\underline{d}^i \tag{70}$$

where

$$\underline{d}^i = \underline{e}(\underline{p}^i) + \beta_{i-1}\,\underline{d}^{i-1}\ ;\quad \underline{d}^1 = \underline{e}(\underline{p}^1) \tag{71}$$

$$\beta_{i-1} \equiv \frac{\sum_{k=0}^{K-1} \underline{e}(\underline{p}^i(k))^T\,\underline{e}(\underline{p}^i(k))}{\sum_{k=0}^{K-1} \underline{e}(\underline{p}^{i-1}(k))^T\,\underline{e}(\underline{p}^{i-1}(k))} \tag{72}$$

$\alpha_i > 0$ is the step length and $\underline{d}^i$ is the search direction in the ith iteration.

set i + 1 → i and go back to step 2.

6.4. Remarks

(1) The above two level algorithm is attractive because at the lowest level only a one dimensional problem has to be solved and even for this one dimensional problem, an analytical solution is available.

(2) Convergence of the second level algorithm is assured since the dual function to be maximised on the second level is convex.

(3) Against these advantages, there is the difficulty that the resulting control is open loop. This means that it is necessary to recalculate the controls every time the initial state changes. Moreover, the control is very sensitive to small parametric variations. Also, the control trajectory needs to be stored before open loop implementation. A constant feedback control matrix is clearly desirable. In the next Section, a simple way of calculating such a constant matrix is described.

7. A MULTILEVEL SOLUTION OF THE INFINITE STAGE REGULATOR

The feedback solution of equation (56) subject to equations (57) and (58) is given by Sage [55] to be

$$\underline{u}(k) = - R^{-1} B^T A^{-1} [P(k) - Q] \underline{x}(k) \tag{73}$$

$$= G \underline{x}(k) \tag{74}$$

where $P(k)$ is the solution of the discrete matrix Riccati equation. For the infinite stage case ($K \to \infty$), one way of obtaining a solution is to solve the Riccati equation for K large enough such that $P(k) = P(k+1)$ and to take this value of $P(k)$ to calculate the constant feedback matrix G in equation (74). In general, if K is several time periods of the system, P does reach a steady state.

Now, although P can be obtained from the Riccati equation, it requires the storage of large matrices and this may not be feasible for large scale systems. However, it is feasible to solve the problem in a hierarchical fashion as described in Section 6. In that case, at the optimum, when the dual function $\emptyset$ is maximised, equations (64) and (65) give the optimal sequences of $\underline{x}$ and $\underline{u}$. It is possible to obtain G in equation (74) from these sequences.

In order to do this, form the matrix

$$X = [\underline{x}(0) \quad \underline{x}(1) \ldots \underline{x}(n)]$$

and

$$U = [\underline{u}(0) \quad \underline{u}(1) \ldots \underline{u}(n)]$$

Then

$$G = U X^{-1} \tag{75}$$

This involves the additional calculation of inverting X but this can be done off-line.

7.1. Extension to the servomechanism case

$$\underset{\underline{u}(k)}{\text{Min}} \; J = \frac{1}{2} \left[\sum_{k=0}^{K-1} \| \underline{x}(k) - \underline{x}^d \|_Q^2 + \| \underline{u} \|_R^2 \right] \tag{76}$$

where $\underline{x}^d$ is a desired reference state and where J is to be minimised subject to

$$\underline{x}(k+1) = A\underline{x}(k) + B\underline{u}(k) + \underline{C} \tag{77}$$

$$\underline{x}(0) = \underline{x}_0 \tag{78}$$

where $\underline{C}$ is a known constant input. It is possible to obtain a similar solution by noting that the standard single level solution is now of the form

$$\underline{u}(k) = G \underline{x}(k) + \underline{d} \tag{79}$$

The two level off-line algorithm is changed slightly at the first level where the analytical solution can now be written as (equation (64) remains unchanged but (65) changes) :

$$\underline{u}^*(0) = -R^{-1} B^T \underline{p}^*(0)$$

$$\underline{x}^*(k) = \underline{x}^d - Q^{-1}\left[-\underline{p}^*(k-1)+A^T \underline{p}^*(k)\right] \tag{80}$$

$$\underline{u}^*(k) = - R^{-1} B^T \underline{p}^*(k)$$

$$k = 0,1,\ldots K-1$$

At the second level, the gradient becomes

$$\nabla_{\underline{p}(k)} \emptyset(\underline{p})\Big|_{\underline{p}=\underline{p}^*} = -\underline{x}^*(k-1) + A\underline{x}^*(k) + B\underline{u}^*(k) + \underline{C}(k)$$

The method of obtaining G and $\underline{d}$ is to solve the problem within a two level structure by duality and decomposition using the initial condition $\underline{x}(0) = \underline{0}$ for K large. Then, the first n values of $\underline{x}$ and $\underline{u}$ can be recorded.From these, form the matrices

$$X = \left[\underline{x}(n) \quad \underline{x}(n-1)\ldots \underline{x}(1)\right]$$

and $$U = \left[[\underline{u}(n)-\underline{u}(0)],[\underline{u}(n)-\underline{u}(1)],\ldots \right]$$

Then $$G = U X^{-1}$$

and $$\underline{d} = \underline{u}(0)$$

8. SIMULATION EXAMPLE

To illustrate the above approach, a two reach river pollution control model was simulated using some data from the River Cam near Cambridge. The model used was the two reach "no delay" model of Tamura [11] . The control problem in this case is to maintain the instream biochemical demand (B.O.D.) and the dissolved oxygen (D.O.) at prespecified levels for a river with multiple polluters using the percentage of the B.O.D. treated at the sewage works as the control variable .

The dynamic behaviour of a two reach system is given for the no delay model by Tamura [11] to be :

$$\underline{x}(k+1) = A\,\underline{x}(k) + B\,\underline{u}(k) + \underline{C}$$

where

$$\underline{x} = \begin{bmatrix} x_1 \\ x_2 \\ x_3 \\ x_4 \end{bmatrix}$$

is such that x_1, x_3 give the B.O.D. concentration (mg/l) in the stream and x_2, x_4 the D.O. concentration (mg/l) . The control is given by

$$\underline{u}(k) = \begin{bmatrix} \pi_1(k) \\ \pi_2(k) \end{bmatrix} \qquad k = 0,1,\dots,kK-1$$

where π_1, π_2 are the maximum fraction of B.O.D. removed from the effluent in the reaches 1,2 A, B, $\underline{C}$ from the Cam data are given by

$$A = \begin{bmatrix} 0.18 & 0 & 0 & 0 \\ -0.25 & 0.27 & 0 & 0 \\ 0.55 & 0 & 0.18 & 0 \\ 0 & 0.55 & -0.25 & 0.27 \end{bmatrix}$$

$$B = \begin{bmatrix} 2.0 & 0 \\ 0 & 0 \\ 0 & -2.0 \\ 0 & 0 \end{bmatrix} \quad \text{and} \quad \underline{C} = \begin{bmatrix} 4.5 \\ 6.15 \\ 2.0 \\ 2.65 \end{bmatrix}$$

A suitable cost function for this system is

$$J = \frac{1}{2} \| \underline{x}(K) \|^2_{I_4} + \sum_{k=0}^{K-1} \frac{1}{2} \left(\| \underline{x}(k) - \underline{x}^d \|^2_{I_4} + \| \underline{u}(k) \|^2_{100\, I_2} \right)$$

where I_4 is the fourth order identity matrix and I_2 is the second order identity matrix. The desired values $\underline{x}^d$ are

$$\underline{x}^d = \begin{bmatrix} 5 \\ 7 \\ 5 \\ 7 \end{bmatrix}$$

This implies that it is desired to maintain the stream near B.O.D. values of 5mg/1 and D.O. values of 7 mg/1 while minimising the treatment at the sewage works.

8.1. Simulation results

The above problem was solved using the hierarchical structure given in Section 6. The initial state was chosen to be $\underline{x}(0) = \underline{0}$ and K was chosen to be 23. The sampling interval here is 0.5 days. K is certainly sufficiently long for the system to settle to a steady state. Convergence to the optimum took place in 89 iterations of the second level which took 30.6 seconds to execute. At this point,

$$\emptyset = J = 1607$$

The first 5 values were then taken of $\underline{x}$ and $\underline{u}$. From this, by inverting a 4 x 4 matrix, the control was found to be $\underline{u} = G\,\underline{x} + \underline{d}$

$$\text{where} \quad G = \begin{bmatrix} 0.0074 & -0.0011 & 0.0006 & -0.0001 \\ 0.0126 & -0.0015 & 0.0042 & -0.0004 \end{bmatrix}$$

and $\underline{d} = \begin{bmatrix} 0.05449 \\ 0.00668 \end{bmatrix}$

using this control law, the system was simulated for the initial states

$$\underline{x}(0) = \begin{bmatrix} 0 \\ 0 \\ 0 \\ 1 \end{bmatrix}$$

Figs. 14, 15 show the B.O.D. and D.O. in reaches 1 and 2 and Fig. 16 the controls.

These trajectories are identical to those found from a global solution.

9. CRITICAL ANALYSIS

In this chapter we have developed methods for computing feedback controls for both discrete time and continuous time linear systems within an off-line decentralised computational structure. The resulting feedback control laws are independent of initial condition disturbances and can thus be usefully implemented for the on-line regulation of large scale systems. The computation required, certainly for the infinite time case which is extensively treated here, is slightly larger than that required for the corresponding open loop hierarchical solution but here all the calculations are done off-line whilst for the open loop hierarchical approach developed in Chapter 2 it is necessary to perform them on-line. It is in fact necessary to perform the open loop hierarchical calculation after measurement of the state $\underline{x}_0$ but before it changes significantly whilst with the feedback laws developed here, we need only multiply the measured state with the gain matrix to obtain the optimal control whatever the initial state was.

The basic idea in the development of all the methods in the chapter was that we were able to obtain off-line the solution of the open loop control problem for various initial conditions and since this off-line calculation was done within a hierarchical structure, it was quite feasible for really large systems and we demonstrated it on our 22nd order river example. Then we substituted the known trajectories into the overall equations to obtain the optimal gains. This general approach has proved to be quite successful. However, it is still somewhat clumsy. It would be interesting to find out if one can generate the feedback matrix directly within the off-line hierarchical structure without having to invert a matrix. This is left as a thought for the reader. In the next chapter we go on with our study of feedback control by considering non-linear systems.

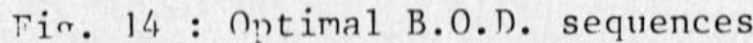

Fig. 14 : Optimal B.O.D. sequences

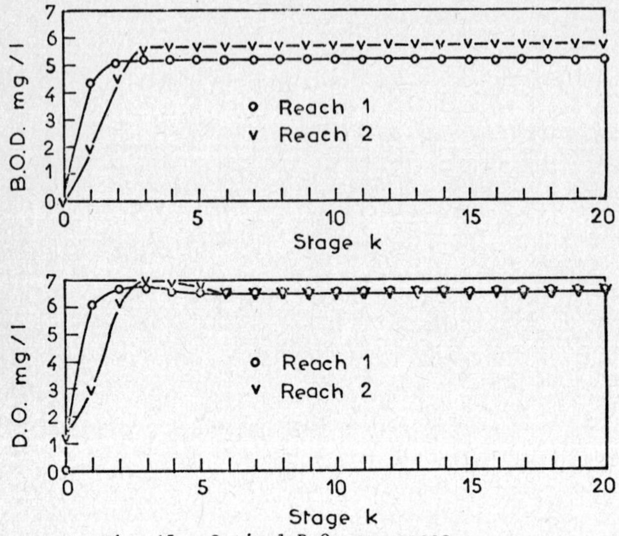

Fig. 15 : Optimal D.O. sequences

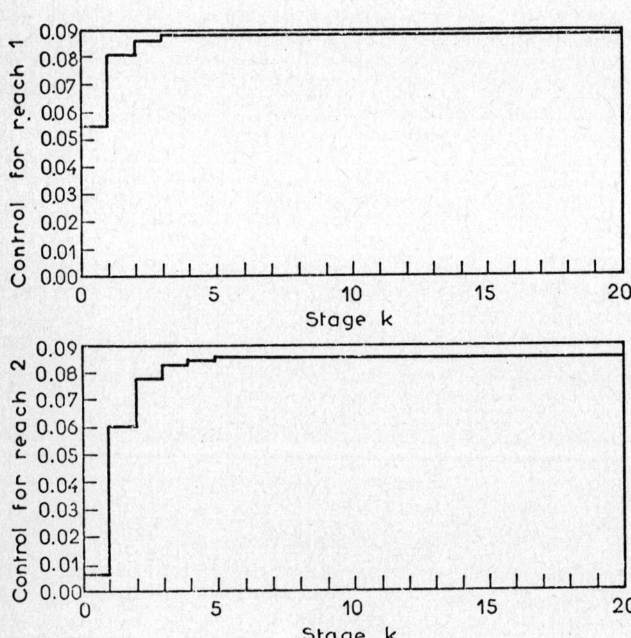

Fig. 16 : Optimal control for reaches one and two

CHAPTER V

HIERARCHICAL FEEDBACK CONTROL FOR NON-LINEAR DYNAMICAL SYSTEMS

1. INTRODUCTION

The problem of computing optimal feedback control for large scale non-linear dynamical systems has received very little attention. This is not surprising since at the present time it is not possible to compute a feedback control law for even the centralised case for non-linear systems if it is desired that the feedback parameters be independent of the initial conditions. For this reason we would not expect to get feedback control laws for non-liner interconnected dynamical systems which are independent of initial condition disturbances. Nevertheless, it may be possible to obtain control laws which do provide feedback, i.e. where the current control is a function of the current state. Such control laws are desirable since they enable us to modify the controls as the process evolves and thus provide some degree of insensitivity to disturbances. In this chapter a method is developed for providing optimal feedback control for large scale non-linear interconnected dynamical systems.

The basis of the approach is that if the problem is solved using one of the methods developed in Chapter 3 for the optimisation of non-linear systems to calculate the optimal open loop control trajectory, then from the related state and costate trajectories it is possible to obtain a control which is a function of the current state.

The open loop method that we will concentrate on is the Goal Coordination method and we will test the feedback calculation on the two non-linear examples treated in Chapter 3 where we know that the Goal Coordination method works. However, the actual open loop method used is not too significant so that we could equally well obtain a feedback control from any open loop control method that works. This idea is examined at the end of the Chapter. We will also consider ways of making the feedback control less sensitive to variations in the initial conditions. We will begin by briefly recapitulating the Goal Coordination method of hierarchical optimisation.

2. THE OVERALL CONTROL PROBLEM AND THE OPEN LOOP HIERARCHICAL CONTROL STRUCTURE

2.1. The optimal control problem

A fairly general problem for the optimal control of interconnected dynamical systems could be formulated as

$$\underset{\text{w.r.t.}\,\underline{u}_i}{\text{Minimise}} \quad I(\underline{x}_i,\underline{u}_i,\underline{z}_i) \qquad i = 1,2,\dots, N \tag{1}$$

where $\underline{x}_i$ is the n_i dimensional state vector of the ith subsystem, $\underline{u}_i$ is the corresponding m_i dimensional control vector and $\underline{z}_i$ is the r_i dimensional vector of interconnection inputs from the other subsystems. I is a scalar functional defined by

$$I = \sum_{i=1}^{N} \left\{ \int_{t_0}^{t_f} f_i[\underline{x}_i(t), \underline{u}_i(t), \underline{z}_i(t), t]dt \right\}, \tag{2}$$

where $f_i\left[\underline{x}_i(t), \underline{u}_i(t), \underline{z}_i(t)\right]$ is the cost at time t for i = 1,2,...N subsystems. The above functional I is to be minimised subject to the constraints which define the subsystem dynamics, i.e.

$$\begin{aligned} \dot{\underline{x}}_i(t) &= \underline{g}_i\left[\underline{x}_i(t), \underline{u}_i(t), \underline{z}_i(t), t\right], \quad t_0 \leqslant t \leqslant t_f \\ \underline{x}_i(t_0) &= \underline{x}_{i0}, \quad i = 1,2,\ldots N \ . \end{aligned} \tag{3}$$

Also, the minimum of I must satisfy the interconnection relationship

$$\sum_{j=1}^{N} \underline{G}_{ij}(\underline{x}_j, \underline{z}_j) = \underline{0} \ . \tag{4}$$

2.2. The open loop hierarchical control structure

Consider the goal coordination or infeasible method of Pearson [7].

The basis of the infeasible approach is the formulation of the dual functional $\xi(\underline{\lambda})$ which is to be maximised w.r.t. $\underline{\lambda}(t)$, $t_0 \leqslant t \leqslant t_f$, where

$$\xi(\underline{\lambda}) = \min_{\underline{x},\underline{u},\underline{z}} \left\{ L(\underline{x},\underline{u},\underline{z},\underline{\lambda}) \ : \text{equation (3)} \right\}$$

where

$$\begin{aligned} L(\underline{x},\underline{u},\underline{z},\underline{\lambda}) &= I + \int_{t_0}^{t_f} \underline{\lambda}_i(t)^T \left\{ \sum_{j=1}^{N} \underline{G}_{ij}(\underline{x}_j, \underline{z}_j) \right\} dt \\ &= \sum_{i=1}^{N} \int_{t_0}^{t_f} [f_i(\underline{x}_i, \underline{u}_i, \underline{z}_i) \\ &\quad + \sum_{j=1}^{N} \underline{\lambda}_j^T(t) \underline{\Psi}_i(\underline{x}_i, \underline{z}_j)] \, dt \end{aligned} \tag{5}$$

Then if

$$\min_{\underline{u}_i} I = \max_{\underline{\lambda}} \xi(\underline{\lambda}), \qquad i = 1,2,\ldots N$$

an alternative way of optimising I would be to maximise $\xi(\underline{\lambda})$. We saw in Chapter 3 that the above assertion is often true.

Now from equation (5), for a given $\underline{\lambda}(t)$, $t_0 \leqslant t \leqslant t_f$, the Lagrangian L is separable into N independent minimisation problems, the ith of which is given by

$$\min_{\underline{x}_i,\underline{u}_i,\underline{z}_i} L_i = \int_{t_0}^{t_f} \left[f_i(\underline{x}_i,\underline{u}_i,\underline{z}_i) + \sum_{j=1}^{N} \underline{\lambda}_j^T(t) \underline{\Psi}_i(\underline{x}_i,\underline{z}_j) \right] dt \tag{6}$$

subject to

$$\begin{aligned} \dot{\underline{x}}_i &= \underline{g}_i(\underline{x}_i,\underline{u}_i,\underline{z}_i), \quad t_0 \leqslant t \leqslant t_f \ , \\ \underline{x}_i(t_0) &= \underline{x}_{i0} \ . \end{aligned} \tag{7}$$

This leads to the two-level structure shown in Fig. 1 where on the first level, for given $\underline{\lambda}$, I_i in equation (6) is minimised subject to equation (7) and on level 2, the $\underline{\lambda}(t)$ $(t_0 \leqslant t \leqslant t_f)$ trajectory is improved using say the steepest ascent method, i.e. from iteration j to j + 1

$$\underline{\lambda}(t)^{j+1} = \underline{\lambda}(t)^{j} + \alpha^{j} \underline{d}^{j} \tag{8}$$

where

$$\underline{d}^{j} = \nabla \xi_{\underline{\lambda}(t)}(\underline{\lambda}) = \sum_{j=1}^{N} G_{ij} (\underline{x}_j, \underline{z}_j) \tag{9}$$

$\nabla \xi (\underline{\lambda})$ is the gradient of $\xi(\underline{\lambda})$, $\alpha^j > 0$ is the step length and $\underline{d}^j$ the steepest ascent search direction. At the optimum $\underline{d}^j \rightarrow \underline{0}$ and the appropriate Lagrange multiplier trajectory is the optimal one.

2.3. Discussion

On the first level, since equation (6) is to be minimised subject to equation (7), the necessary conditions, lead to a two point boundary value problem from which an open loop control could be calculated. However, such open loop optimum control is too sensitive for practical implementation. It is clearly desirable to calculate a closed loop control. Now, one possible method for resolving the two point boundary value problem of the subsystem which arises on minimising (6) subject to (7), is by the use of the quasilinearisation approach. In this method, a sequence of linear two point boundary value problems need to be solved. It is possible to obtain a closed loop control from a linear two point boundary value problem, as we saw in Chapter 4.

The calculation procedure that is envisaged is as follows :

Step 1 : guess a $\underline{\lambda}(t)$, $t_0 \leqslant t \leqslant t_f$, trajectory at level 2 and provide to level 1

Step 2 : formulate the two point boundary value problem. Solve by quasilinearisation

Step 3 : send state and control trajectories of all the subsystems to level 2. At level 2, test if $\underline{d}^j(t)$ $(t_0 \leqslant t \leqslant t_f)$ in equation (9), is acceptably near to zero. If not, calculate new $\underline{\lambda}(t)$ using equation (8). Use new $\underline{\lambda}(t)$ in step 2.

However, if $\underline{d}^j(t)$ is acceptably near zero, use the last linearised two point boundary value problem from step 2 to calculate the parameters of the closed loop controllers. The actual procedure to be adopted is described in Section 3.

Fig. 2 shows the information transfers.

The most significant point to note here is that the closed loop controller's parameters would be such that by using them a control which is arbitrarily close to the optimum is achieved. The reason for this is that :

(a) In the quasilinearisation procedure, the final linear approximation to the non-linear two point boundary value problem must be such that it actually solves the non-linear problem to an acceptable degree.

(b) Since at this point $\underline{d}^j(t)$ is effectively zero for all $t_0 \leqslant t \leqslant t_f$, the max of $\xi(\underline{\lambda})$ has actually been achieved. Therefore, if $\text{Max}\, \xi(\underline{\lambda}) = \text{Min}\ I$, the primal problem is solved.

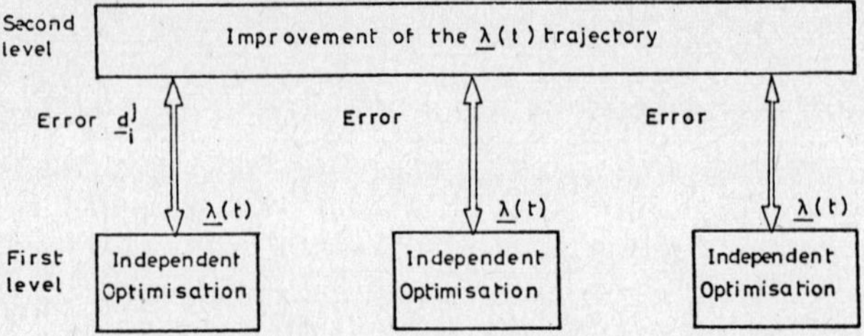

Fig. 1 : The two level open loop control computation

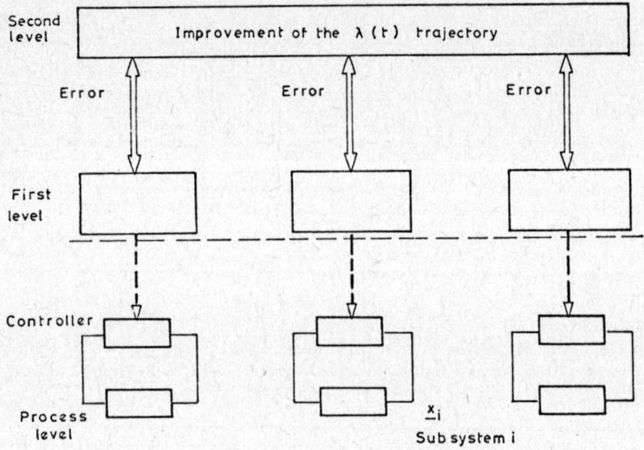

Fig. 2 : The closed loop controllers

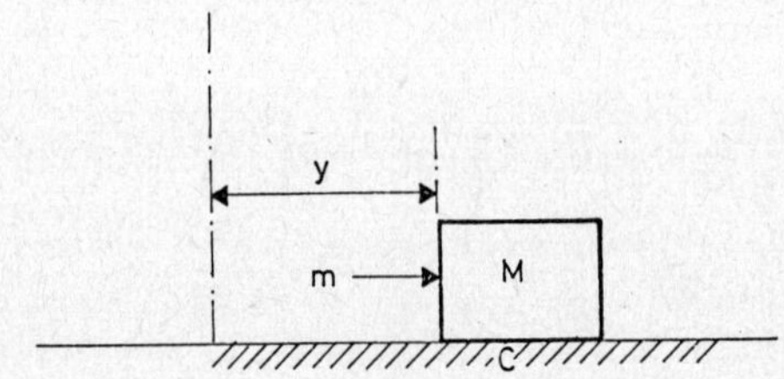

Fig. 3 : The sliding mass sytem

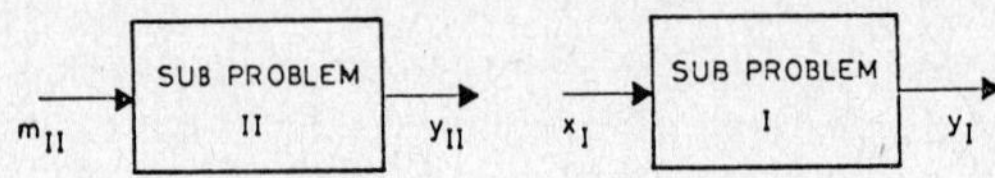

Fig. 4 : Decomposition of the sliding mass problem

3. THE CLOSED LOOP CONTROLLERS FOR THE SUBSYSTEMS

As pointed out in the last Section, the closed loop controllers are obtained at the first level by solving the final linearised equation in the quasilinearisation procedure for solving two point boundary value problems of the subsystems. The actual first level problem for the ith subsystem is

For given $\underline{\lambda}(t)$, $t_0 \leqslant t \leqslant t_f$,

$$\min_{\underline{x}_i,\underline{u}_i,\underline{z}_i} \int_{t_0}^{t_f} \left\{ f_i(\underline{x}_i,\underline{u}_i,\underline{z}_i) + \sum_{j=1}^{N} \underline{\lambda}_i^T \underline{\psi}_j(\underline{x}_i,\underline{z}_j) \right\} dt$$

subject to

$$\dot{\underline{x}}_i = \underline{g}_i(\underline{x}_i,\underline{u}_i,\underline{z}_i), \qquad t_0 \leqslant t \leqslant t_f ,$$

$$\underline{x}_i(0) = \underline{x}_{i0} .$$

For this problem, the Hamiltonian H_i is given by

$$H_i = f_i(\underline{x}_i,\underline{u}_i,\underline{z}_i) + \underline{\lambda}^T \psi_i(\underline{x}_i, \underline{z}_j) + \underline{p}_i^T \underline{g}_i(\underline{x}_i,\underline{u}_i,\underline{z}_i)$$

Then for a given $\underline{\lambda}$, the state and costate equations become

$$\dot{\underline{x}}_i = \underline{g}_i(\underline{x}_i, \underline{u}_i, \underline{z}_i)$$

$$\dot{\underline{p}}_i = -\frac{\partial H_i}{\partial \underline{x}_i} = -\left[\frac{\partial f_i}{\partial \underline{x}_i} + \frac{\sum_{j=1}^{N} \partial \underline{\psi}_i^T}{\partial \underline{x}_i} \underline{\lambda}_i + \frac{\partial \underline{g}_i^T}{\partial \underline{x}_i} \underline{p}_i \right] \tag{10}$$

with

$$\partial H_i/\partial \underline{u}_i = \underline{0} \ ; \quad \partial H_i/\partial \underline{z}_i = \underline{0} \tag{11}$$

The assumption is made at this point that using equation (11) it is possible to obtain the control $\underline{u}_i$ and pseudo control $\underline{z}_i$ which is an explicity function of $\underline{p}_i$ and $\underline{x}_i$, i.e.

$$\begin{aligned} \underline{u}_i &= \underline{c}_i(\underline{x}_i, \underline{p}_i) \\ \underline{z}_i &= \underline{d}_i(\underline{x}_i, \underline{p}_i) \end{aligned} \tag{12}$$

Then substituting for $\underline{u}_i$ and $\underline{z}_i$ in equation (10), the state-costate equations could be written as

$$\begin{aligned} \dot{\underline{x}}_i &= \underline{a}_i(\underline{x}_i, \underline{p}_i), \quad t_0 \leqslant t \leqslant t_f , \\ \dot{\underline{p}}_i &= \underline{b}_i(\underline{x}_i, \underline{p}_i), \quad t_0 \leqslant t \leqslant t_f , \end{aligned} \tag{13}$$

with the boundary conditions

$$\underline{x}_i(t_0) = \underline{x}_{i0} \tag{14}$$

and from the transversality conditions

$$\underline{p}_i(t_f) = \underline{0} . \tag{15}$$

3.1. The quasilinearistation procedure for solving the two point boundary problem on level 1.

The two point boundary value problem of the ith subsystem is given by equation (13) subject to the boundary conditions given by (14) and (15). This problem is solved by the quasilinearisation technique as follows

Define $\underline{y} = \begin{bmatrix} \underline{x}_i \\ \underline{p}_i \end{bmatrix}$ and rewrite equation (13) as

$$\dot{\underline{y}}(t) = F[\underline{y}(t)] \tag{16}$$

In the quasilinearisation procedure, starting from an initial guessed trajectory for $\underline{y} = y^0(t)$, successive linearisations are peformed of equation (16) in such a way that the final linear equation for $\underline{y}$ solves equation (16) to an acceptable degree subject to the boundary conditions (14) and (15) which could be rewritten in a more general form as

$$\begin{aligned} \underline{y}(t_0)^T A_0 &= \underline{b}_0^T \\ \underline{y}(t_f)^T A_f &= \underline{b}_f^T \end{aligned} \tag{17}$$

where A_0, A_f are 2 n x n matrices and $\underline{b}_0$, $\underline{b}_f$ are n x 1 vectors.

The linearised equation of (16) about a trajectory $\underline{y} = \underline{y}^0(t)$ can be obtained by an expansion in a Taylor series about $\underline{y}^0$, i.e.

$$\frac{d\underline{y}}{dt} = F(\underline{y}^0) + J(\underline{y}^0)(\underline{y} - \underline{y}^0) + \underline{\Psi}, \tag{18}$$

where $J(\underline{y}^0)$ is the Jacobian of the function $\underline{F}[\underline{y}(t)]$, $t_0 \leq t \leq t_f$, at the point $\underline{y}^0$ and $\underline{\Psi}$ represents all the terms of second or higher order. Neglecting these terms, a linear equation is obtained, i.e.

$$\frac{d\underline{y}}{dt} = F(\underline{y}^0) + J(\underline{y}^0)(\underline{y} - \underline{y}^0). \tag{19}$$

If the initial guessed trajectory $\underline{y}^0$ while satisfying equations (19) and (17) does not satisfy equation (16) to an acceptable degree, then a new linearising trajectory can be calculated as follows :

From iteration m to m + 1 integrate numerically equation (19) in two parts the homogeneous part and the particular solution, i.e. solve

$$\frac{d\hat{y}^{(m+1)}}{dt} = J(\underline{y}^m)\,\hat{y}^{(m+1)} \quad \text{with} \quad \hat{y}^{(m+1)}(t_0) = I \tag{19a}$$

where I is the 2 n x 2 n identity matrix and to distinguish between the homogeneous part which is a matrix equation and the particular solution, define the vector $\underline{M}$ such that

$$(d/dt)\,(\underline{M}^{(m+1)}) = J(\underline{y}^{(m)})\,\underline{M}^{(m+1)} + F(\underline{y}^m) - J(\underline{y}^m)\underline{y}^m \tag{19b}$$

with

$$\underline{M}^{(m+1)}(t_0) = \underline{0}\,.$$

Then by superposition, the complete solution of equation (19) in order to obtain the (m+1) th trajectory is given by

$$\underline{y}^{(m+1)} = \underline{M}^{(m+1)} + \hat{y}^{(m+1)}\,\underline{C}^{m+1}\,, \tag{20}$$

where $\hat{y}$ is the 2n x 2n matrix solution of equation (19a) and where $\underline{C}^{m+1}$ is a 2n x 1 vector of integration constants which are obtained from the boundary conditions (17) as follows.

From equation((17)

$$A_0^T \underline{C}^{m+1} = \underline{b}_0 \tag{21}$$

and from equation (20)

$$A_f^T \hat{y}^{(m+1)}(t_f) \underline{C}^{m+1} + \underline{M}^{(m+1)}(t_f) = \underline{b}_f \tag{22}$$

From equations (21) and (22), $\underline{C}^{(m+1)}$ can be obtained i.e.

$$\begin{bmatrix} A_0^T \\ \\ A_f^T \hat{y}^{(m+1)} \end{bmatrix} \underline{C}^{m+1} = \begin{bmatrix} \underline{b}_0 \\ \\ \underline{b}_f - A_f^T \underline{M}^{m+1} \end{bmatrix} \tag{23}$$

This $\underline{C}^{m+1}$ can be substituted into equation (20) in order to obtain the new linearised trajectory which satisfies the boundary values. The conditions for the convergence of the quasilinearisation method have been extensively studied by McGill and Kenneth [56] .

3.2. Modifications to the quasilinearisation procedure at level 1 for closed loop control

The basis of the closed loop control is the use of the time-varying linear equation (20) to obtain an explicit relationship between $\underline{x}_i$ and $\underline{p}_i$ and then to substitute for $\underline{p}_i$ in equation (12) in order to obtain a control $\underline{u}_i$ which is only a time-varying function of the state, i.e. a closed loop control. This control is to be calculated only for that $\underline{\lambda}$ trajectory which maximises $\xi(\underline{\lambda})$ for that iteration of the quasilinearisation procedure where the linearised trajectory solves equation (16).

In order to obtain the closed loop control, write the solution of (19) as

$$\underline{y}(t_f) = \emptyset(t_f,t)\, \underline{y}(t) + \int_t^{t_f} \emptyset(t_f,\tau)\, [\underline{F}(\tau) - J\, \underline{y}(\tau)]\, d\tau \tag{24}$$

where $\emptyset$ is the transition matrix of the system (19).

Rewriting equation (24) in partitioned form where the integral is replaced by $\underline{\omega}_i(t)$

$$\begin{bmatrix} \underline{x}_i(t_f) \\ \\ \underline{p}_i(t_f) \end{bmatrix} = \begin{bmatrix} \emptyset_{11}(t_f,t) & \emptyset_{12}(t_f,t) \\ \\ \emptyset_{21}(t_f,t) & \emptyset_{22}(t_f,t) \end{bmatrix} \begin{bmatrix} \underline{x}_i(t) \\ \\ \underline{p}_i(t) \end{bmatrix} + \begin{bmatrix} \underline{\omega}_{i1}(t) \\ \\ \underline{\omega}_{i2}(t) \end{bmatrix}$$

using equation (15)

$$\underline{p}_i(t_f) = \underline{0} = \emptyset_{21}(t_f,t)\, \underline{x}_i(t) + \emptyset_{22}(t_f,t)\, \underline{p}_i(t) + \underline{\omega}_{i2}(t)$$

so that

$$\underline{p}_i(t) = - \emptyset_{22}^{-1} \left[\emptyset_{21} \underline{x}_i + \underline{\omega}_{i2} \right]$$

$$= - \emptyset_{22}^{-1} \quad \emptyset_{21} \underline{x}_i(t) - \emptyset_{22}^{-1} \underline{\omega}_{i2} \tag{25}$$

Note that $\emptyset_{22}^{-1}$ always exists since it is a principal minor of a transition matrix.

If this $\underline{p}_i(t)$ trajectory is substituted into equation (12), it is possible to obtain the control $\underline{u}_i$ which is an explicity function of $\underline{x}_i$, i.e.

$$\underline{u}_i(t) = \underline{C} \; (\underline{x}_i, t) \tag{26}$$

Note that the calculation of $\emptyset_{22}(t_f,t)$, $\emptyset_{21}(t_f,t)$, $\underline{\omega}_{i2}(t)$ imposes a very minor additional computational burden since the $\emptyset$ matrix in equation (24) can be calculated from y in equation (20) as*

$$\hat{y} \; (t_0, t) = \emptyset \; (t_0, t) \tag{27}$$

From this, it is possible to calculate $\emptyset(t_f,t)$ since

$$\emptyset \; (t_f,t) \; \emptyset(t, t_0) = \emptyset(t_f,t_0) \tag{28}$$

i.e. $$\emptyset \; (t_f,t) = \emptyset \; (t_f,t_0) \; \emptyset \; (t_0,t)^{-1} \tag{29}$$

Then, knowing $\emptyset(t_f,t)$ and the F and J, the convolution integral in equation (24) can be easily calculated and this gives $\underline{\omega}_{i2}$ directly.

In the following Section, the calculation procedure is demonstrated on an interesting example of a non-linear dynamical system which has previously been treated by the open loop Goal Coordination method by Bauman.

4. EXAMPLE 1 : CLOSED LOOP CONTROL FOR A SLIDING MASS SYSTEM

Consider the sliding mass system shown in Fig. 3 which was previously considered in Chapter 3. The dynamic behaviour of this system could be described by

$$M \ddot{y} + C \dot{y}^2 \text{ sgn } \dot{y} = m \tag{30}$$

where M is the mass of the sliding solid, C, the coefficient of friction, m, the control force, and y the displacement.

In equation (30)

$$\text{sgn } \dot{y} = \begin{cases} +1 & \text{if} \quad y > 0 \\ -1 & \text{if} \quad y < 0 \end{cases}$$

For convenience, let M = 1 ; C = 1.

---

* To see this, note that the fundamental or transition matrix obeys

$$(d/dt) \; \emptyset(t_0,t) = J \; (t) \; \emptyset(t_0,t)$$

subject to $\emptyset(t_0,t_0) = I$, (cf. Bryson and Ho [59] p. 450). Thus this equation is identical to equation (19a). Hence $\hat{y}(t_0,t) = \emptyset(t_0,t)$.

Then equation (30) could be written in state space form as

$$\dot{y}_1 = y_2$$
$$\dot{y}_2 = m - y_2^2 \operatorname{sgn} y_2 \tag{31}$$

The optimisation problem to be solved in this case is the minimisation of J subject to equation (31) where

$$J = \frac{1}{2}\int_0^T (y_1^2 + y_2^2 + m^2)\,dt$$

Let the period of optimisation T be 1 and the initial conditions be

$$y_1(0) = 2 \quad ; \quad y_2(0) = -2$$

In fact it is possible to decompose this system into two subsystems as shown in Fig . 4.

The coupling relationships for this decomposition is definied by introducing the coupling variable x_I such that *

$$y_{II} = x_I$$

Then the two independent optimisation problems for the two subsystems are given by the following equations for a given λ trajectory of the Lagrange multiplier .

Subproblem I

$$\min \int_0^1 \left[\frac{1}{2}(y_I^2 + x_I^2) + \lambda x_I\right] dt$$

subject to $\dot{y}_I = x_I$.

Subproblem II

$$\min \int_0^1 \left(\frac{1}{2} m_{II}^2 - \lambda y_{II}\right) dt$$

subject to $\dot{y}_{II} = m_{II} - y_{II}^2 \operatorname{sgn} y_{II}$

In order to solve this overall optimisation problem using a hierarchical structure, it is necessary to solve a two point boundary value problem on the first level provided that a $\lambda(t)$ trajectory is provided by the second level.

4.1. Simulation results

This hierarchical problem was solved on the IBM 370/165 digital computer at LAAS. Integration of the subsystem state-costate equations was performed by using a 4th order Runge-Kutta routine. The first level problem was solved using the quasilinearisation technique and for the second level, a simple gradient coordinator was used. The optimal λ trajectory which maximised $\xi(\lambda)$ was obtained in 7 second level iterations. Using the resulting state and control trajectories, I in equation (2) was evaluated and it was found that $I = \xi(\lambda)$. For the 7th iteration, the closed loop control law was, for initial conditions (2, - 2) :

$$m_{II} = p_{II} = -\phi_{22}(t_f,t)^{-1}\left[\phi_{21}(t_f,t)\, y_{II} + \omega_{12}\right] \tag{32}$$

* Such a coupling relationship and the subsequent analysis avoids singular problems at the lowest level, as we saw in Chapter 3.

This is a linear control law with the gain H given by $H=-\emptyset_{22}(t_f,t)^{-1}\emptyset_{21}(t_f,t)$ and the disturbance given by $q = -\emptyset_{22}(t_f,t)^{-1}\omega_{12}$ where $\emptyset_{22}$, $\emptyset_{21}$, ω_{12} are defined in equation (25) and the control law is of the form $m_{II} = H\, y_{II} + q$.

Fig. 5 shows the gain and disturbance over the optimisation interval and Fig. 6 the resulting state trajectories. The control trajectory and the Lagrange multiplier trajectories are also shown in this figure. These trajectories are, as expected, identical to those found by Bauman [44].

To test the sensitivity of this feedback control law, the gain and disturbance calculated above were used to calculate the control trajectories using equation (32) for the initial conditions $y_I(0) = 3$, $y_{II}(0) = -3$.

Fig.7 shows the state, control and Lagrange multiplier trajectories for this case . The overall open loop problem was also solved for these initial conditions and it was found that the resulting optimal control trajectory was virtually identical to that found using the precalculated control law. However, the initial condition used is symmetrical. In the following Table we summarise the result of varying the initial conditions and using first the control law calculated with the initial conditions (2, -2) and then, for comparison, the value of the cost for the optimal open loop control using the true initial condition.

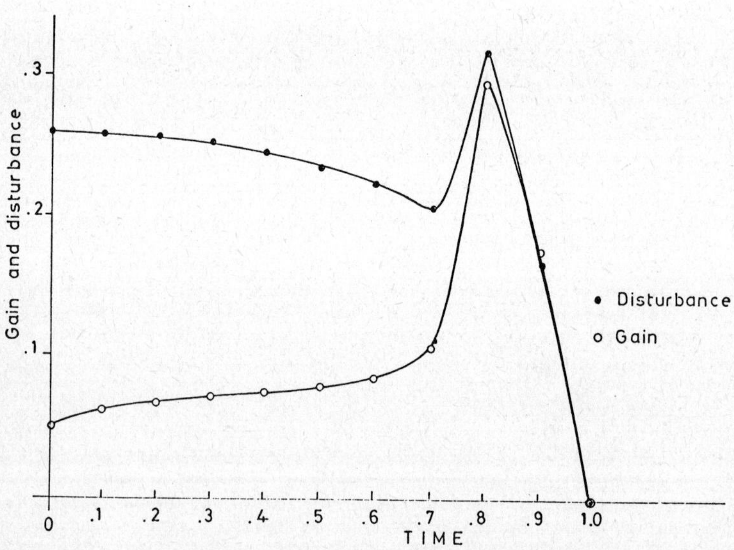

Fig. 5 : The gain and disturbance trajectories for the initial conditions (2, -2)

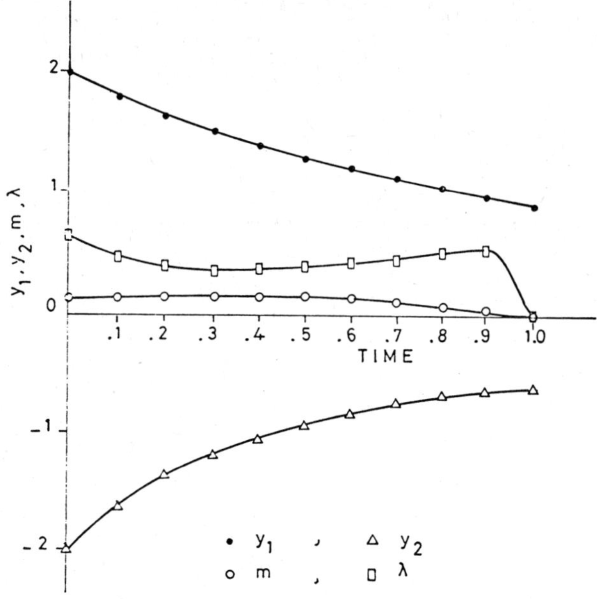

Fig. 6 : The optimal trajectories for the initial conditions (2, -2)

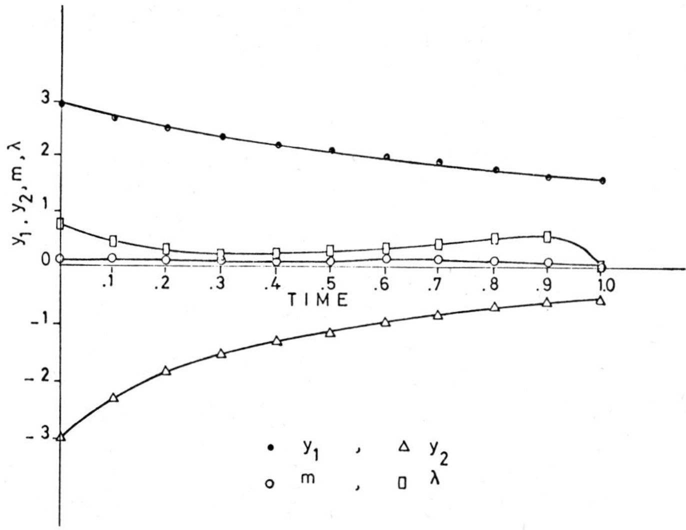

Fig. 7 : The optimal trajectories for the initial conditions (3, -3)

Initial condition	$y_1(0)=2$ $y_2(0)=-2$	$y_1(0)=3$ $y_2(0)=-3$	$y_1(0)=1$ $y_2(0)=-2$	$y_1(0)=2$ $y_2(0)=-10$	$y_1(0)=4$ $y_2(0)=1$
Optimal cost for this initial condition	1.617	3.506	0.741	4.734	9.474
Cost using control law derived from the initial conditions $y_1=2$, $y_2=-2$	1.617	3.506	0.749	4.784	10.137
Loss of optimality	-	0 %	1.02 %	1.06 %	6.99 %

TABLE 1

Remark

(1) The above results show that it is possible to calculate a feedback control quite easily.

(2) This control does provide some degree of insensitivity and is thus more practical than the corresponding open loop control.

We next consider the more practical 2 machine example that we studied in Chapter 3.

4.2. The feedback control of two coupled synchronous machines [28, 48]

The problem is to control the excitation voltages of two coupled synchronous machines optimally. A model for the system is given by the 6 non-linear differential equations

$$\begin{aligned}
\dot{y}_1 &= y_2 \\
\dot{y}_2 &= B_1 - A_1 y_2 + A_2 y_3 \sin y_1 - \frac{B_2}{2} \sin 2\, y_1 \\
\dot{y}_3 &= M_1 - C_1\, y_3 + C_2 \cos y_1 \\
\dot{y}_4 &= y_5 \\
\dot{y}_5 &= B_4 - A_4 y_5 - A_5 y_6 \sin y_4 - \frac{B_5}{2} \sin 2\, y_4 \\
\dot{y}_6 &= M_2 - C_4 y_6 - C_5 \cos y_4
\end{aligned}$$

where y_1-y_6 are the 6 state variables and M_1, M_2 are the controls. The constants are given by

$$A_1 = A_4 = 0.2703,\ A_2 = 12.012,\ A_5 = 14.4144$$

$$B_1 = B_4 = 39.1892,\ B_2 = -48.048,\ B_5 = -57.6576$$

$$C_1 = C_4 = 0.3222,\ C_2 = 1.9,\ C_5 = 2.28$$

and the system comprises two subsystems coupled by $y_1 = y_4$.

It is desired to minimise J where

$$J = \int_0^2 \tfrac{1}{2}\left[\|\underline{y}-\underline{y}_p\|_Q^2 + \|\underline{M} - \underline{M}_c\|_R^2\right] dt$$

where $\underline{y}_c^T = [0.7461 \quad 0 \quad 7.7438 \quad 0.7461 \quad 0 \quad 7.7438]$

$\underline{M}_c^T = [1.1 \quad 1.1]$

$R = I_2$ the second order identity matrix and Q is a diagonal matrix with the diagonal given by Q_D where

$$Q_D = [20 \quad 20 \quad 2 \quad 20 \quad 20 \quad 2]$$

Results

This problem was solved using the infeasible hierarchical method for the initial conditions.

$$\underline{y}(0)^T = [0.7347 \quad -0.2151 \quad 7.7443 \quad 0.7347 \quad -0.2151 \quad 6.9483]$$

and the optimum was reached in 10 second level iterations at this point.

$$J = \xi = 1.1658$$

From the final iteration, the time varying gain and disturbance vectors were calculated and these controlled the system optimally as expected. The control law was of the form

$$M_1 = H_{11}\, y_1 + H_{12}\, y_2 + H_{13}\, y_3 + q_1$$
$$M_2 = H_{21}\, y_1 + H_{22}\, y_2 + H_{23}\, y_3 + q_2$$

Fig. 8 shows the control parameters for machine 1, i.e.

H_{11}, H_{12}, H_{13} and q_1.

Next the initial conditions were changed to

$$\underline{y}(0)^T = [1 \quad 0.1 \quad 10 \quad 1 \quad 0.1 \quad 8.69]$$

Note that these new I.C.s are far from the old ones. Here again, optimal control was calculated in 10 iteration and at this point

$$J = \xi = 78.5048$$

Using the previously calculated gains and disturbances, the control was recalculated and this gave a cost of

$J' = 80.1304$, i.e. a loss of 2 %

For the new initial conditions, the controls M'_{1B}, M'_{2B} using the previously calculated feedback elements, were calculated by the formulae

$$M'_{1B} = H_{11}\, y_1 + H_{12}\, y_2 + H_{13}\, y_3 + q_1$$
$$M'_{2B} = H_{21}\, y_1 + H_{22}\, y_2 + H_{23}\, y_3 + q_2$$

and these controls are shown in Figs. 9 and 10 respectively.

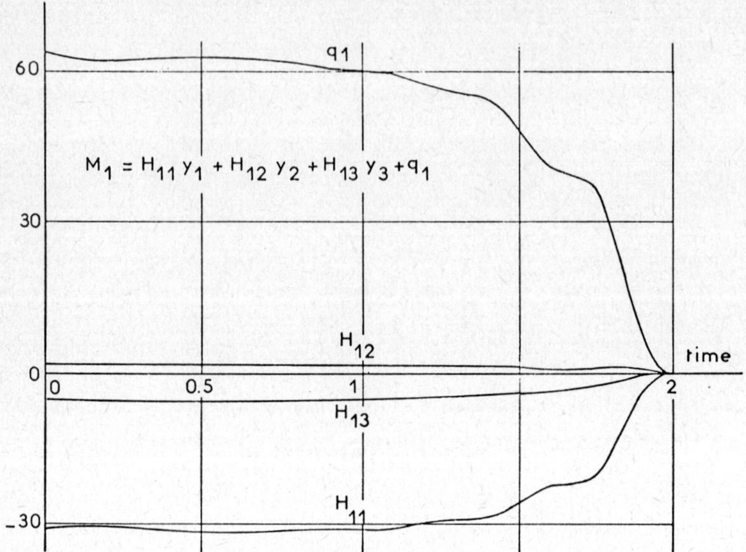

Fig. 8 : The control parameters for machine one

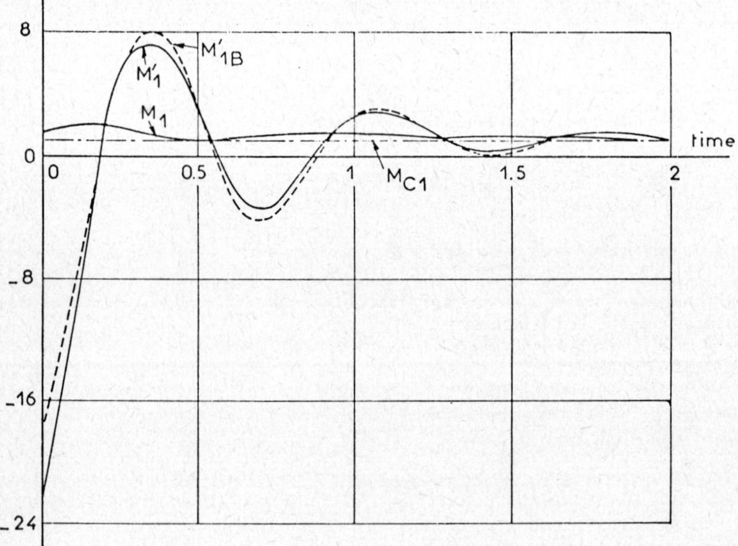

Fig. 9 : The feedback controls for machine one

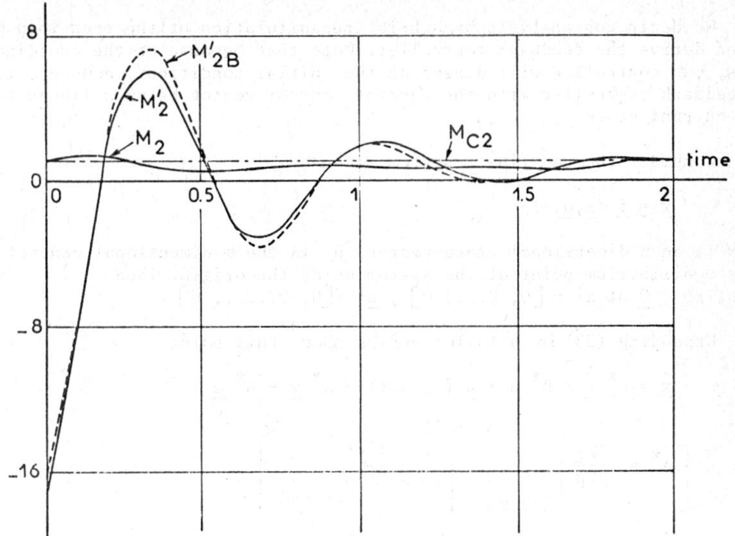

Fig. 10 : The feedback controls for machine 2.

The optimal open loop controls M'_1, M'_2 for the new initial conditions are also shown for comparison. We see that the feedback control trajectory is quite close to the optimal open loop one.

These results for the two examples show that feedback control for non-linear systems using hierarchical methods could prove to be practical.

Remark

So far we have considered the Goal Coordination Method and used it to compute the feedback controls. However, as we discussed in Chapter 3, the Goal Coordination Method may not work in all cases due to the possible existence of duality gaps. We could nevertheless compute a feedback control because the open loop method used is not that significant. For example, we know that if the cost function is a quadratic function of the subsystem states and controls then the method of Hassan and Singh [47] or the modified prediction principle could be used. Since the latter is in general a method with slightly faster convergence characteristics, we will briefly develop the feedback control law using this approach.

5. FEEDBACK CONTROL USING THE MODIFIED PREDICTION PRINCIPLE

As we discussed in Chapter 3, the basis of the modified prediction principle is that if an equilibrium point of a non-linear system is known then it is possible to expand the non-linear dynamics about this point and then use a prediction of the states, controls and their associated Lagrange multipliers to simultaneously fix the non-linearities as well as to decompose the system. One of the main advantages of the approach is that only a linear-quadratic problem needs to be solved at the lowest level. For a linear-quadratic problem, of course, it is easy to calculate a feedback control. This means that as in the Goal Coordination Method modified in the previous Section, it will be possible to obtain a feedback control at the final iteration before overall convergence.

We begin our analysis by a brief recapitulation of the open loop method and then derive the feedback controller. Note that because of the coordination process, our controller will depend on the initial conditions. However, it will be a feedback controller with the current control vector being a linear function of the current state.

Consider the non-linear system given by

$$\dot{\underline{x}} = \underline{f}\ (\underline{x},\underline{u},\ t) \tag{33}$$

where $\underline{x}$ is an n dimensional state vector, $\underline{u}$ is the m dimensional control vector. Let the equilibirium point of the system be at the origin. Then $\underline{f}\ (\underline{x},\ \underline{u},\ t) = \underline{0}$ at $\underline{x}^T = [0,\ 0\ldots,\ 0]$, $\underline{u}^T = [0,\ 0,\ldots,\ 0]$.

Expanding (33) in a Taylor series about this point

$$\dot{\underline{x}} = A^* \underline{x} + B^* \underline{u} + \underline{f}\ (\underline{x},\ \underline{u},t) - A^* \underline{x} - B^* \underline{u}$$

where

$$\left[A^* = \frac{\partial \underline{f}^T}{\partial \underline{x}}\bigg|_{\underline{x}=\underline{u}=\underline{0}}\right]^T,\quad \left[B^* = \frac{\partial \underline{f}^T}{\partial \underline{u}}\bigg|_{\underline{x}=\underline{u}=\underline{0}}\right]^T$$

or

$$\dot{\underline{x}} = A\ \underline{x} + B\ \underline{u} + \underline{D}(\underline{x},\underline{u}) \tag{34}$$

where A, B are respectively the block diagonal parts of A^*, B^*

$$\underline{D}\ (\underline{x},\underline{u}) = C_1\underline{x} + C_2\underline{u} + \underline{f}(\underline{x},\underline{u},t) - A^*\underline{x} - B^*\ \underline{u} \tag{35}$$

and C_1,C_2 are the off-diagonal parts of A^*, B^*.

Let it be desired to minimise the separable cost function

$$J = \sum_{i=1}^{N} \int_0^T \frac{1}{2}\ (\|\underline{x}_i\|^2_{Q_i} + \|\underline{u}_i\|^2_{R_i})\ dt \tag{36}$$

where it is assumed that there are N blocks in A and B, Q_i is assumed to be positive semidefinite, R_i to be positive definite and T is a fixed final time.

The basis of the approach for solving the problem is to predict $\underline{x}^0$,$\underline{u}^0$ at the higher level and use these values in $\underline{D}(\underline{x},\underline{u}) = \underline{D}(\underline{x}^0,\underline{u}^0)$ to fix the non-linear terms. If the higher level forces $\underline{x}^0$, $\underline{u}^0$ towards, $\underline{x}$, $\underline{u}$ then eventually if $\underline{x}^0 = \underline{x}$, $\underline{u}^0 = \underline{u}$ the resulting $\underline{u}$ is the optimal open loop control. Fixing $\underline{x}^0$ and $\underline{u}^0$ also enables us to decompose the problem into subproblems. To see this, write the Hamiltonian H^0 as

$$H^0 = \frac{1}{2}\|\underline{x}\|^2_Q + \frac{1}{2}\|\underline{u}\|^2_R \tag{37}$$

$$+ \underline{\lambda}^T\left[A\underline{x} + B\underline{u} + \underline{D}(\underline{x}^0,\underline{u}^0)\right] + \underline{\pi}^T\left[\underline{x}-\underline{x}^0\right] + \underline{\beta}^T\left[\underline{u}-\underline{u}^0\right]$$

where $\underline{\lambda}$ is the costate vector and $\underline{\pi}$, $\underline{\beta}$ are Lagrange multipliers*. Then from the necessary conditions.

$$\dot{\underline{x}} = A\underline{x} + BR^{-1}\left[-B^T\underline{\lambda} - \underline{\beta}\right] + C_1\underline{x}^0 + C_2\underline{x}^0 + \underline{f}(\underline{x}^0,\underline{u}^0,t)$$

$$- A^*\ \underline{x}^0 - B^*\ \underline{u}^0 \tag{38}$$

---

* These Lagrange multiplier vectors are necessary to force the eventual satisfaction of the equality constraints $\underline{x} = \underline{x}^0$, $\underline{u} = \underline{u}^0$.

with $\underline{x}(0) = \underline{x}_0$ (39)

and $\dot{\underline{\lambda}} = -Q\underline{x} - A^T\underline{\lambda} - \underline{\pi}$ (40)

with $\underline{\lambda}(T) = \underline{0}$. (41)

Also, using

$$\frac{\partial H^0}{\partial \underline{\pi}} = \underline{0} \quad \text{one obtains } \underline{x}^0 = \underline{x} \tag{42}$$

Similarly

$$\frac{\partial H^0}{\partial \underline{\beta}} = \underline{0} \quad \text{gives } \underline{u}^0 = \underline{u}$$

$$= -R^{-1}B^T\underline{\lambda} - R^{-1}\underline{\beta} \tag{43}$$

$$\frac{\partial H^0}{\partial \underline{x}^0} = \underline{0} \text{ gives } \underline{\pi} = \left[C_1^T + \left.\frac{\partial \underline{f}^T(\underline{x}^0,\underline{u}^0,t)}{\partial \underline{x}}\right|_{\substack{\underline{x}=\underline{x}_0^0 \\ \underline{u}=\underline{u}}} - A^{\star T} \right] \underline{\lambda}(t) \tag{44}$$

$$\frac{\partial H^0}{\partial \underline{u}^0} = \underline{0} \text{ gives } \underline{\beta} = \left[C_2^T + \left.\frac{\partial \underline{f}^T}{\partial \underline{u}}\right|_{\substack{\underline{x}=\underline{x}_0^0 \\ \underline{u}=\underline{u}}} - B^{\star T} \right] \underline{\lambda}(t) \tag{45}$$

The method involves solving (38, 39, 40, 41) independently at the first level for the N subproblems for given $\underline{x}^0$, $\underline{u}^0$, $\underline{\beta}$, $\underline{\pi}$ and using the resulting $\underline{x}$, $\underline{u}$, $\underline{\lambda}$ in the R.H.S. of equations (42), (43), (44), (45) to get a new prediction for $\underline{x}^0$, $\underline{u}^0$, $\underline{\beta}$, $\underline{\pi}$. The iterations are started with an initial guess of $\underline{x}^0 = \underline{\pi} = \underline{0}$ $\underline{u}^0 = \underline{\beta} = \underline{0}$.

We have proved the convergence of this scheme in Chapter 3.

5.1. Feedback control

In order to calculate the feedback control let us consider the first level problems. These are given by equations (38-41). For given $\underline{\pi}$, $\underline{\beta}$, $\underline{x}^0$, $\underline{u}^0$, this is a set of N independent two point boundary value problems.

Let us assume a solution of the form

$$\underline{\lambda} = P\underline{x} + \underline{s} \quad , \tag{46}$$

where P is a block diagonal matrix.

Then $\dot{\underline{\lambda}} = P\dot{\underline{x}} + \dot{P}\underline{x} + \dot{\underline{s}}$

Substituting this solution into the two point boundary value problem in equation (39) we have

$$P\dot{\underline{x}} + \dot{P}\underline{x} + \dot{\underline{s}} = -Q\underline{x} - A^T\left[P\underline{x} + \underline{s}\right] - \underline{\pi}$$

substituting from equation (38) for $\dot{x}$

$$\left[\dot{P} + PA - PBR^{-1}B^TP + A^TP + Q\right]\underline{x} + \left[\dot{\underline{s}} + A^T\underline{s} - PBR^{-1}B^T\underline{s}\right.$$

$$\left. -PBR^{-1}\underline{\beta} + PC_1\underline{x}^0 + PC_2\underline{u}^0 + P\underline{f}(\underline{x}^0,\underline{u}^0,t) - PA^{\star}\underline{x}^0 - PB^{\star}\underline{u}^0 + \underline{\pi}\right] = 0$$

from which we obtain

$$\dot{P} + A^T P + PA - PBR^{-1} B^T P + Q = 0 \tag{47}$$

and

$$\dot{\underline{s}} + A^T \underline{s} - PBR^{-1} B^T \underline{s} + P\, C_1 \underline{x}^0 + P\, C_2 \underline{u}^0 - PBR^{-1} \underline{\beta} + Pf(\underline{x}^0, \underline{u}^0, t)$$
$$- P\, A^* \underline{x}^0 - P\, B^* \underline{u}^0 + \underline{\pi} = \underline{0} \tag{48}$$

with $P(T) = 0$, $\underline{s}(T) = \underline{0}$.

Then the feedback control law is given by

$$\underline{u} = - R^{-1} \left[B^T P\underline{x} + B^T \underline{s} + \underline{\beta} \right]. \tag{49}$$

To obtain this feedback law, it is necessary to integrate the N blocks of equation (47) independently, backwards in time from $P(T) = 0$ and equation (48) also backwards from $\underline{s}(T) = \underline{0}$ using the given values for the trajectories for $\underline{x}^0$, $\underline{u}^0$, $\underline{\pi}$, $\underline{\beta}$ supplied by the second level. When $\underline{x}^0$, $\underline{u}^0$, $\underline{\pi}$, $\underline{\beta}$ are very close to their values at the last iteration then the resulting P, $\underline{x}$, $\underline{s}$, $\underline{\beta}$ enable us to calculate the feedback control law given by equation (49).

Remarks

1) The control law of equation (49) does provide feedback control since it depends on the current state $\underline{x}$.

2) The law is dependent upon the initial state $\underline{x}(0)$ through $\underline{s}$ and $\underline{\beta}$.

6. SENSITIVITY WITH RESPECT TO INITIAL CONDITIONS [48]

With all the methods that we have considered so far, the optimal feedback control law depends on the initial conditions. With the examples that we have treated, this dependence is quite weak so that the same feedback controller could be used for small variations in the initial conditions. However it is desirable to know a priori the sensitivity of the cost function to variations in the initial conditions. Calvet [48] has developed an expression which enables us to calculate the sensitivity matrix. Let us assume that the optimal solution of the problem of minimising I in equation (2) subject to equations (3), (4) is given by $\underline{X}^*(t) = \begin{bmatrix} \underline{x}^*(t) \\ \underline{u}^*(t) \end{bmatrix}$. Let us expand the cost function I in a Taylor series about this point upto the second order i.e.

$$I\left[\underline{X}^* + \Delta \underline{X}\right] = I(\underline{X}^*) + \frac{\partial I}{\partial X}^T (\underline{X}^*) \Delta \underline{X} + \Delta \underline{X}^T \frac{\partial^2 I}{\partial \underline{X}^2} (\underline{X}^*) \Delta \underline{X} + \ldots \tag{50}$$

since $\underline{X}^*$ is optimal, $\dfrac{\partial I}{\partial \underline{X}} = \underline{0}$

$$\text{or } \Delta I = I(\underline{X}^* + \Delta \underline{X}) - I(\underline{X}^*) \simeq \frac{1}{2} \Delta \underline{X}^T \frac{\partial^2 I}{\partial X^2} (\underline{X}^*) \Delta \underline{X} \tag{51}$$

Now from equation (2) in the overall system

$$I = \int_{t_0}^{t_f} f(\underline{x}, \underline{u}, \underline{z}, t)\, dt \tag{52}$$

Then

$$\Delta I = \frac{1}{2} \int_{t_0}^{t_f} \left[\Delta \underline{x}^T \;\; \Delta \underline{u}^T\right] \begin{bmatrix} f_{xx} & f_{xu} \\ f_{ux} & f_{uu} \end{bmatrix} \begin{bmatrix} \Delta \underline{x} \\ \Delta \underline{u} \end{bmatrix} \tag{53}$$

Now the control law used is linear, i.e. of the form

$$\underline{u}^* = H^* \underline{x}^* + \underline{q}^* \tag{54}$$

If we could write the optimal $\Delta \underline{u}$ as

$$\underline{u} = H^* \Delta \underline{x} \tag{55}$$

then it is merely necessary to express $\Delta \underline{x}(t)$ as a function of $\Delta \underline{x}(t_0)$ to evaluate ΔI as the initial conditions vary.

Now from equation (16) for the two point boundary value problem, i.e. $\dot{\underline{y}} = F(\underline{y}(t))$ where $\underline{y} = \begin{bmatrix} \underline{x} \\ \underline{p} \end{bmatrix}$ it is possible to expand about the optimal solution

$$\dot{\underline{y}}^* + \Delta \dot{\underline{y}} = F(\underline{y}^* + \Delta \underline{y}) \simeq F(\underline{y}^*) + I(\underline{y}^*) \Delta \underline{y} + \ldots$$

from which $\Delta \dot{\underline{y}} = I(\underline{y}^*) \Delta \underline{y}$ (56)

or

$$\Delta \underline{y} = \emptyset(t, t_0) \Delta \underline{y}(t_0) \tag{57}$$

where $\emptyset$ is a transition matrix.

Using the expanded form

$$\begin{aligned} \Delta \underline{x}(t) &= \emptyset_{11}(t,t_0) \Delta \underline{x}(t_0) + \emptyset_{12}(t,t_0) \Delta \underline{p}(t_0) \\ \Delta \underline{p}(t_f) &= \emptyset_{21}(t_f,t) \Delta \underline{x}(t) + \emptyset_{22}(t_f,t) \Delta \underline{p}(t) \end{aligned} \tag{58}$$

If the solution remains optimal for the perturbed system then as

$$\underline{p}(t_f) = \underline{0}, \quad \Delta \underline{p}(t_f) = \underline{0}$$

so that

$$\Delta \underline{p}(t) = \emptyset_{22}^{-1} \emptyset_{21} \Delta \underline{x} \tag{59}$$

from which we deduce that

$$\begin{aligned} \Delta \underline{x}(t) &= \left[\emptyset_{11}(t,t_0) + \emptyset_{12}(t,t_0) \emptyset_{22}^{-1}(t_f,t_0) \emptyset_{21}(t_f,t_0)\right] \Delta \underline{x}(t_0) \\ &= S \,\Delta x(t_0) \end{aligned} \tag{60}$$

where

$$S = \emptyset_{11} + \emptyset_{12} \emptyset_{22}^{-1} \emptyset_{21} \tag{61}$$

This matrix S can be treated as a sensitivity matrix for the state $\underline{x}$.

Then

$$\Delta I = \frac{1}{2} \Delta \underline{x}(t_0)^T S_J \Delta \underline{x}(t_0) \tag{62}$$

where

$$S_J = \int_{t_0}^{t_f} \begin{bmatrix} S \\ HS \end{bmatrix}^T \begin{bmatrix} f_{xx} & f_{xu} \\ f_{ux} & f_{uu} \end{bmatrix} \begin{bmatrix} S \\ HS \end{bmatrix} dt$$

Note that S_J is easy to calculate once the feedback law has been calculated.

For the 2 machine example, these sensitivity matrices were calculated. These were found to be of the form

$$S_J = \begin{bmatrix} S_{J1} & 0 \\ 0 & S_{J2} \end{bmatrix} \quad \text{where}$$

$$S_{J1} = \begin{bmatrix} 261.6 & -7.2 & 29.5 \\ -7.2 & 4.9 & -1.7 \\ 29.5 & -1.7 & 5.0 \end{bmatrix} ; \quad S_{J2} = \begin{bmatrix} 245.7 & -7.2 & 31.0 \\ -7.2 & 4.5 & -1.9 \\ 31.0 & -1.9 & 5.7 \end{bmatrix}$$

The matrices show that the feedback control is very sensitive to variations in the states y_1 and y_4.

For the sliding mass system, the corresponding sensitivity matrix was computed to be

$$S_J = \begin{bmatrix} 0.9852 & 0.2139 \\ 0.2139 & 0.2111 \end{bmatrix}$$

This shows that the cost function is much more sensitive to variations in $y_1(0)$ than to those in $y_2(0)$. This is confirmed by the results obtained in the simulations as shown in Table 1.

7. IMPROVEMENT OF THE FEEDBACK CONTROL [48]

We have seen, at least on our examples, that the controller can accept some variation in the initial conditions without a significant loss in optimality. However, for particular cases, it may prove necessary to improve the control if the region of initial state variations is too large or if the system is subject to disturbances which change the state at any particular instant. To be able to use a better control, recall from equation (54) that the control law is of the form

$$\underline{u} = H\underline{x} + \underline{q} \tag{63}$$

where H is a block diagonal matrix . It should therefore be possible to improve the control by modifying $\underline{q}$ if we find that the control is too suboptimal. This can be done by introducing an additional level for improving $\underline{q}$ whilst on level 1, each subsystem is regulated by a local feedback of the state $\underline{x}_i$ (i=1,2,...N) via H_i. Calvet [48] has developed a "feasible" approach for improving $\underline{q}$ such that at each iteration an improved $\underline{q}$ results which can be applied on-line.

7.1. The feasible method of Calvet

Using the linear control law of equation (63), let us rewrite the cost function I in a global form as

$$\underset{\underline{q}}{\text{Min}} \left\{ \int_{t_0}^{t_f} f(\underline{x}, H\underline{x} + \underline{q}, t)\, dt \right\} \tag{64}$$

subject to

$$\dot{\underline{x}} = \underline{g}(\underline{x}, H\underline{x} + \underline{q}, t) \quad ; \underline{x}(t_0) = \underline{x}_0 \tag{65}$$

in equations (64,65), the interaction variables $\underline{z}$ have been substituted to form the integrated system.

Then we can write the Hamiltonian as

$$H^{*} = f(\underline{x}, H\underline{x} + \underline{q}, t) + \underline{\psi}^{T} \underline{g}(\underline{x}, Hx + \underline{q}, t) \tag{66}$$

and minimise it w.r.t. $\underline{q}$.

Then $-\dot{\underline{\psi}} = \frac{\partial H^{*}}{\partial \underline{x}}$

$$\frac{\partial H^{*}}{\partial \underline{q}} = \underline{0} \quad \text{and} \quad \underline{\psi}(t_f) = \underline{0}. \tag{67}$$

We essentially want to find a method of improving $\underline{q}$ iteratively which is such that at each iteration we are able to satisfy the system dynamics since then we could use the method on-line and could actually implement the control obtained for each new value of $\underline{q}$. One possible approach is to use the precalculated $\underline{q}$ as initial guess and the actual measured state to integrate the state equation forward in time, the costate equation backward in time and to use these to provide a new $\underline{q}$ and thus a new control which is implemented on-line after each iteration.

This general approach can be used to define a second level for improving the control. Suppose therefore that our system is being run on the feedback control which was previously calculated when at time τ a perturbation affects the system thus changing the state. We should like to calculate an improved control by modifying $\underline{q}$ over the interval $[\tau, t_f]$ using the above algorithm. Fig. 11 shows the calculation structure.

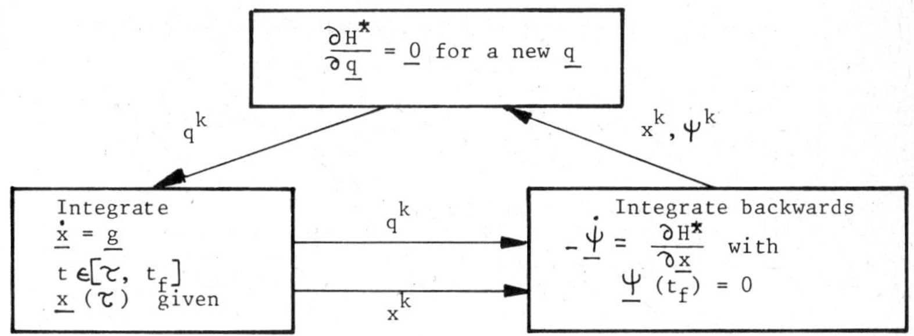

FIGURE 11

The main advantage of such an approach will arise if the time to calculate the optimal $\underline{q}$ is quite small in relation to the dynamics of the system. Even if this is not so, one can still use the improved control which is calculated at each iteration. Let us illustrate the approach by applying it to the sliding mass system.

7.2. Application to the sliding mass system

Recall that the control law developed was of the form

$$m_{II} = H\, y_{II} + q_2 \qquad \text{where } q_2 = - \emptyset_{22}^{-1}\, \omega_2$$

and $\qquad H = - \emptyset_{22}^{-1} \quad \emptyset_{21}$

H and q_2 were calculated using the initial conditions $y_1 = 2$, $y_2 = -2$.

Let us substitute this control into the sliding mass problem's functions i.e. we now wish to minimise

$$\underset{q_2}{\text{Min}} \int_{\tau}^{T} \frac{1}{2}\left[y_1^2 + y_2^2 + (H\, y_2 + q_2)^2\right] dt$$

subject to $\dot{y}_1 = y_2$

$$\dot{y}_2 = H\, y_2 + q_2 - y_2^2 \operatorname{sgn}(y_2)$$

with $\underline{y}(\tau)$ assumed known, possibly through measurement. The Hamiltonian for the problem now becomes

$$H^* = \frac{1}{2}(y_1^2 + y_2^2 + (H\, y_2 + q_2)^2 + p_1\, y_2$$

$$+ p_2\left[H\, y_2 + q_2 - y_2^2 \operatorname{sgn}(y_2)\right]$$

From the necessary conditions

$$\frac{\partial H^*}{\partial q_2} = 0 \quad = H\, y_2 + q_2 + p_2 \quad \text{or} \quad q_2 = -\left[H\, y_2 + p_2\right]$$

$$-\dot{p}_1 = y_1$$

$$-\dot{p}_2 = y_2 + H^2\, y_2 + p_1 + p_2 H - 2y_2 \operatorname{sgn}(y_2) + Hq_2$$

with $\begin{bmatrix} p_1(T) \\ p_2(T) \end{bmatrix} = \underline{0}$

Note that $q_2(t_f) = p_2(t_f) + H_2(t_f)\, y_2(t_f) = 0$

Let us use a two level algorithm as shown in Fig. 12 to improve q_2 where we use the direct prediction type algorithm described above.

This two level algorithm was applied to a simulation of the system where the initial conditions were changed from $\begin{bmatrix} 2 \\ -2 \end{bmatrix}$ to $\begin{bmatrix} 4 \\ -1 \end{bmatrix}$ which represents the most unfavourbale case considered. Convergence to the new optimum took place in 3 iterations which took 0.13 seconds to execute. This is about 25 % of the time for the globally optimal solution. This means that it was possible to calculate a new optimal feedback control before the initial conditions had changed significantly.

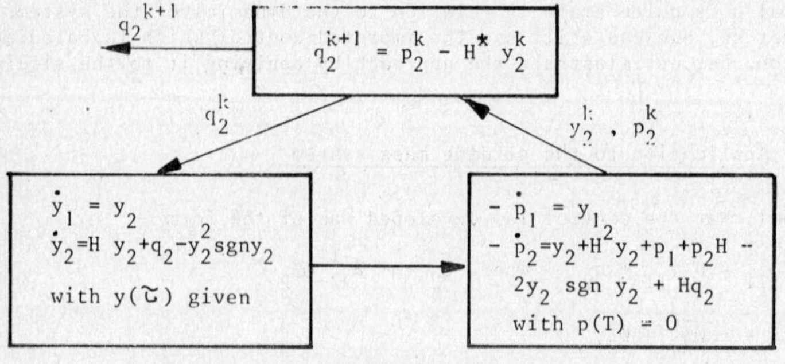

FIGURE 12

Thus the present method of improving the feedback control on-line is both fast and efficient. Thus overall, we envisage a two-stage procedure for the feedback regulation of non-linear systems. In the first stage, the problem is solved off-line for a reasonable initial condition using the Goal Coordination or prediction principle methods. From the final iteration, the feedback controller's parameters H and $\underline{q}$ are calculated where the control $\underline{u}$ is of the form.

$$\underline{u} = H\underline{x} + \underline{q} \cdot$$

The sensitivity matrix is also calculated to give some idea of the relative sensitivity of the overall cost to variations in initial conditions. From this matrix,it is possible to decide whether to use on-line coordination or not. If it is decided that on-line coordination is necessary, then in stage 2 the two level procedure discussed in this section could be implemented to compute the improved $\underline{q}$ and thus $\underline{u}$. If the system has fast dynamics, it will be necessary to use each new $\underline{q}$ as it is calculated. Otherwise, one could wait until the optimum $\underline{q}$ has been calculated. Note that the introduction of the second level for impro--ing $\underline{q}$ is useful in providing a robust controller since if at time τ a disturbance occurs which changes the actual state, as long as the new state can be measured, an improved $\underline{q}$ can be calculated and implemented to provide a better control.

8. COMMENTS

In this chapter, we have examined all the currently available methods for the feedback control of large non-linear interconnected dynamical systems. Although the methods that have been described are quite practical and could prove to be extremely useful, much remains to be done. For example, it would be interesting to compute feedback laws for special cases where use can be made of any favourable properties that the system possesses. Also, convergence of the coordination for on-line improvement should be studied. In this regard Calvet [48] suggests using the approach of Gibson et al.[57] or of Sew Hoy and Gibson [58] for the on-line coordination since there convergence can often be assured.

In this second part of the book, we have looked at feedback control. However, our discussions were limited to optimal control. In the next part of the book, we examine some techniques for providing near optimal control.

PART III

SUBOPTIMAL CONTROL FOR LARGE SCALE SYSTEMS

In the first two parts of this book we have examined the methods for computing optimal control for large interconnected dynamical systems using hierarchical computational structures. We found that although it was possible to compute optimal control, it required a lot of calculation which could only be done on a single digital computer if the order of the overall system was not too large. Now, although computers are getting cheaper so that in the not too distant future it will be economically feasible to have small mini-computers to control every subsystem, at the present time this is not economically feasible. It is interesting to investigate whether it is possible to simplify the calculations in some manner by restricting the demand for complete optimality to one of acceptable suboptimal performance. Certainly, optimality in itself is not always a virtue since the system equations are rarely known well enough for the computed optimal solution to mean very much in practical terms. It may well be that a suboptimal solution could yield better practical results particularly if it was computationally less demanding. It seems reasonable that such simpler solutions, when they exist, will occur because of some favourable properties of the system structure. In this third part of the book we examine some particular structures. The most useful of these is the system structure where the subsystems are serially connected.

Serial processes are quite common in an industrial society : production lines, steel rolling mills, water resource or quality control schemes, etc. all represent dynamical systems that are to some extent serially structured.In Chapter VII we examine the serial systems concept when applied to a non-linear example of a hot steel rolling mill.

CHAPTER VI

HEURISTIC APPROACHES TO THE CONTROL OF LARGE SERIAL AND OTHER SYSTEMS

1. INTRODUCTION

In this first chapter on suboptimal approaches to the hierarchical optimisation of large scale systems we begin by considering a class of problems which have a special structure, i.e. serially connected dynamical systems. Such problems arise in many real life applications. For example, most production processes in the manufacturing industries, water resource and quality control schemes are examples of dynamical systems which are, to some extent, serially structured. Moreover, this serial structure is often composed of recognisable subsystems separated by transportation delays, so that the dynamic behaviour can be represented quite well by a series of lumped parameter subsystem models connected by pure time delays.

It is with such large, serially structured systems in mind that the approach to multilevel systems analysis described in this chapter has been developed. A control strategy has been formulated for serial systems, with and without time delays between the subsystems. Although the basis of the strategy is purely heuristic, it appears to combine near optimal performance with only modest computational requirements. This is demonstrated by the results obtained in a series of experiments in which the suboptimum solutions are compared to the optimum ones for a number of examples by digital simulation.

Although, for simplicity, this chapter will deal only with linear constant coefficient subsystems, it should be noted that the basic idea of the strategy also applies to time variable and non-linear problems. In fact, the steel millcase study in Chapter VII is a good example of the application of the concept to non-linear systems. Let us now see what serial systems are.

2. SERIAL DYNAMICAL SYSTEMS

This chapter will be concerned primarily with the control of serial systems with time delays between the subsystems, as shown in Fig. 1. It is assumed that the blocks in Fig. 1 are recognisable subsystems of lower order than the overall system ; these could represent stands in a metallurgical rolling process, defined reaches in a river system or elements in a production line. For simplicity, assume that the subsystems are linear in form and can be described by the following set of linear differential-difference equations :

$$
\begin{aligned}
\dot{\underline{x}}_1(t) &= A_{11}\underline{x}_1(t) + B_1\underline{u}_1(t) + \underline{w}_1(t) \\
\underline{y}_1(t) &= C_{11}\underline{x}_1(t) \\
\dot{\underline{x}}_2(t) &= A_{21}\underline{x}_1(t-\theta_1) + A_{22}\underline{x}_2(t) + B_2\underline{u}_2(t) + \underline{w}_2(t) \qquad (1)
\end{aligned}
$$

$$\underline{y}_2(t) = C_{22}\underline{x}_2(t$$

$$\vdots$$

$$\dot{\underline{x}}_n(t) = A_{n,n-1}\underline{x}_{n-1}(t-\theta_{n-1})+A_{nn}\underline{x}_n(t) + B_n\underline{u}_n(t) + \underline{w}_n(t)$$

$$\underline{y}_n(t) = C_{nn}\underline{x}_n(t)$$

Here $\underline{x}_i, \underline{u}_i, \underline{w}_i$ and $\underline{y}_i$, $i = 1,2,\ldots, n$ are respectively the ℓ_i dimensional state vector, m_i dimensional control vector , ℓ_i dimensional deterministic disturbance vector and p_i dimensional output or observation vector of the ith subsystem. θ_i are the pure time delays between subsystems and the subsystem matrices A_{ij}, B_i, C_{ii} are of appropriate order with respect to the orders of the state, control and output vectors $\underline{x}_i$, $\underline{u}_i$ and $\underline{y}_i$ of the individual subsystems.

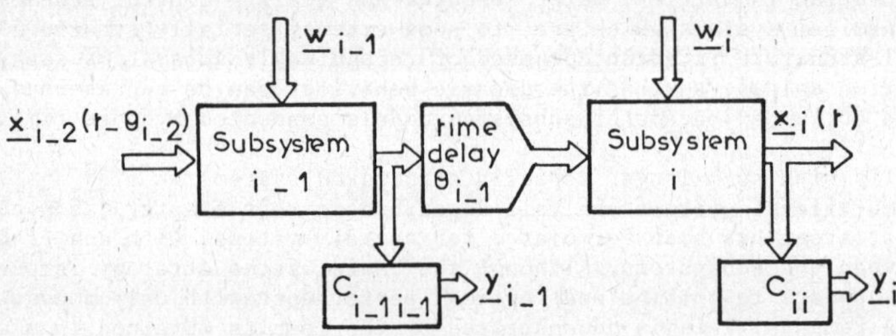

Fig. 1 : Serially connected systems

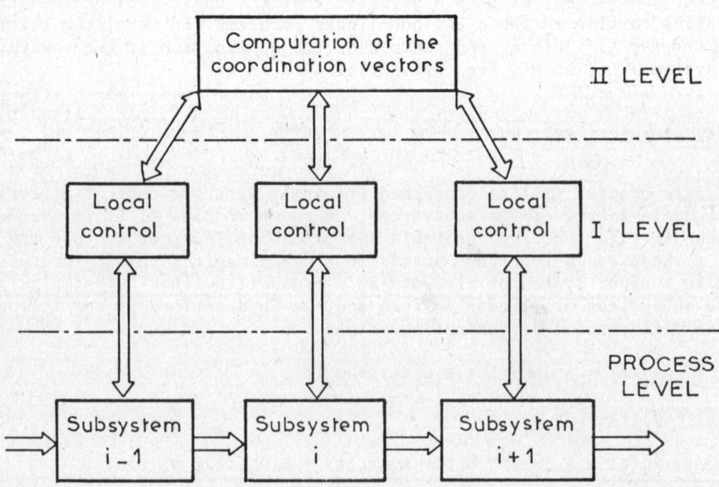

Fig. 2 : A possible two level control structure for serial systems

2.1. Cost functions

It is desired to optimise the system described by equation (1) with respect to a cost function I of the form

$$I = \min_{\underline{u}_1(t),\ldots,\underline{u}_n(t)} \left[\int_0^T \left\{ \|\underline{y}_1-\underline{y}_1^*\|^2_{Q_1} + \|\underline{u}_1\|^2_{R_1} + \ldots + \|\underline{y}_n-\underline{y}_n^*\|^2_{Q_n} + \|\underline{u}_n\|^2_{R_n} \right\} dt \right] \quad (2)$$

where $\underline{y}_i^* = \underline{y}_i^*(t)$, $i = 1,2,\ldots n$, are desired output reference trajectories for the n subsystems while Q_i, R_i are weighting matrices to be specified by the designer. Such a cost function could be used for both the regulator and the tracking cases, but in the latter it is assumed that $\underline{y}_i^*$ are known over the whole of the optimisation interval $(0 \rightarrow T)$.

3. BASIS OF THE SUBOPTIMAL CONTROL STRATEGY

It is desired to minimise equation (2) subject to the constraints given by equation(1). The only case of interest is when the period of optimisation T, is greater than the sum of the delays, i.e.

$$T > \theta_1 + \theta_2 + \ldots + \theta_{n-1}$$

If this condition is not satisfied then an input into the first subsystem would not affect some of the other subsystems, whilst the fundamental property of serial systems is that an input "upstream" affects all subsystems "downstream".

At first sight, the control of a system described by equation (1) in the above manner would appear formidable indeed : as Fuller [60] has pointed out, pure time delays are nominally of infinite dimension in the state space. While it is true that finite order approximations based on discretisation in time (Noton [39]) can be used to obviate this problem to some extent, the state vector still has to be augmented and this can be rather unwieldy.

To illustrate the kind of problem involved in the straightforward minimisation of I in equation (2) subject to equation (1) consider the application of dynamic programming. This involves lumping the system equations (1) into the following matrix form

$$\dot{\underline{X}} = A\underline{X} + B\underline{U} + \underline{W} \quad ; \quad \underline{Y} = C\underline{X}$$

where $\underline{X}$ is the overall state vector of order $\sum_{i=1}^{n} (\ell_i + \ell'_i)$ and ℓ'_i are the additional states due to the delays. Similarly , $\underline{U}$, $\underline{W}$, and $\underline{Y}$ are respectively the overall control, deterministic disturbance and output vectors.

The individual cost functions of the subsystems must also be lumped together so that I in equation (2) becomes

$$I = \min_{\substack{\underline{U}(t) \\ 0 \leq t \leq T}} \int_0^T \left\{ \|\underline{Y} - \underline{Y}^*\|^2_Q + \|\underline{U}\|^2_R \right\} dt$$

and the minimisation is performed by considering small intervals of time ΔT, as the stages in an N-stage optimisations procedure, where $N \Delta T = T$, i.e.

$$I = \min_{\substack{\underline{U}(t)\\ 0\leq t\leq \Delta T}} \left\{ \int_0^{\Delta T} \left\{ \|\underline{Y}-\underline{Y}^*\|_Q^2 + \|\underline{U}\|_R^2 \right\} dt + \ldots + \left\{ \min_{\substack{\underline{U}(t)\\ (N-1)\Delta T\leq t\leq N\Delta T}} \int_{(N-1)\Delta T}^{N\Delta T} \left\{ \|\underline{Y}-\underline{Y}^*\|_Q^2 + \|\underline{U}\|_R^2 \right\} dt \right\} \ldots . \right\} .$$

The enormity of this single level problem for anything but the most trivial example is apparent upon inspection ; not only is the computational burden excessive, but also the structural simplicity of the problem has been obscured during the problem formulation. It is interesting to ask, therefore, whether we can formulate the problem in some other manner, so that its structural simplicity is utilised to ease the computational burden. For example, since we know that the process is serial in nature, so that the effects of control actions flow only in one direction in space, it seems reasonable to consider the subsystems themselves as the stages in the optimisation process. In other words, write the cost function I in equation (2) in the following form :

$$I = \min_{\substack{\underline{u}_1(t)\\ 0\leq t\leq T}} \left\{ \int_0^T \left\{ \|\underline{y}_1-\underline{y}_1^*\|_{Q_1}^2 + \|\underline{u}_1\|_{R_1}^2 \right\} dt + \min_{\substack{\underline{u}_2(t)\\ 0\leq t\leq T}} \left\{ \int_0^T \|\underline{y}_2-\underline{y}_2^*\|_{Q_2}^2 + \|\underline{u}_2\|_{R_2}^2 \right\} dt + \ldots + \min_{\substack{\underline{u}_n(t)\\ 0\leq t\leq T}} \int_0^T \|\underline{y}_n-\underline{y}_n^*\|_{Q_n}^2 + \|\underline{u}_n\|_{R_n}^2 \; dt \right\} \ldots . \right\} . \tag{3}$$

Although the optimisation problem posed by this equation is still formidable if the overall state vector is of large dimension, the formulation is more acceptable because the structural peculiarities of the serial system are emphasised by the nature of the cost function I in equation (3). Moreover, this formulation now suggests a possible two level approach to the optimisation problem in which the second level coordinates the actions of the individual first level subsystem controllers as shown in Fig. 2.

The idea here is that each controller at the first level performs a local minimisation, i.e. for the ith subsystem the local cost function I_i, where

$$I_i = \min_{\substack{\underline{u}_i(t)\\ 0\leq t\leq T}} \int_0^T \left\{ \|\underline{y}_i-\underline{y}_i^*\|_{Q_i}^2 + \|\underline{u}_i\|_{R_i}^2 \right\} dt$$

is minimised subject to the constraints

$$\dot{\underline{x}}_i(t) = A_{i,i-1}\underline{x}_{i-1}(t-\theta_{i-1}) + A_{ii}\underline{x}_i(t) + B_i\underline{u}_i(t) + \underline{w}_i(t)$$

$$\underline{y}_i = C_{ii}\underline{x}_i(t)$$

In order to perform this local minimisation, the ith first level controller requires $\underline{x}_{i-1}(t-\theta_{i-1})$ and $\underline{w}_i(t)$ over the interval $(0 \rightarrow T)$. If $\underline{w}_i(t)$ is known a priori over this interval, and this seems a reasonably non-restrictive assumption, then the local controller only requires $\underline{x}_{i-1}(t-\theta_{i-1})$. Bearing this in mind, one possible two-level approach to the optimisation problem would be to assume that some initial estimates $\hat{\underline{x}}_{i-1}(t-\theta_{i-1})$ of $\underline{x}_{i-1}(t-\theta_{i-1})$, i=1,2,...,n be supplied by the second level controller. First level local optimisation of the subsystems could then proceed using these initial estimates, and the resulting state trajectories could provide the second level controller with the information necessary to update $\hat{\underline{x}}_{i-1}(t-\theta_{i-1})$; which could then be used in a second level optimisation stage. Ideally, this iterative procedure could continue until, hopefully, an overall optimal solution was achieved. The actual calculations on the second level could be performed using one of the methods described in Chapter 2.

Of course, such an iterative scheme is beset with many problems as discussed in Chapter 2. For the problem which can be tackled, the computational burden might well be excessive and would almost certainly exclude the possibility of on-line implementation at the present time if the system was sufficiently large and only one computer was available. With this in mind it is important to ask if it is possible to simplify the computations in some manner by restricting the demand for complete optimality to one of acceptable suboptimal performance. Certainly, optimality in itself is not always or even often a virtue, since the system equations are hardly ever known well enough for the computed optimal solution to mean very much in practical terms. In fact, it may well be that a suboptimal solution could yield better practical results, particularly if it was computationally less demanding.

One heuristic approach to the problem, which will certainly lead to a suboptimal solution, but which is attractive in intuitive terms, is to stop the procedure described above after the first step, i.e. when subsystem one performs the minimisation

$$I_1 = \min_{\substack{\underline{u}_1(t) \\ 0 \leq t \leq T}} \int_0^T \left\{ \| \underline{y}_1 - \underline{y}_1^* \|^2_{Q_1} + \| \underline{u}_1 \|^2_{R_1} \right\} dt$$

subject to

$$\dot{\underline{x}}_1(t) = A_{11}\underline{x}_1(t) + B_1\underline{u}_1(t) + \underline{w}_1(t) \quad ; \quad \underline{y}_1 = C_{11}\underline{x}_1$$

If the second level controller then computes and feeds forward an estimate of the state trajectory $\hat{\underline{x}}_1(t-\theta_1)$, $0 \leq t \leq T$, to subsystem two, the second subsystem will be able to perform its local minimisation, i.e.

$$I_2 = \min_{\substack{\underline{u}_2(t) \\ 0 \leq t \leq T}} \int_0^T \left\{ \| \underline{y}_2 - \underline{y}_2^* \|^2_{Q_2} + \| \underline{u}_2 \|^2_{R_2} \right\} dt$$

subject to

$$\dot{\underline{x}}_2 = A_{21}\hat{\underline{x}}_1(t-\theta_1) + A_{22}\underline{x}_2(t) + B_2\underline{u}_2(t) + \underline{w}_2(t)$$

We could continue this process along the whole set of subsystems ; each subsystem starting from the first, performing its local optimisation and the second level controller then feeding forward an estimate of the resulting local optimal trajectory which is used as an additional forcing term for the next "downstream" optimisation. Clearly, this is only possible for serial systems, since otherwise even the first local optimisation is not practicable.

By utilising these two level control strategies it is assumed that the cost function I in equation (3) can often be approximated by

$$I = \left[\begin{array}{l} \min\limits_{\substack{\underline{u}_1(t) \\ 0 \leq t \leq T}} \left\{ \int_0^T \left\{ \| \underline{y}_1 - \underline{y}_1^* \|^2_{Q_1} + \| \underline{u}_1 \|^2_{R_1} \right\} dt \right\} + \dots + \\ \min\limits_{\substack{\underline{u}_n(t) \\ 0 \leq t \leq T}} \left\{ \int_0^T \left\{ \| \underline{y}_n - \underline{y}_n^* \|^2_{Q_n} + \| \underline{u}_n \|^2_{R_n} \right\} dt \right\} + \dots + \end{array} \right] \qquad (4)$$

Since, in the kind of serial systems considered here, there is often little conflict between the goals of the neighbouring controllers, this seems a reasonable assumption* and this is confirmed by the simulation results discussed in subsequent sections. Of course, particularly adverse initial conditions may degrade the performance of the local optimisations in relation to the overall theoretically optimal trajectory. However, in any practical case it is envisaged that the controllers will optimise the system from 0 to T and then from T to 2T, etc., so that the effects of the adverse initial conditions will eventually die away. One of the numerical examples will illustrate this problem of adverse initial conditions.

One of the principal advantages of the control structure described above is its computational simplicity and its ability to account for the delays without increasing the dimensionality of the problem. On the contrary, the delays actually help the on-line controllers since they provide extra time for computations.

4. IMPLEMENTATION OF THE STRATEGY

Except for the feedforward task of the second level controller the implementation of the suboptimal procedure outlined in the previous section is the same as that required for a normal optimal tracking problem [55] : each subsystem utilises a local optimum control law of the form

$$\underline{u}_i^0(t) = - R_i^{-1} \; B_i^T \left[- \underline{z}_i + P_{ii}\,(t)\; \underline{x}_i(t) \right] \tag{5}$$

where $P_{ii} = P_{ii}(t)$ are the solutions of the matrix Riccati equations for the subsystems, i.e.

$$\dot{P}_{ii} = -A_{ii}^T P_{ii} - P_{ii} A_{ii} + P_{ii} B_i R_i^{-1} \; B_i^T P_{ii} \; - C_{ii}^T Q_i \; C_{ii} \tag{6}$$

subject to the final condition

$$P_{ii}(T) = 0$$

whilst $\underline{z}_i = \underline{z}_i(t)$ are the solutions of the disturbance equations

$$\dot{\underline{z}}_i = - \left[A_{ii} - B_i R_i^{-1} \; B_i^T P_{ii} \right] \underline{z}_i + P_{ii} \; \underline{w}_i^* - C_{ii}^T Q_i \; \underline{y}_i^* \tag{7}$$

subject to

$$\underline{z}_i(T) = 0$$

In equation (7) $\underline{w}_i^*(t)$ is an augmented disturbance vector for the subsystem, i.e.

$$\underline{w}_i^*(t) = \underline{w}_i(t) + A_{i,i-1} \hat{\underline{x}}_{i-1}(t - \theta_{i-1})$$

Sometimes, it may be necessary to insert end constraints on the subsystem states by utilising a local cost function of the form,

$$I_i = \min_{\substack{\underline{u}_i(t) \\ 0 \leq t \leq T}} \; \| \underline{y}_i(T) - \underline{y}_i^*(T) \|^2_{F_i} + \int_0^T \left\{ \| \underline{y}_i - \underline{y}_i^* \|^2_{Q_i} + \| \underline{u}_i \|^2_{R_i} \right\} dt$$

---

* Admittedly there are systems where there is a conflict in the goals of neighbouring controllers. An example of this would be when the weights in the cost function are such that the "downstream" subsystems are much more important than the "upstream" ones. However, it is felt that the approximation applies for many cases of practical interest. At the end of this chapter we will describe a possible modification to the strategy to take some account of conflicts.

In this case, the local control law is exactly the same as that given in equations (5), (6) and (7) but the end conditions on P_{ii} and $\underline{z}_i$ equations are modified to the following form,

$$P_{ii}(T) = C_{ii}^T F_i C_{ii}$$

$$\underline{z}_i(T) = C_{ii}^T F_i \underline{y}_i^*(T) .$$

5. COMPUTATIONAL REQUIREMENTS FOR THE SUBOPTIMAL CONTROLLER

To balance the loss of optimality resulting from the suboptimal hierarchical strategy for control described in previous sections, there are substantial computational savings. To illustrate this, let it be assumed that the computational burden can be measured in terms of the number of elementary multiplication operations required for both the optimal and suboptimal strategies. Suppose that the overall state vector is of order ℓ ,i.e. if

$$\ell = \sum_{i=1}^{n} (\ell_i + \ell_i')$$

where ℓ_i and ℓ_i' are, respectively, the orders of the states of the individual subsystems and the additional states dues to the delays. If the overall control vector is of order $m = \sum_{i=1}^{m} m_i$ and the output vector of order $p = \sum_{i=1}^{p} p_i$, then by merely adding up the number of elementary multiplication steps involved in the solution of equations (5), (6) and (7) and the system equation for all the subsystems, using fourth order Runge Kutta integration, the suboptimal strategy requires the following number of elementary multiplication operations for each integration step

$$\sum_{i=1}^{n}\Big\{20\,\ell_i^3 + 4m_i^3 + 4\,\ell_i^2 m_i + 9\,\ell_i m_i^2 + 15\,\ell_i^2 + \ell_i m_i + \ell_i p_i^2 + p_i^2\Big\} \tag{8}$$

On the other hand, the optimal strategy requires

$$20\,\ell^3 + 4m^3 + 4\,\ell^2 m + 9\ m^2 + 15\,\ell^2 + \ m + \ell\, p2 + p^2 \tag{9}$$

It is clear from these expressions that since $\ell \gg \ell_i$, $m \gg m_i$ and $p \gg p_i$, large computational savingswill normally result which increase with n. Some numerical examples which illustrate the computational efficiency are given in the following section.

6. NUMERICAL EXAMPLES

Since the suboptimal control strategy for serial systems discussed in this chapter is based on heuristic reasoning, it is important that a detailed simulation study should be conducted in order to assess its performance in typical applications. In this section we discuss the results from a number of simulation experiments and, in each case, we consider both the computational savings and loss in optimality associated with the suboptimal strategy.

6.1. Serial Systems Without Time Delays Between the Subsytems

In the first set of examples, consider the regulatory control of a serial system in which the subsystems are directly connected together ; the output of one subsystem providing the input to the next without any intervening pure delays.

Example 1

This is the simplest possible example : the overall system consists of two linear subsystems each of first order.
The system equations are :

$$\dot{x}_1 = x_1 + u_1$$

$$\dot{x}_2 = x_1 + x_2 + u_2$$

and the overall cost function is chosen as,

$$I = \int_0^T \left\{ x_1^2 + x_2^2 + u_1^2 + u_2^2 \right\} dt$$

i.e. $$I_1 = \int_0^T \left\{ x_1^2 + u_1^2 \right\} dt \quad ; \quad I_2 = \int_0^T \left\{ x_2^2 + u_2^2 \right\} dt$$

(a) Computational requirements

Here $\ell_1 = 1$, $m_1 = 1$, $\ell_2 = 1$, $m_2 = 1$, $\ell = m = 2$. Thus for $T = 4$, $\Delta T = 0.1$ seconds, there are $N = 40$ integration steps. As a result the optimal strategy requires 40 x 372 multiplications, whilst the suboptimal strategy requires only 40 x 110 multiplications. In other words, the computational saving is 372/110 x 100 = = 340 %.

(b) Simulation results

The optimal and suboptimal strategies were simulated on the ICL 4130 digital computer of the Cambridge University Control Group. A number of tests were performed and the following results were obtained :

i) Initial conditions $x_1(0) = 1$, $x_2(0) = 1$

Cost of optimal control, $I = 6.40$
Cost of suboptimal control $= 6.49$
Loss of optimality $= 1.6$ %

The resulting optimal and suboptimal state trajectories are shown in Fig. 3. Note that the suboptimal state trajectories are somewhat "superior" to the optimal ones in that there is no steady state offset or overshoot. But this is balanced by an increase in the control effort which is probably the major reason for the 1.6 % loss in optimality.

The suboptimal cost for subsystem one is 2.38 and that for subsystem two is 4.12 whilst the optimal strategy has a cost of 3.20 for each subsystem. In other words, the decreased cost in subsystem one is compensated, as expected, by the increased cost in subsystem two.

ii) Initial conditions $x_1(0) = 1$, $x_2(0) = -1$

Cost of optimal control $I = 3.32$
Cost of suboptimal control $= 3.54$
Loss in optimality $= 6.6$ %

The resulting optimal and suboptimal trajectories are shown in Fig. 4 . In this case the suboptimal cost for subsystem one is 2.38 while that for subsystem two is 1.16

In the first example, the initial conditions (1,1) are favourable because the trajectory from subsystem one "helps" subsystem two. Although this is not the

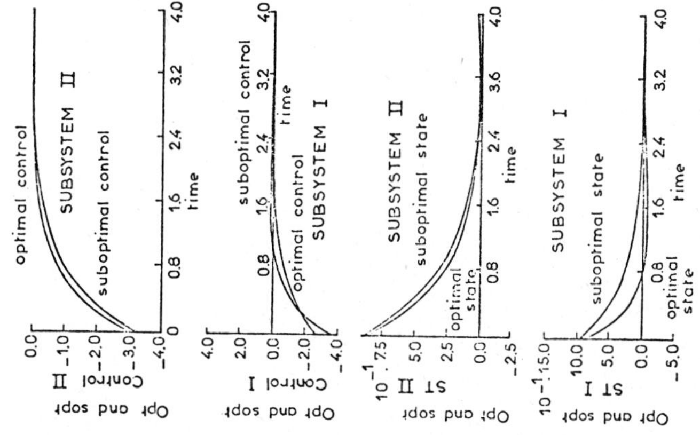

FIGURE 3

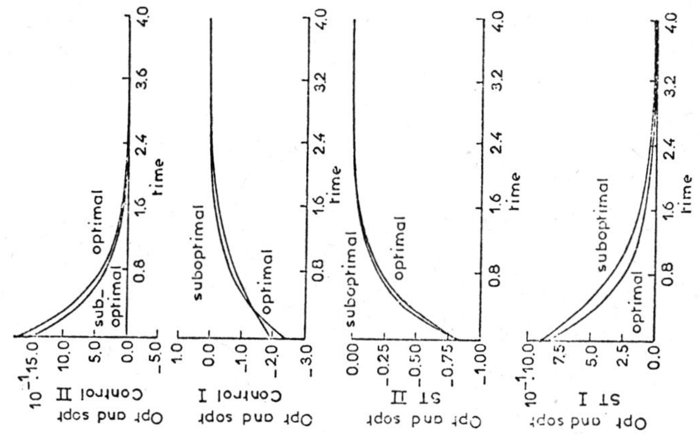

FIGURE 4

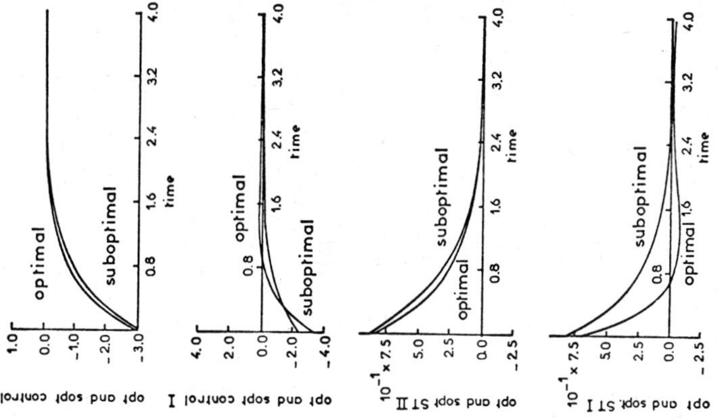

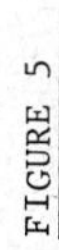

FIGURE 5

case for the initial conditions (1, -1), the optimal and suboptimal trajectories are still very similar, demonstrating to some extent the lack of sensitivity to initial conditions.

iii) In another test, subsystem one was given a unit step disturbance for an initial period of 0.1 seconds. Fig. 5 shows the optimal and suboptimal state trajectories. Here, the suboptimal cost is almost identical to the equivalent optimal cost, and once again, the suboptimal state trajectories are quite close to the optimal ones.

iv) In a final test, the period of optimisation T was chosen to be 1.0 seconds. This is so short that the system states do not have a chance to settle down to their steady state values. Even in this case, however, the loss of optimality is only 3.6 %. It should be noted that such a situation often arises when the upstream disturbance vector $\underline{w}$ for the first subsystem can only be measured for a short period of time ahead.

Example 2

In this example, the overall system consists of four first order subsystems in series. The system equations are :

$$\dot{x}_1 = x_1 + u_1$$
$$\dot{x}_i = x_{i-1} + x_i + u_i \qquad i = 2, 3, 4$$
$$y_i = x_i$$

and the overall cost function is chosen as

$$I = \min_{\substack{u_i \\ i=1,2,3,4}} \int_0^T \sum_{i=1}^{4} \left\{ y_i^2 + u_i^2 \right\} dt$$

(a) Computational requirements

Here $\ell_i = m_i = 1$ $(i = 1,\ldots,4)$. Thus for T = 4, $\Delta T = 0.05$, the integration steps N are 80 so that the optimal strategy requires 80 x 2700 multiplications whilst for the suboptimal strategy, the figure is 80 x 220 multiplications. Consequently, the computational saving in this case is 1200 %.

(b) Simulation results

i) Initial conditions $x_i(0) = 1$; i = 1,2,3,4

Cost of optimal control I = 14.86
Cost of suboptimal control = 15.54
Loss of optimality = 3.5 %

ii) For the same initial conditions but with T = 3 seconds

Cost of optimal control I = 14.856
Cost of suboptimal control = 15.482
Loss of optimality = 4.2 %

iii) For the same initial conditions but with T = 2 seconds

Cost of optimal control I = 14.77
Cost of suboptimal control = 15.59
Performance loss = 5 %

The above results show that as the period of optimisation T increases so the difference between the optimum and suboptimum cost decreases. And even for very short optimisation intervals, the performance loss is still acceptably small.

Example 3

This is the final test example for a number of serial subsystems without timelags. The overall system is in this case of 10th order and consists of ten first order subsystems in cascade. The system equations are :

$$\dot{x}_1 = x_1 + u_1$$
$$\dot{x}_i = x_{i-1} + x_i + u_i \qquad i = 2, 3, \ldots, 10$$

while the overall cost function is chosen to be :

$$I = \min_{\substack{u_i(t) \\ i=1,2,\ldots 10}} \int_0^T \sum_{i=1}^{10} \left\{ x_i^2 + u_i^2 \right\} dt$$

(a) Computational requirements

Optimal strategy I = 60 x 39700 multiplications
Suboptimal strategy = 60 x 550 multiplications
Computational saving = 7200 %

(b) Simulation Results

In this case the following results were obtained for initial conditions $x_i(0) = 1$; $i = 1,2,\ldots, 10$, and T = 3 seconds

Cost of optimum control I = 40.55
Cost of suboptimum control = 42.03
Loss of optimality = 3.2 %

6.2. Application of the strategy to the two reach river system

Let us next consider the application of the strategy to the river Cam system that we have previously considered in Part I. We will consider only the "no delay" model which is given by the following state space equations.

$$\frac{d}{dt}\begin{bmatrix} z_1 \\ q_1 \\ z_2 \\ q_2 \end{bmatrix} = \begin{bmatrix} -1.32 & 0 & 0 & 0 \\ -0.32 & -1.2 & 0 & 0 \\ 0.9 & 0 & -1.32 & 0 \\ 0 & 0.9 & -0.32 & -1.2 \end{bmatrix} \begin{bmatrix} z_1 \\ q_1 \\ z_2 \\ q_2 \end{bmatrix}$$

$$+ \begin{bmatrix} 0.1 & 0 \\ 0 & 0 \\ 0 & 0.1 \\ 0 & 0 \end{bmatrix} \begin{bmatrix} \Delta m_1 \\ \Delta m_2 \end{bmatrix} + \begin{bmatrix} 5.35 \\ 10.9 \\ 4.19 \\ 1.9 \end{bmatrix}$$

and the cost function could be written as

$$J = \min_{\Delta m_1, \Delta m_2} \int_0^4 \Big[\left\{ 2(z_1 - 4.06)^2 + (q_1 - 8)^2 + \Delta m_1^2 \right\}$$

$$+ \left\{ 2\left(z_2 - 5.94\right)^2 + (q_2-6)^2 + \Delta m_2^2 \right\} \Big] dt$$

where $\Delta m_1 = 53.4 + m_1$, $\Delta m_2 = 41.9 + m_2$ and m_1, m_2 are the steady state discharges of B.O.D. and D.O. into the stream.

This cost function implies that it is desired to maintain reach 1 around B.O.D. = 4.06 mg/1, D.O. = 8 mg/1 and for reach 2, B.O.D. = 5.94 mg/1, D.O. = 6 mg/1.

For this example, the computational requirements of the op:imal single level strategy are 3.4 times those of the suboptimum one. If the time delays are included, these rise to 28 times those of the suboptimum one.

6.2.1. Simulation Results

In a typical test, a situation in which the first reach was initially polluted while the second reach was "clean" was investigated. The initial values of B.O.D. and D.O. in reach 1 were chosen to be $z_1(0) = 5$ mg/1, $q_1(0) = 5$ mg/1 and for reach 2 these equalled the desired values,i.e.

$$z_2(0) = 5.94 \text{ mg/1}, \quad q_2(0) = 6 \text{ mg/1}$$

The simulation results obtained for this example are shown in Fig. 6. The optimum and suboptimum trajectories are virtually identical showing that for this case the simple hierarchical strategy does provide near optimal performance. This is further confirmed by the value of the cost J for the two policies. The optimal cost is 10.62 and the suboptimum cost is 10.74. Many other tests were performed and results substantially similar to the ones reported here were obtained [42] .

6.3. Serial Systems with Time Delays between the Subsystems

As pointed out previously, time delays between the subsystems present no problems to the proposed control strategy ; on the contrary they provide more time for the second level controller to compute the feedforward information. This is a very favourable property of the proposed suboptimal control strategy since most practical systems include distributed effects which can often be modelled as pure delay elements between lumped parameter blocks.However, in order to compute the cost of the optimal strategy for the purposes of comparison, it is necessary to approximate the time delays in some manner. Here the time delay was approximated in the frequency domain by

$$e^{-s\theta} = \left[1 + s\theta + s^2 \frac{\theta^2}{2} + \ldots\right]^{-1}$$

Example 1

The first example to be considered here is the same as example 1 of Section 6.1 but with a delay of θ seconds between the two subsystems. The system equations are :

$$\dot{x}_1(t) = x_1(t) + u_1(t)$$

$$\dot{x}_4(t) = x_1(t-\theta) + x_4(t) + u_2(t)$$

And the cost function is chosen as

$$I = \min_{u_1(t),u_2(t)} \int_0^T \left\{ x_1^2 + x_4^2 + u_1^2 + u_2^2 \right\} dt$$

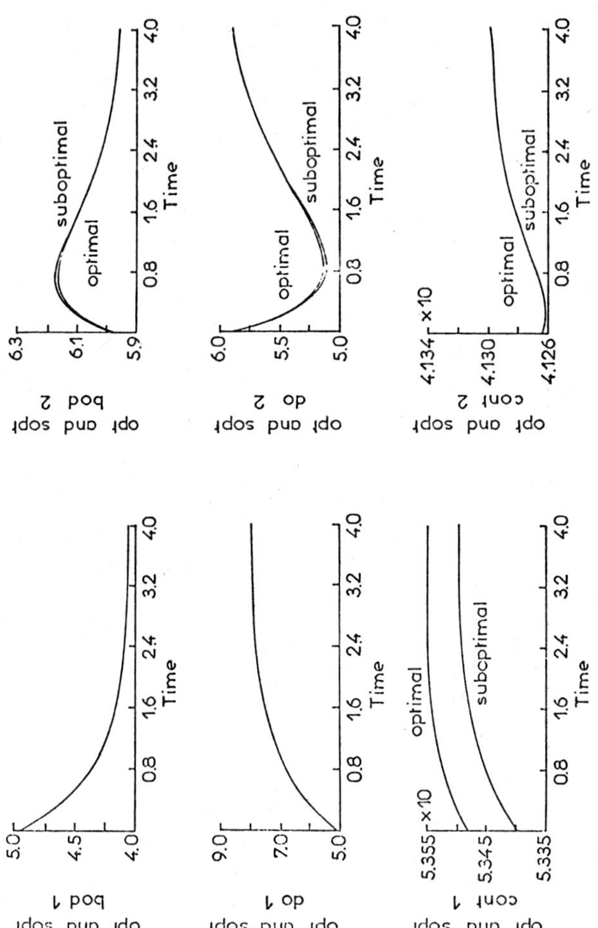

Fig. 6 : Optimal and suboptimal trajectories for the river example

In order to compute the optimal cost, a second order approximation to the time delays was used.* In other words, two extra variables x_2 and x_3 were introduced and the state equations were modified to the following form,

$$\dot{x}_1 = x_1 + u_1$$
$$\dot{x}_2 = x_3$$
$$\dot{x}_3 = \frac{2}{\theta^2} x_1 - \frac{2}{\theta^2} x_2 - \frac{2}{\theta} x_3$$
$$\dot{x}_4 = x_2 + x_4 + u_2$$

For a time delay of $\theta = 0.05$ seconds and initial conditions given by $x_i(0) = 1$, $i = 1,2,3,4$, the optimal cost for $T = 4$ seconds, $\Delta T = 0.05$ seconds, was found to be 6.50 while the suboptimal cost was 6.81 giving a performance loss of 4.5 %

For the same optimisation interval of $T = 4$ seconds, $\Delta T = 0.05$ seconds the optimal and suboptimal costs were computed for a number of different time delays and the results are tabulated below.

Delay	Cost of optimal control	Cost of suboptimal control	% Difference
0.1 seconds	6.77	7.02	3
0.25 seconds	7.30	7.47	2.5
0.5 seconds	8.03	8.09	0.07

Example 2

In the second example, the system is assumed to consist of 3 first order subsystems so that the system equations are of the form

$$\dot{x}_1(t) = x_1(t) + u_1(t)$$
$$\dot{x}_2(t) = x_1(t-\theta_1) + x_2(t) + u_2(t)$$
$$\dot{x}_3(t) = x_2(t-\theta_2) + x_3(t) + u_3(t)$$

and the cost function is

$$I = \sum_{i=1}^{3} \int_0^T (x_i^2 + u_i^2)\, dt$$

Once again, a second order delay approximation was used to compute the optimal strategy and the simulation yielded the following results for a time delay $\theta_1 = \theta_2 = 0.1$ seconds, $T = 4$ seconds, $\Delta T = 0.05$, $x_i(0) = 1$, $i = 1,2,\ldots, 8$

(a) Computational requirements

The optimal strategy required 80 x 12909 multiplications while the suboptimal strategy only required 80 x 165 giving a saving of roughly 7 500 %.

(b) Simulation results

Cost of optimal control = 11.43
Cost of suboptimal control = 11.76
Loss of optimality = 3.5 %

* Higher order approximations yield very little change in the optimal cost so that the second order approximation was considered adequate.

7. BOUNDS ON SUBOPTIMALITY

In the previous section, a number of studies have illustrated the performance of the simple hierarchical strategy and it appears to provide good suboptimal performance for all the conditions investigated. In this section, a method is developed which enables bounds to be put on the degree of suboptimality of the strategy for any particular application without actually calculating the optimum as done in the preceding simulation studies. The method arises from an idea of Pearson [61] that finding the lowest point of a functional subject to constraints has a dual of finding the highest tangent under the curve as shown in Fig. 7. This concept can be used to find the upper and lower bounds for the performance of an approximate solution such as that developed in this chapter.

When the dual function of a primal problem such as the one defined by the serial systems class exists then by the saddle value theoremof Lagrange Duality*

$$\emptyset_s \leq \emptyset^* = I^* \leq I_s$$

where $\emptyset^*$ and I^* are the optimal values of the primal and dual functionals. I_s is the cost of the suboptimal solution and $\emptyset_s$ is the value of the dual function using the suboptimal control trajectory and the corresponding state and Lagrange multiplier trajectories. Given thus the suboptimal state and control trajectories, it is possible to compute two numbers which bound the optimal performance $I^* = \emptyset^*$. The measure of the deviation $I_s - \emptyset_s$, if used "sparingly" can be used to predict the optimum cost I^*. It will be a measure of the degree of suboptimality.

In this formulation, the cost I_s associated with the suboptimal control trajectory $\underline{u}_s(t)$ can be computed when the suboptimal strategy is put on-line and this provides the upper bound on the cost. The lower bound can be calculated from the dual function $\emptyset$ derived below.

7.1. The Lower Bound Calculation

The primal problem is defined as

$$I = \min_{\substack{\underline{U}(t) \\ 0 \leq t \leq T}} \frac{1}{2} \int_0^T (\| \underline{X}-\underline{X}^* \|_Q^2 + \| \underline{U} \|_R^2)\, dt$$

subject to

$$\dot{\underline{X}} = A\underline{X} + B\underline{U} + \underline{W} \quad , \quad \underline{X}(0) = \underline{X}_0$$

where $\underline{X}$ and $\underline{U}$ refer to the integrated one level problem. Here, the more general servomechanism formulation is given and the regulator results can be obtained by setting the desired trajectories $\underline{X}^*$ to zero.

For this primal problem, the dual function $\emptyset$ can be written as

$$\emptyset = \max_{\underline{\lambda}} \left[\operatorname*{infimum}_{\underline{U},\, \underline{X}} \left\{ \int_0^T \left\{ \| \underline{X}-\underline{X}^* \|_Q^2 + \|\underline{u}\|_R^2 + \underline{\lambda}^T (A\underline{X}+B\underline{U}+\underline{W}-\dot{\underline{X}}) \right\} dt \right\} \right] \quad (10)$$

In order to obtain an explicit relationship for the dual function, it is necessary to evaluate the infimum w.r.t. $\underline{X}$ and $\underline{U}$ in equation (10).

---

* See the appendices for a discussion of the application of Lagrange Duality theory to optimal control problems.

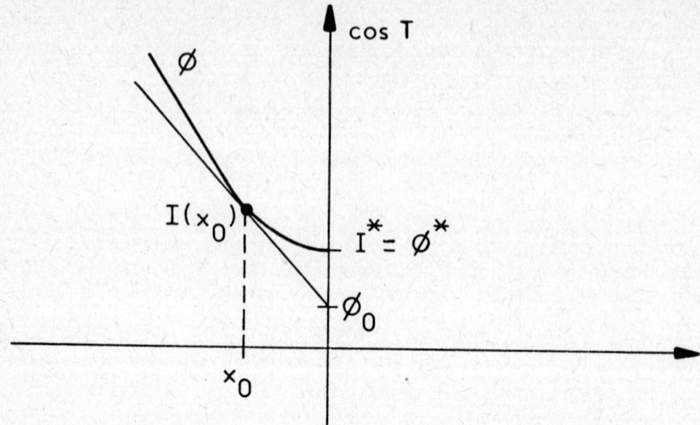

Fig. 7 : Geometric interpretation of the lower bound

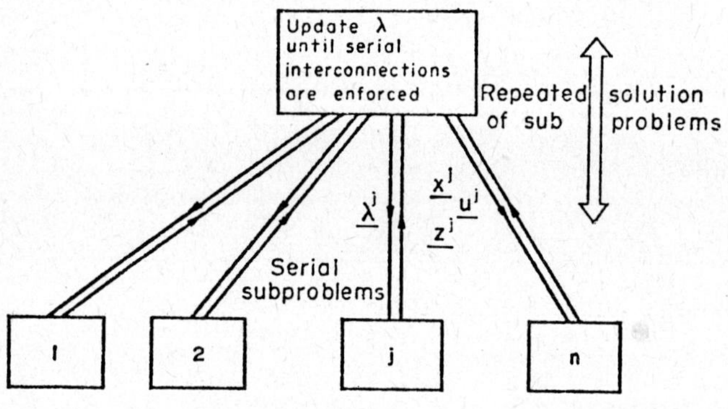

Fig. 8 : The serial controller for systems with conflicts

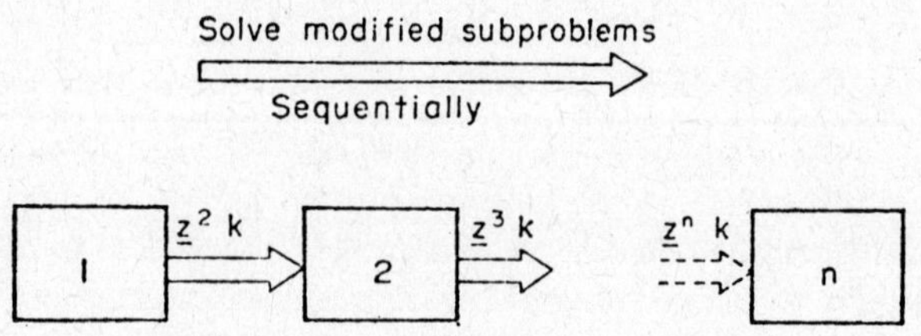

Fig. 9 : The modified structure

The Hamiltonian H is given by

$$H = \frac{1}{2} \|\underline{X}-\underline{X}^*\|^2_Q + \|\underline{U}\|^2_R + \underline{\lambda}^T \left[A\underline{X} + B\underline{U} + \underline{W}\right]$$

The necessary conditions for the optimum are :

$$\frac{\partial H}{\partial \underline{U}} = \underline{0} \text{ and } \frac{\partial H}{\partial \underline{X}} = -\dot{\underline{\lambda}} \qquad \underline{\lambda}(T) = \underline{0}$$

from the first of these

$$\underline{U} = -R^{-1} B^T \underline{\lambda}$$

and from the second,

$$\dot{\underline{\lambda}} = -\frac{\partial H}{\partial \underline{X}} = -Q\underline{X} - A^T \underline{\lambda} + Q\underline{X}^*$$

Since

$$\int_0^T \underline{\lambda}^T \dot{\underline{X}}\, dt = \underline{\lambda}^T(T)\, \underline{X}(T) - \underline{\lambda}^T(0)\, \underline{X}_0 + \int_0^T \underline{X}^T \frac{\partial H}{\partial \underline{X}}\, dt$$

the dual function $\emptyset$ in equation (10) can be written as

$$\emptyset = \max_{\underline{\lambda}} \left[\inf_{\underline{U}} \left[\underline{\lambda}^T(0)\, \underline{X}(0) + \int_0^T \left\{ \frac{1}{2} \|\underline{U}\|^2_R + \|\underline{X}-\underline{X}^*\|^2_Q + \right.\right.\right.$$

$$\left.\left.\left. + \underline{\lambda}^T \left[A\underline{X}+B\underline{U}+\underline{W}\right] - \underline{X}^T Q\underline{X} - \underline{X}^T A^T \underline{\lambda} + \underline{X}^T Q\underline{X}^* \right\} dt \right]\right]$$

using $\underline{U} = -R^{-1} B^T \underline{\lambda}$

the above integral becomes

$$-\frac{1}{2} \|\underline{\lambda}\|^2_{BR^{-1}B^T} - \frac{1}{2} \|\underline{X}-\underline{X}^*\|^2_Q + \underline{\lambda}^T \underline{W}$$

therefore

$$\emptyset = \max_{\underline{\lambda}} \left[\underline{\lambda}^T(0)\, \underline{X}_0 + \int_0^T \left\{ \underline{\lambda}^T \underline{W} - \frac{1}{2} \|\underline{\lambda}\|^2_{BR^{-1}B^T} + \|\underline{X}-\underline{X}^*\|^2_Q) \right\} dt \right] \tag{11}$$

where

$$\dot{\underline{\lambda}} = -Q\underline{X} - A^T\underline{\lambda} + Q\underline{X}^*$$
$$\underline{\lambda}(T) = \underline{0} \tag{12}$$

For the suboptimum dual function $\emptyset_s$, the maximisation w.r.t. $\underline{\lambda}$ in equation (11) is not performed. Thus to compute the lower bound $\emptyset_s$, given a suboptimal state trajectory, it is necessary to integrate equation (12) backwards from the final condition and then substitute the $\underline{\lambda}$ trajectory computed into equation (11) ignoring the outer maximisation w.r.t. $\underline{\lambda}$. Since $\underline{\lambda}$ is of the same order as the overall system (as opposed to the square symmetrical matrix in the Riccati equation), it is possible to calculate this lower bound with a fairly modest computational effort.

There is one point to note, however, and that is the asymmetry of the dual and primal functionals which is the reason why $I_s - \emptyset_s$ gives an estimate of the optimum only if used "sparingly". A simple calculation is given below to illustrate the lower bound calculation.

7.2. Numerical example

The problem for which the worst results were obtained was example 1 in Section 6.1 where the initial conditions on the states were (1, -1) and the corresponding optimal and suboptimal costs were

optimal = 3.32 suboptimal = 3.54

The suboptimal cost of 3.54 serves as an upper bound on the cost. For the lower bound, calculations on the ICL 4130 digital computer at Cambridge University showed that the corresponding value was 1.99, so that

$$1.99 \leq I^* \leq 3.54$$

It should be noted that the above bounds give only a rough idea of the degree of suboptimality of the strategy. The reason for this is that the primal and dual functionals are essentially asymmetrical so that it is only at the optimum that $\emptyset^* = I^*$. Nevertheless, the lower bound is useful in that it does fix the lowest possible level above which the optimal cost must lie and therefore gives some idea of the possible efficacy of the strategy prior to simulation.

8. DISCUSSION

In this chapter so far we have formulated the important concept of serially connected systems and developed a simple hierarchical strategy for the control of such serial systems with and without time delays between the subsystems. The strategy can be used to provide on-line control for this important class of problems. Although the basis of the strategy is purely heuristic, it appears to combine near optimal control performance with only modest computational requirements. In addition it has been found possible to put bounds on the suboptimality of the control scheme using the basic theorem of Lagrange Duality.

9. REFINEMENT OF THE SERIAL CONTROL SCHEME FOR LINEAR QUADRATIC SYSTEMS [14]

In this section a development of the serial scheme due to Drew [62] will be described which makes some allowance for conflicts which may be present. Such conflicts may arise when there is competition between subsystems for limited resources or the goals themselves are in opposition. Such a difficulty is not uncommon in industrial and managerial situations, e.g. bottlenecks of a production line.

The class of systems examined here is that of the discrete time linear quadratic problem.

Let the optimal solution for those serially connected systems be obtained using the three-level method described in Chapter 2.

The problem is to

$$\text{Minimise } \frac{1}{2} \| \underline{x}_i (K) - \underline{x}_i^* (K) \|_{Q_i(K)}$$

$$+ \sum_{k=1}^{K-1} \Big[\frac{1}{2} \| \underline{x}_i(k) - \underline{x}_i^* (k) \|^2_{Q_i(k)}$$

$$+ \frac{1}{2} \| \underline{u}_i(k) - \underline{u}_i^*(k) \|^2_{R_i(k)} +$$

$$\frac{1}{2}\| \underline{z}_i(k) - \underline{z}_i^*(k) \|^2_{S_i(k)} \Big] \tag{13}$$

subject to

$$\begin{aligned} \underline{x}_i(k+1) &= A_i(k)\,\underline{x}_i(k) + B_i(k)\,\underline{u}_i(k) + \underline{z}_i(k) \\ \underline{z}_{i+1}(k) &= M_{i+1}(k)\,\underline{x}_i(k) + N_{i+1}(k)\,\underline{u}_i(k) \\ \underline{x}_i(0) &= \underline{x}_{i0} \end{aligned} \tag{14}$$

for i = 1,2,..., n subsystems.
The serial interconnection is apparent from the constraints. A Lagrangian function can be constructed for this overall system, i.e.

$$\begin{aligned} L(\underline{x},\underline{u},\underline{z},\underline{\lambda},\underline{p}) = \sum_{i=1}^{n} \Big\{ \frac{1}{2}\| \underline{x}_i(K) - \underline{x}_i^*(K) \|^2_{Q_i(K)} + \sum_{k=1}^{K-1} \Big\{ \frac{1}{2}\| \underline{x}_i(k) - \underline{x}_i^*(k) \|^2_{Q_i(k)} \\ + \frac{1}{2}\| \underline{u}_i(k) - \underline{u}_i^*(k) \|^2_{R_i(k)} + \frac{1}{2}\| \underline{z}_i(k) - \underline{z}_i^*(k) \|^2_{S_i(k)} + \\ + \underline{p}_i(k+1)^T \big[\underline{x}_i(k+1) - A_i(k)\,\underline{x}_i(k) - B_i(k)\,\underline{u}_i(k) - \underline{z}_i(k) \big] \\ + \underline{\lambda}_{i+1}(k)^T \big[\underline{z}_{i+1}(k) - M_{i+1}\underline{x}_i(k) - N_{i+1}\underline{u}_i(k) \big] \Big\} \Big\} \end{aligned} \tag{15}$$

This problem could be solved using the three-level method described in Chapter 2. In that case the necessary conditions are :

$$\begin{aligned} &\underline{x}_i(k+1) = A_i(k)\,\underline{x}_i(k) + B_i(k)\,\underline{u}_i(k) + \underline{z}_i(k) \\ &\underline{z}_{i+1}(k) = M_{i+1}(k)\,\underline{x}_i(k) + N_{i+1}(k)\,\underline{u}_i(k) \\ &Q_i(k)\big[\underline{x}_i(k) - \underline{x}^*(k) \big] \\ &\quad + \underline{p}_i(k) - A_i(k)^T\,\underline{p}_i(k+1) \\ &\quad - M_{i+1}(k)^T\,\underline{\lambda}_{i+1}(k) = \underline{0}\,, \\ &R_i(k)\big[\underline{u}_i(k) - \underline{u}_i^*(k) \big] - B_i(k)^T\,\underline{p}_i(k+1) \\ &\quad - N_{i+1}(k)^T\,\underline{\lambda}_{i+1}(k) = \underline{0}\,, \\ &S_i(k)\big[\underline{z}_i(k) - \underline{z}_i^*(k) \big] - \underline{p}_i(k+1) + \underline{\lambda}_i(k) = 0 \end{aligned} \tag{16}$$

It is desired that the suboptimal scheme to be used will proceed in the same manner as that described in this chapter, each subsystem performing its local optimisation and feeding forward the resulting local optimum trajectories to the next subsystem.

To allow for the conflicting requirements of the subsystems "down the line" each subproblem has a modified cost function. Quadratic terms in the dependent interconnection variables are added, but the cost does not include terms in the interconnection from the previous subsystem.

The problem for subsystem i could thus be written as

$$\text{Minimise } \frac{1}{2}\|\underline{x}_i(K) - \underline{x}_i^*(K)\|^2_{Q_i(K)} + \sum_{k=1}^{K-1}\Big[\frac{1}{2}\|\underline{x}_i(k) - \underline{x}_i^*(k)\|^2_{Q_i(k)} + \frac{1}{2}\|\underline{u}_i(k) - \underline{u}_i^*(k)\|^2_{R_i(k)} + \frac{1}{2}\|\underline{z}_{i+1}(k) - \hat{\underline{z}}_{i+1}(k)\|^2_{T_i(k)}\Big] \tag{17}$$

subject to

$$\underline{x}_{i+1}(k) = M_{i+1}(k)\,\underline{x}_i(k) + N_{i+1}(k)\,\underline{u}_i(k) + \underline{z}_i(k) \tag{18}$$

$$\underline{z}_{i+1}(k) = M_{i+1}(k)\,\underline{x}_i(k) + N_{i+1}(k)\,\underline{u}_i(k)$$

$$\underline{x}_i(0) = \underline{x}_{i0}\ .$$

Suppose that the interconnections $\underline{z}_i(k)$ are known through calculation at the previous subsystem. The constraints (18) may be used to construct a Lagrangian for this problem using the multipliers $\underline{\pi}_i(k)$ and $\underline{\beta}_i(k)$ and the necessary conditions for this lead to the equations

$$\underline{x}_i(k+1) = A_i(k)\,\underline{x}_i(k) + B_i(k)\,\underline{u}_i(k) + \underline{z}_i(k)$$

$$\underline{z}_{i+1}(k) = M_{i+1}(k)\,\underline{x}_i(k) + N_{i+1}(k)\,\underline{u}_i(k)$$

$$Q_i(k)\left[\underline{x}_i(k) - \underline{x}_i^*(k)\right] + \underline{\pi}_i(k) - A_i(k)^T\underline{\pi}_i(k+1) - M_{i+1}(k)^T\underline{\beta}_{i+1}(k) = \underline{0}$$

$$R_i(k)\left[\underline{u}_i(k) - \underline{u}_i^*(k)\right] - B_i(k)^T\underline{\pi}_i(k+1) - M_{i+1}(k)^T\underline{\beta}_{i+1}(k) = \underline{0}$$

$$T_i(k)\left[\underline{z}_{i+1}(k) - \hat{\underline{z}}_{i+1}(k)\right] + \underline{\beta}_{i+1}(k) = \underline{0}$$

It will be noticed that these equations are identical in form to equations (16) except for the last one involving interconnections.

Using (16) for subsystem i + 1

$$S_{i+1}(k)\left[\underline{z}_{i+1}(k) - \underline{z}_{i+1}^*(k)\right] - \underline{p}_{i+1}(k+1) + \underline{\lambda}_{i+1}(k) = \underline{0} \tag{20}$$

If $T_i(k)$ and $\hat{\underline{z}}_{i+1}(k)$ can be chosen such that

$$T_i(k)\left[\underline{z}_{i+1}(k) - \hat{\underline{z}}_{i+1}(k)\right] = S_{i+1}(k)\left[\underline{z}_{i+1}(k) - \underline{z}_{i+1}^*(k)\right] - \underline{p}_{i+1}(k+1) \tag{21}$$

The equations are identical in form and will have identical solutions. The difficulty is that this requires foreknowledge of the multipliers $\underline{p}_{i+1}(k+1)$ belonging to the next subproblem.

For the purposes of clarity development will now be restricted to interconnections of the form :

$$\underline{z}_{i+1}(k) = N_{i+1}(k)\ \underline{u}_i(k).$$

Note that the more general problem is easily treated by simple transformation.

For this case the added quadratic terms to each subsystem are quadratic in $\underline{u}_i(k)$.

Consider subsystem i where the extra terms in $\underline{u}_{i+1}(k)$ for subsystem i+1 have already been determined and incorporated in $R_{i+1}(k)$ and $\underline{u}^*_{i+1}(k)$.

The necessary equations of subsystem (i+1) are then given by

$$\begin{aligned}\underline{x}_{i+1}(k+1) &= A_{i+1}(k)\ \underline{x}_{i+1}(k)\\ &\quad + B_{i+1}(k)\ \underline{u}_{i+1}(k) + \underline{z}_{i+1}(k)\\ Q_{i+1}(k)\left[\underline{x}_{i+1}(k) - \underline{x}^*_{i+1}(k)\right] &+ \underline{\pi}_{i+1}(k) - A_{i+1}(k)^T\underline{\pi}_i(k+1) = \underline{0}\ , \qquad (24)\\ R_{i+1}(k)\left[\underline{u}_{i+1}(k) - \underline{u}^*_i(k)\right] &- B_{i+1}(k)^T\underline{\pi}_i(k+1) = \underline{0}\end{aligned}$$

Here the relation $\underline{z}_{i+2}(k) = N_{i+1}(k)\ \underline{u}_{i+1}(k)$ has been directly substituted in the equations so the multipliers $\underline{\beta}(k)$ are not needed.

Elementary manipulation of these equations gives the second-order difference equation :

$$\begin{aligned}\underline{z}_{i+1}(k) = &\left[Q_{i+1}(k+1)\ A_{i+1}(k+1)^T\right]\underline{p}_{i+1}(k+1) + \left[A_{i+1}(k)\ Q_{i+1}(k)\right.\\ &\left.A_{i+1}(k)^T\right]\underline{p}_{i+1}(k) - \left[Q_{i+1}(k+1)^{-1} + A_{i+1}(k)\right.\\ &\left.Q_{i+1}(k)^{-1}\ A_{i+1}(k)^T + B_{i+1}(k)\ R_{i+1}(k)^{-1}\ B_{i+1}(k)^T\right]\\ &\underline{p}_{i+1}(k+1) - A_{i+1}(k)\ Q_{i+1}(k)^{-1}\ \underline{x}^*_{i+1}(k)\\ &+ Q_{i+1}(k+1)^{-1}\ \underline{x}^*_{i+1}(k+1) - B_{i+1}(k)\ R_{i+1}(k)^{-1}\\ &\underline{u}^*_{i+1}(k)\end{aligned} \tag{25}$$

This set of equations for k = 1,..., K may in principle be inverted to obtain $\underline{p}_{i+1}(k+1)$ as a function of $\underline{z}_{i+1}(k)$ (k=1,2,...,K).

The development is much simplified, however, if the terms in $\underline{p}_{i+1}(k)$ and $\underline{p}_{i+1}(k+1)$ are ignored. In this case the following relationship is obtained :

$$\underline{p}_{i+1}(k+1) = S_{M_{i+1}}(k) - \left[z_{i+1}(k) + S_{ML_{i+1}}(k)\right] \tag{26}$$

where

$$\begin{aligned}&S_{M_{i+1}}(k)\\ &= \left[Q_{i+1}(k+1)^{-1} + A_{i+1}(k)\ Q_{i+1}(k)^{-1}\ A_{i+1}(k)^T\right.\\ &\quad\left.+ B_{i+1}(k)\ R_{i+1}(k)^{-1}\ B_{i+1}(k)^T\right]^{-1}\end{aligned} \tag{27}$$

$$S_{ML_{i+1}}(k) =$$
$$= - A_{i+1}(k)\, Q_{i+1}(k)^{-1}\, \underline{x}^*_{i+1}(k)$$
$$+ Q_{i+1}(k+1)^{-1}\, \underline{x}^*_{i+1}(k+1)$$
$$- B_{i+1}(k)\, R_{i+1}(k)^{-1}\, \underline{u}^*_{i+1}(k)\,. \tag{28}$$

Substituting (26), (27) and (28) in (21), expressions are obtained for $T_i(k)$ and $\hat{\underline{z}}_{i+1}(k)$

$$T_i(k) = S_{i+1}(k) + S_{M_{i+1}}(k) \tag{29}$$

$$\hat{\underline{z}}_{i+1}(k) = \underline{z}^*_{i+1}(k) + S_{M_{i+1}}(k)\, S_{ML_{i+1}}(k)\,. \tag{30}$$

It will be noticed that the terms $T_i(k)$ and $\hat{\underline{z}}_{i+1}(k)$ contain all the relevant parameters of the immediately upstream system . $T_i(k)$ is also a symmetric positive definite matrix.

If these relationships for $T_i(k)$ and $\hat{\underline{z}}_{i+1}(k)$ are used the solutions will be suboptimal since certain terms have been ignored. The degree of suboptimality was investigated for several examples by Drew [62] and the method appeared to give good results. Figs.8 and 9 show the algorithmic structure of the optimal and suboptimal schemes.

10. MORE GENERAL STRUCTURES

We have so far considered an important class of systems and developed useful control algorithms for this class. In the next chapter we will consider the application of the basic idea to a practical steel rolling problem. Here we continue our study of suboptimal methods for large scale systems by considering more general structures than serially connected systems. Most of the techniques that we shall describe are fairly well known in the literature so our study will be quite brief. We shall consider essentially three different approaches. The first of these is the aggregation approach which was first considered in the control context by Aoki [63] . The second is the singular perturbation method described by Kokotovic [64, 65] and the final one is the suboptimal constrained decentralised controller of Wang [67] .

10.1. Aggregation [63]

In the aggregation approach of Aoki [63] an attempt is made to represent the overall system of high order n by another system of much lower order l. The state vector $\underline{x}$ and $\underline{y}$ of the large system model and the low order model are assumed to be related by

$$\underline{y} = H\underline{x} \tag{31}$$

where H is an l x n constant matrix called the aggregation matrix. Thus if the system model with state vector $\underline{x}$ is a description of a physical or non-physical object according to some classification of variables then the system model with the state vector $\underline{y}$ is a description of the same object using a coarser grid of classification. This is the intuitive reason why $n \gg l$.

Let the high order system be described by

$$\dot{\underline{x}} = A\underline{x} + B\underline{u} \tag{32}$$

where the control $\underline{u}$ is to be chosen such that the following quadratic performance index is minimised

$$J = \int_0^\infty (\|\underline{x}\|_Q^2 + \|\underline{u}\|_R^2)\, dt \tag{33}$$

The lower dimensional system which is related to the above system by the aggregation matrix can be written as

$$\dot{\underline{y}} = F\underline{y} + G\,\underline{u} \tag{34}$$

where it is desired to minimise

$$J = \int_0^\infty (\|\underline{y}\|_{Q_M}^2 + \|\underline{u}\|_R^2)\, dt \tag{35}$$

The low order optimisation problem can be solved and its optimal solution can be transformed back to the original system. Aoki [63] has shown that if the original system is weakly coupled as defined by Milne [68] then the optimal control for the aggregated system maps into a good suboptimal control for the original system.

It remains to choose the aggregation matrix H. For $\underline{y}$ to satisfy equation (34) subject to $\underline{y}(0) = H\underline{x}(0)$, F and G must be related to A and B by

$$FH = HA \tag{36}$$

$$G = HB \tag{37}$$

where if A and H satisfy the matrix equation

$$HA = HAH^T (HH^T)^{-1} H$$

then

$$F = HAH^T (HH^T)^{-1} \tag{38}$$

the matrix F given by equation (36) retains some of the characteristic values of A.

One method of choosing H is by considering the controllability matrices, (for more details of the concept of controllability cf. [55]) i.e.

$$W_A = [B,\ AB, \ldots\ A^{n-1}B]$$

$$W_F = [G,\ FG, \ldots\ F^{n-1}G]$$

then

$$H = W_F W_A^T (W_A W_A^T)^{-1} \tag{39}$$

Thus by specifying $F = \mathrm{diag}\,(\lambda_1, \ldots, \lambda_1)$ and choosing G so as to make (34) completely controllable, C is given by (39). We also need to have a Q_M in equation (35) for the low order controller. Aoki shows that a good choice of Q_M is

$$Q_M = (HH^T)^{-1} HQH^T (HH^T)^{-1} \tag{40}$$

Comment

The above approach works rather well for weakly coupled systems. The main idea differs from our underlying concern of providing decentralised control in the sense that the present method considers the overall system as such without bothering about decomposition or utilising any subsystem structure which may exist. We next consider the perturbation methods which have been formulated in the same centralised spirit although as with the aggregation approach, they enable us to obtain solutions to large scale problems.

11. SOLUTION OF RICCATI EQUATIONS BY PERTURBATION METHODS

Since in solving the optimisation problem of large scale systems, the main computational difficulty arises in the solution of the high order Riccati equation, it may be worthwhile to approximate the solution in some way. Consider for example the nth order system

$$\dot{\underline{x}} = F\underline{x} + G\underline{u} \qquad (41)$$

and it is desired to find the control $\underline{u}$ which minimises

$$J = \int_0^T (\underline{x}^T Q\underline{x} + \underline{u}^T\underline{u})\, dt \qquad (42)$$

Then the Riccati equation for this overall system is

$$\begin{aligned} \dot{P} &= - PF - F^T P - PG\, G^T P + Q \\ P(T) &= 0 \end{aligned} \qquad (43)$$

Let us assume that the overall system consists of two subsystems which are weakly coupled,i.e. they can be described by

$$\begin{bmatrix} \dot{x}_1 \\ \dot{x}_2 \end{bmatrix} = \begin{bmatrix} F_{11} & F_{12} \\ F_{21} & F_{22} \end{bmatrix} \begin{bmatrix} x_1 \\ x_2 \end{bmatrix} + \begin{bmatrix} G_{11} & \epsilon G_{12} \\ \epsilon G_{21} & G_{22} \end{bmatrix} \begin{bmatrix} u_1 \\ u_2 \end{bmatrix} \qquad (44)$$

where ϵ is a scalar parameter which is assumed to be small. The matrix Q in the performance index could be partitioned as

$$Q = \begin{bmatrix} Q_{11} & \epsilon Q_{12} \\ \epsilon Q_{12}^T & Q_{22} \end{bmatrix} \qquad (45)$$

and the associated Riccati equation solution as

$$P = \begin{bmatrix} P_{11} & P_{12} \\ P_{12}^T & P_{22} \end{bmatrix} \qquad (46)$$

Let $P^* = P$ when $\epsilon = 0$ and $P^*_\epsilon = \frac{\partial P}{\partial \epsilon}$ when $\epsilon = 0$. Then it is easy to show that P is analytic in ϵ and can be expanded by a MacLaurin's series, i.e.

$$P = P^* + \epsilon P^*_\epsilon + \text{higher order terms} \qquad (47)$$

Note that $$P^* = \begin{bmatrix} P^*_{11} & 0 \\ 0 & P^*_{22} \end{bmatrix} \qquad (48)$$

and

$$P_\epsilon^* = \begin{bmatrix} 0 & P_{12\epsilon}^* \\ P_{12\epsilon}^{*T} & 0 \end{bmatrix} \tag{49}$$

where

$$-\dot{P}_{11}^* = P_{11}^* F_1 + F_1^T P_{11}^* - P_{11}^* G_1 G_1^T P_{11}^* + Q_{11} \tag{50}$$

with $P_{11}^*(T) = 0$

$$-\dot{P}_{22}^* = P_{22}^* F_{22}{}^T P_{22}^* - P_{22}^* G_{22} G_{22}{}^T P_{22}^* + Q_{22} \tag{51}$$

with $P_2^*(T) = 0$

and

$$-\dot{P}_{12\epsilon}^* = P_{12\epsilon}^* (F_{22} - G_{22} G_{22}^T P_{22}^*) + (F_1 - G_1 G_1^T P_1^*)^T P_{12\epsilon}^*$$

$$+ P_{11}^* F_{12} + F_{21}^T P_{22}^* - P_{11}^* (G_{11} G_{21}^T + G_{12} G_{22}^T) P_{22}^* + Q_{12} \tag{52}$$

Thus the zeroth order approximation to the high order Riccati equation is given by solving equations (50), (51) and the 1st order by also solving equation (52) in which case

$$P = P^* + \epsilon P_\epsilon^* \tag{53}$$

It is possible to add further terms in the MacLarin's series without too much additional computation. Examples of the use of the technique are given in [64, 65] .

12. SYSTEMS WITH STRONG COUPLING

In the previous section we considered the approximate control of weakly coupled dynamical systems. However, a much more interesting class of problems is the one where the system dynamics are strongly coupled. In such cases also it is possible to use singular perturbation methods. In this context, the methods are conceptually quite closely related to the aggregation approach described in Section 10. The idea behind the approximation is that physically systems have some time constants which are much faster than others so that their effect on the system dynamics is negligible. In frequency domain terms, some of the poles of the system transfer function may be far to the left in the left half plane with their residues in a partial fraction expansion being very small. The approximation involves neglecting these poles.

As a first step let us express all the time constants in terms of parameter ϵ where ϵ is assumed to have a known small value for the given system. When the states associated with the small time constants are denoted by $\underline{z}$, the high order system description turns out to have the form

$$\begin{bmatrix} \dot{\underline{x}} \\ \epsilon \dot{\underline{z}} \end{bmatrix} = \begin{bmatrix} F_1 & F_2 \\ F_3 & F_4 \end{bmatrix} \begin{bmatrix} \underline{x} \\ \underline{z} \end{bmatrix} + \begin{bmatrix} G_1 \\ G_2 \end{bmatrix} \underline{u}$$

where ϵ is very much less than unity.

If we set $\epsilon = 0$, this has the effect of neglecting the fast time constants in equation (54). This reduces the order of the system since $\underline{z}$ in now related to $\underline{x}$ and $\underline{u}$ through an algebraic equation. Thus if F_4 is invertible

$$F_3\underline{x} + F_4\underline{z} + G_2\underline{u} = 0$$

or

$$\underline{z} = - F_4^{-1} (F_3\underline{x} + G_2\underline{u}) \tag{55}$$

so that

$$\underline{\dot{x}} = (F_1 - F_2F_4^{-1} F_3)\, \underline{x} + (G_1 - F_2\, F_4^{-1}\, G_2)\, \underline{u} \tag{56}$$

It can be shown [66] that the solutions $\underline{x}(t,\epsilon)$, $\underline{z}(t,\epsilon)$ of equation (54) approach the solutions $\underline{x}(t)$, $\underline{z}(t)$ of (55) and (56) as $\epsilon \rightarrow 0$ if the eigenvalues of $F\ \underline{u}$ have -ive real parts for all t as one would expect. This approximation where we neglect the fast poles is called the zeroth order approximation. In [65] Kokotovic has shown that this zeroth order approximation can be improved by the method of matched asymptotic expansions.

Desoer and Shensa [66] developed this idea further by considering systems of the form

$$\begin{bmatrix} \underline{\dot{x}} \\ \epsilon\underline{\dot{y}} \\ \mu\underline{\dot{z}} \end{bmatrix} = \begin{bmatrix} A_{11} & A_{12} & A_{13} \\ A_{21} & A_{22} & A_{23} \\ A_{31} & A_{32} & A_{33} \end{bmatrix} \begin{bmatrix} \underline{x} \\ \underline{y} \\ \underline{z} \end{bmatrix} \tag{57}$$

where the states $\underline{x}$, $\underline{y}$ and $\underline{z}$ correspond to the normal, high and low frequency parts of the system. Then it is possible to have the following approximations

$$\text{Mid Frequency Approximation :} \begin{cases} \underline{\dot{x}} = A_{11}\underline{x} + A_{12}\underline{y} \\ \underline{0} = A_{21}\underline{x} + A_{22}\underline{y} \end{cases} \tag{58}$$

High Frequency Approximation :

$$\epsilon\, \underline{\dot{y}} = A_{22}\underline{y} \tag{59}$$

and Low Frequency Approximation

$$\begin{aligned} \underline{0} &= A_{11}\underline{x} + A_{12}\underline{y} + A_{13}\underline{z} \\ \underline{0} &= A_{21}\underline{x} + A_{22}\underline{y} + A_{23}\underline{z} \\ \underline{\dot{z}} &= A_{31}\underline{x} + A_{32}\underline{y} + A_{33}\underline{z} \end{aligned} \tag{60}$$

Each of these approximations could be useful, depending on the region of interest.

Desoer and Shensa also show that if the approximations in equations (58), (59) and (60) represent stable systems then there exist some positive numbers ϵ_0 and μ_0 such that the overall system given by equations (57) is asymptotically stable for any ϵ in $(0, \epsilon_0)$ and any μ in (μ_0, ∞). This result is useful in that it provides justification for separately designing the high, low and normal frequency components of large scale systems. A good example of this would be the independent design of the boiler, turbine, etc. of a steam generation plant.

12.1. Comment

In the last three sections we have considered more general dynamical systems and outlined some approaches to providing good suboptimal control. In the various approximations considered, no attempt was made to utilise the underlying subsystem structure of the system. In each case we were able to solve our problem by reducing the order of the model and thus the complexity of the calculation. However, the controls for the overall system were eventually implemented centrally. We next consider a decentralised control scheme where the controls are implemented in a completely decentralised fashion.

13. THE DECENTRALISED SUBOPTIMAL CONTROLLER OF WANG [67]

We found in our optimal hierarchical control studies that although the overall systems control calculation was performed within a decentralised hierarchical structure, the implementation was either open loop as in Part I or centralised as in Part II where a feedback control was developed. In fact if we want to implement optimal feedback control for large scale systems it must necessarily be centralised. The reason for this is that optimal control requires a feedback of all the states and this means that each subsystem controller not only has a feedback of its own states but also a feedback of the other subsystem's states. Decentralisation of implementation requires the severance of the feedback links from the other subsystems and this will clearly provide suboptimal control which may not even be able to stabilise the subsystems.

Hence it is not meaningful to talk of providing optimal control if the implementation has to be decentralised. It is sometimes necessary to use a decentralised implementation scheme because for large scale systems which are widely distributed in space like our river example, the main cost of implementation of the control may well lie in the telemetry links necessary to transmit the current state of the various subsystems to each other. For example, the subsystems in the case of the river could easily be separated by a few kilometers. Thus the actual subsystem controllers might consist of a few inexpensive electronic components, whilst the main cost lies in the transmission of the B.O.D. and D.O. data between the subsystems.

With this in mind, let us consider the overall system described by the state space equations

$$\dot{\underline{x}} = A\underline{x} + B\underline{u}$$
$$\underline{x}(t_0) = \underline{x}_0 \tag{61}$$

where $\underline{x}$ and $\underline{y}$ could be partitioned as

$$\underline{x} = \begin{bmatrix} \underline{x}^1 \\ \underline{x}^2 \\ \cdot \\ \cdot \\ \underline{x}^r \end{bmatrix}, \qquad \underline{u} = \begin{bmatrix} \underline{u}^1 \\ \underline{u}^2 \\ \cdot \\ \cdot \\ \underline{u}^r \end{bmatrix}$$

and

$$A = \begin{bmatrix} A_{11} & A_{12} & \cdots\cdots & A_{1r} \\ A_{21} & A_{22} & \cdots\cdots & A_{2r} \\ \vdots & \vdots & & \vdots \\ A_{r1} & A_{r2} & & A_{rr} \end{bmatrix}$$

$$B = \begin{bmatrix} B_{11} & & 0 \\ & B_{22} & \\ 0 & & B_{rr} \end{bmatrix}$$

For the decentralised "optimal" control of such a system w.r.t. a suitable criterion function one would expect the control law to be in general non-linear, time varying and initial state dependent, i.e. of the form

$$\underline{u} = \underline{f}\ (\underline{x}, \underline{x}_0, t)$$

However, it is difficult to implement such a control law because (a) it is necessary to use complex non-linear function generators in the feedback path which are expensive, (b) the time varying nature of the feedback parameters means that it will be necessary to store them on tapes or generate them in some way by a computer. Moreover, they have to be in sychronisation with each other and with real time and (c) the dependence on the initial condition means that whenever these change, it will be necessary to recalculate the control.

For all these reasons, it is desirable that the control law be constrained to be of the form

$$\underline{u} = K\underline{x} \tag{62}$$

where K is time invariant and independent of the initial state. Also, decentralisation requires that K be of the form

$$K = \begin{bmatrix} K_{11} & & 0 \\ & \ddots & \\ 0 & & K_{rr} \end{bmatrix}$$ i.e. that it be block diagonal.

So far we have not specified how we should calculate the feedback matrix K since clearly just any diagonal matrix will not do. It is useful to choose a K which minimises a suitable objective function. If the objective function is chosen to be

$$J = \int_0^\infty (\tfrac{1}{2}\, \|\underline{x}\|_Q^2 + \tfrac{1}{2}\, \|\underline{u}\|_R^2)\, dt \tag{63}$$

as in the case of the standard regulator then we know that it is not possible to find a decentralised control law which minimises J and which is linear and independent of $\underline{x}_0$.

However, for an arbitrary K (decentralised or otherwise), the minimum cost is given by

$$J = (\underline{u}, \underline{x}_0) = \underline{x}_0^T P\, \underline{x}_0 \qquad \text{for all} \quad \underline{x}_0 \tag{64}$$

where

$$P = \int_0^\infty \left[e^{(A+BK)t}\right]^T (Q + K^T RK) \left[e^{(A+BK)t}\right] dt \qquad (65)$$

and where P is the constant positive definite symmetric solution of the linear equation

$$(A + BK)^T P + P(A + BK) + K^T RK + Q = 0 \qquad (66)$$

This suggests one useful way of finding K is that if K is determined by minimising the trace of P then this has the effect of minimising the average value of J in equation (63) as x_0 varies over the surface of a unit sphere (cf. Athans and Kleinman [69]).

This has another useful property that the trace of P^* corresponding to the optimal K which minimises (63) is a lower bound on the trace of the suboptimal P which we are trying to find. Wang [67] gives a set of necessary conditions and a suitable algorithm for solving these to give the suboptimal decentralised gain matrix. However, his main method requires an iterative solution of a centralised problem for a decentralised implementation. The latter may not always be feasible Thus here we see the converse of the optimal approach of Part II where the calculation was decentralised although the implementation was centralised.

14. DISCUSSION

In this chapter we have considered a number of suboptimal control methods for large scale systems. In some of these, the structure of the overall system was used to provide approximate control which required little calculation whilst in others the state space was reduced in some way. In the first category we could put the analysis of serial systems and the decentralised controller of Wang. The aggregation approach of Aoki and the singular perturbation methods are good examples of the second. In each case the resulting control is not far from optimal so such approaches are well worth considering if one is confronted with a practical problem which

(a) has a special structure (for example a serial structure)
or (b) where it is necessary to implement a decentralised control
or (c) where suitable model reduction through aggregation or singular perturbations is feasible.

In the next chapter we discuss the application of the serial systems concept for the control of a practical problem, i.e. a hot steel rolling mill.

CHAPTER VII

HOT STEEL ROLLING

1. INTRODUCTION

In this chapter we describe the application of the concept used in Chapter VIto a practical problem. The problem is that of controlling the output temperature and thickness of the strip from the roughing process of a hot steel rolling mill. The mill concerned is at the Spencer Works, Newport of the British Steel Corporation. The problem is that the finishing process, which is linked to the output of the roughing mill, is computer controlled and has good control performance provided the output temperature and thickness of the slabs from the roughing process are accurate. At present the temperature and thickness control of the roughing process is manual and for most steels good control can be achieved by trial and error on the part of experienced operators, but there is much wastage and such manual control is uneconomic for small batch rollingfrom several furnaces. Automation of the roughing process would eliminate these disadvantages. However, on-line dynamic optimisation for this process is not possible for two reasons :

(a) because of the high dimensionality,and

(b) the actual time available for the calculations is very small since four stands have to be processed through six roll slabs in less than a minute.

It is therefore necessary to use decomposition techniques to achieve decentralised control. For optimal decentralised control infeasible methods are inapplicable because of the fast dynamics of the system whilst feasible methods are also inapplicable since the subsystems (rollstands) have two interconnection variables (temperature and thickness) but only one control (screw down). There are therefore no existing methods which can be used in practice to achieve the overall optimum control on-line so here again one has to resort to suboptimum control. However, the system is of the favourable serial type and the strategy of Chapter VI can be applied so that near optimal control may be achieved. The work described in this chapter used the model and detailed digital simulation of the roughing process of Spencer Works developed by Eaglen [70] .

1.1. A Description of the Roughing Process at Spencer Works

The hot strip rolling process of the Spencer Works, Newport of British Steel Corporation consists of a set of reheating furnaces, a roughing process, an automated finishing process and a coiler. The main difficulty at present associated with the automated finishing process is that of temperature disturbances which occur at the finishing process input. These disturbances are caused by skid marks, the longitudinal temperature gradient and the resulting average temperature of the slab. In the steel rolling industry compensation for roughing process output temperature variations is usually achieved by controlling the finishing mill thread speed and the spread of these variations is reduced by computer control of furnace heating. At Spencer Works, both of these methods are employed but do not give the degree of control demanded by close specification of finishing requirements on small batches. In fact, skid marks can be removed only by redesigning the reheating furnace supporting skids, but the longitudinal temperature gradient can be controlled by modulating either the water descaling sprays or the thickness reduction pattern or both ; these also determine the mean temperature level. The primary purpose of the water descaling sprays is the removal of oxide scale, however, and temperature control through the sprays may reduce the efficiency of this process. It was decided here, therefore, to control the output temperature from the last roll stand of the roughing process by changing the thickness reduction pattern*. The roughing process consists of a set of six horizontal rolls and six vertical rolls as shown in Fig. 1.Each set of horizontal rolls is powered by a large (7000 H.P.) synchronous motor and the vertical rolls by smaller (100 H.P.) D.C. motors. In front of each set of horizontal rolls is a pair of water descaling sprays which have the side effect of cooling the slabs.

Slabs entering the roughing process are 5 inches to 10 inches thick, 30 inches to 60 inches wide and 15 to 30 feet long. If the output material from the roughing process is 1 inch thick then the present control system of the subsequent finishing process at Spencer Works is capable of operating effectively. Therefore 1 inch is taken as the desired output thickness from the roughing process, whilst the desired output temperature is determined indirectly by the desired gauge from the finishing process. It should be noted that large reductions of thickness at earlier stands of the roughing process reduce the temperature of slabs at the entry to the finishing process and increase the power level at the earlier stands. Smaller reductions at the earlier stands reduce the rate of heat loss and this results in higher temperature at the later roughing stands. Thus there is sufficient flexibility within the roughing process operation for all but the largest slabs and this flexibility allows the output temperature from the last roughing stand to be controlled by changing the thickness reduction pattern within the process constraints, thereby minimising the temperature disturbances at the finishing process input. Objections to schemes which attempt to vary the roughing process reduction patterns to control temperatures often centre on their acceptability to operators. However on-line computer control should allow the operators to intervene only in special cases such as for bent slabs, thereby reducing their work load.

2. OFF-LINE CALCULATION OF THE ROUGHING PROCESS THICKNESS REDUCTION PATTERN

The overall control strategy adopted here consists basically of two parts. In the first nominal "optimum" settings for the control parameters are computed off-line. In the second part of the strategy the deviations of temperatures from their nominally optimal values are measured as the process evolves and used to adjust, on-line, the control parameters using the serial systems control approach developed in Chapter VI.

To achieve the desired temperature and thickness out of the last roughing stand, R5, it is necessary to have a controller which changes the thickness reduction pattern in the roughing process. Initially a nominal thickness reduction pattern is chosen which transforms a slab of thickness H_0 and average temperature T_0 into a slab of thickness h^*_{R5} and temperature T^*_{R5} at the roughing process output. This choice can be made either by storing the reduction pattern used in present practice for each transformation, or by designing an algorithm to calculate automatically the reduction pattern for a minimum value of some cost function. At the same time, this algorithm could also compute the desired values of power, output temperature and thickness at each roughing stand.

The actual algorithm used was one of steepest descent with a penalty function for the violation of process constraints. These process constraints arise sin-

* It should be note that this is an unusual way of controlling the rolling mill. However, with all the control mechanisms used at present, closed output specification is not achieved for small batches and this provided the main motivation for using the thickness reduction pattern in the roughing process as an additional control mechanism.

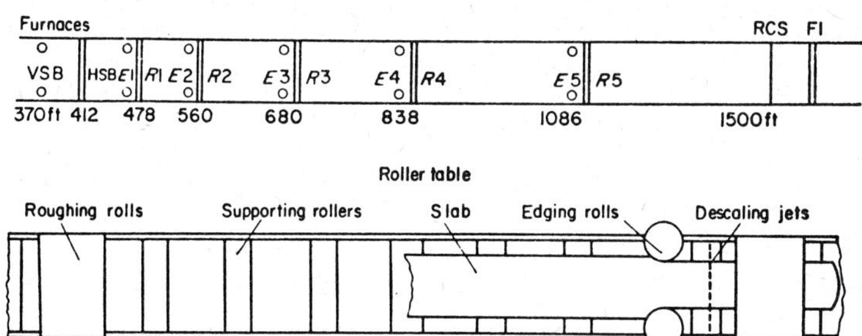

Fig. 1 : Spencer works, roughing process layout and roller-table detail

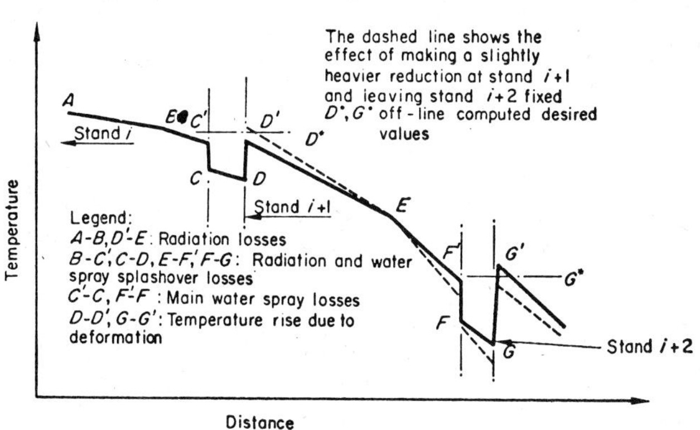

Fig. 2 : Temperature profile of a slab element over the (i+1)th stage

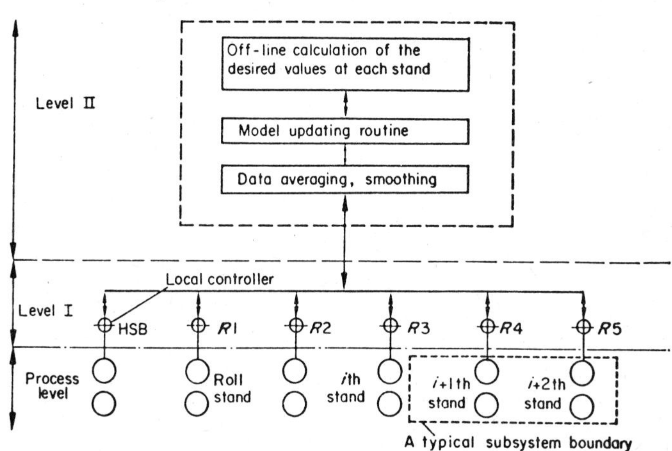

Fig. 3 : The hierarchical structure showing the (i+1)th stage or subsystem

ce roll-gaps can never produce negative reductions and there are maximum reductions, determined by entry conditions, or power constraints, which must never be exceeded.

2.1. The Cost Function

It is desired to find reduction patterns which transform slabs from their initial state, i.e. slab thickness and temperature, to the required state of output temperature T^{*}_{R5} and thickness h^{*}_{R5}. At Spencer Works, a constant output thickness is preferred as this enables better control of the finishing process. In obtaining the reduction pattern, it is desirable to maintain a power pattern along the roughing stands so as not to overload the driving motors. In addition, the "shape" of the finished strip appears to be unfavourably influenced by large departures from a base roughing reduction pattern (and the corresponding power pattern) which is similar to the one used in current mill practice.

Several different cost functions, all based upon the error-squared form, were tried and the one given below was found to be most satisfactory for calculating the roughing process reduction patterns corresponding to present practice.

$$C = C_1 \cdot (T_{R5}-T^{*}_{R5})^2 + C_2 \cdot \sum_{i=1}^{6} (P_i-\overline{P}) - (c_i-\overline{c})^{2} \qquad (1)$$

where the symbols have the following meaning :

- C : cost
- C_1 : temperature error weighting coefficient
- T_{R5} : R5 calculated output temperature averaged along the slab
- T^{*}_{R5} : desired R5 output temperature averaged along the slab
- P_i : calculated rolling power at each roughing stand averaged along the slab
- P : average calculated rolling power for the six roughing stands ,i.e. $\frac{1}{6} \sum_{i=1}^{6} P_i$
- c_i : power shaping coefficient for each stand corresponding to the desired power pattern
- $\overline{c}$: average shaping coefficient for each stand $c = \sum_{i=1}^{6} c_i/6$
- c_2 : power error weighting coefficient
- i : stand index number 1 : HSB;2 ; R1;3 ; R2;4 ; R3;5 ; R4;6 ; R5

(in current mill practice stand 1 is called the horizontal scale breaker (H.S.B.) and stands 2-6 are called the Roughers 1 to 5).

In choosing C_1 and C_2 greater weight can be given either to errors in the R5 output temperature or errors in the power pattern. The power pattern of the roughing stands is determined by the coefficients c_i and $\overline{c}$ in equation (1) and all these coefficients are independent of the slab being rolled. Therefore by manipulating these coefficients, a power pattern corresponding to good mill practice can be achieved.

When rolling thinner slabs the HSB reduction can be set to zero and then the optimisation can be performed with respect to four thicknesses instead of five. Although the desired output thickness from R5 is at present 1 inch, this could be included as a control input by the addition of a term $C_3\ (h_{R5}-h^{*}_{R5})^2$ in the cost function. Further improvements, such as holding the slabs on the roller tables to reduce the temperature and the minimisation of rolling energy $\sum_{i=1}^{6} p_i . t_i$ where t_i is the time during which stand i is operating on the slab, could also be included at the expense of longer computation.

2.2. The Model

Mathematical equations have been developed by Eaglen [70] to represent the characteristics of the Spencer Works roughing process. Each equation is derived in terms of the average values of the process variables along a pre-determined length of each slab, and the coefficients of the process equations are estimated by an on-line algorithm. The process equations used to calculate the powers and temperatures at each stand are :

The temperature drop equation :

$$T_{1i} = T_{0(i-1)} + 460 - \sqrt[3]{\frac{(T_{0(i-1)} + 460)^3 H_i}{H_i + 6k_i I_i (T_{0(i-1)} + 460)^3}} \qquad (2)$$

Input temperature to next stand :

$$T_{3i} = T_{0(i-1)} - T_{1i} - T_{2i} \qquad (3)$$

Stand power :

$$P_i = \frac{n_i s_i (H_i - h_i) W_i}{T_{3i}} \qquad (4)$$

Temperature rise due to deformation ;

$$T_{4i} = \frac{I_i P_i}{W_i (H_i - h_i)} \sqrt[2]{\frac{H_i}{h_i}} \qquad (5)$$

Slab temperature at the stand output

$$T_{5i} = T_{3i} + T_{4i} - T_{6i} \qquad (6)$$

Note that $T_{5i} = T_{0i}$

where the symbols indicate the following :

i	:	label number of the stand about to roll
i-1	:	label number of the previous stand
T_{0i}	:	i^{th} stand output temperature (°F)
T_{1i}	:	radiation temperature drop from the $(i-1)^{th}$ stand to the ith stand (°F)
T_{2i}	:	i^{th} stand water spray temperature drop (°F)
T_{3i}	:	i^{th} stand input temperature (°F)
T_{4i}	:	i^{th} stand temperature rise due to deformation (°F)

* In equation (2), time appears explicity as I_i. This equation is the solution to the non-linear differential equation called the Stefan's radiation equation.

T_{5i} : i^{th} stand output temperature (°F)

T_{6i} : i^{th} stand temperature drop due to conduction to the rolls (°F)

H_i : slab input thickness at the ith stand (inches)

h_i : slab output thickness at the ith stand (inches)

I_i : time between stages i and i +1 (secs.)

P_i : roll power to stand i (Kw)

W_i : slab width at stand i output (inches)

k_i : radiation heat loss coefficient from the $(i-1)^{th}$ to the ith stand $(in/(°F)^3 sec.)$

l_i : coefficient for temperature rise due to deformation at output of ith stand $(in/(°F)^3$ sec.)

n_i : roll speed coefficient for i^{th} stand (ft.rad/sec.)

s_i : slab hardness coefficient at the output of ith stand ($n_i.s_i$ in Kw.°F $(in)^{-2}$)

The slab temperatures are averaged both along and across the cross section of each slab. Estimates of the coefficients describing the physical properties of each slab are required as input data.

This simple model has been developed by Eaglen [70] in addition to a more detailed digital simulation of the Spencer Works roughing process. The simple model is quite adequate for both the off-line and on-line control studies as shown by the examples in this and the next section. The detailed simulation, however, is valuable in assessing the performance of the controls.

2.3. Off-Line Optimisation

In order to establish a reasonable set of component cost coefficients, a series of roughing process simulation tests were undertaken with the specific reduction patterns used at Spencer Works. The powers, thicknesses and temperatures at each stand, corresponding to an element half way along each slab, were recorded and the coefficients necessary for the above mathematical equations were then calculated. With these coefficients incorporated into the process equations, a series of hill-climbing trials were undertaken to determine the set of cost function component coefficientsso that the reduction patterns corresponding to minimum costs were similar to those used at present at Spencer Works. When a suitable set of cost function coefficients had been determined, another series of tests were used to ensure that the reduction patterns computed for slabs with different input states and different demanded R5 output temperatures to the ones used in the first tests, corresponded to reduction patterns that would be used in practice. From the reductions,the corresponding nominal (optimal) screw position pattern is easily computed using equation (9) below. This allows for a stand-housing stretch of approximately one tenth of an inch. (Usually the loaded roll-gap equation is derived in terms of the roll-force. However, since the Spencer Works roughing process does not have load-cells on the first five roughing stands, Eaglen [70] derived this equation as a function of the roll-power).

2.4. Results of the Off-Line Optimisation

Table 0 gives measured rougher roll powers which have been used to calculate the coefficients of the cost function in equation (1). These measured values are also used for comparing the departure of the calculated roll powers from the measured ones where the departure at any stand is referred to as the power pattern error.

Tables 1 to 4 show how the calculated R5 output temperature approaches the desired value T^*_{R5} when the cost is minimised by hill-climbing on the reduction pattern for various conditions.

Table 1 shows the output thickness, temperature and roll power at each stand for the minimum cost solution for the test where the average cross-sectional temperature at furnace release is 2200°F and the desired R5 output temperature is 2065°F. The calculated R5 temperature error for the minimum cost is +0.4 °F, and the errors in the power pattern are approximately 5 %. The thickness reduction pattern and temperature pattern from this test are used in the on-line control system developed in Section 3.

Table 2 is for the test where the desired R5 output temperature is now reduced to 2050° F. In this test the temperature cost coefficient is unchanged. With this value the output temperature error is 3.8°F and the maximum power patterns error is 30 %.

When a lower R5 output temperature is required, improvements in the power pattern can be obtained either by delaying the slab on a roller-table or releasing the slab from the furnace at a lower temperature. However, the present off-line control strategy increases the thickness reductions at earlier stands to decrease the R5 output temperature and decreases these reductions to produce higher R5 output temperatures. It is interesting to note that the R4 output temperature is greater in this test than in the test shown in Table 1, but as the R4 output gauge is less, the faster cooling of thinner material results in a lower R5 output temperature so that the desired effect is achieved.

Table 3 is for a slab with a lower furnace release temperature of 2180°F and a desired R5 output temperature of 2065°F. A comparison of this reduction pattern with that from Table 1 shows that the reductions at earlier stands have been reduced in order to conserve heat. An output temperature of 2062°F is obtained and the power pattern error is 10 % for every stand.

Table 4 shows that in some cases, even when the weight of the temperature cost function component is reduced, it is still possible to reach the desired R5 output temperature by correctly choosing the power level at each stand. The temperature error is 3°F and the power pattern error is less than 3 %.However, if the desired R5 temperature is now changed, the minimisation of the cost function will not yield a thickness reduction pattern to produce a slab near the desired R5 temperature, as the demanded power pattern dominates the total cost.

Now that the static desired values for the temperature, thickness and power at each roll have been determined, it is possible to apply on-line control in order to attenuate the effects of disturbances to which the process is normally subjected.

O/P Output
O/P gauge in inches
O/P temperature in °F
Roll-power in Kwatts

Table 0

Desired Roll Power	Stand
2800 Kw	HSB
2811 Kw	R1
4690 Kw	R2
6333 Kw	R3
4630 Kw	R4
5170 Kw	R5

O/P Gauge	O/P Temperature	Roll-power	Stand
7.59	2186.5	2840	HSB
5.76	2172.5	2997	R1
4.17	2159.7	4672	R2
2.60	2150.8	6204	R3
1.70	2117.3	4433	R4
1.00	2065.4	4791	R5

Table 1

Minimum Cost 20.216

Slab dimensions 9.4 in. x 38.5 in x 30 ft.
Furnace release temperature 2200°F
Desired R5 output temperature 2065°F
Initial reduction pattern 9.4 5.58 4.02 2.16 1.57 1.0
Cost function coefficients C_1=5, C_2 = 0.0001
Step length 0.01 in.

O/P Gauge	O/P temperature	Roll-power	Stand
7.65	2185.9	2717	HSB
5.56	21.74.6	3449	R1
3.90	2163.9	4936	R2
2.34	2157.0	6115	R3
1.51	2122.1	4077	R4
1.00	2053.8	3464	R5

Table 2

Minimum Cost 399.6

Furnace release temperature 2200°F
Desired R5 output temperature 2050°F
Cost function coefficients C_1=5, C_2=0.0001

O/P Gauge	O/P Temperature	Roll-power	Stand
7.79	2186.9	2525	HSB
6.21	2149.3	2643	R1
4.58	2136.2	4820	R2
2.92	2127.3	6621	R3
1.92	2097.1	5063	R4
1.00	2062.2	6241	R5

Table 3

Minimum Cost is 156.13

Cost function coefficients C_1=5, C_2=0.0001
Furnace release temperature : 2180°F
Desired R5 temperature : 2065°F

O/P Gauge	O/P Temperature	Roll-power	Stand
7.56	2186.9	2862	HSB
5.84	2171.7	2846	R1
4.25	2158.5	4645	R2
2.67	2149.8	6316	R3
1.74	2116.9	4551	R4
1.00	2067.8	5035	R5

Table 4

Minimum costs is 2.65

Cost function coefficients C_1=0.1, C_2=0.0001
Furnace release temperature : 2200°F
Desired R5 temperature : 2065°F

3. ON-LINE HIERARCHICAL STRATEGY FOR TEMPERATURE CONTROL IN THE ROUGHING PROCESS

3.1. Description of the Hierarchical Control Strategy

The slab furnace release temperature can only be estimated to within ± 20°F. In addition, the metallurgical properties of successive slabs are different and the system is subjected to random disturbances, especially from the water sprays. It is therefore necessary to update the screw positions on-line in order to achieve the required output temperature from R5 (T^*_{R5}). One possible contról strategy would be to start from the off-line screw positions and update these with an on-line procedure after surface temperature measurements* have been made with a pyrometer at the output of the HSB. This would be repeated after each succeeding stand**.

If a hill-climbing method similar to the one developed for the off-line calculation was applied, these screw positions could then be updated after each slab has passed through successive stands. However, in the process computer cycle, there are other functions which must be executed, such as finishing mill control and data-logging, and these reduce the amount of computing time that may be used for roughing process control and optimisation. Since there are up to four slabs in the roughing process at any one time, and for each slab it is necessary to solve a problem with five unknown parameters and up to thirty constraints, it is most probable that this hill-climbing method can never be applied on-line because of its dimensionality.

It is possible to apply the simple hierarchical strategy of Chapter VI, however, since the system has the necessary serial structure. The time lags bet-

* In practice the slab surface temperature can only be reliably estimated at the output of each stand since scale and steam contaminate the pyrometer measurement on the input to each stand.

** Although the hill-climbing procedure is derived in terms of the average cross-sectional output temperature from a stand, Eaglen[70] has shown that this can be accurately related to the surface temperature provided that the surface temperature is measured within 2 seconds of leaving the stand. A simple linear relationship has been derived by him between the slab surface output temperature from a stand and the pyrometer measurement a small distance ahead.

ween the rolls should help by providing extra time for computations. In order to use the strategy, it is necessary to define the serially structured subsystems. The obvious choice is that each subsystem should consist of one roll stand, but this may yield less than near optimal control and it is possible that enough control action may not be available at each stand. For this reason it is necessary to choose the subsystem structure very carefully as discussed in the following subsection.

3.2. Roughing Process Subsystem

It is desired to define a subsystem structure which is such that all the subsystems have a similar level of importance since deviation from this condition would mean that the basic serial systems strategy of Chapter VI may possibly yield somewhat less than optimal performance. The obvious choice of using each roll stand as a subsystem has the undesirable characteristic that more weight may not be placed on performance near the end of the roughing process since it is the final stand's output temperature which is the most important aspect of the control. Another disadvantage of such a subsystem structure is that there may not be enough control action available at latter stands. This is illustrated in Fig. 2 where two temperature trajectories show the effect of perturbing the output thickness at the $(i+1)^{th}$ stand for an element of a slab as it travels from the output of the ith stand to the output of the $(i+2)^{th}$ stand. The dashed line corresponds to a slab with a larger thickness reduction from the $(i+1)^{th}$ stand than that shown by the continuous line. It is seen that the reduction at the $(i+1)^{th}$ stand influences the value of the ordinate D' as well as the rate of fall in temperature between the $(i+1)^{th}$ and $(i+2)^{th}$ stands. Also the temperature deviations $D'-D^*$ and $G'-G^*$ change as the reduction at the $(i+1)^{th}$ stand is modified. D^* and G^* are the values computed off-line.

If a subsystem had been defined from the output of the ith stand to the output of the $(i+1)^{th}$ stand, it would have been possible to achieve the desired output temperature D^* at the $(i+1)^{th}$ stand output by choosing the appropriate reduction at this stand. However, this would not have guaranteed that sufficient control action would be available at the $(i+2)^{th}$ stand to achieve the desired output temperature G^* also, since the fall in temperature between the $(i+1)^{th}$ and $(i+2)^{th}$ stands is a function of the output thickness from the $(i+1)^{th}$ stand.

An alternative subsystem structure which does not suffer from any of the above disadvantages is one where the region between the output of the ith stand and the output of the (i+2)th stand is considered and the control variable is taken to be the screwdown at the (i+1)th stand and the screwdown at the (i+2)th stand is kept constant at the pre-computed desired values as calculated in Section 2. The (i+1)th subsystem is indicated in Fig. 3. The actual control can then be computed by minimising the deviations from the desired temperatures as discussed in the next subsection.

Thus the relationship between the subsystems or stages and the stands is :

Subsystem 1 : corresponds to the region from the output of the furnace to the output of stand 2 (i.e. output of 0 to output of 2)
Subsystem 2 : output of stand 1 to the output of stand 3
subsystem 3 : output of stand 2 to the output of stand 4
subsystem 4 : output of stand 3 to the output of stand 5
subsystem 5 : output of stand 4 to the output of stand 6

The proposed hierarchical control structure for the roughing process as shown in Fig. 3 is described in detail below.

3.3. The Hierarchical Control Structure

The hierarchical control structure consists of two levels. Level I is the lower level, consisting of a local controller for each of the five subsystems. Each controller computes the necessary control action (output thickness) in order to minimise the cost function given by equation (7) below.

Level II, the higher level controller, has three tasks which enable the Level I controllers to compute the local control action. A general description of the hierarchical structure is given here and its implementation on the roughing process simulation is discussed in Section 4.

Level II Controller

The first task of the Level II controller is to compute the arithmetic mean values of thickness, temperature and roll-power from on-line measurements along a part of the slab length at the output of the ith stand for each slab. It has been found by Eaglen [70] that it is quite adequate to take the arithmetic mean values of temperature, thickness and roll-power if the front end of each slab is not considered. These average values are then used as input data for the Level I controller and input data for the computation of the process parameters at the $(i+1)^{th}$ stand. In the second task of the level II controller, the slab hardness and water-descaling spray effectiveness (cooling capability) are updated from stand to stand and slab to slab by inverting the deterministic process equations (2 to 6). The updated values for the $(i+1)^{th}$ subsystem are calculated from an equation of the form

$$P_n = P_0 + K (p_c - P_0)$$

where the symbols are as follows :

P_n : updated value of the process parameter

P_0 : previous values of the parameter of the kth subsystem

p_c : computed value for the kth subsystem derived from the first task

K : weighting coefficient to limit the speed of adaptation. 0.25 is approximately the magnitude of this coefficient, as larger values would cause wrongly identified slabs to update the stored values out of range.

In practice, the updating of the process parameters could be done "laterally" from stand to stand and also "vertically" from slab to slab. In this way the off-line calculation would be improved by using the most recently computed values for the process parameters.

The second task of Level II is then to pass the updated parameters, determined at the ith stand to the Level I controller so that the control action at the $(i+1)^{th}$ stand can be quickly computed with these updated parameters.

In the third task, the process parameters incorporated in the off-line hill-climbing procedure are replaced by updated values thereby aiming to reduce the degree of on-line correction.

Level I Controller

The Level I controller for the $(i+1)^{th}$ subsystem or stage uses average values of the slab output thickness and temperature and the updated values of the process parameters supplied by the Level II controller after the slab has left the

i^{th} stand. The Level I controller then computes the desired output thickness from the $(i+1)^{th}$ stand by minimising the cost function :

$$C = c_4 \left| T_{i+1} - T^*_{i+1} \right| + c_5 \left| T_{i+2} - T^*_{i+2} \right| \tag{7}$$

where the symbols are as follows :

C : cost function

c_4 : temperature error coefficient at the $(i+1)^{th}$ stand

c_5 : temperature error coefficient at the $(i+2)^{th}$ stand

T : output temperature from a stand (°F)

T^* : desired output temperature (°F)

i : stand number

$|\cdot|$: the modulus

Here the desired temperature T^* is obtained from the off-line strategy as discussed in Section 2.
The constraint (equation (8)) must also be satisfied :

$$tol^1_{i+1} \leq h_{i+1} \leq tol^2_{i+1} \tag{8}$$

where h represents stand output thickness, tol represents tolerance derived from process constraints.

The output thickness h_{i+2} from the $(i+2)^{th}$ stand is maintained at the previously computed off-line value during this minimisation. The output temperatures T_{i+1} and T_{i+2} are calculated from a simplified set of equations derived by Eaglen. This set of equations is in terms of average values of the process variables over the slab length, rather than in terms of particular values for each slab element. In the simplified set of equations, the temperature loss due to the water sprays at each stand, T_{2i} is assumed constant for the relatively small slab thickness and velocity changes resulting from modifications to the reductions at the previous and current stands. Although the average value of T_{2i} was determined by off-line experimentation this is also updated on-line once the water-descaling spray effectiveness parameter has been updated. Stefan's equation is used to calculate the temperature drop due to radiation from stand to stand. These equations are given in Section 2 (equations (2 to 6)).

The tolerances for each output thickness are chosen such that the process constraints are not violated. If the minimum cost from equation (7) lies outside the constrained region, the value taken for h_{i+1} is the appropriate boundary value. The cost function given by equation (7) uses the modulus of the temperature errors and is considered an equally appropriate choice as one of quadratic form, since the on-line hill-climbing is undertaken with a simple direct search and derivatives are not computed. The cost component coefficients c_4 and c_5 are chosen to give different levels of importance to the output temperatures from the $(i+1)^{th}$ and $(i+2)^{th}$ stands and, at the same time, place different levels of confidence upon the process parameters used for successive subsystems. During the simulation tests, a choice of $c_5/c_4 = 100$ was found to be satisfactory. Note that although a high weight is placed on the $(i+2)^{th}$ stand, all the subsystems are of equal importance so that it has been possible, with this subsystem structure, to achieve the main condition under which the serial systems strategy of Chapter VI provides near optimal performance.

4. REALISATION OF THE HIERARCHICAL CONTROL STRATEGY WITH THE ROUGHING PROCESS SIMULATION

The hierarchical control strategy described in Section 3 was incorporated into a detailed digital simulation of the Spencer Works roughing process developed by Eaglen [70]. The controller, however, used only the simplified model equations (2) to (6). The on-line adaptive controller was then tested on the ICL 4100 computer of the Cambridge University Control Group. The realisation of the control strategy was divided into three parts :observation, process parameter updating and control. Initial values for the process parameters necessary for the equations described in Section 2 (equations (2) to (6)) were provided by Eaglen from simulation tests (reference [70]) when no control was applied to the process.

4.1. Observation

As stated previously, the observation procedure operates for approximately ten seconds and commences two seconds after each stand starts to roll a slab. This avoids the temperature transients at the head of each slab. The roll-power, slab output thickness and slab output temperature are recorded every 0.5 seconds and at the end of the obervation interval, the average values of these process variables are computed. It is necessary to average these variables because the variables are not constant during the rolling period. In practice, process noise contaminates these measurements and filtering or averaging techniques have to be employed.

4.2. Process Parameter Updating

The process parameter updating procedure uses an inverted form of the process equations to compute the process parameters, hardness and water-descaling spray effectiveness. Average values for the process variables computed by the observation procedure are used to compute the process parameters and the updated values are obtained by adding a proportion of the difference between the previous and currently calculated values to the previous value as described in Section 3. This method is employed in place of more sophisticated parameter estimation techniques, since no knowledge is available concerning the characteristics of the measurement noise within the roughing process and little time is available for the adaptation. The updated process parameters computed from the deterministic equations are fed forward to the following subsystems and also usedfor the next slab entering this subsystem.

4.3. Control

The control procedure uses the average values from the ith stand as well as the updated process parameters from the updating algorithm to calculate h_{i+1} corresponding to the minimum costs given by equation (7) for the $(i+1)^{th}$ subsystem. The minimum cost obtained by allowing the slab thickness (h_{i+1}) to vary between the tolereances at the $(i+1)^{th}$ stand is found. An example of the cost function plotted against the output thickness corresponding to the minimum cost calculated on-line almost equals the off-line calculation for R4 output thickness (Fig. 4). In addition, another example is given where the minimum lies outside the tolerance range. When this condition occurs, the optimal thickness is taken as the boundary value. The screw settings corresponding to the desired thickness are then obtained from equation (9) below which was derived by Eaglen [70] in terms of the roll-power at each stand

$$h_i = g_i + \frac{m_i \; P_i}{\sqrt[2]{(H_i - h_i)}} \qquad (9)$$

where the symbols have the following mean :

h_i : unloaded gap (in.)
P_i : roll-power (Kw)
H_i : input thickness (in.)
h_i : output thickness (in.)
m_i : coefficient related to roll-speed and stand modulus.

4.4. Simulation Results when On-Line Control is Applied

Using the hierarchical control strategy outlined in Section 3, the series of tests in this section show the output thickness and output temperatures at each stand for different simulation runs, subjected to different process disturbances*. Fig. 5a gives the slab temperature at the output of each stand for three slabs. For the purposes of comparison a standard slab has a furnace release temperature of 2200°F. In this particular test the furnace release temperatures of the two other slabs have been estimated incorrectly by + 10°F. For the standard slab, the R5 output slab temperature is higher than the off-line predicted value. This is caused by initial errors between the control model and the detailed simulation in the water spray effectiveness. When this is corrected as in Fig.6a the R5 output slab temperature is withing 0.6°F of the desired value of 2120°F. In Fig. 5b it is seen

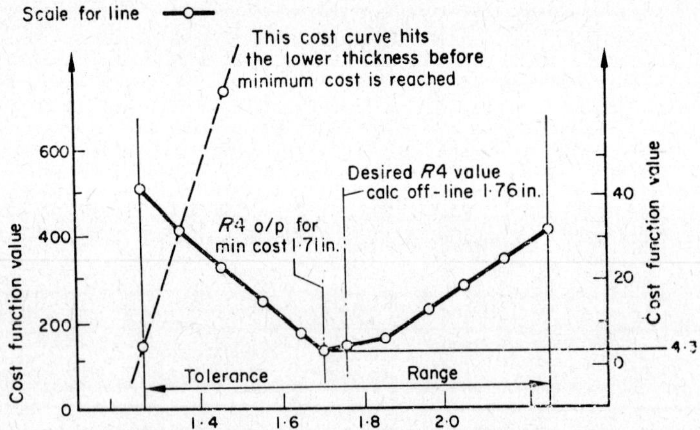

Fig. 4 : A cost function calculated at R

* It should be noted that since there is no on-line control on the Spencer Works roughing process at the present time, temperature deviations of ± 40 °F occur at the output of R5. A controller which reduces this deviation to ± 10 °F is satisfactory for the finishing process input.

that the hotter slab released from the furnace undergoes larger reductions at the earlier stands and the cooler slab undergoes smaller reductions at these stands. This control action restores each slab to the required trajectory. Fig. 5b also shows that the slab temperature deviation for the "hotter" and "standard" slab at R4 results in the reduction at R4 being limited by the upper constraint set at this stand. In this particular example, most of the reductions are limited by the constraint imposed on the output thickness from each stand.

Fig. 6a shows how the slab output temperature from R5 is almost equal to the desired temperature (within 0.4°F), when the estimate of the water-descaling spray effectiveness is improved. The thickness reduction pattern computed for this slab lies within the interior of the constrained region of each stand as shown in Fig. 6b.

Fig. 7a illustrates the slab output temperatures at each stand for both a "standard" and a "harder" slab where the effectiveness of the water sprays was also over-estimated. Despite these inaccurate estimates of the water-spray effectiveness and hardness coefficient, the adaptive control system minimises the output temperature error at R6 by re-estimating the process parameters. For the "harder" slab, the temperature rise due to deformation increases and this offsets the extra temperature loss due to the more effective water sprays. Fig. 7b shows the corresponding reduction pattern for these slabs.

In Fig. 8a the updated values of the water spray effectiveness are used with a slab producing less temperature rise due to deformation, than the "standard" slab. This figure shows that the R5 output temperature is less than the desired value by 8.7°F. This case arises because the deformation temperature rise coefficient is not re-estimated during the process. Re-estimation of the slab hardness does not improve the R5 output temperature error. Fig. 8b shows the corresponding thickness reduction patterns.

In Fig. 9a changes to the desired slab temperature at the output of R5 are investigated. A change of ± 5°F in the trajectory causes a similar deviation in the R5 temperature. From the results for the "standard" slab with and without error in the estimate of the water-spray effectiveness it is seen that inaccuracies in determining the water spray effectiveness are more important than errors in the values calculated for the desired off-line trajectory. The thickness reduction patterns for these slabs are shown in Fig. 9b.

In Fig. 10a the hardness coefficient is initially underestimated and the R5 output temperature error is still less than 4°F. This emphasises how the control system adapts to errors in the estimate of the hardness coefficient. For the slab rolled with inaccurate estimates in the water-spray effectiveness and the coefficient of temperature rise due to deformation, it is seen that the on-line estimation of the hardness coefficient compensates for some of these errors.

4.5. Discussion

The above tests have shown that the hierarchical control strategy of Chapter VI, outlined for this system in Section 3, enables the R5 output temperature T^*_{R5} to be maintained at "any" required value by suitably modulating the reduction pattern. As a result, temperature disturbances into the finishing process are reduced. During the initial application of this scheme, errors may arise in the R5 output temperature due to inaccurate estimation of the water-descaling spray effectiveness. However, these errors will be quickly reduced by updating the effectiveness coefficient after the first few slabs have been rolled through each stage. Initial errors in the estimation of the slab parameters are easily identified and updated on-line as shown in the examples above.

Thus the serial systems strategy appears to provide good control perfor-

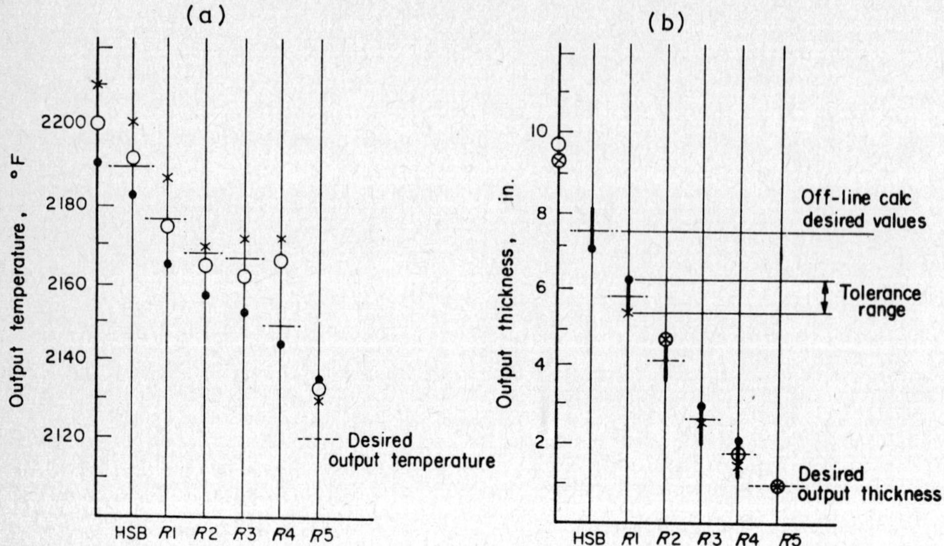

Fig. 5 a : Output temperature from each stand. ✕ 1 Assumed hotter by 10°F. ● 2 Assumed cooler by -10°F ○ 3 2200°F standard, inaccurate water sprays.

Fig. 5 b : Output thickness from each stand

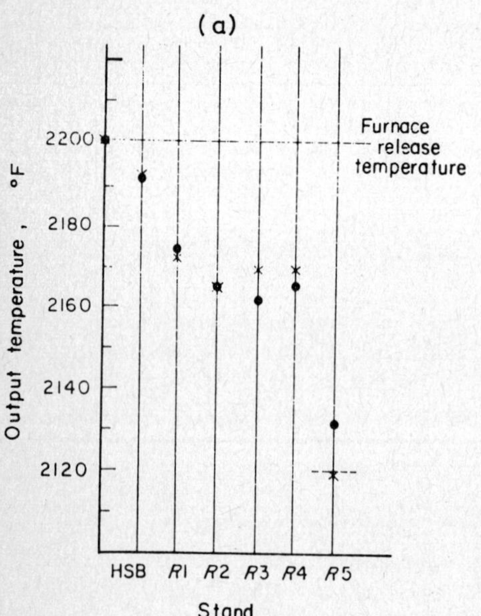

Fig. 6 a : Output temperature from each stand. ● 3 standard with inaccurate water spray estimate. ✕ 6 standard with better spray estimate.

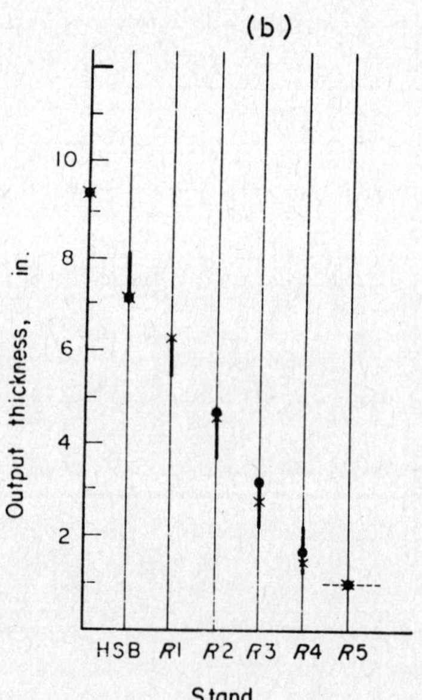

Fig. 6 b : Output thickness from each stand.

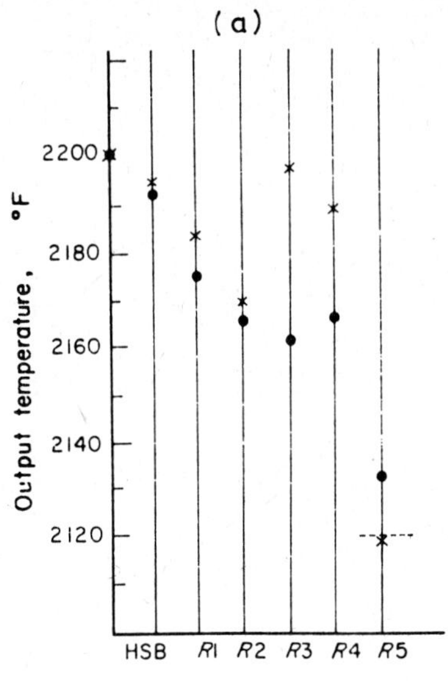

Fig. 7 a : Output temperature from each stand. ● 3 standard, inaccurate water sprays. ✕ 4 harder inaccurate water sprays

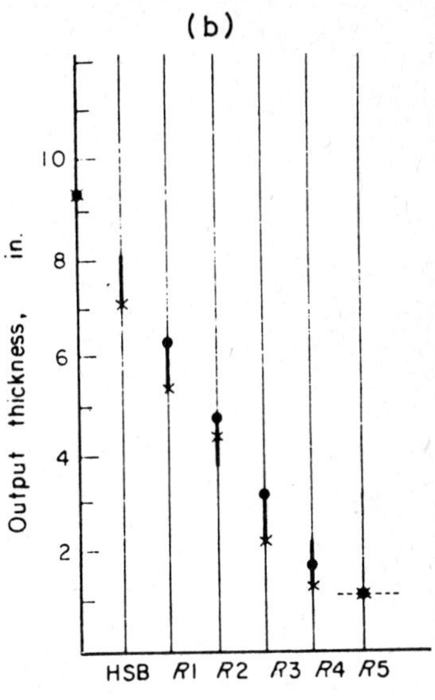

Fig. 7 b : Output thickness from each stand

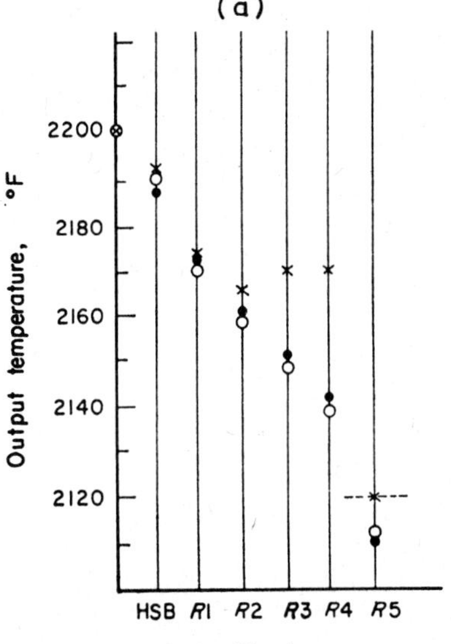

Fig. 8 a : Output temperature from each stand. ✕ 6 standard. O 7 less temperature rise from rolling. ● 8 as for 7 and lower estimate of slab hardness

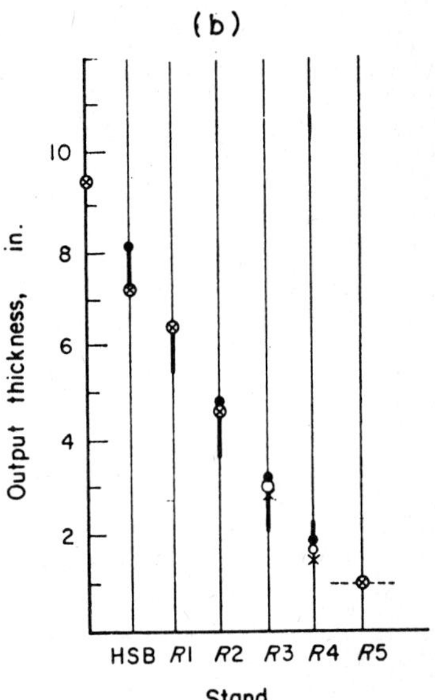

Fig. 8 b : Output thickness from each stand

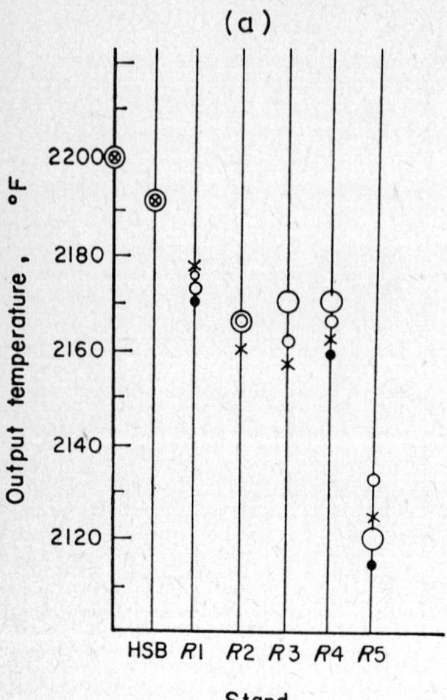

Fig. 9 a : Output temperature from each stand. O 3 standard inaccurate water sprays. O 6 standard x 10 change in trajectory. ● 11 as for 10,5°F down.

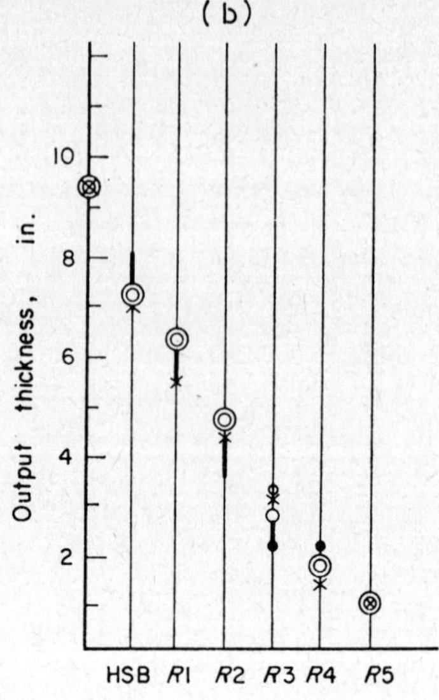

Fig. 9 b : Output thickness from each stand

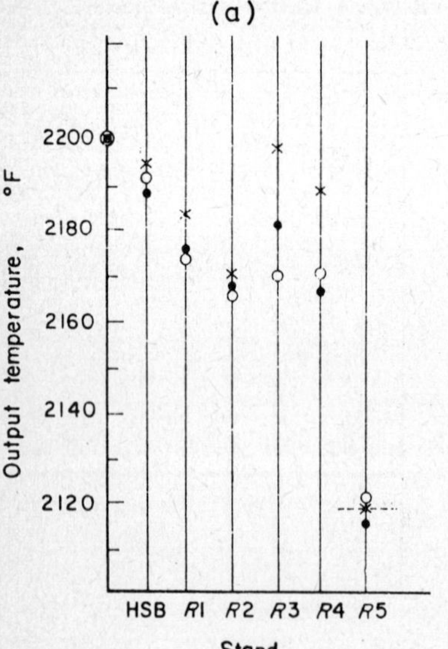

Fig. 10 a : Output temperature from each stand. x 4 harder, inacurrate water sprays, O 6 standard. ● 9 assumed softer

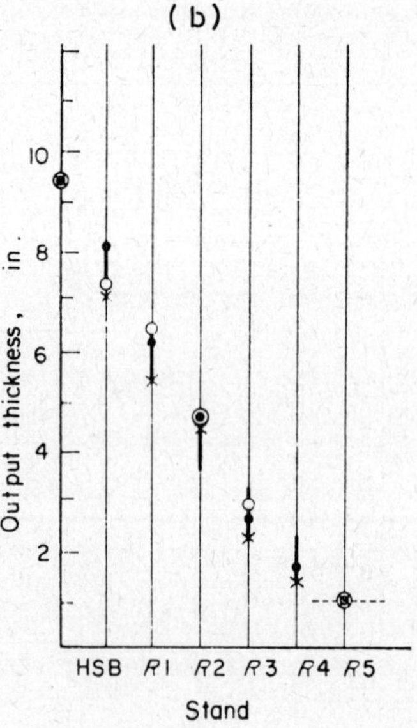

Fig. 10 b : Output thickness from each stand.

mance despite the many uncertainties that characterise the system. An overall optimal strategy may have provided a marginally better control but it would not have been possible to implement it on even multiple processors since the time available for the computation of the deterministic control and the adaptation is very small. The serial systems strategy used here, on the other hand, has extremely modest computational requirements. To give some measure of these, consider the comparative computing tasks of the strategy.

This study required :

(i) a detailed simulation of the roughing process which was taken to be the real process here
(ii) off-line trajectory determination
(iii) on-line observation of the process variables
(iv) on-line estimation of the process parameters
(v) on-line optimisation and control

The roughing process simulation was implemented digitally on the computing system (CASSANDRA) at Cambridge University. This computer had a 32 K store and a 2μsec store cycle.

(i) was effectively computed in real-time
(ii) required approximately ten seconds to reach the minimum cost for a random initial estimate of the thickness reduction pattern
(iii) (iv) required only a few milliseconds since the estimates were computed from average values of the process variables and time-series analysis was not included
(v) needed approximately 0.25 seconds when a direct search method was used with a step-length of 0.01 inches in output thickness. Obviously this computation time would be reduced if a more sophisticated search method was used.

Thus, the on-line hierarchical strategy requires very little computation and is therefore easy to implement.

If the method used for off-line determination of the reduction pattern trajectory had been extended to on-line control, it is estimated that the computation time for the case when four slabs are being rolled in the roughing process would have been approximately 60 seconds, which is more than the time available.

Thus this study shows that the hierarchical control strategy which has been applied is simple, effective and uses very little computer time. It has adaptive features and is able to track the variations in the parameters of individual slabs on-line. Simulation results show that the control variables remain very close to their desired value, despite fluctuations in the hardness, water descaling spray flow rate and furnace release temperatures. The present approach is thus able to provide an "Engineering" solution to this important practical problem and through this further practical aspects of hierarchical control have been illustrated.

PART IV

STOCHASTIC CONSIDERATIONS

In this final part of the book we examine the effect of relaxing the assumption that the models used in the first three parts of the book are perfect and that perfect noise free measurements of the states are available. We will be concerned primarily with linear systems subject to Gaussian disturbances since this is virtually the only class of problems for which some preliminary results are available. We will be mainly concerned with state estimation although some of the algorithms that we will discuss are also applicable to the identification of parameters. It should be emphasised that very little work has been done in this area and in view of the practical importance of state and parameter estimation, this subject should prove to be very fruitful for research in the coming years.

CHAPTER VIII

MULTI-LEVEL STATE AND PARAMETER ESTIMATION

1. INTRODUCTION

All real systems operate in a stochastic environment where they are subject to unknown disturbances and in addition, the controller has to rely, in practice, on imperfect measurements. In the case of linear dynamical systems, these difficulties can be overcome, at least in principle, by using the Kalman filter [71], since this will provide optimal state estimates. Further, from the separation theorem (Joseph and Tou [72]), stochastic optimum control can be achieved by cascading the optimal filter with the optimal deterministic controller as shown in Fig. 1

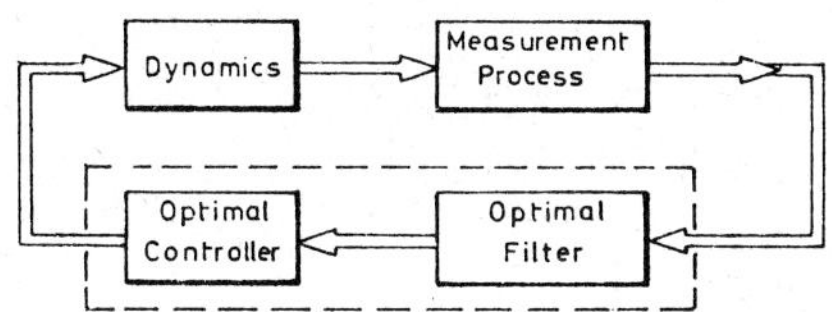

Fig. 1 : Stochastic optimal control system

The disadvantage of applying the single-level Kalman filter, however, is that the computational burden associated with the implementation of the filter is proportional to the cube of the system order. Consequently, if such a filter were used with a hierarchical controller to provide stochastic control, then the computational advantage gained in the controller would be lost. In order to overcome this, there is clearly a need for finding ways of decomposing the optimal Kalman filter.

The problem of decomposition-coordination of the optimal Kalman filter has received increasing attention in the last few years [7, 77, 75, 76, 78, 53, 54] However, up to the present time no satisfactory approach exists which yields the optimal solution. We will describe in the beginning of this chapter some of the attempts which have been made at solving the problem and outline the nature of the difficulties. We shall then describe various suboptimal approaches which nevertheless yield near optimal filtered estimates.

2. THE SINGLE LEVEL KALMAN FILTER AND THE MULTI-LEVEL PEARSON FILTER

2.1. The Kalman filter [71]

In view of the importance of the single-level Kalman filter in the work we shall describe in this chapter, it will be useful to start with a brief description of the optimal Kalman filter :

Consider the system :

$$\dot{\underline{x}} = A\underline{x} + B\underline{u} + \underline{\eta}$$

$$\underline{y} = C\underline{x} + \underline{\xi}$$

where $\underline{x}$ and $\underline{y}$ are, respectively, the state and output vectors. $\underline{\eta}$ and $\underline{\xi}$ are assumed to be drawn from Gaussian white noise processes and have zero mean and

$$E\{\underline{\eta}(t)\underline{\eta}^T(\tau)\} = Q\delta(t-\tau)$$

$$E\{\underline{\xi}(t)\underline{\xi}^T(\tau)\} = R\delta(t-\tau)$$

where δ is the Dirac delta function. $\underline{\eta}$, $\underline{\xi}$ and $\underline{x}(0)$ are assumed to be uncorrelated. For such a system, given an initial estimate of the state $E\{\underline{x}(0)\} = \hat{\underline{x}}_0$ and the initial covariance of the error $P(0) = P_0$, the optimal estimate $\hat{\underline{x}}$ of the state $\underline{x}$ evolves according to the equation

$$\dot{\hat{\underline{x}}} = A\hat{\underline{x}} + B\underline{u} + K\{\underline{y} - C\hat{\underline{x}}\}$$

where K is a gain matrix and is defined by

$$K = PC^T R^{-1}$$

and where P is the error covariance matrix and is a solution of the matrix Riccati equation

$$\dot{P} = AP + PA^T - PC^T R^{-1} CP + Q \quad ; \quad P(0) = P_0$$

Thus the main part of the computational burden is in computing the above Riccati equation since this is an lxl matrix where l is the order of the overall state vector $\underline{x}$. Clearly, if $\underline{x}$ could be partitioned into vectors of a lower order, much computational saving may result. This is essentially the basic principle behind the Pearson filter which we describe below.

2.2. The optimal multi-level filter of Pearson [7]

The Pearson filter was perhaps the first formulation of the multi-level state estimation problem for interconnected dynamical systems. But, as will become clear during the analysis, the filter cannot be used for the practical solution of the optimal multi-level filtering problem. However, the basic thinking behind it is of considerable interest since it would appear to be a direct extension of some of the ideas on the control of interconnected dynamical systems which we have described in this book.

The first limitation of the analysis of Pearson [7] is that his filter is formulated in continuous time and this leads to difficulties in the system description. However, these difficulties can be circumvented by considering a discrete-time version of Pearson's multi-level filter. In this section, following along the lines of Pearson's paper [7], we give an interpretation of his filter for the case of a discrete-time system.

The model that Pearson uses has a well-defined interconnection structure.

It consists of subsystems which are linked through an interconnection matrix L from the outputs $\underline{y}$ of the other subsystems, i.e.

$$\underline{z}(k) = L\underline{y}(k) \tag{1a}$$

where $\underline{z}(k)$ is an interconnection input and L is a matrix of ones and zeros. The interconnection inputs are assumed to be completely measurable through certain corrupted measurements $\underline{w}$, i.e.

$$\underline{w}(k) = \underline{z}(k) + \underline{\xi}(k) \tag{1b}$$

where $\underline{\xi}$ is a zero mean Gaussian white noise vector of known covariance R

$$E\left\{\underline{\xi}(j)\,\underline{\xi}(k)^T\right\} = R\delta_{jk} \tag{1c}$$

where δ is the Kronecker delta function, i.e.

$$\delta_{jk} = \begin{cases} 1 & (j=k) \\ 0 & (j\neq k) \end{cases}$$

In addition, the system state $\underline{x}$ evolves according to the equation

$$\underline{x}(k+1) = A\underline{x}(k) + B\underline{m}(k) + C\underline{z}(k) \tag{1d}$$

where $\underline{z}$ provides the interconnections from other subsystems and $\underline{m}$ is a noise input which is assumed to be drawn from a zero mean Gaussian process with known covariance, i.e.

$$E\left\{\underline{m}(j)\,\underline{m}(k)^T\right\} = S\delta_{jk} \tag{1e}$$

The system also has a number of outputs $\underline{y}$ which were used above to define the interconnection inputs $\underline{z}$ and these are related to the states $\underline{x}$ by

$$\underline{y}(k) = M\underline{x}(k) + N\underline{m}(k) \tag{1f}$$

It should be noted that the outputs $\underline{y}$ in Pearson's filter in fact are not used as observations but merely to provide the interconnections $\underline{z}$. For the observation of the state, there is postulated another message process $\underline{v}$ where

$$\underline{v}(k) = H\underline{x}(k) + \underline{\eta}(k) \tag{1g}$$

where $\underline{\eta}$ is also drawn from a zero mean Gaussian process of known covariance Q, i.e.

$$E\left\{\underline{\eta}(j)\,\underline{\eta}(k)^T\right\} = Q\delta_{jk} \tag{1h}$$

Thus the model describes an interconnected system with corrupted measurements of all the interactions as well as of a part of the state vector. It should be noted that within this model, the only interactions that exist between the subsystems arise through the interconnection matrix L and that the matrices A, B, C M, N, Q, R, S are all block diagonal.

The basis of the method is to convert the problem of finding the best estimate $\hat{\underline{x}}$ of $\underline{x}$ to a functional minimisation problem and then to solve this using one of the decentralised hierarchical optimisation methods outlined in this book. In order to do this, we could eliminate variables between the subsystem equations to put the problem into a standard form. Thus, the overall state equation becomes

$$\underline{x}(k+1) = (A + CLM)\,\underline{x}(k) + (B + CLN)\,\underline{m}(k)$$

$$\begin{bmatrix} \underline{v}(k) \\ \underline{w}(k) \end{bmatrix} = \begin{bmatrix} H \\ LM \end{bmatrix} \underline{x}(k) + \begin{bmatrix} \underline{\eta}(k) \\ LN\,\underline{m}(k) + \underline{\xi}(k) \end{bmatrix} \tag{2}$$

i.e.

$$\underline{x}(k+1) = A^{*}\underline{x}(k) + B^{*}\,\underline{m}(k)$$
$$\underline{v}^{*} = H^{*}\underline{x} + \underline{\eta}^{*} \tag{3}$$

where $\underline{m}$ and $\underline{\eta}^{*}$ are zero mean correlated sources with

$$E\left[\begin{Bmatrix}\underline{m}(j)\\ \underline{\eta}^{*}(j)\end{Bmatrix}\begin{Bmatrix}\underline{m}(k)\\ \underline{\eta}^{*}(k)\end{Bmatrix}^{T}\right] = \begin{bmatrix} S & 0 & SN^{T}L^{T} \\ 0 & Q & 0 \\ LNS & 0 & R+LNSN^{T}L^{T}\end{bmatrix}\delta_{jk}$$

$$= \begin{bmatrix} S & (S^{*})^{T} \\ S^{*} & Q^{*}\end{bmatrix}\delta_{jk} \tag{4}$$

where

$$A^{*} = A + CLM \; ; \; H^{*} = \begin{bmatrix} H \\ LM \end{bmatrix} \; ; \; \underline{\eta}^{*} = \begin{bmatrix} \underline{\eta} \\ LN\underline{m} + \underline{\xi} \end{bmatrix} ; \quad B^{*} = B + CLN \; ; \; \underline{v}^{*} = \begin{bmatrix} \underline{v} \\ \underline{w} \end{bmatrix}$$

$$S^{*} = \begin{bmatrix} LNS \\ 0 \end{bmatrix} \; ; \quad Q^{*} = \begin{bmatrix} Q & 0 \\ 0 & R + LNSN^{T}L^{T} \end{bmatrix}$$

Now, for this problem Cox [73] has shown that the a posteriori Gaussian Probability density function has a negative exponential argument of

$$\frac{1}{2}\left\|\underline{x}(t_0)-\bar{\underline{x}}_0\right\|^{2}_{P_0^{-1}} + \frac{1}{2}\sum_{k=0}^{n}\left[\left\|\begin{matrix}\underline{m} \\ \underline{v}^{*} - H\underline{x}^{*}\end{matrix}\right\|^{2}_{\begin{bmatrix} S & (S^{*})^{T} \\ S^{*} & Q^{*}\end{bmatrix}^{-1}}\right] \tag{5}$$

where $\underline{x}$ and $\underline{m}$ satisfy the integrated model of the process. Thus the maximum likelihood estimate of $\underline{x}$ can be obtained by formally minimising the expression in equation (5) with respect to $\underline{x}(k)$ and $\underline{m}(k)$; $k = 0,\ldots,n$. If a standard solution such as the one proposed by Cox [73] is used then the filter equations which emerge do not decompose at the subsystem level due to the arbitrary structure of L. The separation can be achieved by introducing the interactions explicitly. To do this, consider first the quadratic form in the cost functional in equation (5). By Gaussian elimination it can be shown that

$$\begin{bmatrix} S & 0 & SN^{T}L^{T} \\ 0 & Q & 0 \\ LNS & 0 & R+LNSN^{T}L^{T}\end{bmatrix}^{-1} = \begin{bmatrix} S^{-1}+N^{T}L^{T}R^{-1}LN & 0 & N^{T}L^{T}R^{-1} \\ 0 & Q^{-1} & 0 \\ -R^{-1}LN & 0 & R^{-1}\end{bmatrix} \tag{6}^{*}$$

So the argument of the summation in the function in equation (5) becomes

---

* It is easy to check that the expression on the right-hand side of equation (6) is indeed the inverse of the matrix on the left-hand side (by multiplying the two matrices and checking that the result is the unit matrix).

$$\left[\underline{m} \quad \underline{v}-H\underline{x} \quad \underline{w}-LM\underline{x}\right]\begin{bmatrix} S^{-1}N^TL^TR^{-1}LN & 0 & -N^TL^TR^{-1} \\ 0 & Q^{-1} & 0 \\ -R^{-1}LN & 0 & R^{-1}\end{bmatrix}\begin{bmatrix}\underline{m} \\ \underline{v}-H\underline{x} \\ \underline{w}-LM\underline{x}\end{bmatrix}$$

$$=\left\{\underline{m}\,(S^{-1}+N^TL^TR^{-1}LN)-(\underline{w}-LM\underline{x})\,R^{-1}\,LN\right\}$$

$$\left\{(\underline{v}-H\underline{x})\,Q^{-1}\right\}\left\{(\underline{w}-LM\underline{x})\,R^{-1}-\underline{m}N^TL^TR^{-1}\right\}\begin{bmatrix}\underline{m} \\ \underline{v}-H\underline{x} \\ \underline{w}-LM\underline{x}\end{bmatrix}$$

$$=\|\underline{m}\|^2_{S^{-1}}+\|\underline{v}-H\underline{x}\|^2_{Q^{-1}}+\left\{\underline{m}N^TL^TR^{-1}\,LN\underline{m}-(\underline{w}-LM\underline{x})\,R^{-1}\,LN\underline{m}+(\underline{w}-LM\underline{x})\,R^{-1}(\underline{w}-LM\underline{x})\right.$$
$$\left.\underline{m}\,(N^TL^TR^{-1})\,(\underline{w}-LM\underline{x})\right\}$$

Now, since $\underline{z} = LN\underline{m} + LM\underline{x}$ it follows that $LM\underline{x} = \underline{z} - LN\underline{m}$. The functional in the summation then becomes

$$\|\underline{m}\|^2_{S^{-1}}+\|\underline{v}-H\underline{x}\|^2_{Q^{-1}}+\left\{\underline{m}N^TL^T-\underline{w}+\underline{z}-LN\underline{m}\right\}R^{-1}\,LN\underline{m}$$
$$+\left[\underline{w}-\underline{z}+LN\underline{m}-LN\underline{m}\right]R^{-1}(\underline{w}-LM\underline{x})$$

$$=\|\underline{m}\|^2_{S^{-1}}+\|\underline{v}-H\underline{x}\|^2_{Q^{-1}}+\left[\underline{z}-\underline{w}\right]R^{-1}LN\underline{m}-\left[\underline{z}-\underline{w}\right]R^{-1}\left[\underline{w}-\underline{z}+LN\underline{m}\right]\}$$

$$=\|\underline{m}\|^2_{S^{-1}}+\|\underline{v}-H\underline{x}\|^2_{Q^{-1}}+\|\underline{z}-\underline{w}\|^2_{R^{-1}}$$

so that the deterministic problem corresponding to finding $\hat{\underline{x}}$ becomes one of minimising

$$\sum_{k=0}^{n}\|\underline{m}(k)\|^2_{S^{-1}}+\|\underline{v}(k)-H\underline{x}(k)\|^2_{Q^{-1}}+\|\underline{z}(k)-\underline{w}(k)\|^2_{R^{-1}}$$

subject to

$$\underline{z}(k) = LM\underline{x}(k) + LN\underline{m}(k)$$

and

$$\underline{x}(k+1) = A\underline{x}(k) + B\underline{m}(k) + C\underline{z}(k)\ .$$

Now, in this formulation, due to the block diagonal nature of A, B, C, Q, R, S, H, the interactions enter into the problem only through the equation for $\underline{z}$. It is therefore possible to decompose the problem as in Chapter II by maximising a function $\phi(\underline{\lambda})$ with respect to $\underline{\lambda}$, where

$$\phi(\underline{\lambda}) = \min_{\underline{x},\underline{m}}\begin{bmatrix} L(\underline{x},\underline{m},\underline{\lambda})\text{ subject to} \\ \\ \underline{x}(k+1) = A\underline{x}(k)+B\underline{m}(k)+C\underline{z}(k)\end{bmatrix}$$

where

$$L(\underline{x},\underline{m},\underline{\lambda}) = \sum_{k=0}^{n}\left\{\|\underline{m}(k)\|^2_{S^{-1}}+\|\underline{v}(k)-H\underline{x}(k)\|^2_{Q^{-1}}+\|\underline{z}(k)-\underline{w}(k)\|^2_{R^{-1}}+\right.$$

$$+ \underline{\lambda}(k)^T \left\{-\underline{z}(k) + LN\underline{m}(k) + LM\underline{x}(k)\right\}\} \tag{8}$$

This decomposes into subproblems due to the additive separability of the Lagrangian L with respect to $\underline{x}$, $\underline{m}$ for given $\underline{\lambda}$. The actual solution of the problem can be done at least in principle by using the two-level goal coordination algorithm described in Chapter II.

2.2.1 Discussion

The above approach yields the optimal smoothed estimate $\hat{\underline{x}}$ (n/0) (for details of smoothing cf. Meditch[86]). Pearson[7] argues that if at any sampling point n the Lagrangian L is minimised subject to the dynamics given by equation (1d) and maximised w.r.t. $\underline{\lambda}$ then at that point, the optimal filtered and smoothed estimates must be identical. Hence if the problem is solved for a succession of "final" intervals, n the resulting sequence $\hat{\underline{x}}$ (n/0) gives the optimal filtered estimate. This approach is obviously quite impractical for on-line estimation since the period of optimisation in equation (8) increases as time increases. Thus the computational requirements keep on increasing since ever larger coordination sequences $\underline{\lambda}$ have to be optimised as n increases.

The real source of the difficulty in the Pearson filter is the need to solve the optimisation problem from the origin k=0 as opposed to from the last estimate. To get around this difficulty, Sage [53] proposed a suboptimal estimator for a slightly more complex class of problems. We next describe the suboptimal approach of Sage and his co-workers.

3. THE MAXIMUM A POSTERIORI APPROACH OF ARAFEH AND SAGE [53]

Arafeh and Sage consider the nth order non-linear discrete time system given by

$$\underline{x}(k+1) = \underline{\phi}\left[\underline{x}(k), k\right] + \underline{w}(k) \tag{9}$$

$$\underline{z}(k) = \underline{h}\left[\underline{x}(k), k\right] + \underline{v}(k) \tag{10}$$

where $\underline{x}(k)$ is the n dimensional state vector where the parameters to be identified are also included in $\underline{x}$. $\underline{\phi}\left[\underline{x}(k), k\right]$ is the n dimensional vector-valued non-linear function which describes the structure of the system and includes any known inputs. $\underline{w}(k)$ is the n dimensional plant noise vector, $\underline{z}(k)$ is the m dimensional observation vector. $\underline{h}\left[\underline{x}(k), k\right]$ is the m dimensional vector-valued non-linear observation function and $\underline{v}(k)$ is the m dimensional noise vector.

The plant and measurement noises are described by Gaussian white sequences with

$$E\{\underline{w}(k)\} = \underline{q}(k) \quad ; \quad E\left\{\underline{w}(k)\ \underline{w}(1)^T\right\} = Q(k)\ \delta\ (k-1)$$

$$E\{\underline{v}(k)\} = \underline{r}(k) \quad ; \quad E\left\{\underline{v}(k)\ \underline{v}(1)^T\right\} = R(k)\ \delta\ (k-1)$$

where δ is the Kronecker delta function $\underline{w}$, $\underline{v}$, $\underline{x}(k_0)$ are assumed to be independent. Q, R are respectively positive semidefinite and positive definite block diagonal matrices. Also

$$E\left\{\underline{x}(k_0)\right\} = \bar{\underline{x}}(k_0) \quad \text{and} \quad E\left\{\underline{x}(k_0)\ \underline{x}(k_0)^T\right\} = P\ (k_0)$$

where P (k_0) is also assumed to be block diagonal.

Then the maximum a posteriori estimate is given by minimising

$$J = \frac{1}{2}\|\underline{x}(k_0)-\underline{x}(k_0)\|^2_{P^{-1}(k_0)} + \frac{1}{2}\sum_{k=k_0}^{k_f-1}\Big\{\|\underline{z}(k+1)-\underline{r}(k+1) - \underline{h}\big[\underline{x}(k+1),k+1\big]\|^2_{R^{-1}(k+1)} + \|\underline{w}(k)-\underline{q}(k)\|^2_{Q^{-1}(k)}\Big\} \quad (11)$$

w.r.t. $\underline{w}(k)$

subject to the dynamic constraint given by equation (9) with k_0, k_f fixed.

To perform this minimisation write the Hamiltonian as

$$H = \frac{1}{2}\|\underline{z}(k+1)-\underline{r}(k+1) - \underline{h}\big[\underline{x}(k+1,k+1\big]\|^2_{R^{-1}(k+1)} + \frac{1}{2}\|\underline{w}(k)-\underline{q}(k)\|^2_{Q^{-1}(k)} + \underline{\lambda}^T(k+1)\Big\{\underline{\phi}\big[\underline{x}(k),k\big] + \underline{w}(k)\Big\}$$

where $\underline{\lambda}$ is the adjoint vector. Using the discrete minimum principle [82] the two point boundary value problem can be written as

$$\underline{x}(k+1)=\underline{\phi}\big[\underline{x}(k),k\big] + \underline{q}(k)-Q(k)\big[\underline{\lambda}(k+1) - \phi(k)\,H^T(k+1)\,R^{-1}(k+1)\,\underline{\nu}(k+1)\big] \quad (12)$$

$$\underline{\lambda}(k) = \phi^T(k)\,H^T(k+1)\,R^{-1}(k+1)\,\underline{\nu}(k+1) + \phi^T(k)\,\underline{\lambda}(k+1) \quad (13)$$

where
$$\underline{\nu}(k+1) = \underline{z}(k+1) - \underline{r}(k+1) - \underline{h}\big[\underline{x}(k+1),\ k+1\big]$$

$$\phi(k) = \frac{\partial\underline{\phi}^T\big[\underline{x}(k),k\big]}{\partial\,\underline{x}(k)}$$

$$H(k+1) = \frac{\partial\,\underline{h}^T\big[\underline{x}(k+1),k+1\big]}{\partial\,\underline{x}(k+1)}$$

and from the transversality conditions

$$\underline{\lambda}(k_0) = P^{-1}(k_0)\big[\underline{x}(k_0) - \bar{\underline{x}}(k_0)\big] \quad (14)$$

$$\underline{\lambda}(k_f) = \underline{0} \quad (15)$$

The solution of this two point boundary value problem yields the fixed interval smoothing solution. To obtain the filtering solution, it is necessary to use the principle of invariant imbedding. Before we do this, let us decompose our system by introducing interconnection variables of the form

$$\underline{\pi}_i(k) = \underline{g}_i(\underline{x}_j,k) \qquad j = 1,2,\dots,N$$

and thus decompose the cost function of equation (11), i.e.

$$J^0 = \sum_{i=1}^{N}\Big\{\frac{1}{2}\|\underline{x}_i(k_0)-\bar{\underline{x}}(k_0)\|^2_{P^{-1}(k_0)} + \sum_{k=k_0}^{k_f-1}\frac{1}{2}\|\underline{z}_i(k+1) - \underline{r}_i(k+1) - \underline{h}_i(\underline{x}_i,\underline{\pi}_i,k+1)\|^2_{R_i^{-1}(k+1)} + \frac{1}{2}\|\underline{w}_i(k) - \underline{q}_i(k)\|^2_{Q_i^{-1}(k)}\Big\}$$

so that $J = \sum_{i=1}^{N} J_i$ where

$$J_i = \frac{1}{2} \| \underline{x}_i(k_0) - \bar{\underline{x}}_i(k_0) \|^2_{P_i^{-1}(k_0)} + \sum_{k=k_0}^{k_f-1} \left\{ \frac{1}{2} \| \underline{z}_i(k+1) - \underline{r}_i(k+1) - \right.$$

$$\left. - \underline{h}_i(\underline{x}_i, \underline{\pi}_i, k+1) \|^2_{R^{-1}(k+1)} + \frac{1}{2} \| \underline{w}_i(k) - \underline{q}_i(k) \|^2_{Q_i^{-1}(k)} \right\}$$

The system model also decomposes, i.e.

$$\underline{x}_i(k+1) = \phi_i[\underline{x}_i, \underline{\pi}_i, k] + \underline{w}_i(k)$$

$$\underline{z}_i(k) = \underline{h}_i[\underline{x}_i, \underline{\pi}_i, k] + \underline{v}_i(k)$$

for $i = 1,2,\ldots, N$

To solve the decomposed problem using say the interaction prediction principle, the ith subsystems Hamiltonian can be written as

$$H_i = \frac{1}{2} \| \underline{z}_i(k+1) - \underline{r}_i(k+1) - \underline{h}_i(\underline{x}_i, \underline{\pi}_i, k+1) \|^2_{R_i^{-1}(k+1)} + \frac{1}{2} \| \underline{w}_i(k) -$$

$$- \underline{q}_i(k) \|^2_{Q_i^{-1}(k)} + \underline{\beta}_j(k)^T [\underline{\pi}_j(k) - \underline{g}_j(\underline{x}_i, k)] + \underline{\lambda}_i^T(k+1) [\underline{\phi}_i(\underline{x}_i, \underline{\pi}_i, k) +$$

$$+ \underline{w}_i(k)] \qquad j = 1,2,\ldots, N$$

where $\underline{\beta}_j$ is a Lagrange multiplier vector which has been introduced to force the eventual satisfaction of the interconnection constraint $\underline{\pi}_j(k) = \underline{g}_j(\underline{x}_i, k)$

From the Hamiltonian, the ith subsystem's two point boundary value problem can be written as

$$\underline{x}_i(k+1) = \underline{\Phi}_i[\underline{x}_i, \underline{\pi}_i, k] + \underline{q}_i(k) - Q_i(k)\, \phi_i^T(k) [\underline{\lambda}_i(k) - \underline{B}_i(k)]$$

$$\underline{\lambda}_i(k+1) = \Phi_i^T [\underline{\lambda}_i(k) - \underline{B}_i(k)] + H_i^T(k+1)\, R_i^{-1}(k+1)\, \underline{\nu}_i(k+1) \qquad (16)$$

where

$$\Phi_i(k) = \frac{\partial \underline{\phi}_i}{\partial \underline{x}_i(k)} [\underline{x}_i, \underline{\pi}_i, k]$$

$$H_i(k+1) = \frac{\partial h_i(\underline{x}_i, \underline{\pi}_i, k+1)}{\partial \underline{x}_i(k+1)}$$

$$\underline{\nu}_i(k+1) = \underline{z}(k+1) - \underline{r}_i(k+1) - \underline{h}_i(\underline{x}_i, \underline{\pi}_i, k+1)$$

$$\underline{B}_i(k) = \frac{\partial}{\partial \underline{x}_i(k)} [\underline{\beta}_j(k)^T [\underline{\pi}_j(k) - \underline{g}_j(\underline{x}_i, k)]]$$

From the transversality conditions, the boundary conditions are given by

$$\begin{aligned} \underline{\lambda}_i(k_0) &= \underline{P}_i^{-1}(k_0)\left[\underline{x}_i(k_0) - \underline{\bar{x}}_i(k_0)\right] \\ \underline{\lambda}_i(k_f) &= \underline{0} \end{aligned} \tag{17}$$

Arafeh and Sage [53] have developed the following sequential estimation algorithm for the ith subsystem by using the principle of invariant imbedding :

$$\left.\begin{aligned} \underline{\hat{x}}_i(k+1) &= \underline{\Phi}_i(\underline{\hat{x}}_i, \underline{\pi}_i, k) + \underline{q}_i(k) + K_i(k+1)\,\underline{\hat{\nu}}_i(k+1) + N_i(k+1)\,\underline{B}_i(k) \\ K_i(k+1) &= P_i(k+1)\,H_i^T(k+1)\,R_i^{-1}(k+1) \\ P_i(k+1) &= P_i(k+1/k) + D_i(k)\left[I - \frac{\partial M_i(k+1)}{\partial \underline{x}_i(k+1/k)}\,P_i(k+1/k) + C_i(k+1)\right]^{-1} \\ P_i(k+1/k) &= \Phi_i(k)\,P_i(k)\,\Phi_i^T(k) + Q_i(k) \end{aligned}\right\} \tag{18}$$

where

$$N_i(k+1) = -\left\{P_i(k+1)\left[I - \frac{\partial M_i(k+1)}{\partial \underline{x}_i(k+1/k)}\,Q_i(k)\right] - Q_i(k)\right\}\,\emptyset_i^{-T}(k)$$

$$C_i(k+1) = \frac{\partial}{\partial \underline{x}_i(k)}\left\{\emptyset^{-T}(k)\,B_i(k) - \frac{\partial M_i(k+1)}{\partial \underline{x}_i(k+1/k)}\,Q_i(k)\,\emptyset^{-T}(k)\,\underline{B}_i(k)\right\}P_i(k)\,\emptyset_i^T(k)$$

$$D_i(k) = \frac{\partial}{\partial \underline{x}_i(k)}\left\{Q_i(k)\,\emptyset_i^{-T}(k)\,\underline{B}_i(k)\right\}P_i(k)\,\emptyset_i^T(k)$$

$$M_i(k+1) = H_i^T(k+1)\,R_i^{-1}(k+1)\,\underline{\nu}_i(k+1)$$

3.1. Suboptimal coordination

Arafeh and Sage [53] make no attempt to optimally coordinate the subsystem filters. Rather, a strategy of "coordination for improvement" is used. The idea is to use sequential coordination for improvement with the passing of time since for many systems initial results are not as important as obtaining acceptable results near the final time.

For this purpose it is possible to use a sequential predictor-corrector scheme for the improvement of the coordination. In this method, first of all the coordination variables $\underline{\pi}_i$ and $\underline{\beta}_i$ can be predicted by linear extrapolation, i.e.

$$\begin{aligned} \underline{\beta}_i(k+1/k) &= \underline{\beta}_i(k) + \underline{\beta}_i^*(k) \\ \underline{\pi}_i(k+1/k) &= \underline{\pi}_i(k) + \underline{\pi}_i^*(k) \end{aligned}$$

where

$$\begin{aligned} \underline{\beta}_i^*(k) &= \underline{\beta}_i(k) - \underline{\beta}_i(k-1) \\ \underline{\pi}_i^*(k) &= \underline{\pi}_i(k) - \underline{\pi}_i(k-1) \end{aligned}$$

The predicted value of $\underline{\beta}_i$ is corrected by a gradient procedure i.e.

$$\underline{\beta}_i(k+1) = \underline{\beta}_i(k+1/k) + \alpha\left[\underline{\pi}_i(k) - \underline{g}_i\left[\underline{x}_j(k), k\right]\right]$$

where α is the step length and $\underline{\hat{x}}_j$ is obtained from solving equation (18) at the

1st level. $\underline{\pi}_i$ is corrected by averaging the predicted and estimated value of $\underline{\pi}_i$ according to

$$\underline{\pi}_i(k+1) = \frac{1}{2}\left[\underline{\pi}_i(k+1/k) + \underline{g}_i(x_j(k), k)\right]$$

Arafeh and Sage [54] have successfully applied this approach to the estimation problem of an interconnected power system.

Let us now consider another suboptimal approach to multi-level state estimation which uses an entirely different approach. This is the supplemented partitioning approach (SPA) of Shah [74] .

4. THE S.P.A. FILTER

For clarity of exposition, a system consisting of only two subsystems will be considered. Extension to multiple interconnected systems is quite straightforward.

The dynamical equations of the system could be written as :

$$\begin{aligned}
\dot{\underline{x}}_1(t) &= A_{11}(t)\,\underline{x}_1 + A_{12}(t)\,\underline{x}_2 + \underline{\eta}_1(t) \\
\underline{y}_1(t) &= C_{11}(t)\,\underline{x}_1(t) + \underline{\xi}_1(t) \\
\dot{\underline{x}}_2(t) &= A_{21}(t)\,\underline{x}_1(t) + A_{22}(t)\,\underline{x}_2(t) + \underline{\eta}_2(t) \\
\underline{y}_2(t) &= C_{22}(t)\,\underline{x}_2(t) + \underline{\xi}_2(t)
\end{aligned} \tag{19}$$

where the symbols have the following meaning : $\underline{x}_1$ is the $l_1 \times 1$ state vector of subsystem I ; $\underline{x}_2$ is the $l_2 \times 1$ state vector of subsystem II ; A_{11}, A_{12}, A_{21}, A_{22} are, respectively, $l_1 \times l_1$, $l_1 \times l_2$, $l_2 \times l_1$, $l_2 \times l_2$ matrices, $\underline{\eta}_1$, $\underline{\eta}_2$ are white noise vectors of dimensions $l_1 \times 1$, $l_2 \times 1$, respectively. $\underline{y}_1$, $\underline{y}_2$ are the output vectors of the two subsystems and are $p_1 \times 1$, and $p_2 \times 1$, respectively. $\underline{\xi}_1$ and $\underline{\xi}_2$ are $p_1 \times 1$ and $p_2 \times 1$ vectors of measurement noises for the two subsystems. C_{11}, C_{12} are measurement matrices of the two subsystems and are of dimension $p_1 \times l_1$ and $p_2 \times l_2$ respectively.

The stochastic processes $\underline{\eta}_i(t)$; $t \geq t_0$ $i = 1,2$ and $\underline{\xi}_i(t)$; $t \geq t_0$, $i = 1,2$ are zero mean Gaussian white noise of known covariance, i.e.

$$E\left[\underline{\eta}_i(t)\,\underline{\eta}_i^T(\tau)\right] = Q_i(t)\,\delta(t-\tau) \quad ; i = 1,2 \tag{20}$$

and

$$E\left[\underline{\xi}_i(t)\,\underline{\xi}_i^T(\tau)\right] = R_i(t)\,\delta(t-\tau) \quad ; i = 1,2 \tag{21}$$

for all $t, \tau \geq t_0$ where E denotes the expected value and δ is the Dirac delta function. The $l_i \times l_i$ $(i = 1,2)$ matrices Q_i are positive semidefinite for $t \geq t_0$ while the $(p_i \times p_i)$ $(i = 1,2)$ matrices R_i are continuous and positive definite for $t \geq t_0$. It is assumed that the stochastic processes $\underline{\eta}_i$, $\underline{\xi}_i$ are independent of each other, i.e.

$$E\left[\underline{\eta}_i(t)\;\underline{\xi}_i^T(\tau)\right] = 0$$

for all τ, $t \geq t_0$.

The initial states $\underline{x}_i(t_0)$ $i = 1,2$, are assumed to be zero mean Gaussian random $(1 \times l_i)$ vectors. They are independent of $\underline{\eta}_i(t)$, $t \geq t_0$, and of $\underline{\xi}_i(t)$ $t \geq t_0$ and their $(l_i \times l_i)$ covariance matrices, $E\left[\underline{x}_i(t_0)\,\underline{x}_i^T(t_0)\right] = P(t_0)$, are positive semidefinite. It is also assumed that the overall system noise covariance matrix is block diagonal, i.e.

$$E\left[\underline{\eta}_i(t)\,\underline{\eta}_j^T(\tau)\right] = 0 \qquad i = 1,2\ ;\quad j = 1,2 \qquad i \neq j$$

This is a realistic assumption for practical systems. The estimation error is defined as :

$$\underline{\tilde{x}}_i(t_1/t) = \underline{x}_i(t_1) - \underline{\hat{x}}_i(t_1/t) \qquad i = 1,\ 2 \tag{22}$$

where $\underline{\hat{x}}_i(t_1/t)$ is the estimate at t_1 given all previous observations. Consider subsystem II. Since $\underline{x}_1(t) = \underline{\hat{x}}_1(t) + \underline{\tilde{x}}_1(t)$ by equation (22) above, the subsystem equations could be written as :

$$\underline{\dot{x}}_2(t) = A_{21}(t)\,\underline{\hat{x}}_1(t) + A_{21}(t)\,\underline{\tilde{x}}_1(t) + A_{22}(t)\,\underline{x}_2 + \underline{\eta}_2(t)$$

$$\underline{y}_2(t) = C_{22}(t)\,\underline{x}_2 + \underline{\xi}_2(t)$$

or

$$\underline{\dot{x}}_2(t) = A_{21}(t)\,\underline{\hat{x}}_1(t) + A_{22}(t)\,\underline{x}_2(t) + \underline{\eta}^*_2(t) \tag{23}$$

where

$$\underline{\eta}^*_2(t) = A_{21}(t)\,\underline{\tilde{x}}_1(t) + \underline{\eta}_2(t)\,. \tag{24}$$

Similarly subsystem I equations could be written as :

$$\underline{\dot{x}}_1(t) = A_{11}(t)\,\underline{x}_1(t) + A_{12}(t)\,\underline{\hat{x}}_2(t) + A_{12}(t)\,\underline{\tilde{x}}_2(t) + \underline{\eta}_1(t)$$

or

$$\underline{\dot{x}}_1(t) = A_{11}(t)\,\underline{x}_1(t) + A_{12}(t)\,\underline{\hat{x}}_2(t) + \underline{\eta}^*_1(t) \tag{25}$$

where

$$\underline{\eta}^*_1(t) = A_{12}(t)\,\underline{\tilde{x}}_2(t) + \underline{\eta}_1(t) \tag{26}$$

Now consider the simple filter structure for this system consisting of two subsystems

$$\dot{\underline{\hat{x}}}_1(t) = A_{11}(t)\,\underline{\hat{x}}_1(t) + K_1\left[\underline{y}_1(t) - C_{11}(t)\,\underline{\hat{x}}_1(t)\right] + A_{12}(t)\,\underline{x}_2(t) \tag{27a}$$

$$\dot{\underline{\hat{x}}}_2(t) = A_{22}(t)\,\underline{\hat{x}}_2(t) + K_2\left[\underline{y}_2 - C_{22}(t)\,\underline{\hat{x}}_2(t)\right] + A_{21}\,\underline{\hat{x}}_1(t) \tag{27b}$$

where

$$K_1 = P_{11}\,C_{11}^T\,R_1^{-1} \tag{27c}$$

$$K_2 = P_{22}\,C_{22}^T\,R_2^{-1} \tag{27d}$$

and P_{11}, P_{22} are the solutions of the subsystem matrix Riccati equations :

$$\dot{P}_{11} = A_{11}P_{11} + P_{11}A_{11}^T\,R_1^{-1}\,C_{11}\,P_{11} + Q_1^* \ ;\ P_{11}(0) = P_{11_0} \tag{27e}$$

$$\dot{P}_{22} = A_{22}P_{22} + P_{22}A_{22}^T - P_{22}C_{22}^T\,R_2^{-1}\,C_{22}P_{22} + Q_2^* \ ;\ P_{22}(0) = P_{22_0} \tag{27f}$$

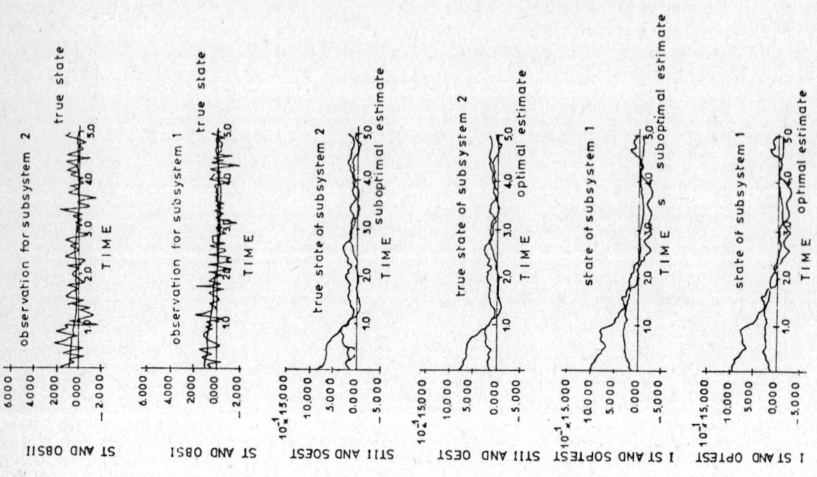

Fig. 3 : Optimal and suboptimal estimates for example 1 in section 4.4.

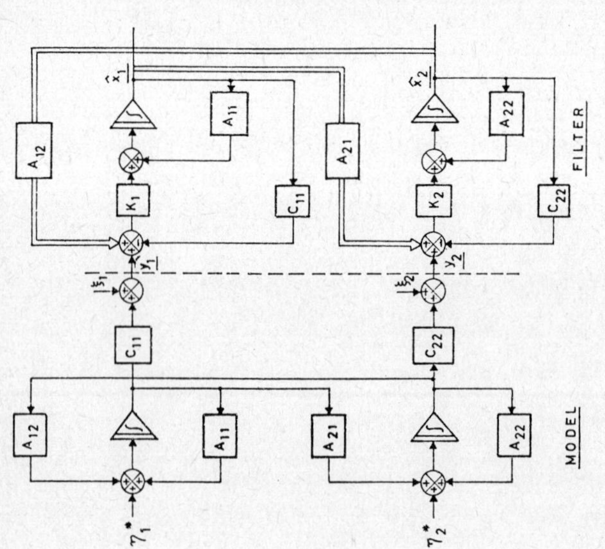

Fig. 2 : The filter structure

where $Q_1^* = Q_1 + A_{12}P_{11}A_{12}^T$; $Q_2^* = Q_2 + A_{21}P_{11}A_{21}^T$

Figure 2 shows the structure of the filter. It should be noted that such a filter does not explicitly account for the interactions which are expressed in the optimal filter by the inclusion of the off diagonal terms in the overall system error covariance matrix P. It should therefore be of considerable interest to see if it is nevertheless possible to get near optimal filtering.

4.1. The suboptimality of the S.P.A. filter

The filter described by equations (27) is an overall optimal filter for the system given by equation (19) if $\underline{\eta}_1^*$ and $\underline{\eta}_2^*$ in equations (24) and (26) are uncorrelated white noise vectors. The reason for this is that the filter formulation in equation (27) is of the standard Kalman filter type and all the information about the subsystem interactions is contained in $A_{12}\hat{\underline{x}}_2(t)$ and $A_{21}\hat{\underline{x}}_1(t)$. Therefore, if $A_{12}\hat{\underline{x}}_2(t)$ and $A_{21}\hat{\underline{x}}_1(t)$ can be provided to subsystem I and II, respectively, the overall filter problem decomposes into two independent filter problems. Since the gains K_1 and K_2 are calculated from optimal Riccati equations for the two independent subsystems, the filter must be optimal.

If $\underline{\eta}_1^*$, $\underline{\eta}_2^*$ are not white, then the filter cannot be optimal since $\underline{\eta}_1^*$, $\underline{\eta}_2^*$ must contain interaction information which can be extracted from them, at least in principle, by modelling these coloured noise processes by differential equations and augmenting the individual state vectors of the subsystems. If these interactions are ignored, then the independence of the two subsystems cannot be justified.

The optimality of the S.P.A. filter, therefore, hinges on the "whiteness" of $\underline{\eta}_1^*$ and $\underline{\eta}_2^*$. In the following it will be shown that for a number of cases of practical interest, $\underline{\eta}_1^*$ and $\underline{\eta}_2^*$ are indeed good approximations to white noise.

4.2. The "whiteness" of $\underline{\eta}_1^*$, $\underline{\eta}_2^*$ [75]

Consider subsystem II. It is desired to see under what conditions, if any,

$$E\{\underline{\eta}_2^*(t_2)\,\underline{\eta}_2^{*T}(t_1)\} = \delta(t_2 - t_1)\,Q_2^*$$

where Q_2^* is a matrix of known covariance, δ is the Dirac delta function and E is the expectation operator. Consider $t_2 = t_1 = t$. Then

$$\begin{aligned} E\{\underline{\eta}_2^*(t)\,\underline{\eta}_2^{*T}(t)\} &= E\{A_{21}(t)\,\tilde{\underline{x}}_1(t) + \underline{\eta}_2(t)\}\{A_{21}(t)\,\tilde{\underline{x}}_1(t) + \underline{\eta}_2(t)\}^T \\ &= E\{A_{21}(t)\,\tilde{\underline{x}}_1^T(t)\,\tilde{\underline{x}}_1^T(t)\,A_{21}^T(t)\} + E\{A_{21}(t)\,\tilde{\underline{x}}_1(t)\underline{\eta}_2^T(t)\} \\ &\quad + E\{\underline{\eta}_2(t)\,\tilde{\underline{x}}_1^T\,A_{21}(t)^T\} + E\{\underline{\eta}_2(t)\underline{\eta}_2^T(t)\} \end{aligned}$$

The second and third terms on the right-hand side of the above expression vanish because the estimation error and white noise are uncorrelated at t. Therefore

$$E\{\underline{\eta}_2^*(t)\underline{\eta}_2^{*T}(t)\} = A_{21}(t)\,P_{11}(t)\,A_{21}^T(t) + Q_2 \tag{28}$$

Thus $\underline{\eta}_2^*$ will be approximately white if $E\{\underline{\eta}_2^*(t_2)\underline{\eta}_2^{*T}(t_1)\}$, $(t_2 \neq t_1)$ is much smaller than the expression in equation (28) or if the spectral density of $\underline{\eta}_2^*$ is approximately constant over a range larger than that for subsystem II.

Consider the case when $t_2 > t_1$. Then

$$E\{\underline{\eta}_2^*(t_2)\ \underline{\eta}_2^*(t_1)^T\} = E\{[A_{21}(t_2)\ \underline{\tilde{x}}_1(t_2) + \underline{\eta}_2(t_2)][A_{21}(t_1)\ \underline{\tilde{x}}_1(t_1)$$

$$+\underline{\eta}_2(t_1)]^T\} = E\{A_{21}(t_2)\ \underline{\tilde{x}}_1(t_2)\ \underline{\tilde{x}}_1^T(t_1)\ A_{21}^T(t_1)\}$$
$$+ E\{A_{21}(t_2)\ \underline{\tilde{x}}_1(t_2)\ \underline{\eta}_2^T(t_1)\}$$
$$+ E\{\underline{\eta}_2(t_2)\ \underline{\tilde{x}}_1^T(t_1)\ A_{21}^T(t_1)\} + E\{\underline{\eta}_2(t_2)\ \underline{\eta}_2^T(t_1)\}$$

The fourth term is zero in the above expression from equation (20). The third term is zero since future noise is uncorrelated with past errors in the state estimates. Thus :

$$E\{\underline{\eta}_2^*(t_2)\ \underline{\eta}_2^*(t_1)^T\} = E\{A_{21}\ \underline{\tilde{x}}_1(t_2)\ \underline{\tilde{x}}_1(t_1)\ A_{21}^T(t_1)\}$$
$$+ E\{A_{21}(t_2)\ \underline{\tilde{x}}_1(t_2)\ \underline{\eta}_2^T(t_1)\} \tag{29}$$

Therefore, in order to evaluate $E\{\underline{\eta}_2^*(t_2)\ \underline{\eta}_2^*(t_1)^T\}$ for $t_2 \neq t_1$ it is necessary to relate $\underline{\tilde{x}}_1(t_2)$ with $\underline{\tilde{x}}_1(t_1)$ and with $\underline{\eta}_2(t_1)$. In order to do this, consider the overall optimal filter

$$\dot{\underline{\hat{x}}} = A\underline{\hat{x}} + K[\underline{y} - C\underline{\hat{x}}]. \tag{30}$$

The overall system equations could also be written as

$$\dot{\underline{x}} = A\underline{x} + \underline{\eta} \tag{31}$$
$$\underline{y} = C\underline{x} + \underline{\xi} \tag{32}$$

substracting equation (30) from equation (31)

$$(\dot{\underline{x}} - \dot{\underline{\hat{x}}}) = A\ (\underline{x} - \underline{\hat{x}}) + \underline{\eta} - K[\underline{y} - C\underline{\hat{x}}]$$

i.e.

$$\dot{\underline{\tilde{x}}} = A\underline{\tilde{x}} + \quad - K[C\underline{x} + \underline{\xi} - C\ \underline{\hat{x}}]$$

i.e.

$$\dot{\underline{\tilde{x}}} = (A - KC)\underline{\tilde{x}} - K\underline{\xi} + \underline{\eta}$$

integrating this estimation error equation

$$\underline{\tilde{x}}(t_2) = \emptyset(t_2-t_1)\ \underline{\tilde{x}}(t_1) + \int_{t_1}^{t_2} \emptyset(t_2,\tau)\left[-K(\tau)\underline{\xi}(\tau) \pm \underline{\eta}(\tau)\right] d\tau$$

where $\emptyset$ is the transition matrix associated with (A - KC).

Then

$$E\{\underline{\tilde{x}}(t_2)\ \underline{\tilde{x}}^T(t_1)\} = \emptyset(t_2,t_1)\ E\{\underline{\tilde{x}}(t_1)\ \underline{\tilde{x}}^T(t_1)\}$$
$$= \emptyset(t_2,t_1)\ P(t_1) \tag{33}$$

and

$$E\left\{\underline{\tilde{x}}(t_2)\,\underline{\eta}^T(t_1)\right\} = \int_{t_1}^{t_2} \phi(t_2,\tau)\left\{-K(\tau)\,\underline{\xi}(\tau)\underline{\eta}^T(t_1) + \right.$$

$$\left. + \underline{\eta}(\tau)\,\underline{\eta}^T(t_1)\right\} d\tau = \phi(t_2,t_1)\;Q(t_1) \qquad (34)$$

Now equation (33) can be written in terms of the component subsystem as

$$E\begin{bmatrix} \underline{\tilde{x}}_1(t_2)\,\underline{\tilde{x}}_1^T(t_1) & \underline{\tilde{x}}_1(t_2)\underline{\tilde{x}}_2^T(t_1) \\ \underline{\tilde{x}}_2(t_2)\,\underline{\tilde{x}}_1^T(t_1) & \underline{\tilde{x}}_2(t_2)\underline{\tilde{x}}_2^T(t_1) \end{bmatrix} = \begin{bmatrix} \phi_{11}(t_2,t_1) & \phi_{12}(t_2,t_1) \\ \phi_{21}(t_2,t_1) & \phi_{22}(t_2,t_1) \end{bmatrix}\begin{bmatrix} P_{11}(t_1) & P_{12}(t_1) \\ P_{12}^T(t_1) & P_{22}(t_1) \end{bmatrix}$$

$$E\left\{\underline{\tilde{x}}_1(t_2)\,\underline{\tilde{x}}_1^T(t_1)\right\} = \phi_{11}(t_2,t_1)\,P_{11}(t_1) + \phi_{12}(t_2,t_1)\,P_{12}^T\,(t_1)$$

Similarly,

$$E\left\{\underline{\tilde{x}}_1(t_2)\,\underline{\eta}_2^T(t_1)\right\} = \phi_{12}(t_2,t_1)\,Q_2(t_1)$$

Then substituting in equation (29)

$$E\left\{\underline{\eta}_2^*(t_2)\,\underline{\eta}_2^*(t_1)^T\right\} = A_{21}(t_2)\,\phi_{11}(t_2,t_1)\,P_{11}(t_1)\,A_{21}{}^T(t_1)$$

$$+ A_{21}(t_2)\,\phi_{12}(t_2,t_1)\,P_{12}^T\,(t_1)\,A_{21}{}^T(t_1)$$

$$+ A_{21}(t_2)\,\phi_{12}(t_2,t_1)\,Q_2(t_1) \qquad (35)$$

Equations (28) and (35) describe the autocorrelation function of the subsystem noise forcing term. The conditions under which the expression on the right-hand side of equation (35) is very much smaller than the expression on the right -hand side of equation (28) will now be examined.

It should be noted that the subsystem equation which produced $P_{12} > P_{11}$ P_{22} would not represent a good decomposition of the overall system and that it should always be possible to find a decomposition such that P_{11}, $P_{22} > P_{12}$. In any practical situation, in fact, P_{11}, P_{22} would be much larger than P_{12}.

Now comparing equations (28) and (35), term by term, the first and third terms of equation (35) are the same as the first two terms of equation (28) except for the multiplicative factors $\phi_{11}A_{21}(t_2)\phi_{12}$. In equation (35), however, there is also the additional term $A_{21}\phi_{12}P_{12}A_{21}^T$. Now $\phi(t_2,t_1)=\exp[(A-KC)\;(t_2-t_1)]$ and this factor will always be very small, provided the overall filter gain matrix K has terms of a large magnitude. In that case, $A_{21}\phi_{12}P_{12}A_{21}{}^T$ will be of negligible magnitude, being a product of small quantities. The other two terms in equation (35) would also be much smaller than the expression on the right-hand side of equation (28) because of the multiplicative factors ϕ_{11},ϕ_{12}.

Thus, the main condition under which $\underline{\eta}_1^*$, $\underline{\eta}_2^*$ are approximately white is when the overall gain K is large. One case of considerable practical significance where this occurs is when the measurement noise spectral density is low compared to the system noise since in that case, the overall steady state gain is indeed quite large. This is best illustrated by the scalar case.

Consider the scalar system :

$$\dot{x} = ax + \eta \quad ; \quad y = cx + \xi$$

In this case the scalar Riccati equation becomes :

$$\dot{p} = 2ap - \frac{p^2 c^2}{r} + q$$

In the steady state, $\dot{p} \rightarrow 0$ so that

$$p^2 - \frac{2\,ar}{c^2}\,p - \frac{r}{c^2}\,q = 0$$

or

$$p = \frac{ar}{c^2} + \frac{2}{c^2}\sqrt{(a^2 r^2 + qr\ )}$$

then

$$K = \frac{pc}{r} = \frac{a}{c} \pm \frac{2}{c}\sqrt{a^2 + \frac{q}{r}}$$

From this equation it is clear that the steady state gain K is large when $q \gg r$.

In a practical case, for a given system, all that is required is that the spectral density of the interaction noise be relatively constant over the period of the system time constants. This will be illustrated in the numerical studies. It should be noted that the covariance of the subsystem noise for the two subsystems from equation (28) is

$$Q_2^* = Q_2 + A_{21}(t)\,P_{11}(t)\,A_{21}^T(t)$$
$$Q_1^* = Q_1 + A_{12}(t)\,P_{22}(t)\,A_{21}^T(t)$$

and these are the values of the subsystem noise which are used in the filter of equation (27). This is the reason why Shah calls the filter the supplemented partitioning approach. However, the above analysis shows that the crucial part of the method is the filter structure where the forcing terms $A_{12}(t)\,\hat{\underline{x}}_2(t)$ into subsystem one filter and $A_{21}(t)\,\hat{\underline{x}}_1(t)$ into subsystem two filter provide the bulk of the interactions. In fact, for the serial systems class, as discussed in Section 6, results which are virtually identical to the S.P.A. filter results can be obtained without supplementing the system covariance matrices.

4.3. Computational requirements

The principal attraction of the above S.P.A. filter is its computational simplicity. Shah [74] derived expressions for the computational requirements of the optimal and suboptimal filter. However, his formulae were for a discrete time system whereas here a continuous time system is being considered. Still it is easy to show (Singh [13]) that the computational requirements, in terms of elementary multiplication operations, for the two continuous time filters, are for each iteration :

Optimal

$$20l^3 + 4p^3 + 5l^2p + 5lp^2 + 4lm^2 + 8l^2 + 12lp + 4l\,m + m^2$$

Suboptimal

$$\sum_{i=1}^{2} (20l_i^3 + 4p_i^3 + 5_i p_i^2 + 5l_i^2 p_i + 5l_i m_i^2 + 5m_i^2 + 8l_i^2 + 4l_i m_i +$$

$$+ 121_i m_i^2) + 101_i^2 1_2 + 101_i 1_2^2$$

since $1 \gg 1_i$, $m \gg m_i$, $p \gg p_i$ the computational savings can be substantial.

4.3.1. Figure of merit

To compare the performance of the optimal and suboptimal filters, the square of the estimation error was taken as the criterion function, i.e. for a particular system, at each iteration, the optimal and suboptimal estimates were compared with the states obtained from a simulation of the overall system. This is a more valid criterion than the trace of the covariance matrix as used by Shah for discrete, dynamical sytems, since in that case the subsystem error covariance matrix does not represent the true covariance of the suboptimal estimates as it is obtained from a suboptimal Riccati equation.

4.4. Simulation Studies

The first example is of a serially connected system. The overall system is of second order and consists of two subsystems. The system equations are :

$$\begin{aligned} \dot{x}_1 &= - x_1 + \eta_1 \\ y_1 &= x_1 + \xi_1 \\ \dot{x}_2 &= - x_1 - x_2 + \eta_2 \\ y_2 &= x_2 + \xi_2 \end{aligned}$$

The optimal and suboptimal filters were simulated on the ICL 4130 digital computer of the Cambridge University Control Group. Since the optimal filter is optimal in a statistical sense, it is necessary to compare the performance of the optimal and suboptimal filters for a number of sample functions of the noise and to take an average.

Results

In the first series of tests, the case when the overall system noise was Q = I and the overall measurement noise, R = 0.5I was investigated were I is the second-order identity matrix. Five different simulations were done for different sample functions of the noise and the average was taken. Each simulation was for 100 iterations. The average optimal cost was 14.43 and the corresponding suboptimal cost was 14.50, giving a performance loss of 0.5 %. The computational requirements for the two filters were :

Optimal = 404 multiplications per iteration

Suboptimal : 88 multiplications per iteration

Computational saving : 460 %

Figure 3 shows the performance of the filters for one of the sample functions of the noise. The states start from 1 and the estimates from zero. The initial error covariance is assumed to be known exactly, being the second-order identity matrix. The top two graphs show the observations and the true state as obtained from the simulation. The measurement noise level is quite high. The next two graphs show the state x_2 and the corresponding optimal and suboptimal estimates. These are virtually identical. Convergence to the true states takes place fairly quickly but this is to be expected since measurement noise covariance is only 50 % of the system noise covariance.

In another test, the case when Q = R = I was examined. Here the optimal and suboptimal costs over five simulations for different sample functions of noise were :

Optimal = 18.25

Suboptimal : 18.76

Performance loss = 2.9 %

Thus, as expected, the suboptimal performance deteriorates as the measurement noise increases.

Example 2

This is a continuous time version of one of Shah's examples. The system equations were :

$$\dot{x}_1 = -0.8\, x_1 + 0.6\, x_2 + \eta_2 \quad ; \quad y_1 = x_1 + \xi_1$$

$$\dot{x}_2 = 0.6\, x_1 - 0.8\, x_2 + \eta_2 \quad ; \quad y_2 = x_2 + \xi_2$$

For this example Shah's results showed virtually optimal performance but with the more realistic performance measure used here, this turns out not to be the case.

For this example, the computational requirements for the two filters are the same as for example 1, i.e.

Optimal = 404 multiplications per iteration

Suboptimal = 88 multiplications per iteration

Saving = 460 %

The filters were simulated for a variety of system and measurement noise levels. In each case, five different simulations were performed for different sample functions of the noise. The initial conditions on the states and estimates were :

$$x_1(0) = x_2(0) = 1 \quad ; \quad \hat{x}_1(0) = \hat{x}_2(0) = 0$$

$$P_{11}(0) = P_{22}(0) = 1$$

Table 1 gives the optimal and suboptimal performances

Q	R	Optimal average cost for 100 iterations	Suboptimal average cost for 100 iterations	Performance loss
I	0.1I	4.47	4.77	6.9 %
I	0.2I	7.59	8.27	9 %
I	0.5I	12.55	13.90	10 %
I	I	15.48	18.51	20 %
I	2I	25.36	31.88	26 %

Table 1

For one of the sample functions of four of the above simulations, equations (28) and (35) were computed to yield the autocorrelation function of the interaction noise for certain values of time when steady state had been reached in each case. Figure 4 gives these values over the effective time constant of 0.8 of subsystem

II. The graphs show that increasing the measurement noise R provides a decreasingly good approximation to white noise. This, taken with the results in Table 1, provides experimental confirmation of the theory developed in Section 4.2.

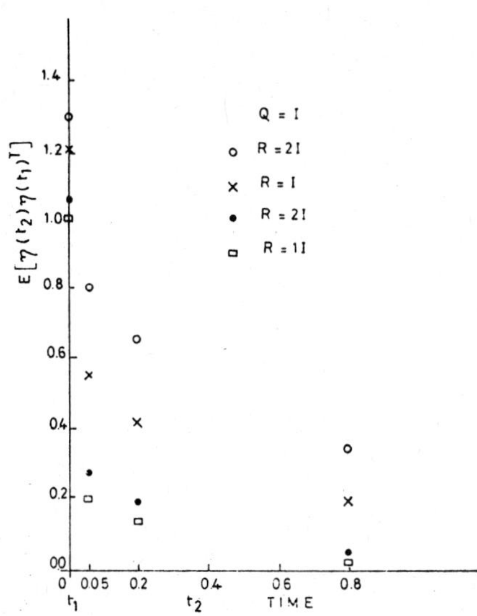

Figure 4

4.5. Discussion

The S.P.A. filter described above has modest computational requirements and yields good filtering performance for a variety of conditions. For the serial systems example, the performance is markedly better than for the second more general example. This is to be expected since, for serial systems, the number of interconnections is smaller. The theory developed in Section 4.2. enables predictions to be made of the expected efficiency of the filter. The main point that emerges is that if the gain K is large, good filter performance will result. The most important case where this occurs is when the measurement noise spectral density is low. Such a situation often arises in practice since the instrumentation on most modern systems is usually fairly accurate.

In the next section, the extension of the filter to the case where time delays exist between the subsystems is described.

5. A DECENTRALISED FILTER FOR TIME LAG SYSTEMS

Since many practical systems are distributed parameter systems which can be approximated fairly well by lumped parameter subsystems separated by pure time delays, it is important to investigate if a decentralised filter such as the S.P.A. filter described above can be extended to cover such systems.

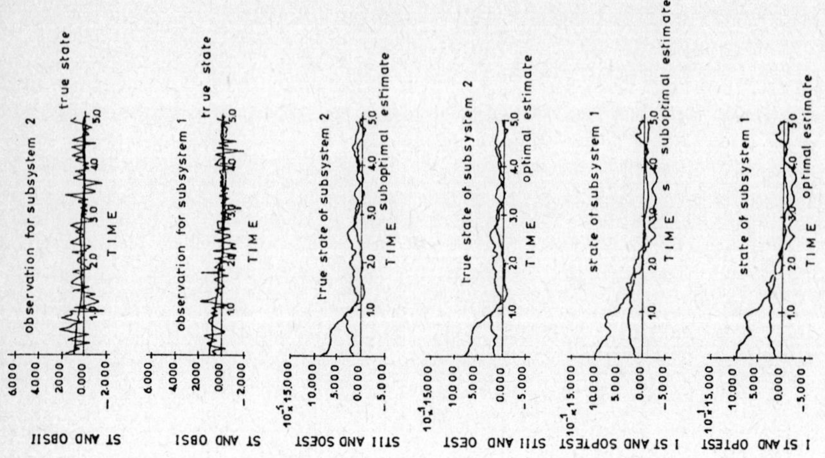

Fig. 6 : Simulation results for example 2

Fig. 5 : A decentralised filter for time lag systems

Consider a system consisting of two subsystems with time lags between them. The dynamical equations of the system could be written as :

$$\dot{\underline{x}}_1(t) = A_{11}(t)\,\underline{x}_1(t) + A_{12}(t)\,\underline{x}_2(t-\theta_2) + \underline{\eta}_1(t)$$

$$\underline{y}_1(t) = C_{11}(t)\,\underline{x}_1(t) + \underline{\xi}_1(t)$$

$$\dot{\underline{x}}_2(t) = A_{21}(t)\,\underline{x}_1(t-\theta_1) + A_{22}(t)\,\underline{x}_2(t) + \underline{\eta}_2(t)$$

$$\underline{y}_2(t) = C_{22}(t)\,\underline{x}_2(t) + \underline{\xi}_2(t)$$

where $\underline{\eta}_1, \underline{\eta}_2, \underline{\xi}_1, \underline{\xi}_2$ are drawn from Gaussian white noise sources as shown in equations (20) and (21). Consider subsystem I. The state equations could be written as :

$$\dot{\underline{x}}_1(t) = A_{11}(t)\,\underline{x}_1(t) + A_{12}(t)\,\hat{\underline{x}}_2(t-\theta_2) + \underline{\eta}_1^*(t)$$

where

$$\underline{\eta}_1^*(t) = A_{12}\,\tilde{\underline{x}}_2(t-\theta_2) + \underline{\eta}_1(t)$$

By the same reasoning* as for the S.P.A. filter in Section 4.2 it is possible to construct independent filters for the two subsystems provided that

(a) $A_{12}\hat{\underline{x}}_2(t-\theta_2)$ is fed into subsystem I and
$A_{21}\hat{\underline{x}}_1(t-\theta_1)$ into subsystem II

(b) the subsystem noise covariance matrices Q_1 and Q_2 are augmented to Q_1^*, Q_2^* where

$$Q_1^* = Q_1 + A_{12}(t)\,P_{22}(t-\theta_1)\,A_{12}(t)^T$$

$$Q_2^* = Q_2 + A_{21}(t)\,P_{11}(t-\theta_2)\,A_{21}(t)^T$$

and these are the values used in the filter equations (27). The filter structure is shown in Fig. 5. Here the first level solves the independent filter problems using equations (27 c-f) and the second level provides

(a) the values of $P_{11}(t-\theta_1)$, $P_{22}(t-\theta_2)$ for the Q_1^*, Q_2^* used for Q_1, Q_2 in equations (27 e,f) ; these Q_1^*, Q_2^* are obtained from equation (28)

(b) the new filtered estimates $\hat{\underline{x}}_1$, $\hat{\underline{x}}_2$ which are delayed and fed into the subsystem filters as shown by the double lines in Fig. 5. The actual estimates are of course obtained from the first level so that the second level in this case serves merely as a communication link.

Numerical example

A simple numerical example was computed to illustrate the performance of this filter. The system equations are for a time lag version of example 2 in Section 4.4., i.e.

$$\dot{x}_1(t) = -0.8x_1(t) + 0.6x_2(t-\theta) + \eta_1(t)$$

$$y_1(t) = x_1(t) + \xi_1(t)$$

$$\dot{x}_2(t) = -0.8x_2(t) + 0.6x_1(t-\theta) + \eta_2(t)$$

$$y_2 = x_2 + \xi_2$$

* A detailed analysis for this time lag case is given by Singh [76] and since the main steps in the theoretical development are virtually identical to the analysis in Section 4.2. it has been omitted here.

The optimal and suboptimal filters were simulated for this example on the ICL 4130 digital computer of the Cambridge University Control Group. The delays in the overall filter were approximated by a second-order Taylor series expansion, i.e.

$$x_1(t-\theta) = L^{-1}\left[x_1 \exp(-s\theta)\right] = L^{-1}\left[x_1(s)/1 + s\theta + s^2 \frac{\theta^2}{2}\right]$$

where L is the Laplace transform, so that the overall system became of sixth order.

The computational requirements for the optimal and suboptimal filters were :

Optimal = 5390 multiplications per iteration

Suboptimal = 156 multiplications per iteration

Savings = 35 times

Simulation results

Table 2 gives an average of five different simulations for each value of the noise covariance matrices Q and R. All the costs are for 100 iterations for delay θ = 0.1 sec.

Q	R	Optimal average cost	Suboptimal average cost	Performance loss
I	0.1I	5.360	5.362	0.4 %
I	0.5I	16.494	17.753	7.5 %
I	I	19.100	21.230	9 %
I	2I	27.508	30.643	10 %

Table 2

5.1. Comment

The decentralised filter for time lag systems is a fairly straightforward extension of the S.P.A. filter. It yields good performance and has small computational requirements. However, as pointed out previously, the most important aspect of the S.P.A. filter is not the supplementation of the covariance matrices but rather the structure of the decentralised filter. This fact is emphasised in the serial systems feedforward filter which we describe in the next section.

6. THE FEEDFORWARD FILTER FOR SERIAL SYSTEMS

Because of the duality of linear estimation and control, it is intuitively reasonable to believe that the simple hierarchical structure which we described in Chapter VI for serial systems can be used to obtain a good suboptimal solution to the state estimation problem for such serially connected systems. To illustrate this, consider the system

$$\begin{aligned}
\dot{\underline{x}}_1(t) &= A_{11}\underline{x}_1(t) + B_1\underline{u}_1(t) + \underline{w}_1(t) + \underline{\eta}_1(t) \\
\dot{\underline{x}}_2(t) &= A_{21}\underline{x}_1(t) + A_{22}\underline{x}_2(t) + B_2\underline{u}_2(t) + \underline{w}_2(t) + \underline{\eta}_2(t) \\
&\vdots \\
\dot{\underline{x}}_n(t) &= A_{nn-1}\underline{x}_{n-1}(t) + A_{nn}\underline{x}_n(t) + B_n\underline{u}_n(t) + \underline{w}_n(t) + \underline{\eta}_n(t)
\end{aligned} \qquad (36)$$

where $\underline{\eta}_i$, i = 1,2,....,n are l_i dimensional Gaussian white noise disturbance vectors with zero mean and covariance matrix Q_i, i.e.

$$E\{\underline{\eta}_i(t)\} = \underline{0} \quad ; \quad E\{\underline{\eta}_i(t)\underline{\eta}_i^T(\tau)\} = Q_i\,\delta(t-\tau)$$

where $\delta(t-\tau)$ is the Dirac delta function and E is the expectation operator. Further let it be assumed that the system is observed via the following linear observation equations,

$$\begin{aligned} \underline{y}_1(t) &= C_{11}\underline{x}_1(t) + \underline{\xi}_1 \\ &\vdots \\ \underline{y}_n(t) &= C_{nn}\underline{x}_n(t) + \underline{\xi}_n \end{aligned} \tag{37}$$

where $\underline{\xi}_i$, i = 1,2,...,n are p_i dimensional Gaussian white noise vectors with zero mean and covariance R_i, i.e.

$$E\{\underline{\xi}_i(t)\} = \underline{0} \quad ; \quad E\{\underline{\xi}_i(t)\underline{\xi}_j^T(\tau)\} = R_i\,\delta(t-\tau)\,.$$

A suboptimal strategy, analogous to the one we used in Chapter VI for the control problem can be used to solve the state estimation problem for the system of equations (36, 37). Sub-system one solves it own local state estimation problem and the second level feeds forward the resulting state estimate to sub-system two where it is considered as a disturbance. Subsystem two then solves its own local state estimation problem and the local estimation-feedforward procedure is continued down the line of subsystems as in the control case. This procedure requires that each subsystem filter implements the following (Kalman [71]) state estimation equations for its own local subsystem

$$\begin{aligned} \dot{\hat{\underline{x}}}_i(t) &= A_{i,i-1}\hat{\underline{x}}_{i-1}(t) + A_{ii}\hat{\underline{x}}_i(t) + B_i\underline{u}_i(t) + \underline{w}_i(t) \\ &\quad + K_i\left[\underline{y}_i(t) - C_{ii}\underline{x}_i(t)\right] \qquad i = 1,2,\ldots,n \end{aligned} \tag{38}$$

where $K_i = P_{ii}C_{ii}^T R_i^{-1}$ and P_{ii} is the solution of the matrix Riccati equation

$$\dot{P}_{ii} = A_{ii}P_{ii} + P_{ii}A_{ii}^T - P_{ii}C_{ii}^T R_i^{-1} C_{ii}P_{ii} + Q_i\,.$$

Using the same heuristic reasoning as in the control case of Chapter VI, it should be expected that the resulting state estimator will often be near optimal, and this has been confirmed by many numerical studies. One such study is described below. Again it is easy to extend the filter to the time lag case.

It should be noted that since it is not required to supplement the system noise covariance matrices Q_i, the number of multiplication operations per iteration in the implementation of the filter is reduced.

Example

Consider the system

$$\begin{aligned} \dot{x}_1 &= -x_1 + \eta_1 \\ y_1 &= x_1 + \xi_1 \\ \dot{x}_2 &= -x_2 + \eta_2 - x_1 \\ y_2 &= x_2 + \xi_2 \end{aligned}$$

This algorithm was previously simulated using the S.P.A. algorithm in

Section 4 whilst here it is computed with the feedforward algorithm for comparison using the same functions of noise. The average optimal and suboptimal costs are :

Optimal = 14.43
Suboptimal = 14.52
Performance loss = 0.5 %

Figure 6 shows the performance of the optimal and suboptimal filters. This is virtually identical to the results from the S.P.A. calculation shown in Fig. 3.

Let us next consider a more practical application of the S.P.A. and feedforward filters to our "no-delay" 2 reach River Cam model.

7. APPLICATION TO THE RIVER SYSTEM

The two reach no-delay river model can be written as

$$\frac{d}{dt}\begin{bmatrix} z_1 \\ q_1 \\ z_2 \\ q_2 \end{bmatrix} = \begin{bmatrix} -1.32 & 0 & 0 & 0 \\ -0.32 & -1.2 & 0 & 0 \\ 0.9 & 0 & -1.32 & 0 \\ 0 & 0.9 & & -1.2 \end{bmatrix}\begin{bmatrix} z_1 \\ q_1 \\ z_2 \\ q_2 \end{bmatrix} + \begin{bmatrix} 0.1m_1 + z_0 + 53.5 + u_1 \\ 1.9 + q_0 + u_2 \\ 0.1m_2 + 41.9 + u_3 \\ 1.9 + u_4 \end{bmatrix} \tag{39}$$

$$\begin{bmatrix} y_1 \\ y_2 \\ y_3 \\ y_4 \end{bmatrix} = \begin{bmatrix} 1 & 0 & 0 & 0 \\ 0 & 1 & 0 & 0 \\ 0 & 0 & 1 & 0 \\ 0 & 0 & 0 & 1 \end{bmatrix}\begin{bmatrix} z_1 \\ q_1 \\ z_2 \\ q_2 \end{bmatrix} + \begin{bmatrix} v_1 \\ v_2 \\ v_3 \\ v_4 \end{bmatrix} \tag{40}$$

where z_1, z_2, q_1, q_2 are respectively the concentrations of B.O.D. and D.O. in reaches 1 and 2 ; m_1, m_2 are the known deterministic controlled discharges of B.O.D. into the river ; z_0, q_0 are respectively the known B.O.D. and D.O. inputs into reach 1 ; $\underline{u}^T = [u_1, u_2, u_3, u_4]$ is a zero mean Gaussian white noise vector of known covariance

$$Q = \begin{bmatrix} Q_1 & 0 \\ 0 & Q_2 \end{bmatrix}$$

where Q_i, Q_2 are 2 x 2 matrices and $\underline{v}^T = [v_1, v_2, v_3, v_4]$ is also a zero mean Gaussian white noise vector of known covariance

$$R = \begin{bmatrix} R_1 & 0 \\ 0 & R_2 \end{bmatrix}$$

$\underline{y}^T = [y_1, y_2, y_3, y_4]$ is vector of the measurements of B.O.D. and D.O. for the two reaches.

Using the overall Kalman filter equations, a filter for the two reach no-delay system could be constructed where the overall optimum state estimates evolve according to the equation :

$$\frac{d}{dt} \begin{bmatrix} \hat{z}_1 \\ \hat{q}_1 \\ \hat{z}_2 \\ \hat{q}_2 \end{bmatrix} = \begin{bmatrix} -1.32 & 0 & 0 & 0 \\ -0.32 & -1.2 & 0 & 0 \\ 0.9 & 0 & -1.32 & 0 \\ 0 & 0.9 & -0.32 & -1.2 \end{bmatrix} \begin{bmatrix} \hat{z}_1 \\ \hat{q}_1 \\ \hat{z}_2 \\ \hat{q}_2 \end{bmatrix} +$$

$$\begin{bmatrix} 0.1m_1 + z_0 + 53.5 \\ 1.9 + q_0 \\ 0.1m_2 + 41.9 \\ 1.9 \end{bmatrix} + \begin{bmatrix} K_{11} & K_{12} & K_{13} & K_{14} \\ K_{21} & K_{22} & K_{23} & K_{24} \\ K_{31} & K_{32} & K_{33} & K_{34} \\ K_{41} & K_{42} & K_{43} & K_{44} \end{bmatrix} \begin{bmatrix} y_1 - \hat{z}_1 \\ y_2 - \hat{q}_1 \\ y_3 - \hat{z}_2 \\ y_4 - \hat{q}_2 \end{bmatrix}$$

where the gain matrix K_{ij} $i = 1,\ldots, 4$; $j = 1,\ldots, 4$ is obtained from the Riccati equation .

Using
$$\begin{bmatrix} \hat{z}_1(0) \\ \hat{q}_1(0) \\ \hat{z}_2(0) \\ \hat{q}_2(0) \end{bmatrix} = \underline{0} \qquad \begin{bmatrix} z_1(0) \\ q_1(0) \\ z_2(0) \\ q_2(0) \end{bmatrix} = \begin{bmatrix} 4.06 \\ 8 \\ 5.94 \\ 6 \end{bmatrix}$$

$$P_0 = \begin{bmatrix} 16 & 0 & 0 & 0 \\ 0 & 64 & 0 & 0 \\ 0 & 0 & 36 & 0 \\ 0 & 0 & 0 & 36 \end{bmatrix}$$

where P_0 is the initial covariance in the Riccati equation,the overall optimum filter was simulated on the ICL 4130 digital computer of the Cambridge University Control Group for a variety of system and measurement noises. For comparison,the S.P.A. filter was also simulated using the same sample function of the noise. It will be recalled that the S.P.A. requires the augmentation of the system noise covariance matrices as follows :

$$Q_1^* = Q_1 + A_{12} P_{22} A_{12}^T \tag{41}$$

$$Q_2^* = Q_2 + A_{21} P_{11} A_{21}^T \tag{42}$$

where Q_1, Q_2 are the system noise covariances of the two subsystems, A_{12}, A_{21} are the off-diagonal parts of the overall system matrix and P_{11}, P_{22} are the solutions of the subsystem filter Riccati equations. Here, since $A_{12} = 0$,

$$Q_1^* = Q_1 \tag{43}$$

In the first test, the overall system noise covariance $Q = 20\ I_4$ was used where I_4 is the fourth order identity matrix. The overall measurement noise was $R = I_4$. The S.P.A. and overall optimum filters were simulated over a period of five days using an integration interval $\Delta T = 0.025$ days.

Fig. 7 shows the optimal and suboptimal S.P.A. results for reach 1. The top two graphs show the true D.O. and B.O.D. for the five day period as calculated from an integration of the system equation, with superimposed system noise generated digitally from a Gaussian white noise generator. The observations of B.O.D. and D.O. which are corrupted by measurement noise are also shown on the same graphs. The third graph shows the state D.O. with the suboptimal S.P.A. state estimate

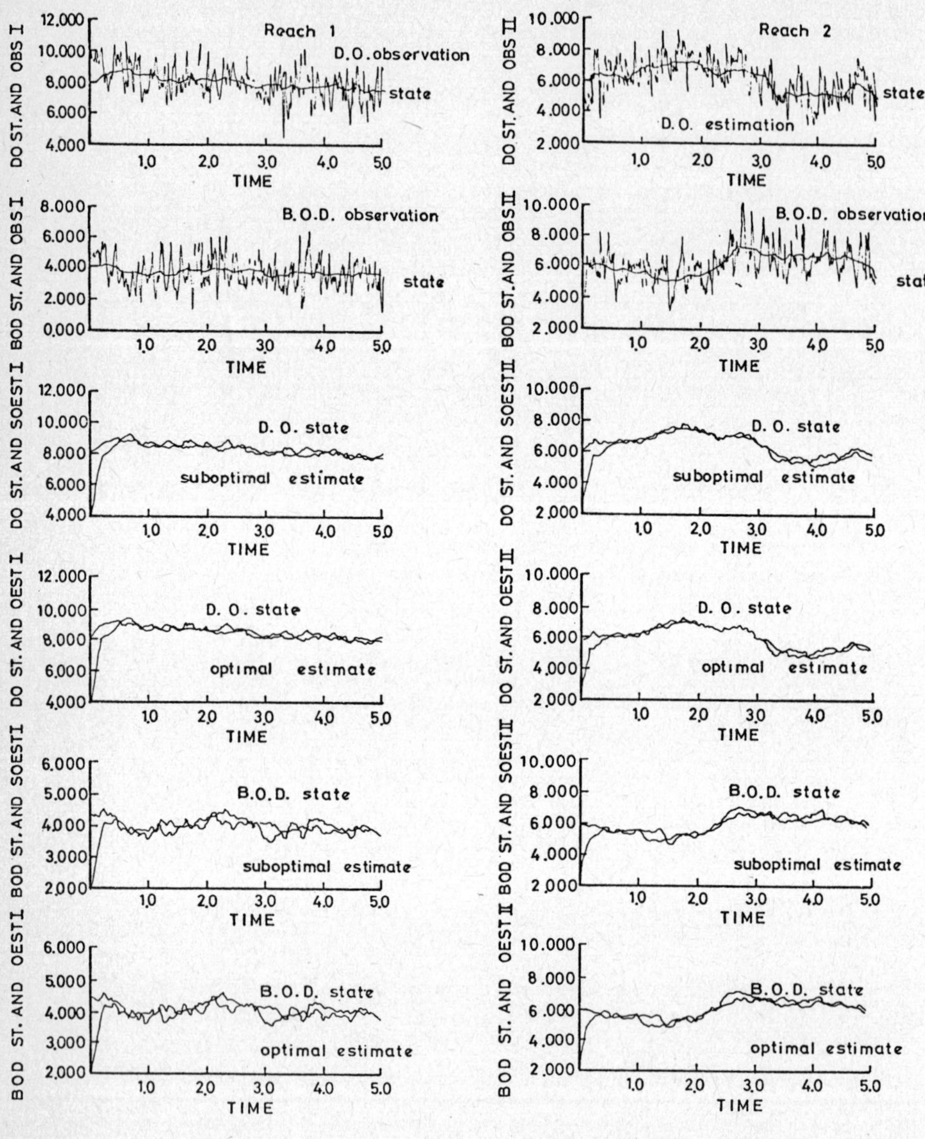

FIGURE 7

FIGURE 8

whereas the fourth one shows the state D.O. and the overall optimal estimate. The bottom two graphs show the same for B.O.D. Note that the optimum and suboptimum estimates for both B.O.D. and D.O. are virtually identical whilst the optimal filter's computational requirements in terms of elementary multiplication operations using the expressions of Section 4.3. are 2608 per iteration compared to 535 for the S.P.A. giving a saving of approximately 500 %. The estimates converge very quickly to the actual state but this is to be expected since the measurement noise is fairly low. Fig. 8 shows the corresponding results for the second reach. Again the optimal and suboptimal estimates are virtually identical. Note that the B.O.D. and D.O. estimates remain around 4.06 and 8 for reach 1 and around 5.94 and 6 for reach 2 after convergence since these are the desired steady state values and there is no bias.

For comparison, the feedforward filter was also simulated for this example. This involved setting $Q_1^{\star} = Q_1$, $Q_2^{\star} = Q_2$ in equations (41) and (42). The feedforward filter in this case gives a computational saving of about 7 % per iteration on even the S.P.A. and this increases if more reaches are considered. The results of the simulation of the feedforward filter are shown in Figs. 9 and 10 for reaches 1 and 2 using the same sample functions of the noise. The optimal estimates and the suboptimal feedforward estimates are virtually identical showing that the feedforward filter is also near optimal. If Fig. 7 is superimposed on Fig. 9, and Fig. 8 on Fig. 10 the results are indistinguishable showing that the S.P.A. filter and the feedforward filter give identical performance for this sytem.

In another series of experiments, a situation in which the overall measurement noise is much higher was investigated, in order to assess the performance of the two suboptimal filters in more difficult conditions*. Note that these levels of measurement noise are fairly unrealistic and represent a sort of worst case design. Figs. 11 and 12 show the results for the two reaches using the S.P.A. filter and Figs. 13 and 14 the same using the feedforward filter. Here convergence to the true states is slower taking about 1.5 days. After that all the filters follow the true states faithfully. The S.P.A., feedforward and the overall optimal filters are again virtually identical.

Many other tests for varying system and measurement noise were performed for this system and they all gave similar results. Some further tests where the S.P.A. and overall optimal filter are compared for the time delay case are given in [76] and have been omitted here.

7.1. Discussion

The simulation results for the two reach river system have shown that it is possible to get virtually optimal performance from the simple decentralised filters for this practical problem. It should be noted that the filter formulation here is important even without the stochastic control implications if only in so far as the smoothing problem is solved with the same algorithms and this should be of interest in the collection and interpretation of river data at the present time.

In this chapter we have considered a number of filters for the decentralised state estimation of large scale systems. The main points which emerge from our study are :

(a) At the present time, optimal decentralised filtering is not a practical proposition for large scale systems since it is necessary, with the only optimal algorithm that has been proposed [7] to solve a succession of optimisation problems where the optimisation sequences get longer as time passes.

(b) For suboptimal filtering, two general approaches have been discussed. The first is the approach of Arafeh and Sage [53] which provides sequential coor-

---

* Here $Q = 20\ I_4$, $R = 10\ I_4$

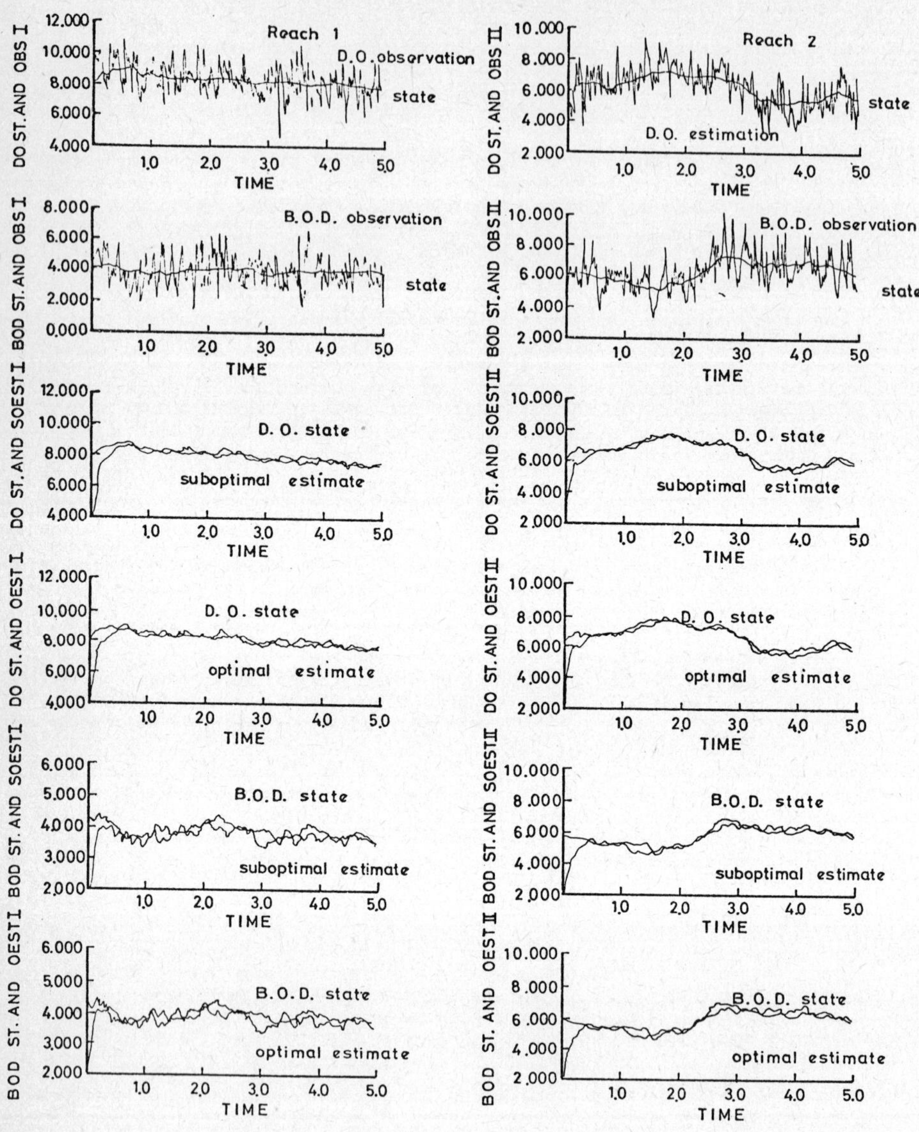

FIGURE 9

FIGURE 10

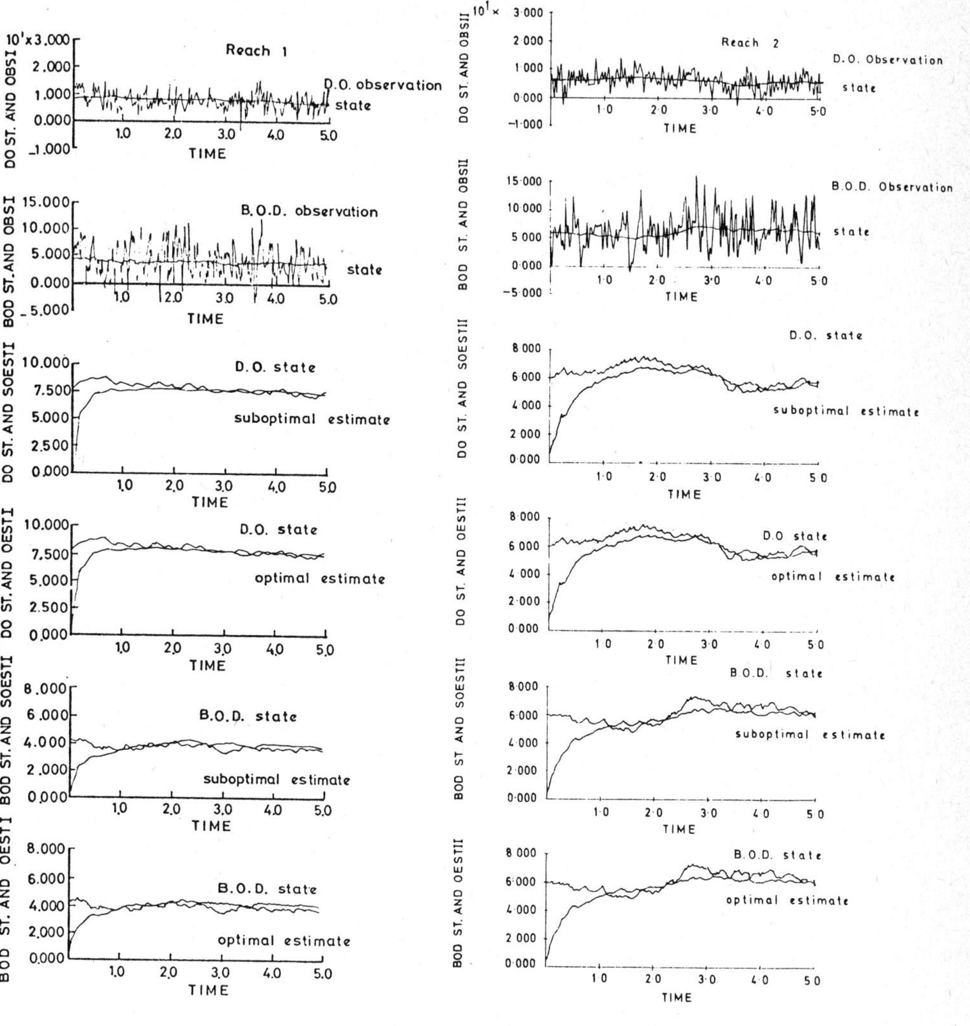

FIGURE 11

FIGURE 12

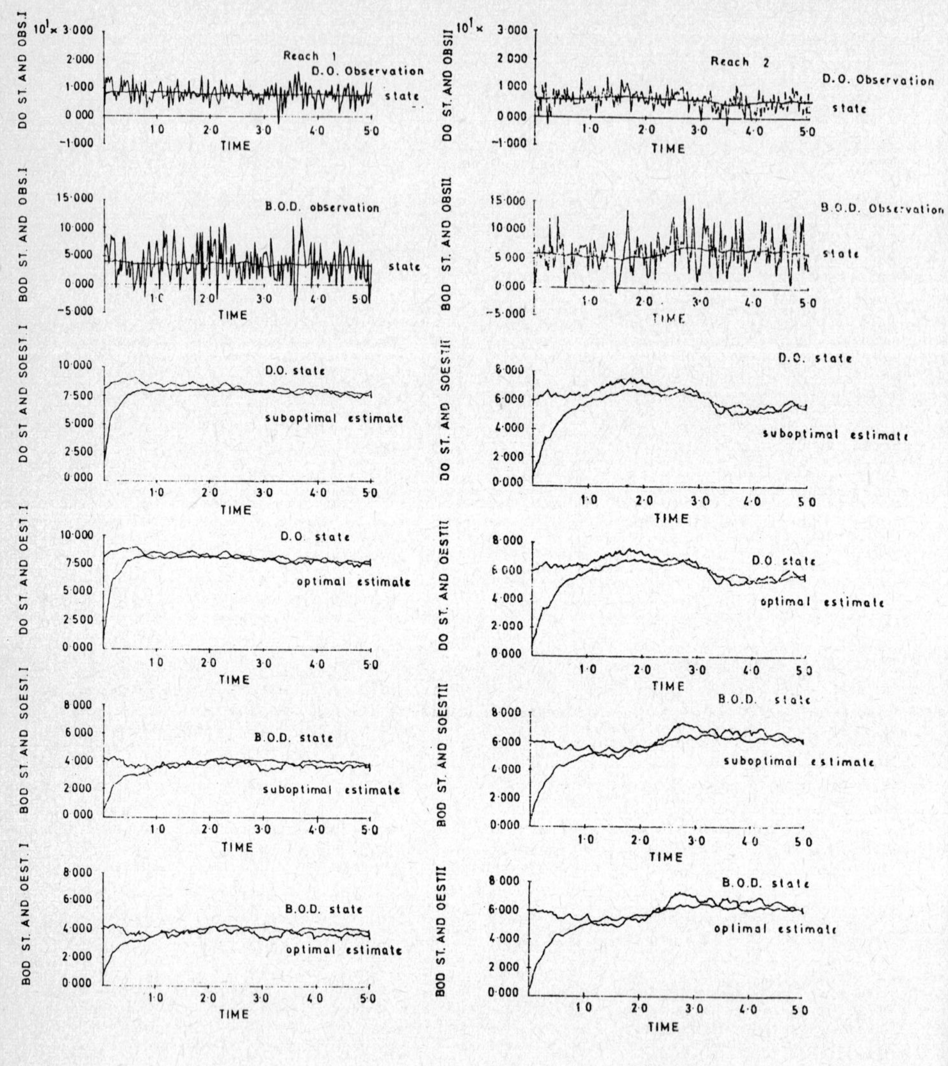

FIGURE 13

FIGURE 14

dination for improvement using the basic framework of Pearson [7] , i.e. by converting the estimation/identification problem to an optimisation problem. In the other approach instead of solving a surrogate optimisation problem, we use direct "primal" decomposition. Here it is necessary to supply the interconnections which have been severed in the decomposition. In the analysis of the S.P.A. filter, we saw that the interconnections consisted of two components, i.e.

(i) the filtered estimates from the other subsystems and
(ii) the rest of the interactions which are present in $\underline{\eta}_1^*$, $\underline{\eta}_2^*$ in equations (24) and (26).

In certain important practical cases, i.e. where the measurement noise is small compared to the system noise, the vectors $\underline{\eta}_1^*$, $\underline{\eta}_2^*$ are fairly good approximations to white noise. This implies that there is little further interaction information in $\underline{\eta}_1^*$ and $\underline{\eta}_2^*$ so that the filter should be near optimal and this has been confirmed by our numerical studies.

(c) Under such conditions, for serial systems, one should expect to achieve particularly good suboptimal filter performance since the total interactions are likely to be "small" because of the smaller number of links.This is confirmed by the numerical studies.

(d) Since the filtered estimates from other subsystems are usually the most important components of the interactions (if $\underline{\eta}_1^*$, $\underline{\eta}_2^*$ are nearly white) the serial feedforward filter should be near optimal and this is also borne out by the simulation studies.

(e) Since direct "primal" decomposition is used, the same filter structure should be applicable for systems with time lags between the subsystems. Again numerical studies confirm this.

The approach of Sage, on the other hand, is useful particularly for parameter estimation since there accurate final values are more important than parameter values obtained near the origin of time.

8. CONCLUSIONS

In this chapter we have considered many approaches for the near optimal estimation and identification of large scale systems. In principle, any of these estimators could be cascaded with a deterministic controller to yield stochastic control. In the next chapter we examine a two level structure for the optimal Kalman filter and show that it indeed yields optimal stochastic control.

An entirely different approach to stochastic control has been suggested by Chong and Athans [77]. In this approach, coordination is only used periodically so that in between the coordination instants, the subsystem's stochastic controllers are essentially independant of each other. For such periodic coordination to work, it is necessary that the subsystem interaction dynamics be very slow. It is also necessary that the interactions be satisfied on average (i.e. not instantaneously). This can perhaps be achieved through the introduction of buffer stores. So far, no practical studies have been performed with such periodic coordination algorithms but the approach is certainly of value for a significant class of problems.

CHAPTER IX

OPTIMAL STOCHASTIC CONTROL USING MULTI-LEVEL TECHNIQUES

1. INTRODUCTION

In this final chapter we describe some recent results in the area of stochastic optimal control using multi-level techniques. We begin the analysis by developing an optimal two level filter which has desirable numerical properties. We then cascade this filter with an optimal deterministic two level controller taken from chapter IV to achieve optimal stochastic control. Both the filter and controller are illustrated on realistic examples. Finally, we examine the joint problem of parameter estimation and optimal control. We develop a four level algorithm for tackling such problems.

2. THE MULTI-LEVEL KALMAN FILTER [103]

The most appealing property of the global Kalman filter from a practical point of view is its recursive nature. Essentially, this recursive property of the filter arises from the fact that if an estimate exists based on measurements up to that instant, then when receiving another set of measurements, one could subtract from these measurements that part which could be anticipated from the results of the first measurements, i.e., the updating is based on that part of the new data which is orthogonal to the old data. In the new filter for systems comprising lower order interconnected subsystems this orthogonalisation is performed subsystem by subsystem, i.e., the optimal estimate of the state of subsystem one is obtained by successively orthogonalising the error based on a new measurement for subsystems 1,2,3,..., N w.r.t. the Hilbert space formed by all measurements of all the subsystems up to that instant. Much computational saving results using this successive orthogonalization procedure since, at each stage, only low-order subspaces are manipulated.

The actual orthogonalisation procedure that is performed in the Kalman filter is based on the following theorem (cf. Luenberger [104 p.92]).

Theorem 1: Let β be a member of space H of random variables which is a closed subspace of L_2 and let $\hat{\beta}_1$ denote its orthogonal projection on a closed subspace y_1 of H (thus, $\hat{\beta}_1$ is the best estimate of β in y_1). Let $\underline{y}_2$ be an m vector of random variables generating a subspace y_2 of H and let $\hat{\underline{y}}_2$ denote the m-dimensional vector of the projections of the components of $\underline{y}_2$ on to y_1 (thus $\hat{\underline{y}}_2$ is the vector of best estimates of y_2 in y_1). Let $\tilde{\underline{y}}_2 = \underline{y}_2 - \hat{\underline{y}}_2$.

Then the projection of β on to the subspace $y_1 \oplus y_2$, denoted $\hat{\beta}$ is

$$\hat{\beta} = \hat{\beta}_1 + E\{\beta \tilde{\underline{y}}_2^T\} \; [E\{\tilde{\underline{y}}_2 \tilde{\underline{y}}_2^T\}]^{-1} \tilde{y}_2$$

where E is the expected value. For proof cf. Luenberger [104 p.92]. The above equation can be interpreted as

$\hat{\beta}$ is $\hat{\beta}_1$ plus the best estimate of β in the subspace $\tilde{y}_2$

generated by $\tilde{y}_2$

Consider next the system comprising N interconnected linear dynamical subsystems defined by

$$\underline{x}_i(k+1) = \phi_{ii}\underline{x}_i(k) + \sum_{j=1;i\neq j}^{N} \phi_{ij}\underline{x}_j(k) + \underline{w}_i(k)$$

$$i = 1,2,\ldots N \tag{1}$$

with the outputs given by

$$\underline{y}_i(k+1) = H_i\underline{x}_i(k+1) + \underline{v}_i(k+1) \quad i = 1,\ldots N \tag{2}$$

where $\underline{w}_i$ $\underline{v}_i$ are uncorrelated zero mean Gaussian white noise sequences with covariances Q_i, R_i, respectively. Consider the Hilbert space y formed by the measurements of the overall systems. At the instant k+1, this space is denoted by y (k+1). The optimal minimum variance estimate $\hat{x}(k+1|k+1)$ is given by

$$\hat{\underline{x}}(k+1|k+1) = E\{\underline{x}(k+1)|\ y(k+1)\}$$

$$= E\{\underline{x}(k+1)|\ y(k)\} + E\{\underline{x}(k+1)|\ \tilde{\underline{y}}(k+1|k)\}. \tag{3}$$

This equation states algebraically the geometrical result of Theorem 1. The idea of the new filter is to decompose the second term i.e., $E\{\underline{x}(k+1)|\tilde{\underline{y}}(k+1|k\}$ such that the optimal estimate $\hat{\underline{x}}(k+1|k+1)$ is given using the two terms by considering the estimate as the orthogonal projection of $\underline{x}_i(k+1)$ taken on the Hilbert space generated by

$$y(k) \oplus \tilde{y}_1(k+1|k) + \tilde{y}_2^{1}(k+1)|k+1)$$

$$+ \tilde{y}_3^{2}(k+1|k+1) + \cdots + \tilde{y}_N^{N-1}(k+1|k+1)$$

where $\tilde{y}_i^{i-1}$ (k+1|k+1) is the subspace generated by the subspace of measurements $y_i(k+1)$ and the projection of it on the subspaces generated by $y(k) + y_1(k+1) + y_2(k+1) + \cdots + y_{i-1}(k+1)$ which leads to Theorem 2.

Theorem 2: The optimal estimate $\hat{\underline{x}}_i(k+1|k+1)$ of the ith subsystem is given by the projection of $\underline{x}_i(k+1)$ on the space generated by all measurements up to k($y(k)$) and the projection of $\underline{x}_i(k+1)$ on the subspace generated by $\tilde{y}_1(k+1|k) + \tilde{y}_2^1(k+1|k+1) + \cdots + \tilde{y}_N^{N-1}(k+1)$.

Proof: Rewrite (3) as

$$\hat{\underline{x}}_i(k+1|k+1) = E\{\underline{x}_i(k+1)|y(k), y_1(k+1), \underline{y}_2(k+1), \cdots$$

$$\underline{y}_i(k+1), \underline{y}_{i+1}(k+1), \cdots y_N(k+1)\}$$

$$= E\{\underline{x}_i(k+1)|\ y(k), \underline{y}_1(k+1), \underline{y}_2(k+1) + \ldots$$

$$+ \underline{y}_i(k+1), \underline{y}_{i+1}(k+1), \cdots \underline{y}_{N-1}(k+1)\}$$

$$+ E\{\underline{x}_i(k+1)|\tilde{\underline{y}}_N^{N-1}(k+1|k+1)\}$$

where

$$\underline{y}_N^{N-1}(k + 1|k + 1) = y_N(k + 1)$$
$$- E\{\underline{y}_N(k + 1)|\ y(k), y_1(k + 1), \cdots y_{N-1}(k + 1)\}$$

or

$$\underline{x}_i(k + 1|k + 1) = E\{\underline{x}_i(k + 1)|\ y(k)\}$$
$$+ E\{x_i(k + 1)|\tilde{\underline{y}}_1(k + 1|k)\}$$
$$+ \sum_{r=2}^{N} E\{\underline{x}_i(k + 1)|\tilde{\underline{y}}_r^{r-1}(k + 1|k + 1)\}$$

which proves the assertion.

Using the idea of successive orthogonalisation of the spaces defined above, the algebraic structure of the new decentralised filter is described in the next section.

2.1 The Algebraic Structure of the New Filter

In order to develop the filter equations for the overall systems comprising N interconnected subsystems, write the equations for the overall systems as

$$\underline{x}(k + 1) = \phi(k + 1,k)\underline{x}(k) + \underline{w}(k)$$

$$\underline{y}(k + 1) = H(k + 1)\underline{x}(k + 1) + \underline{v}(k + 1)$$

where the subsystems structure is seen more clearly by decomposing those equations as

$$\underline{x}_i(k + 1) = \sum_{j=i}^{N} \phi_{ij}(k + 1,k)\underline{x}_j(k) + \underline{w}_i(k)$$

$$\underline{y}_i(k + 1) = H_i(k + 1)\underline{x}_i(k + 1) + \underline{v}_i(k + 1).$$

Then the optimal state prediction for the ith subsystem is given by

$$\hat{\underline{x}}_i(k + 1|k) = \sum_{j=1}^{N} \phi_{ij}(k + 1,k)\hat{\underline{x}}_j(k|k) \tag{4}$$

Now, by definition of the prediction errors, $\tilde{\underline{x}}_i(k + 1|k) = \underline{x}_i(k + 1) - \hat{\underline{x}}_i(k + 1|k)$. A recursive expression for the co-variance of the prediction error can be written as

$$P_{ii}(k+1|k) = \sum_{j=1}^{N}\sum_{r=1}^{N} \phi_{ij}(k + 1,k)$$

$$P_{\tilde{x}_j\tilde{x}_r}\phi_{ir}^T(k + 1,k + Q_i(k)$$

$$= \sum_{j=1}^{N} \phi_{ij}(k + 1,k).$$

$$\left\{\sum_{r=1}^{N} P_{\tilde{x}_j\tilde{x}_r}(k|k)\phi_{ir}^{T}(k+1,k)\right\} + Q_i(k). \tag{5}$$

Also,

$$P_{ij}(k+1|k) = \sum_{r=1}^{N}\sum_{l=1}^{N} \phi_{ir}(k+1,k)P_{rl}(k|k)\phi_{jQ}^{T}(k+1,k)$$

$$= \sum_{r=1}^{N} \phi_{ir}(k+1,k)\left\{\sum_{l=1}^{N} P_{rl}(k|k)\phi_{jl}^{T}(k+1,k)\right\}. \tag{6}$$

Now, using the proof of Theorem 2, it is easy to show that

$$\hat{\underline{x}}_i(k+1|k+1) = \hat{\underline{x}}_i(k+1|k+1)_l + \sum_{r=l+1}^{N} P_{x\tilde{y}_r^{r-1}}(k+1|k+1)$$

$$P^{-1}_{\tilde{y}_r^{r-1}\tilde{y}_r^{r-1}}(k+1)\tilde{\underline{y}}_r^{r-1}(k+1|k+1) \tag{7}$$

where

$$\hat{\underline{x}}_i(k+1|k+1)_l = \hat{\underline{x}}_i(k+1|k+1)_{l-1} \cdot K_{ij}^{l-1}(k+1)\tilde{y}_l^{l-1}(k+1|k+1) \tag{8}$$

and

$$P_{ii}(k+1|k+1)_l = P_{ii}(k+1|k+1)_{l-1} - K_{i_l}^{l-1}(k+1)P_{\tilde{y}_l^{l-1}\tilde{x}_{l-1}}(k+1|k+1) \tag{9}$$

where

$$K_{i_l}^{l-1}(k+1) = P_{\tilde{x}_{i_{l-1}}\tilde{y}_l^{l-1}}(k+1|k+1)\cdot P^{-1}_{\tilde{y}_l^{l-1}\tilde{y}_l^{l-1}}(k+1|k+1) \tag{10}$$

$$\tilde{y}_l^{l-1}(k+1|k+1) = \tilde{\underline{y}}_l^{l-2}(k+1|k+1) - K_{l_{l-1}}^{l-2}(k+1)\tilde{\underline{y}}_{l-1}^{l-2}(k+1|k+1) \tag{11}$$

$$K_{l_{l-1}}^{l-2} = P_{\tilde{y}_l^{l-2}\tilde{y}_l^{l-2}}(k+1|k+1)P^{-1}_{\tilde{y}_{l-1}^{l-2}\tilde{y}_{l-1}^{l-2}}(k+1|k+1) \tag{12}$$

$$P_{\tilde{y}_l^{l-1}\tilde{y}_l^{l-1}}(k+1|k+1) = P_{\tilde{y}_l^{l-2}\tilde{y}_l^{l-2}}(k+1|k+1) - K_{l_{l-1}}^{l-2}(k+1)P_{\tilde{y}_{l-1}^{l-2}\tilde{y}_{l-1}^{l-2}}(k+1|k+1) \tag{13}$$

$$P_{\tilde{y}_l^{l-1}\tilde{y}_l^{l-1}}(k+1|k+1) = H_l P_{\tilde{x}_l^{l-1}\tilde{x}_l^{l-1}}\cdot(k+1|k+1)H_l^{T} + R_l(k+1)$$

$$P_{\tilde{x}_{l-1}\tilde{y}_l^{l-1}}(k+1|k+1) = P_{\tilde{x}_l^{l-1}\tilde{x}_l^{l-1}}(k+1|k+1)\cdot H_l^{T}(k+1) \tag{14}$$

$$P_{ij}(k + 1|k + 1)_l = P_{ij}(k + 1|k + 1)_{l-1} - K_{i_l}^{l-1}(k + 1)P_{\tilde{y}_l}^{-1}{}^{l-1}_{\tilde{x}_j}{}^{l-1}(k + 1|k + 1). \quad (15)$$

Thus, (4)-(6) and (8)-(15) give the algebraic equations of the new filter.

Mechanisation of the algorithm for one step of filter is: 1) From (4), (5), and (6) we calculate the prediction estimate as well as its covariance matrix. 2) Put l=1 (note that $\hat{x}_i(k+1|k+1)_o = \hat{x}_i(k+1|k)$ and $P_{ij}(k+1|k+1)_o = P_{ij}(k+1|k)$ i=1,...,M; j=1,...,N). From (8)-(15) calculate the filtered estimate $x_i(k+1|k+1)_l$ and the corresponding covariance matrix. 3) If l=N the resulting estimate is the optimal Kalman estimate and the covariance matrix is the minimum error covariance matrix, otherwise go to Step 2.

Note that although the new algorithm and the global Kalman filter are algebraically equivalent the numerical properties of the decomposed filter are significantly better.

Next consider the computational requirements of this new filter as compared tothose of the global Kalman filter.

2.2 Computational Requirements

The computational requirements of the new filter as compared to those of the global Kalman filter can be divided into two categories, i.e., storage requirements and computational time requirements. The storage requirements of the new filter are roughly similar to those of the global Kalman filter although if the processing is done on a multiprocessor then the new filter's storage can be conveniently distributed between the computers. The computational time advantage of the new filter requires further elaboration.

Now, a good measure of the computation time requirements of the global Kalman filter and the new decentralised filter is given by the number of elementary multiplication operations involved. Consider first the number of elementary multiplications required for the global Kalman filter.

A. Number of Multiplications Required for the Global Kalman Filter

Assume that x is if dimension n, y is of dimension m, then the number of multiplications required under the assumption that H is block diagonal and each subsystem has the same number of states and outputs is

$$1.5n^2 + 1.5m^3 + nm \cdot \left[\frac{1}{N} + \frac{m + 1}{2N} + m + 1 + \frac{n + 1}{2} + \frac{m^2(3m + 1)}{2}\right]$$

where N is the number of subsystem:

B. The number of Multiplications Required for the New Filter

Assume that all subsystem have an equal number of state variables n/N and equal number of measurements m/N where N is the number of subsystems. Then the number of multiplications required is

$$1.5n^2 + 1.5n^3 + N \left\{ \frac{mn}{N^2} + \frac{mn(m + N)}{2N^3} + \frac{m^2 \frac{3m}{N} + 1}{2N^2} \right.$$

$$+ N \left| \frac{n^2m}{N^3} + \frac{nm^2}{N^3} + \frac{nm}{N^2} + \frac{nm(n + N)}{2N^3} \right|$$

$$\left. + \frac{N(N-1)}{2} \cdot \frac{n^2m}{N^3} \right\}$$

It is easy to show that for high-order systems, the new filter will give substantial savings in computation time.

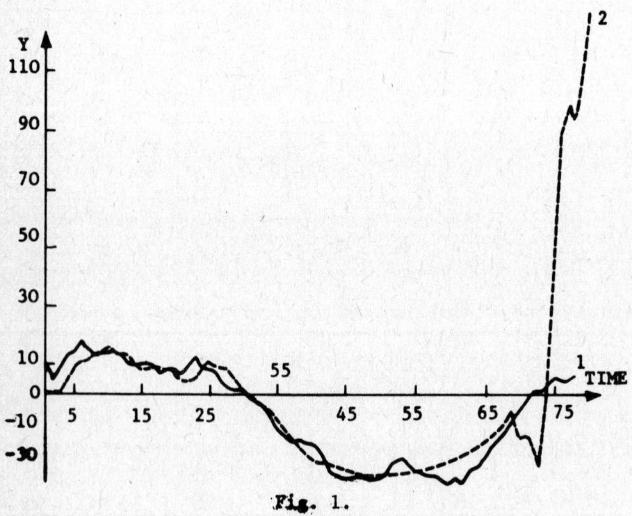

Fig. 1.

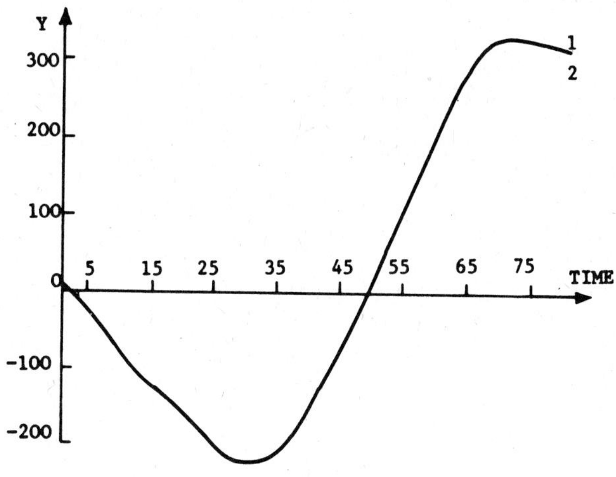
Y
300
200
100
0
-100
-200
5
15
25
35
45
55
65
75
TIME
1
2

Fig. 2.

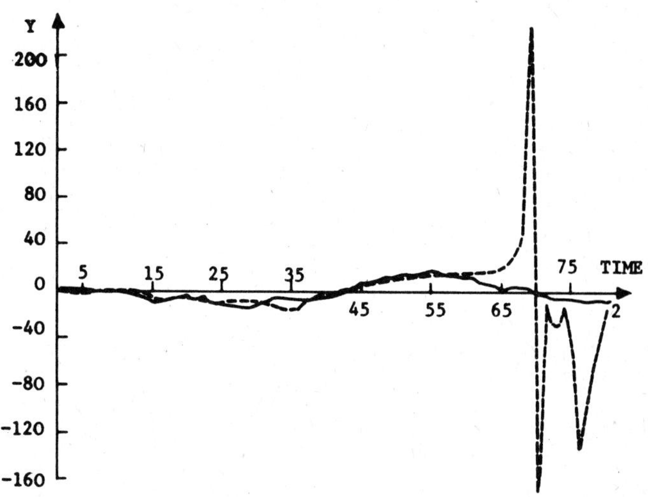
Y
200
160
120
80
40
0
-40
-80
-120
-160
5
15
25
35
45
55
65
75
TIME
2

Fig. 3.

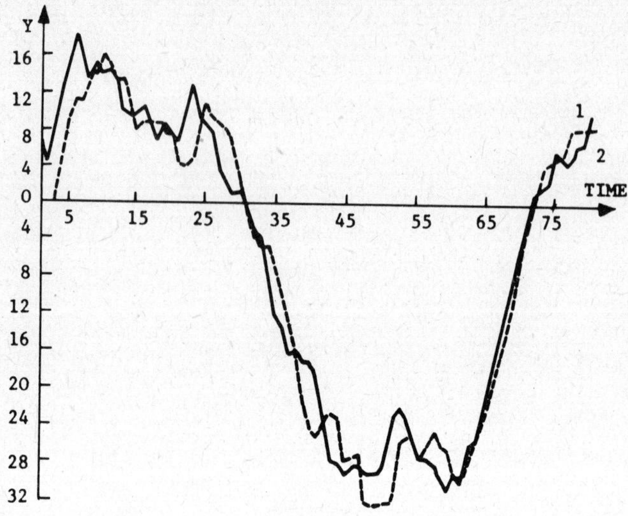
Y
16
12
8
4
0
4
8
12
16
20
24
28
32
5
15
25
35
45
55
65
75
TIME
1
2

Fig. 4.

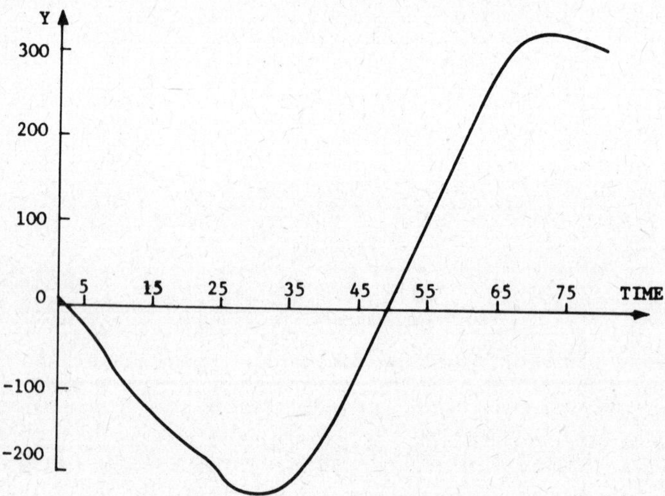
Y
300
200
100
0
-100
-200
5
15
25
35
45
55
65
75
TIME

Fig. 5.

3. STATE ESTIMATION FOR A SYSTEM COMPRISING 11 COUPLED SYNCHRONOUS MACHINES

The multimachine power system under consideration consists of 11 coupled machines. The model of an n-machine system consists of a set of nonlinear equations which can be written for the ith machine as (cf. Darwish and Fantin |105| for further details on modelling of such systems).

$$M_i\ddot{\delta}_i = P_i - \sum_{\substack{j=1\\ j\neq i}}^{n} b_{ij}\sin\delta_{ij} \qquad i=1,\ldots,n$$

where M is the inertia, P is the power injected, b_{ij} is the interconnection variable and δ is the angle.

For the system to be completely controlable and completely observable the nth machine is taken as reference. Then, by subtracting the nth equation from the equation of each machine, a model can be constructed for the n machine system.

For small perturbations, the nonlinear model can be linearized about the equilibrium point so that the linear equations which result can be written in discrete form.

$$x(k+1) = Ax(k) + \xi.$$

For the 11 machine system, A is the 20X20 matrix [103] and ξ is a zero mean Gussian white noise vector. For the ith machine, the observation equation is given by

$$y_i = \begin{bmatrix} 0 & 1 \end{bmatrix} \begin{bmatrix} x_{1i} \\ x_{2i} \end{bmatrix} + \begin{bmatrix} u_i \end{bmatrix}$$

where y_i is the speed of the ith machine and u_i is also a zero mean Gussian white noise vector sequence.

The covariances of $\underline{\xi}$ and $\underline{u}$ are given by Q_i and R_i respectively and these were taken to be $R_i = 1$ and Q_i diagonal with the diagonal elements given by 5, P_o the initial covariance was also taken to be diagonal with the diagonal given by 25. The initial estimate was taken to be zero while the initial states were all taken to be 10.0.

3.1 Simulation Results

The global and the new decentralised filter were simulated on the IBM 370/165 digital computer at LAAS Toulouse over a time horizon of 80 discrete points.

Figs. 1-3 show the first three states and the corresponding estimates using the global Kalman filter and Figs. 4-6 the corresponding states and estimates using the new decentralised filter. Note that the global Kalman filter is numerically unstable while the hierarchical solution is stable. Essentially, numerical errors build up to make the global 20th order filter unstable while in the case of the hierarchical solution, since only second order subsystems are used at each stage, these numerical inaccuracies are avoided so that the resulting filter remains stable.

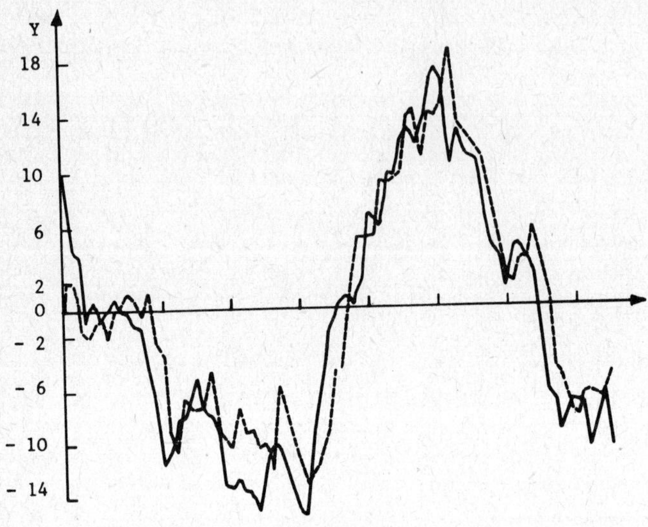

Fig. 6.

3.2 Remark

In this chapter we have described a decentralised algorithm for optimal state estimation in large scale linear interconnected dynamical systems. The algorithm uses a series of successive orthogonalisatons on the measurement subspaces for each subsystem within a hierarchical structure in order to provide the optimal estimate. This ensures substantial savings in computation time. Also, since only low-order subsystem equations are manipulated at each stage, numerical inaccuracies are reduced and the filter remains stable for even high-order systems as illustrated by the machine example. The hierarchical structure is ideally suited for implementation using a multiprocessor system since then the computational savings can be even more substantial although it should be pointed out that the computational time savings in the multiprocessor implementation arise due to a tradeoff between low calculation time due to parallel processing and relatively long time for communication between the processors. Thus, the savings can be substantial only if the communications are very efficient.

4. OPTIMAL STOCHASTIC CONTROL

Next, let us see how the above filter hierarchy can be incorporated into a two level deterministic control hierarchy to yield optimal stochastic control.

The basic stochastic control problems can be written as:

minimise $$J = E\left\{ \frac{1}{2} \sum_{k=k_o}^{k_f-1} ||\underline{x}(k+1)||^2_{Q_1} + ||\underline{u}(k)||^2_{R_1} \right\} \tag{16}$$

subject to the constraints

$$\underline{x}(k+1) = \phi\underline{x}(k) + \psi\underline{u}(k) + c\underline{z}(k) + n(k) \tag{17}$$

where $$\underline{z}(k) = LM\underline{x}(k) + LN\underline{u}(k) \tag{18}$$

and $$\underline{y}(k) = H\underline{x}(k) + \underline{u}(k) \tag{19}$$

Here $\underline{u}$, u are uncorrelated zero mean Gussian random white noise vectors of known covariance. Q_1, R_1, ϕ, ψ, M, N, H are all block diagonal matrices with the blocks corresponding to a distinct subsystem structure whilst L is a full matrix. Thus essentially we have a system comprising N linear interconnected dynamical systems whose outputs are corrupted by noise as shown in equation (19) and whose interaction inputs are formed by a linear combination of the states and controls of all the other subsystems.

In order to develop the optimal stochastic controller, we begin by examining the deterministic problems. Thus we have

Theorem 3

For large scale linear interconnected dynamical systems with quadratic cost functions of the type

$$\text{Min } J = \frac{1}{2}\left[\sum_{k=ko}^{kf-1} ||\underline{x}(k+1)||^2_{Q_1} + ||\underline{y}(k)||^2_{R_1} \right]$$

and subject to the constraints given by equations (16-18), the optimal control paw is given by $\underline{u}(k_f - k) = S_1(k_f - k)\,\underline{x}(k_f - k) + S_2(k_f - k)\,\underline{x}(k_f - k)$ where S_1 is a time varying block diagonal matrix and S_2 is a full matrix.

Comment

The calculation of S_1 and S_2 can be done using the deterministic control hierarchy of Singh [29] that we outlined in chapter IV. Essentially, we calculate S_1 from local riccati equations whilst S_2 is calculated off-line by storing the states and controls at certain points of the trajectories obtained using a standard hierarchical method and then inverting a matrix.

Next, we move to the stochastic case and use the fact that we have a classical information pattern in the sense of Witsenhausen [106]. Therefore, the separation principal [72] applies so that the following Lemma becomes self evident.

Lemma

For large scale linear interconnected dynamical systems with an average quadratic cost function of the type

$$J = E\left\{\frac{1}{2}\sum_{k=k_o}^{kf-1} ||\underline{x}(k+1)||^2_{Q_1} + \underline{u}(k)||^2\right\}$$

the optimum control law is given by

$$\underline{u}(k_f - k) = S_1(k_f - k)\ \hat{\underline{x}}\ (k_f - k \mid k_f - k)$$

$$+ S_2(k_f - k)\ \hat{\underline{x}}\ (k_f - k \mid k_f - k) \tag{20}$$

where S_1 and S_2 are the same as those given in theorem 3 while $\hat{\underline{x}}\ (k_f - k|k_f - k)$ is the optimal filtered estimate of $\hat{\underline{x}}\ (k_f - k)$.

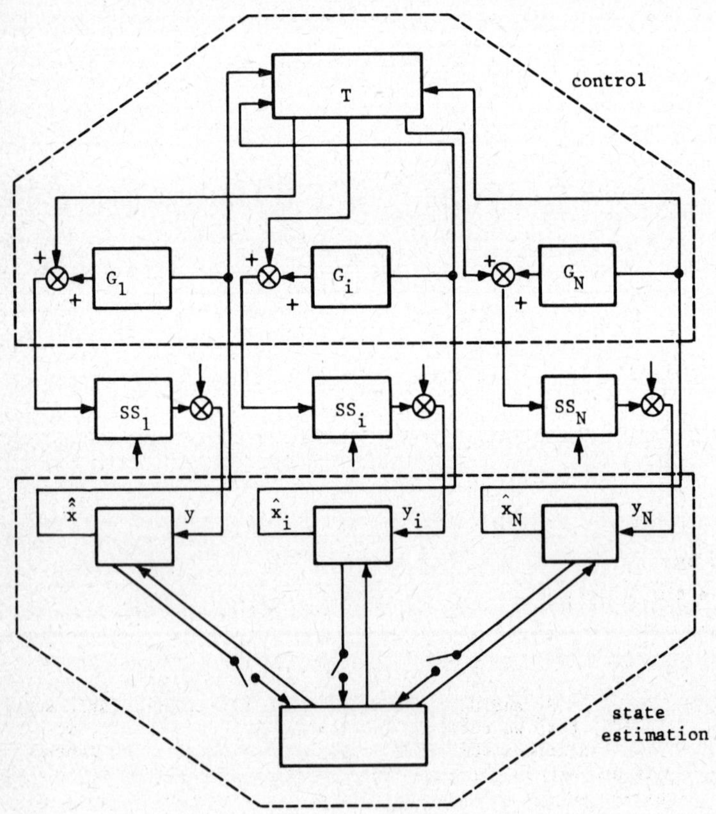

Fig. 7. Stochastic control structure

Comment

With this Lemma, we see that it is possible to compute optimal stochastic control by superposing the deterministic control hierarchy on the decentralised filter hierarchy as shown in Fig.7.

Example

As an example, consider the 6 reach distributed delay model for a river pollution control system for the discrete time case. This leads to a model of order 52 of the form

$$\underline{x}(k+1) = A\,\underline{x}(k) + B\,\underline{u}(k) + C + \underline{\xi}(k)\,;\ \underline{y}(k+1) = D\,\underline{x}(k+1) + y(k+1)$$

Where $\underline{\xi}$ and $\underline{y}$ are uncorrelated zero mean Gussian random vectors. Here, we make the realistic assumption that BoD is not measurable whilst Do is

The control is given by

$$\underline{u}(k) = \begin{bmatrix} \pi_1(k) \\ \vdots \\ \pi_6(k) \end{bmatrix} \quad k = 0, 1, --- K-1$$

where π --- π_6 are the maximum fractions of BoD removed from the effluent in reaches 1 to 6. A suitable cost function is of the form:

$$J = \underset{\underline{u}}{\text{Min}}\ E\ \frac{1}{2}\ ||\,\underline{x}(400)||^2_{I_{52}} + \sum_{k=0}^{399} \frac{1}{2}\left(||\,\underline{x}(k) - \underline{x}^d\,||^2_{I_{52}} + ||\,\underline{u}(k)||^2_{100I_2}\right)$$

Where $\underline{x}^d$ are the desired values which are taken to be steady state values of BoD and Do for each reach, I_{52} is the 52nd order identity matrix whilst I_2 is the 2nd order one.

Results

The filter and the control hierarchies for this 52nd order river pollution control problem were simulated on an IBM 370/165 digital computer at LAAS Toulouse over a period of 4 days divided into 100 sampling periods per day. Figs 8-13 show the real and estimated BoD and Do in each of the 6 reaches. Fig. 14 shows the 6 controls.

As expected, the estimation of BoD is not very good since it is not measured. We also see that in each case the state approaches its desired value although as we go further downstream, it takes much longer to reach the steady state value.

5. THE JOINT PROBLEM OF IDENTIFICATION AND OPTIMISATION [107]

We note that a pre-requisite for the calculation of optimum controls for a dynamical system is the existance of a well defined mathematical model. Ifit's parameter values correspond closely to the pre-calculated ones, then the optimal controls based on such a model should provide a good performance. However, the parameters of most realistic systems vary considerably so that a control based on the fixed pre-calculated parameter values may often be inadequate. It is therefore more desirable to perform the parameter estimation and the dynamic optimisation simultaneously.

Basically, two possible categories of this simultaneous study arise depending on the nature of the systems description. One category results when considering the mathematical description of the system problem on a probabilistic basis and this leads to the optimal stochastic control problem as we have seen. The other category in an average sense is an asymptotic steady-state version of the first and is obtained if the system dynamic optimisation and parameter identification are approached simultaneously within a deterministic framework. The computational load of both approaches will be excessive when dealing with high dimensional problems. To reduce this load, the hierarchical control methodology seems to provide an elegant and systematic procedure by suitably partioning the problem at hand into smaller, easily solvable subproblems and properly coordinating their solutions in an iterative manner so as to achive the original (integrated) solution.

The deterministic combined problem of system identification and optimisation has been tackled previously by Haimes et al [108-111] with particular emphasis on water resources planning and management. Although their approach is interesting and has proved useful on simulation studies, it has some drawbacks. Firstly, only a rudimentary form of a hierarchical methodology is used in that they have stressed only the traditional feasible and non feasible decomposition methods without partitioning the state vector. However other more recent decomposition and coordination methods are intuitively appealing and readily available as we have seen in chapter III. Secondly, for one reason or another they have always assumed that the system parameters, to be identified, are constants and have ignored the possibility of incorporating suitable models for the parameters. Thirdly and more important, the interaction among system variables is not considered which in turn tends to increase the overall computational efforts.

Here we provide a hierarchical control approach to the deterministic joint problem of systems identification and optimisation. We treat nonlinear control problems with the constant but unknown parameters subject to quadratic performance indices. Assuming the possibility of observing an output vector, a weighted integral error is then formulated as an identification criterion. We further construct a parametric performance measure to combine the optimisation and identification problems. Application of the minimum principle yields a set of necessary conditions whose solution can be performed by a four-level hierarchical computational structure. The convergence analysis of this algorithm is demonstrated to show how the iteractive procedure will approach the integrated solution of the joint identification and optimisation problem. Finally, we illustrate the new approach on an example.

5.1 Development of the Joint Problem

5.1.1 Dynamic Optimisation Problem

The basic dynamical optimisation problem is:

Given $\underline{\alpha}$ (t), determine u* (t) ; t ϵ $[t_o, t_f]$ such that

$$\min J = \frac{1}{2} ||\underline{X}(t_f)||^2_S + \frac{1}{2} \int_{t_0}^{tf} \left\{ ||\underline{X}(t)||^2_Q + ||\underline{u}(t)||^2_R \right\} dt \tag{21}$$

Subject to

$$\underline{X}(t) = \underline{f}\,[\underline{X}(t), \underline{u}(t), \underline{\alpha}(t)| \quad ; \quad \underline{X}(t_0) = \underline{X}_0 \tag{22}$$

where $||.||^2_S = .^T S\ .$

$\underline{X}(t) \in R^n$ is the state vector

$\underline{u}(t) \in R^m$ is the control vector

$\alpha(t) \in R^p$ is the unknown parameters vector

f is an n-vector of functions $f_i \epsilon\ C^2$.

The matrices S, Q and R are block-diagonal.

5.1.2 Parameter Identification Problem

The parameter estimation problem is:

Determine $\underline{\alpha}^*(t)$; t ϵ $[t_0, t_f]$ such that

$$\min V = \frac{1}{2} \int_{t_0}^{tf} (||\underline{Y}_0(t) - \underline{Y}(t)||^2_{W(t)}) \, dt \tag{23}$$

Subject to

$$\underline{Y}(t) = \underline{D}\ [\underline{X}(t), \underline{u}(t), \underline{\alpha}(t)] \tag{24}$$

where

$Y \in R^r$ is the output vector

$\underline{Y}_0 \in R^r$ is the vector of observations

W(t) is a suitable r x r weighting matrix.

Due to the tight interdependence between the dynamic optimisation and parameter identification problems, simultaneous study and solution of them are essential. Therefore, a "joint problem" which combines reasonably both problems can be formulated as: "Determine $\underline{\alpha}^*(t)$, $u^*(t)$; $t \in [t_0, t_f]$ so as to minimise $[J, V]$ subject to the equality constraints (22) (24)[*]

5.2 A Parametric Solution Procedure

An appropriate combined form of the twin objective function J and V can be obtained using the parametric approach [112]:

$$Z = \beta V + (1-\beta) J \; ; \; 0 < \beta < 1 \tag{25}$$

and the parametric joint problem becomes:

$$\min_{\underline{u}(t),\alpha(t)} \quad Z = \frac{1}{2}(1-\beta) \; ||\underline{X}(t_f)||^2_S + \frac{1}{2}(1-\beta)\int_{t_0}^{t_f} \left[\, ||\underline{X}(t)||^2_Q + \right.$$

$$\left. + \; ||\underline{u}(t)||^2_R \right] dt + \frac{1}{2}\beta \int_{t_0}^{t_f} ||\underline{Y}_0(t) - D\left[\underline{X}(t), \underline{u}(t), \underline{\alpha}(t)\right]||^2_{W(t)} \; dt \tag{26}$$

Subject to $\quad \dot{\underline{X}} = \underline{f}\,(\underline{X}, \underline{u}, \,) \; ; \; \underline{X}_0 = \underline{X}(t_0)$

$$0 < \beta < 1 \tag{27}$$

5.3 Remark

β is defined over the open interval $]0,1[$ to combine both the optimisation and identification problems. Note that at $\beta = 0$ we have an optimisation problem only whereas at $\beta = 1$ we have only an identification problem.

This parametric from is amenable to handling by the standard methods of dynamic optimisation. Our aim form here onwards is to utilise the basic concepts of dynamic hierarchical control.

5.4 The Hierarchical Control Approach

To decompose the parametric problem at hand, let us define predicted patterns labelled by superscript 0 as follows:

$$\underline{X}^0(t) = \underline{X}(t) \tag{27a}$$

$$\underline{u}^0(t) = \underline{u}(t) \tag{28}$$

$$\alpha^0(t) = \alpha(t) \tag{29}$$

We will use these patterns to subdivide the problem into N subproblems. To further ensure proper identification, and to avoid singularity we add the penality term $||\underline{\alpha}(t) - \underline{\alpha}^0(t)||^2_P$ to the joint functional (26) and expand the model dynamics (27) around the predicted trajectories. Thus :

---

[*] J and V are scalars. For notational simplicity the symbol $[J,V]$ represents any possible scalar combination of J. and V. Thus $[J,V]$ means $\beta V + (1-\beta)J$ for all $0 < \beta < 1$.

$$\min_{\underline{u}(t),\alpha(t),\alpha^0(t),\underline{u}^0(t),\underline{X}^0(t)} Z = \sum_{i=1}^{N} \Bigg[\frac{1}{2}(1-\beta)\Big[||\underline{X}_i(t_f)||^2_{S_i} +$$

$$\int_{t_0}^{t_f} \Big[||\underline{X}_i||^2_{Q_i} + ||\underline{u}_i||_{R_i} \Big] dt \Big] + \frac{1}{2}\beta \Big[\int_{t_0}^{t_f} \Big[||\underline{Y}_{0i} - \underline{D}_i(\underline{X}^0,\underline{u}^0,\alpha^0)||^2_{W_i} +$$

$$+ \quad ||\underline{\alpha}_i(t) - \underline{\alpha}_i^2||^2_{P_i} \Big] dt \Big] \Bigg] \tag{30}$$

Subject to:

$$\begin{aligned} \dot{\underline{X}}_i = \; & \Phi_{1i} \; (\underline{X}^0,\underline{u}^0,\alpha^0)\underline{X}_i + \\ & \Phi_{2i} \; (\underline{X}^0,\underline{u}^0,\underline{\alpha}^0)\underline{u}_i + \\ & \Phi_{3i} \; (\underline{X}^0,\underline{u}^0,\underline{\alpha}^0)\underline{\alpha}_i + \\ & \Psi \; (\underline{X}^0,\alpha^0,u^0) \end{aligned} \tag{31}$$

and equations (27) through (29)

where
$$\Phi_{1i}(\underline{X}^0,\underline{u}^0,\alpha^0) = \left[\frac{\partial \underline{f}_i^T}{\partial \underline{X}_i} \Bigg|_{\substack{\underline{X} = X^0 \\ \underline{u} = \underline{u}^0 \\ \underline{\alpha} = \underline{\alpha}^0}} \right]^T \tag{32}$$

$$\Phi_{2i}(\underline{X}^0,\underline{u}^0,\alpha^0) = \left[\frac{\partial \underline{f}_i^T}{\partial \underline{u}_i} \Bigg|_{\substack{\underline{X} = \underline{X}^0 \\ \underline{u} = \underline{u}^0 \\ \underline{\alpha} = \underline{\alpha}^0}} \right]^T \tag{33}$$

$$\Phi_{3i}(\underline{X}^0,\underline{u}^0,\underline{\alpha}^0) = \left[\frac{\partial \underline{f}_i^T}{\partial \underline{\alpha}_i} \Bigg|_{\substack{\underline{X} = X^0 \\ \underline{u} = \underline{u}^0 \\ \underline{\alpha} = \underline{\alpha}^0}} \right]^T \tag{34}$$

$$\underline{\Psi}(\underline{X}^0,\underline{u}^0,\underline{\alpha}^0,) = f\,(\underline{X}^0,\underline{u}^0,\underline{\alpha}^0) - \Phi_1\,(\underline{X}^0,\underline{u}^0,\underline{\alpha}^0)\underline{X} - \Phi_2(\underline{X}^0,\underline{u}^0,\underline{\alpha}^0)\,\underline{u} - - \Phi_3(\underline{X}^0,\underline{u}^0,\underline{\alpha}^0)\,\underline{\alpha} \tag{35}$$

where

$$\Phi_1 = \text{diag}\,[\Phi_{1i}]\,;\quad \Phi_2 = \text{diag}\,[\Phi_{2i}] \quad \text{and} \quad \Phi_3 = \text{diag}\,[\Phi_{3i}]\,.$$

The hierarchical solution starts by formulating the Hamiltonian:

$$\begin{aligned} H = {} & \tfrac{1}{2}(1-\beta)\,||\underline{X}||_Q^2 + \tfrac{1}{2}(1-\beta)\,||\underline{u}||_R^2 + \tfrac{1}{2}\beta\,||\underline{Y}_0 - \underline{D}(\underline{X}^0,\underline{u}^0,\underline{\alpha}^0||_W^2 \\ & + \tfrac{1}{2}\beta\,||\underline{\alpha} - \underline{\alpha}^0||_P^2 + \underline{\lambda}^T[\Phi_1(\underline{X}^0,\underline{u}^0,\underline{\alpha}^0)\underline{X} + \phi_2(\underline{X}^0,\underline{u}^0,\underline{\alpha}^0)\underline{u} \\ & + \Phi_3(\underline{X}^0,\underline{u}^0,\underline{\alpha}^0)\underline{\alpha} + \underline{\Psi}(\underline{X}^0,\underline{u}^0,\underline{\alpha}^0)] + \underline{\pi}^T(\underline{X}-\underline{X}^0) + \underline{\theta}^T(\underline{\alpha}-\underline{\alpha}^0) \\ & + \underline{\gamma}^T(\underline{u}-\underline{u}^0) \end{aligned} \tag{36}$$

where $\underline{\pi}$, $\underline{\theta}$ and $\underline{\gamma}$ are appropriate Lagrange Multipliers.

Then writing the necessary conditions for optimality as follows:

$$\frac{\partial H}{\partial \underline{u}} = \underline{0}$$

$$= (1-\beta)R\underline{u} + \Phi_2^T(\underline{X}^0,\underline{u}^0,\underline{\alpha}^0)\underline{\lambda} + \underline{\gamma}$$

Thus,

$$\underline{u} = -\frac{1}{(1-\beta)}R^{-1}[\underline{\gamma} + \Phi_2^T(\underline{X}^0,\underline{u}^0,\underline{\alpha}^0)\underline{\lambda}] \tag{37}$$

$$\frac{\partial H}{\partial \underline{\alpha}} = \underline{0}$$

gives

$$\underline{\alpha} = -\frac{1}{\beta}P^{-1}[\underline{\theta} + \Phi_3^T(\underline{X}^0,\underline{u}^0,\underline{\alpha}^0)\underline{\lambda} - \beta P\underline{\alpha}^0] \tag{38}$$

Notice that from equations (37), (38), β can neither take the value 1 nor 0.

$$\frac{\partial H}{\partial \underline{\lambda}} = \dot{\underline{X}}$$

$$= \Phi_1(\underline{X}^0,\underline{u}^0,\underline{\alpha}^0)\underline{X} + \Phi_2(\underline{X}^0,\underline{u}^0,\underline{\alpha}^0)\underline{u} + \Phi_3(\underline{X}^0,\underline{u}^0,\underline{\alpha}^0)\underline{\alpha} + \underline{\Psi}(\underline{X}^0,\underline{\alpha}^0,\underline{u}^0) \tag{39}$$

$$\frac{\partial H}{\partial \underline{X}} = -\dot{\underline{\lambda}}$$

$$= \underline{\pi} + \Phi_1^T(\underline{X}^0,\underline{u}^0,\underline{\alpha}^0)\underline{\lambda} + (1-\beta)Q\,\underline{X} \tag{40}$$

$$\frac{\partial H}{\partial \underline{\pi}} = \underline{0} \quad \text{gives} \quad \underline{X} = \underline{X}^0 \tag{41}$$

$$\frac{\partial H}{\partial \underline{\theta}} = \underline{0} \quad \text{gives} \quad \underline{\alpha} = \underline{\alpha}^0 \tag{42}$$

$$\frac{\partial H}{\partial \gamma} = \underline{0} \quad \text{gives} \quad \underline{u} = \underline{u}^0 \tag{43}$$

$$\frac{\partial H}{\partial \underline{X}^0} = \underline{0} \quad \text{gives}$$

$$\underline{\pi} = -\beta \frac{\partial \underline{D}^T}{\partial \underline{X}^0} W \left[\underline{Y}_0 - \underline{D}(\underline{X}^0,\underline{u}^0,\underline{\alpha}^0)\right] + \left[\frac{\partial \underline{F}_1^T}{\partial \underline{X}^0} + \frac{\partial \underline{F}_2^T}{\partial \underline{X}^0} + \frac{\partial \underline{F}_3^T}{\partial \underline{X}^0}\right] \underline{\lambda} + \frac{\partial \underline{\Psi}^T}{\partial \underline{X}^0} \underline{\lambda} \tag{44}$$

$$\frac{\partial H}{\partial \underline{u}^0} = \underline{0} \quad \text{gives} \quad \underline{\gamma} = -\beta \frac{\partial \underline{D}^T}{\partial \underline{u}^0} W \left[\underline{Y}_0 - \underline{D}(\underline{X}^0,\underline{u}^0,\underline{\alpha}^0)\right] + \left[\frac{\partial \underline{F}_1^T}{\partial \underline{u}^0} + \frac{\partial \underline{F}_2^T}{\partial \underline{u}^0} + \frac{\partial \underline{F}_3^T}{\partial \underline{u}^0} + \frac{\partial \underline{\Psi}^T}{\partial \underline{u}^0}\right] \underline{\lambda} \tag{45}$$

$$\frac{\partial H}{\partial \underline{\alpha}^0} = \underline{0} \quad \text{gives} \quad \underline{\theta} = -\beta \frac{\partial \underline{D}^T}{\partial \underline{\alpha}^0} W \left[\underline{Y}_0 - \underline{D}(\underline{X}^0,\underline{u}^0,\underline{\alpha}^0)\right] - \beta P(\underline{\alpha}-\underline{\alpha}^0) - \left[\frac{\partial \underline{F}_1^T}{\partial \underline{\alpha}^0} + \frac{\partial \underline{F}_2^T}{\partial \underline{\alpha}^0} + \frac{\partial \underline{F}_3^T}{\partial \underline{\alpha}^0} + \frac{\partial \underline{\Psi}^T}{\partial \underline{\alpha}^0}\right] \underline{\lambda} \tag{46}$$

where

$$\underline{F}_1(\underline{X}^0,\underline{\alpha}^0,\underline{u}^0) = \Phi_1(\underline{X}^0,\underline{u}^0,\underline{\alpha}^0)\underline{X} \tag{47}$$

$$\underline{F}_2(\underline{X}^0,\underline{\alpha}^0,\underline{u}^0) = \Phi_2(\underline{X}^0,\underline{u}^0,\underline{\alpha}^0)\underline{u} \tag{48}$$

$$\underline{F}_3(X^0,\underline{\alpha}^0,\underline{u}^0) = \Phi_3(\underline{X}^0,\underline{u}^0,\underline{\alpha}^0)\underline{\alpha} \tag{49}$$

Next, we see how we can tackle these equations using a four level hierarchical structure.

6. A FOUR-LEVEL COMPUTATIONAL ALGORITHM

The basic guide lines we will use in developing our algorithm are:

(1) Each level of the hierarchy should perform a reasonable amount of calculation.
(2) A predictive co-ordination routine is always employed to lessen the order of information processing and storage requirements.

We have synthesized a four-level hierarchical computational algorithm as follows.

Level 4

An initial value of the parameter β is guessed and sent downwards to the remaining three levels. Set $I = 1$.

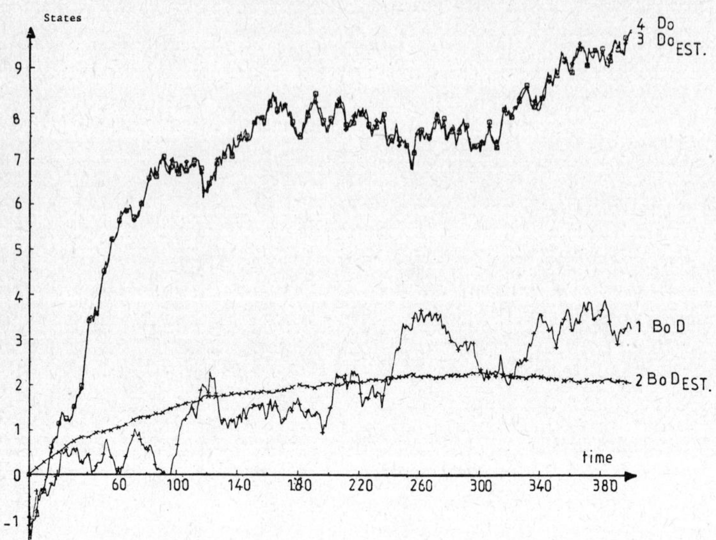

Fig. 8 : Concentrations of BOD and DO (actual and estimated) for reach 1

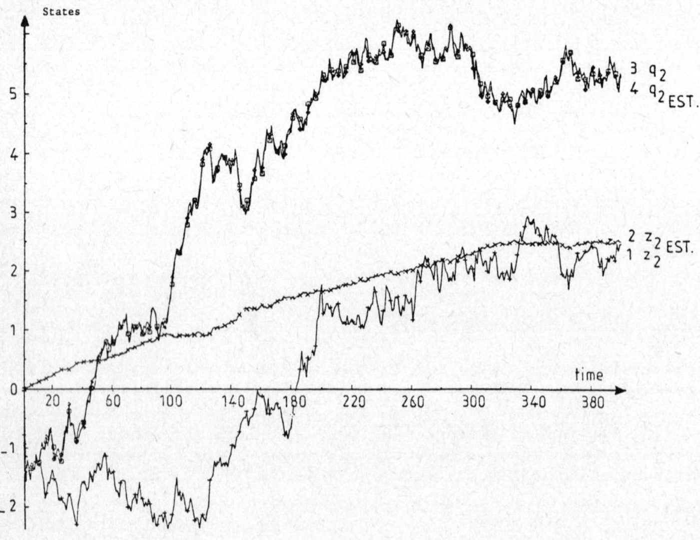

Fig. 9 : Concentrations of BOD and DO (real and estimated) for reach 2

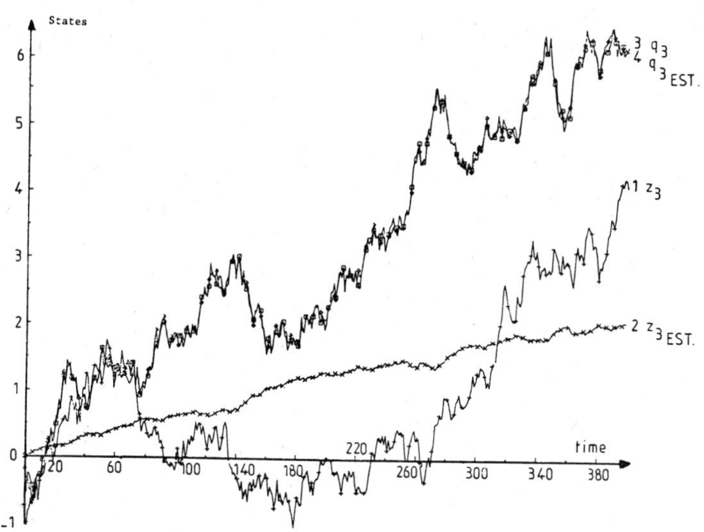

Fig. 10 : Concentrations of BOD and DO for reach 3

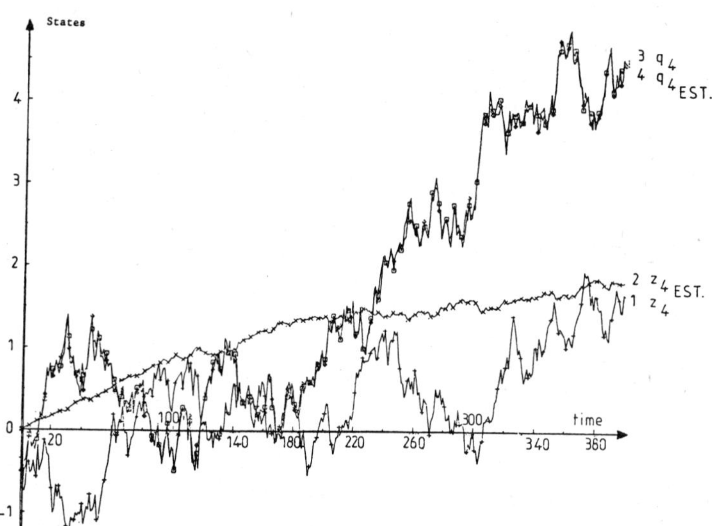

Fig. 11: Concentrations of BOD and DO for reach 4

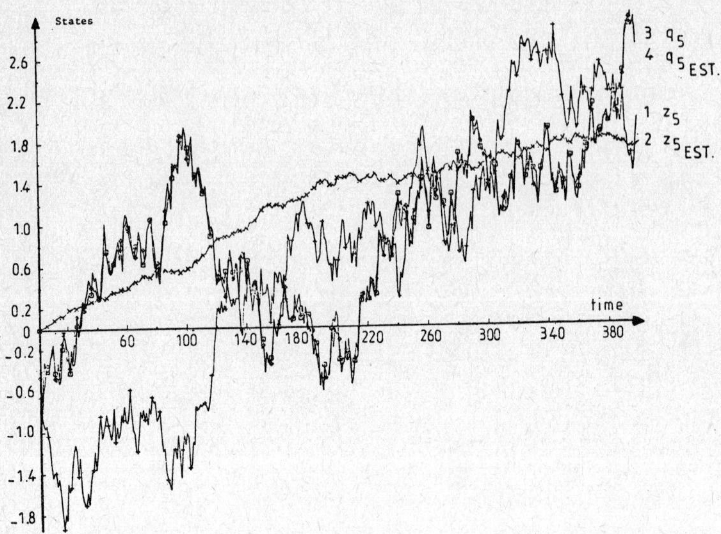

Fig. 12 : Concentrations of BOD and DO for subsystem 5

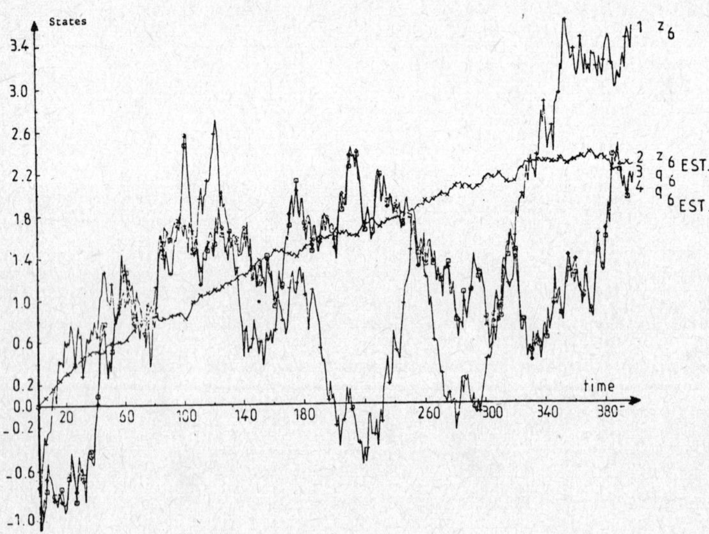

Fig. 13: Concentrations of BOD and DO for reach 6

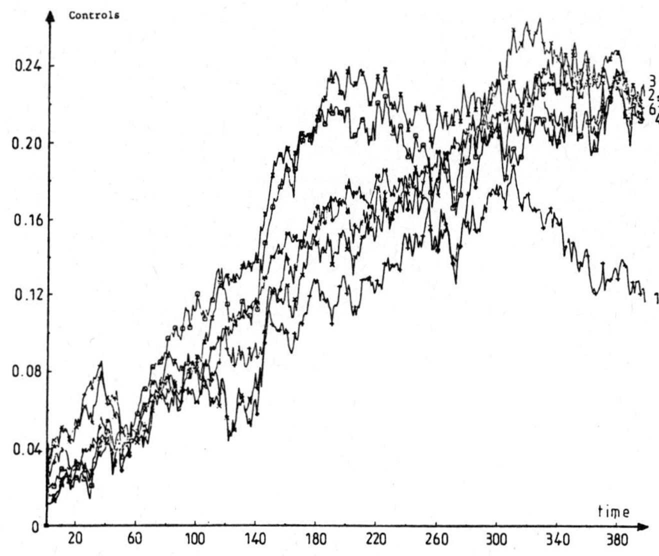

Fig. 14: The optimal stochastic controls for the 6 reaches

Level 3

An initial pattern of the components $(\underline{X},\underline{\alpha},\underline{u},\underline{\pi},\underline{\gamma},\underline{\theta})$ is predicted and conveyed to the first two levels. Fix $J = 1$.

Level 2

An initial trajectory of the costate vector $\underline{\lambda}$ is assumed and delivered to level 1. Set $K = 1$.

Level 1

Using the supplied information, the control $\underline{u}$ is determined from equation (37) and the unknown vector $\underline{\alpha}$ is obtained from equation (38). Afterwards, the state $\underline{X}$ is calculated from equation (39). These results are transferred upwards to level 2.

Level 2

With K replaced by $K+1$, the new costate trajectory $\underline{\lambda}^{K+1}$ is obtained from equation (40) and the following test is made:

$$\int_{t_0}^{t_f} ||\underline{\lambda}^{K+1} - \underline{\lambda}^{K}||^2 \, dt \leq \varepsilon_\lambda$$

If it is satisfied, $[\underline{X},\underline{u},\underline{\alpha},\underline{\lambda}]$ will be transferred to level 3. If not, $\underline{\lambda}^{K+1}$ will be sent to level 1 and the iterations will be repeated.

Level 3

A new pattern $L^T = [\underline{X}^{0^T} \ \underline{\alpha}^{0^T} \ \underline{u}^{0^T} \ \underline{\pi}^T \ \underline{\gamma}^T \ \underline{\theta}^T]$ is determined from equations (41) through (46) and the test:

$$\int_{t_0}^{t_f} ||L^{J+1} - L^{J}||^2 \, dt < \varepsilon_L$$

is performed. In case the test fails we send L^{J+1} to the first two levels. If it is successful, we move to level 4.

Level 4

We update β by

$$\beta^{I+1} = \beta^{I}(1-\Delta\beta)$$

where $\Delta\beta$ is the relative step size.

If $C(\beta^{I+1}) > C(\beta^{I})$ stop. If not, go to Level 3.

6.1 Remarks

(1) The first level calculations are performed in a sequential manner and these involve the least mathematical manipulations. This important property makes the algorithm easy for practical realization and amenable to software synthesis based on microprocessors.

Figure (15) shows a block diagram of the four-level hierarchical structure.

Next we study the convergence of the algorithm.

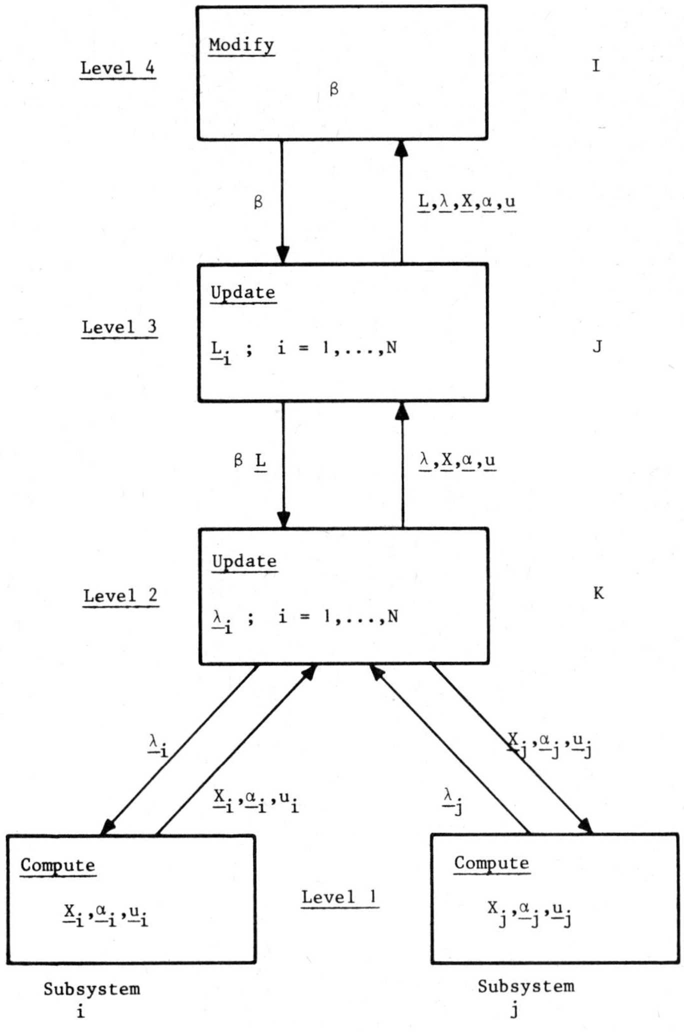

Fig. (15) A Four-Level Hierarchical Structure.

7. CONVERGENCE ANALYSIS

We note that for a given β, fixed by the fourth level, the iterative procedure of the remaining three-levels resembles, with very minor modifications, the control structures developed in Chapter III. Therefore, we are going to concentrate our efforts on demonstrating that the sequence of β-iterates is gradually approaching the solution of the joint problem provided that the remaining three-levels always attain a local solution.

Recall that the parameteric joint problem can be simplified to:

$$\min_{\underline{c}} \beta V[\underline{c}] + (1-\beta) J[\underline{c}] \tag{50}$$

subject to $\dot{\underline{X}} = \underline{f}(\underline{X},\underline{\alpha},\underline{u}) \qquad 0 < \beta < 1$

where $\underline{c} = [\underline{X}^T \ \underline{\alpha}^T \ \underline{U}^T]^T$

Define $C = [\beta,\underline{c} \mid$ equations (37-49) are satisfied$]$ as the set containing the allowable solutions of the first three-levels. Clearly $c(\beta) \in C$ for $0 < \beta < 1$ is an optimal solution for problem (50).

7.1 Lemma 1

If $\underline{c}(\beta)$ is an optimal solution for problem (50), then $V[\underline{c}(\beta)] \triangleq V(\beta)$ and $J[\underline{c}(\beta)] \triangleq J(\beta)$ are unimodal over $]0,1[$.

Proof:

Let $\underline{c}(\beta_i)$, $i = 1,2,3$, solve (50) with $0 < \beta_1 < \beta_2 < \beta_3 < 1$. Then the lemma implies that there exists an S, $0 \leq S \leq 1$ such that:

$$J(\beta_2) \leq S\, J(\beta_1) + (1-S)\, J(\beta_3) \tag{51a}$$

$$V(\beta_2) \leq S\, V(\beta_1) + (1-S)\, V(\beta_3) \tag{51b}$$

Obviously if $S \in [0,1]$ exists, then the following linear programming problem:

$$\min_{S} \tag{52}$$

subject to $[J(\beta_3) - J(\beta_1)]S \leq J(\beta_3) - J(\beta_2)$

$[V(\beta_3) - V(\beta_1)]S \leq V(\beta_3) - V(\beta_2)$

and $S \leq 1$

has a solution. By duality, the problem

$$\max_{\underline{N}} [J(\beta_3) - J(\beta_2)]N_1 + [V(\beta_3) - V(\beta_2)]N_2 + N_3 \tag{53}$$

subject to $N_i \geq 0 \qquad i = 1,2,3$

$[J(\beta_3) - J(\beta_1)]N_1 + [V(\beta_3) - V(\beta_1)]N_2 + N_3 \geq 0$

where N_i are the dual variables, must also have a solution. Therefore, if the solutions to (52) and (53) exist, they must be identical. Let us assume that the theorem is false. Thus, there exist no $S \geq 0$ that solves (52) and the values of

(52) and (53) are strictly less than zero. Hence, we have:

$$[J(\beta_3) - J(\beta_2)]N_1 + [V(\beta_3) - V(\beta_2)]N_2 + N_3 < 0 \tag{54a}$$

$$[J(\beta_3) - J(\beta_1)]N_1 + [V(\beta_3) - V(\beta_1)]N_2 + N_3 \geq 0 \tag{54b}$$

$$N_i \geq 0 \qquad i = 1,2,3$$

Eliminating N_3 gives:

$$[J(\beta_2) - J(\beta_1)]N_1 + [V(\beta_2) - V(\beta_1)]N_2 \geq 0 \tag{55a}$$

$$[J(\beta_3) - J(\beta_2)]N_1 + [V(\beta_3) - V(\beta_2)]N_2 < 0 \tag{55b}$$

Normalizing equations (35), using $K = \frac{N_2}{N_1+N_2}$, and rearranging:

$$[KV(\beta_2) + (1-K)J(\beta_2)] - [KV(\beta_1) + (1-K)J(\beta_1)] \geq 0 \tag{56a}$$

$$[KV(\beta_3) + (1-K)J(\beta_3)] - [KV(\beta_2) + (1-K)J(\beta_2)] < 0 \tag{56b}$$

Let $$E_i(\beta_j) = \beta_j V(\beta_i) + (1-\beta_j)J(\beta_i) \tag{57}$$

then $$E_i(\beta_i) = E^* \quad \text{and} \quad E_i(\beta_j) \geq E^* .$$

Using (57) in (56) one arrives at:

$$E_1(K) - E_2(K) \leq 0 \tag{58a}$$

$$E_3(K) - E_2(K) < 0 \tag{58b}$$

Observe that $E_i(\beta_j)$ is linear in β_j. Since $\beta_1 < \beta_2$, (58a) implies $K \leq \beta_2$. Likewise, since $\beta_2 < \beta_3$, (58b) implies $K > \beta_2$. This is a contradiction. Hence, the conclusion of the Lemma is true.

7.2 Lemma 2

If $\underline{c}(\beta)$ is an optimal solution for problem (50), then $J(\beta)$ is non-decreasing and $V(\beta)$ is non-increasing over $(0,1)$.

Proof:

By definition $\underline{c}(\beta)$ solves

$$\min_{\underline{c}} \beta V[\underline{c}] + (1-\beta) J[\underline{c}]$$

Obviously, for $\beta = 0$, $\underline{c}(0)$ is at the global minimum of $J[\underline{c}]$. We have seen previously that $J(\beta)$ is unimodal over $(0,1)$ hence it is non-decreasing over the same interval. Similarly, at $\beta = 1$, $\underline{c}(1)$ is at the global minimum of $V(\beta)$; and, by Lemma 1, $V(\beta)$ must be non-increasing over $]0,1[$.

Notice that up to now we have established that an increasing-type of β-sequence produces improved solutions to the joint problem. It remains to give an upper bound to this sequence.

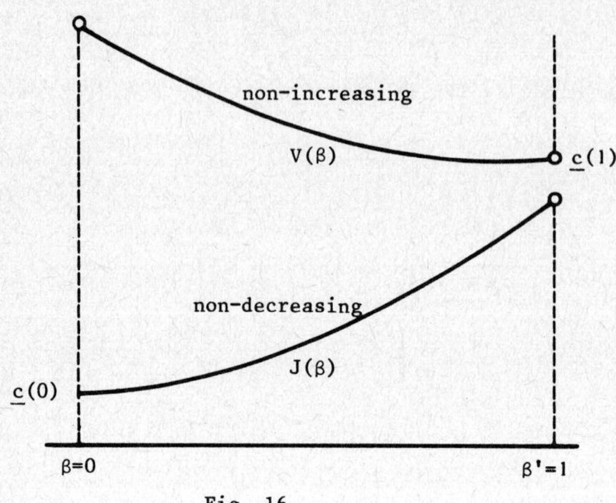

Fig. 16

7.3 Theorem

For an optimal solution $\underline{c}(\beta)$, the point $\lim_{\beta\to 0^+} \underline{c}(\beta)$ solves the joint problem.

Proof:

As β approaches 0 from above, logically $\lim_{\beta\to 0^+} \underline{c}(\beta) \in C$. Suppose that $\underline{c}(0^+)$ is not a candidate solution to the joint problem; then there exist a point $\underline{c}' \in$ such that

$$J[\underline{c}'] < J[\underline{c}(0^+)] \tag{59a}$$

$$V[\underline{c}'] > V[\underline{c}(0^+)] \tag{59b}$$

By inspection, this is not true, since $\underline{C}(0^+)$ solves problem (50) with $\beta = 1$. Thus, $\underline{c}' \in C\ (0^+)$. Let $\tilde{\beta} > 0^+$ be such that $J[\underline{c}'] > J[\underline{c}(\tilde{\beta})]$. This contradicts the montonicity of $J[\underline{c}(\beta)]$. Consequently, $\underline{c}(0^+)$ minimizes $J[\underline{c}]$ and is a solution to the joint problem.

The above theorem implies that the solution to the joint optimization and identification problem may be obtained by choosing the parameters α as:

$$\lim_{\beta\to 0^+} \underline{\alpha}(\beta)$$

which is guaranteed by the unimodality of $J(\beta)$ and $V(\beta)$ over $0 < \beta < 1$.

Finally, we consider an illustrative example.

8. EXAMPLE

Consider the problem with the dynamics given by:

$$\begin{bmatrix} \dot{X}_1 \\ \dot{X}_2 \end{bmatrix} = \begin{bmatrix} \alpha_1 & \alpha_2 \\ \alpha_2 & \alpha_4 \end{bmatrix} \begin{bmatrix} X_1 \\ X_2 \end{bmatrix} + \begin{bmatrix} 1 & 0 \\ 0 & 1 \end{bmatrix} \begin{bmatrix} u_1 \\ u_2 \end{bmatrix} \qquad X_1(0) = 2 \ ; \ X_2(0) = 1$$

where

$\alpha_1,\ldots,\alpha_4$ are unknown parameters.

The performance index is:

$$\min_{x_1,x_2,u_1,u_2} \quad J = \int_0^1 (X_1^2 + X_2^2 + u_1^2 + u_2^2)\, dt$$

The observations are:

K	0	1	2	3	4	5	6	7	8	9
X_{1_m}	1.2	1.3	1.4	1.5	1.6	1.5	1.4	1.3	1.2	1.1
X_{2_m}	2.	1.8	1.6	1.4	1.2	1.	.8	.6	.4	.2

K	10	11	12	13	14	15	16	17	18	19
X_{1_m}	1.	.9	.8	.7	.6	.5	.4	.4	.4	.4
X_{2_m}	.0	-.1	-.2	-.3	-.4	-.5	-.5	-.5	-.5	-.5

The identification measure is:

$$V = \sum_{k=0}^{20} ||\underline{X}(k) - \underline{X}_m(k)||_W^2$$

$$\underline{X}(k) = [X_1(k)X_2(k)]^T, \quad W = \text{diag}\,[1.0 \quad 1.5]$$

A FORTRAN program was written and implemented using

(1) $\beta^0 = 0.995$ at $I = 1$

(2) at $J = 1$ and $K = 1$ all the predicted patterns were set to zero

$\forall\, t \in 0, 1$.

The results of implementation are plotted in Figures (17-19). At the optimal solution, β^* has a value of 0.1 . The following table gives some additional computational statistics.

Accuracy	No. of second level iterations	No. of third level iterations	No. of fourth level iterations	C P U sec
10^{-4}	5	8	6	9.15

8.1 Remarks

In this part a new four level hierarchical algorithm has been developed for solving the joint dynamic optimisation and parameter estimation problems. The first three levels use a prediction type algorithm whilst in the fourth level a certain parameter which links the two problems is gradually increased from zero. We have studied the convergence of the algorithm and we have illustrated the algorithm on a realistic example with constant parameters. The hierarchical nature of the algorithm makes it particularly suitable for implementation on a distributed computing facility. Also, it could enable one to solve realistic large scale problems.

9. CONCLUSIONS

In this revised version of the book we have updated some of the chapters in order to provide a more coherent view of the subject of hierarchical control for dynamical systems. We see that controlling systems using hierarchies is a realistic way of tackling large scale systems problems. Some of the other approaches to tackling large scale problems are described in [113,114].

The main weakness of the hierarchical approach, as developed up to now, is the emphasis it places on the use of optimisation techniques. It may perhaps be desirable to develop frequency domain methods for use in hierarchies. Some work in this direction is already developing. In addition, future work must take into consideration: reliability factors, communication costs, particularly in micro-processor based distributed controllers, computer interfaces, etc. The work in this book provides nevertheless a framework for distributed control using micro-processors for large scale systems.

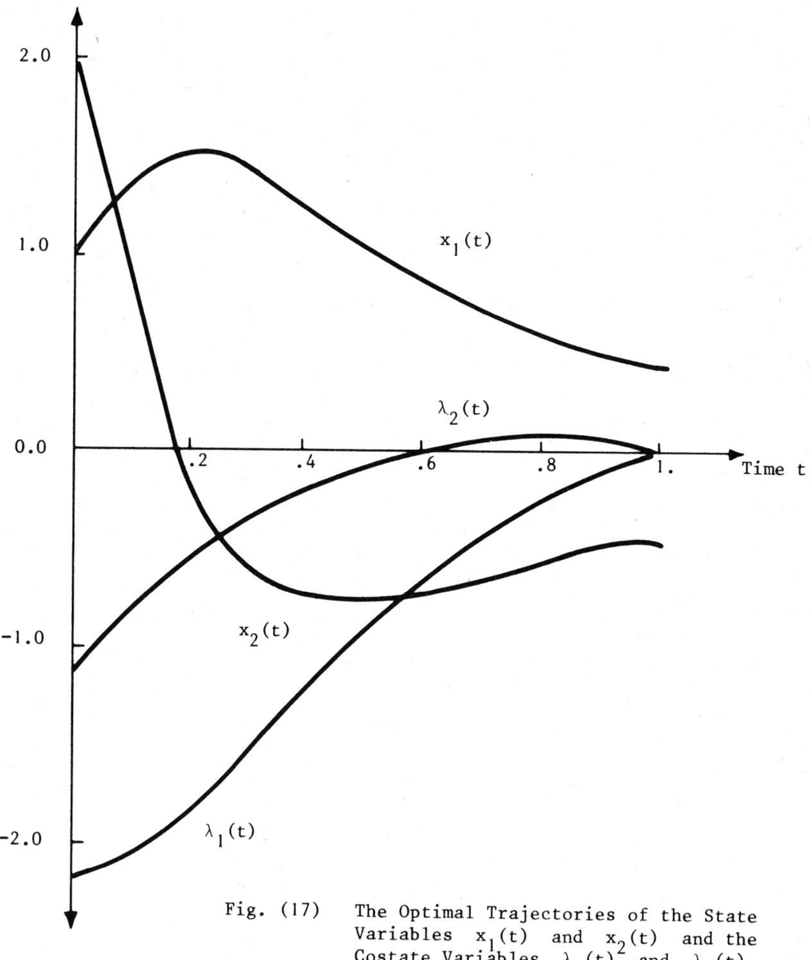

Fig. (17) The Optimal Trajectories of the State Variables $x_1(t)$ and $x_2(t)$ and the Costate Variables $\lambda_1(t)$ and $\lambda_2(t)$.

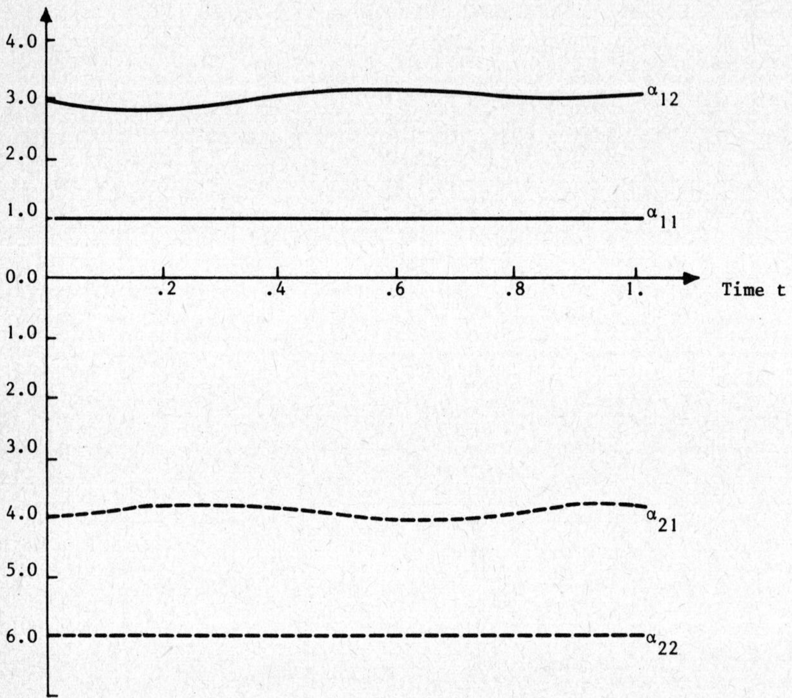

Fig. (18) The Time History of the Unknown Parameters
α_{11}, α_{12}, α_{21}, α_{22}

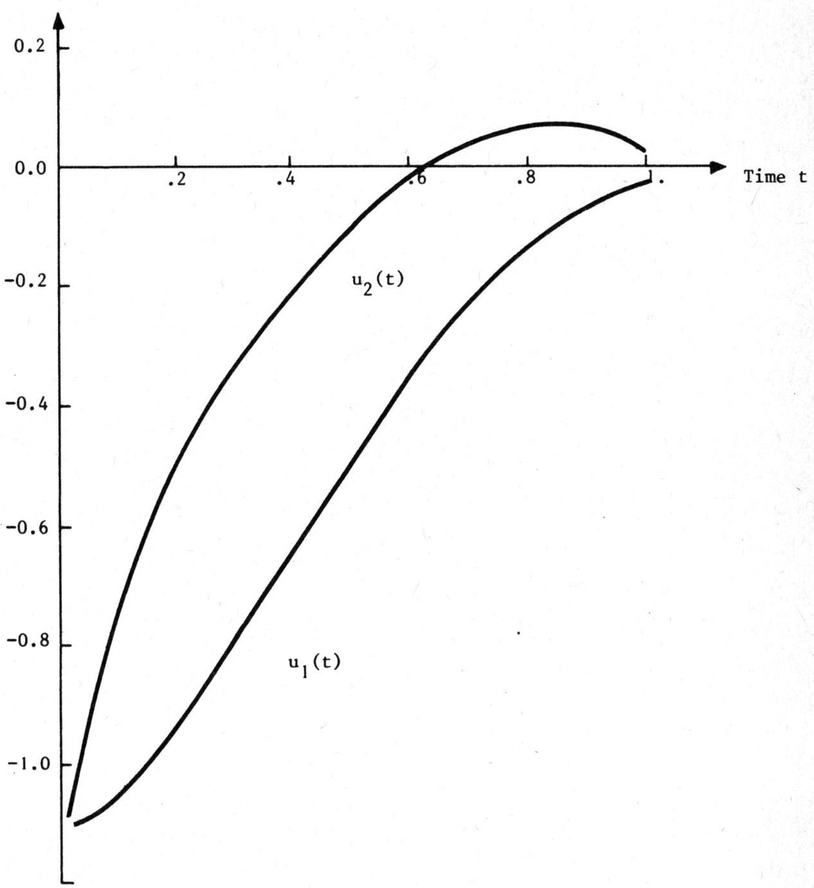

Fig. (19) The Optimal Profile of the Control Signals $u_1(t)$ and $u_2(t)$

APPENDIX 1

STANDARD FUNCTIONAL OPTIMISATION TECHNIQUES

In this appendix we give a brief overview of the standard techniques that exist for the optimisation of dynamical system. These techniques are covered in great detail in a number of excellent text books [55,87] so our treatment here is necessarily brief.

1. THE OPTIMISATION PROBLEM

The basic problem that we have attempted to tackle in this book is of the following form :

Find an admissible control $\underline{u}^*$ which causes the system

$$\dot{x}(t) = \underline{a}\ (\underline{x}(t),\ \underline{u}(t),\ t) \tag{1}$$

to follow an admissible trajectory $\underline{x}^*$ that minimises the performance measure

$$J = h(\underline{x}\ (t_f),t_f) + \int_{t_0}^{t_f} g\ (\underline{x}(t),\ \underline{u}(t),\ t)\ dt \tag{2}$$

where an admissible trajectory $\underline{x}^*$ is one that satisfies at each point in time any additional state constraints that may exist (aside from the dynamical constraints (1)) whilst an admissible control trajectory is one which satisfies at every point in time any additional control constraints which may exist. We will denote admissible states by $\underline{x} \in X$ and admissible controls by $u \in U$ where X and U are respectively the sets of admissible states and controls over the period $(t_0,\ t_f)$.

These admissibility constraints are often physical bounds on the states or control effort. For example most physical controls are limited by saturation effects and any control which is greater than the maximum saturated constraint is clearly not admissible.

There are a number of points which should be noted about the above optimal control problem. The first of these is the existance of the optimal control. In a number of important cases, the optimal control may not exist. Now, usually it is very difficult to tell a priori whether an optimal control will exist or not for a particular problem so that it is often easier to just try and solve the problem and if we are able to find the optimal control, it obviously exists.

The second important consideration is that except for a limited class of problems, the optimal control may be non-unique.

It should be emphasised that what we are seeking is basically the "global" optimum i.e. the $\underline{u}^*$ that is such that

$$J^{*} = h(\underline{x}^{*}(t_f),t_f) + \int_{t_0}^{t_f} g(\underline{x}^{*}(t),\ \underline{u}^{*}(t),\ t)\ dt$$
$$\leq h\ (\underline{x},(t_f),t_f) + \int_{t_0}^{t_f} g(\underline{x}(t),\ \underline{u}(t),\ t)\ dt$$

for all $\underline{u} \in U$ which makes $\underline{x} \in X$.

In practice, except for the special case of linear-quadratic problems that we will discuss and with the method of Dynamic Programming, it is not possible to obtain the global optimal control numerically. We can however, obtain local optima and in principle, if we obtain all the local optima, we could obtain the global optimum control by choosing from among the local optima the control that gives minimal cost J. We next describe the various standard techniques that exist for solving the problem.

2. STANDARD FUNCTIONAL OPTIMISATION TECHNIQUES

2.1. Variational techniques and the Maximum Principle

In this section we will develop the necessary conditions for the solution of our dynamical optimisation problem using the calculus of variations. Satisfaction of these conditions will yield a local optimum.

Assume that the admissible state and control regions are not bounded and that the initial conditions $\underline{x}(t_0) = \underline{x}_0$ and the initial time t_0 are specified. $\underline{x}$ is an n x 1 state vector and $\underline{u}$ is an m x 1 control vector.

Let us begin by noting that if in the cost function of equation (1) h is a differentiable function, then

$$h\ (\underline{x}(t_f),\ t_f) = \int_{t_0}^{t_f} \frac{d}{dt}\left[h(\underline{x}(t),t)\right] dt + h(\underline{x}(t_0),t_0) \tag{3}$$

so that we can rewrite equation (2) as

$$J = \int_{t_0}^{t_f} \left\{g(\underline{x}(t),\ \underline{u}(t),\ t) + \frac{d}{dt}\left[h(\underline{x}(t),\ t))\right]\right\} dt + h\ (\underline{x}\ (t_0),\ t_0) \tag{4}$$

Since $\underline{x}(t_0)$, t_0 are fixed, these will not affect the minimisation of J in equation (4) so we need only consider the minimisation of

$$J(\underline{u}) = \int_{t_0}^{t_f} \left\{ g(\underline{x}(t),\ \underline{u}(t),\ t) + \frac{d}{dt}\left[h(\underline{x}(t),t)\right]\right\} dt \tag{5}$$

$$= \int_{t_0}^{t_f} \left\{ g(\underline{x}(t),\ \underline{u}(t),\ t) + \left[\frac{\partial h}{\partial \underline{x}}(\underline{x}(t),t)\right]^T \dot{\underline{x}}(t) + \frac{\partial h}{\partial t}(\underline{x}(t),\ t)\right\} dt \tag{6}$$

by the chain rule of differentiation.

Now if we include the differential equation constraints by introducing the Lagrange Multipliers $p_1(t), \ldots\ p_n(t)$ then the cost function must be augmented to

$$J^* = \int_{t_0}^{t_f} \Big\{ g(\underline{x}(t), \underline{u}(t), t) + \Big[\frac{\partial h}{\partial \underline{x}}(\underline{x}(t),t)\Big]^T \dot{\underline{x}}(t) + \frac{\partial h}{\partial t}(\underline{x}(t),t) + \underline{p}^T(t)\Big[\underline{a}(\underline{x}(t), \underline{u}(t),t) - \dot{x}(t)\Big]\Big\} dt \quad (8)$$

Define $G[\underline{x}(t), \dot{\underline{x}}(t), \underline{u}(t), \underline{p}(t),t]$ as the term inside the integral in the augmented cost functions J^* so that

$$J^* = \int_{t_0}^{t_f} \Big\{ G\,[\underline{x}(t), \dot{\underline{x}}(t), \underline{u}(t), \underline{p}(t), t)]\Big\} dt$$

Now if we have small variations $\delta \underline{x}$, $\delta \dot{\underline{x}}$, $\delta \underline{u}$, $\delta \underline{p}$ and δt_f, then on an extremal (i.e. on a local optimal solution), the variation of J^* i.e. δJ^* must vanish. It is easy to show that δJ^* is given by

$$\begin{aligned}
\delta J^* = 0 = &\Big[\frac{\partial G}{\partial \underline{x}}(\underline{x}^*(t_f), \dot{\underline{x}}^*(t_f), \underline{u}^*(t_f), \underline{p}^*(t_f), t_f)\Big]^T \delta \underline{x}_f \\
&+ \Big[G(\underline{x}^*(t_f), \dot{\underline{x}}^*(t_f), \underline{u}^*(t_f), \underline{p}^*(t_f), t_f) \\
&- \Big[\frac{\partial G}{\partial \dot{\underline{x}}}(\underline{x}^*(t_f),\dot{\underline{x}}^*(t_f),\underline{u}^*(t_f),\underline{p}^*(t_f),t_f)\Big]^T \dot{\underline{x}}^*(t_f)\Big]\delta t_f \\
&+ \int_{t_0}^{t_f}\Big\{\Big[\Big[\frac{\partial G}{\partial \underline{x}}(\underline{x}^*(t), \dot{\underline{x}}^*(t), \underline{u}^*(t), \underline{p}^*(t), t\Big]^T \delta \underline{x} \qquad (9) \\
&- \frac{d}{dt}\Big[\frac{\partial G}{\partial \underline{x}}(\underline{x}^*(t), \dot{\underline{x}}^*(t),\underline{u}^*(t),\underline{p}^*(t), t)\Big]^T\Big]\delta \underline{x}(t) \\
&+ \Big[\frac{\partial G}{\partial \underline{u}}(\underline{x}^*(t), \dot{\underline{x}}^*(t), \underline{u}^*(t), \underline{p}^*(t), t)\Big]^T \delta \underline{u}(t) \\
&+ \Big[\frac{\partial G}{\partial \underline{p}}(\underline{x}^*(t), \dot{\underline{x}}^*(t), \underline{u}^*(t), \underline{p}^*(t), t)\Big]^T \delta \underline{p}(t)\Big\} dt \qquad (9)
\end{aligned}$$

Consider next the terms inside the integral which involve the function h ; these terms contain

$$\frac{\partial}{\partial \underline{x}}\Big[\Big[\frac{\partial h}{\partial \underline{x}}(\underline{x}^*(t),t)\Big]^T \dot{\underline{x}}^*(t) + \frac{\partial h}{\partial t}(\underline{x}^*(t), t)\Big] - \frac{d}{dt}\Big\{\frac{\partial}{\partial \dot{\underline{x}}}\Big[\Big[\frac{\partial h}{\partial \underline{x}}(\underline{x}^*(t), t)\Big]^T \dot{\underline{x}}^*(t)\Big]\Big\} \quad (10)$$

Writing out the above partial derivatives gives

$$\Big[\frac{\partial^2 h}{\partial \underline{x}^2}(\dot{\underline{x}}^*(t),t)\Big]\dot{\underline{x}}^*(t) + \Big[\frac{\partial^2 h}{\partial t \partial \underline{x}}(\underline{x}^*(t), t)\Big] - \frac{d}{dt}\Big[\frac{\partial h}{\partial \underline{x}}(\underline{x}^*(t), t)\Big] \quad (11)$$

Applying the chain rule to the last term

$$\Big[\frac{\partial^2 h}{\partial \underline{x}^2}(\dot{\underline{x}}^*(t),t)\Big]\dot{\underline{x}}^*(t) + \Big[\frac{\partial^2 h}{\partial t \partial \underline{x}}(\underline{x}^*(t), t)\Big] - \Big[\frac{\partial^2 h}{\partial \underline{x}^2}(\underline{x}^*(t),t)\Big]\dot{\underline{x}}^*(t) - \Big[\frac{\partial^2 h}{\partial \underline{x}\partial t}(\underline{x}^*(t), t)\Big] \quad (12)$$

Now if we assume that the second partial derivatives are continuous, the order of differentiation can be interchanged, and these terms add to zero. In the integral term we therefore have

$$\int_{t_0}^{t_f} \Big\{ \Big[\Big[\frac{\partial g}{\partial \underline{x}} (\underline{x}^*(t), \underline{u}^*(t), t \Big]^T + \underline{p}^{*T}(t) \Big[\frac{\partial \underline{a}^T}{\partial \underline{x}} (\underline{x}^*(t), \underline{u}^*(t), t) \Big] - \frac{d}{dt} \Big[- \underline{p}^{*T}(t) \Big] \Big] \delta \underline{x}(t) + \Big[\Big[\frac{\partial g}{\partial \underline{u}} (\underline{x}^*(t), \underline{u}^*(t), t) \Big]^T + \underline{p}^{*T}(t) \Big[\frac{\partial \underline{a}^T}{\partial \underline{u}} (\underline{x}^*(t), \underline{u}^*(t), t) \Big] \delta \underline{u}(t) + \Big[\Big[\underline{a}(\underline{x}^*(t), \underline{u}^*(t), t) - \dot{\underline{x}}^*(t)^T \Big] \delta \underline{p}(t) \Big] \Big\} dt \tag{13}$$

Now this integral must vanish on an extremal trajectory. In addition, since the dynamic constraints

$$\dot{\underline{x}}^*(t) = \underline{a} (\underline{x}^*(t), \underline{u}^*(t), t) \tag{14}$$

must be satisfied on an extremal, the coefficient of $\delta \underline{p}$ must be zero.

Again, since the Lagrange multipliers are arbitrary, we can select them to make the coefficient of $\delta \underline{x}(t)$ zero i.e.

$$\dot{\underline{p}}^*(t) = - \Big[\frac{\partial \underline{a}^T}{\partial \underline{x}} (\underline{x}^*(t), \underline{u}^*(t), t) \Big]^T \underline{p}^*(t) - \frac{\partial g}{\partial \underline{x}} (\underline{x}^*(t), \underline{u}^*(t), t) \tag{15}$$

This equation is referred to in the main text as the costate equation and $\underline{p}(t)$ as the costate vector.

Since the remaining variation $\underline{u}(t)$ is independent, its coefficient must be zero, i.e.

$$\frac{\partial g(\underline{x}^*(t), \underline{u}^*(t), t)}{\partial \underline{u}} + \Big[\frac{\partial \underline{a}^T(\underline{x}^*(t), \underline{u}^*(t), t}{\partial \underline{u}} \Big]^T \underline{p}^*(t) = \underline{0} \tag{16}$$

For the terms outside the integral, since the variations must be zero, we have

$$\Big[\frac{\partial h}{\partial \underline{x}} (\underline{x}^*(t_f), t_f) - \underline{p}^*(t_f) \Big]^T \delta \underline{x}_f + \Big[g(\underline{x}^*(t_f), \underline{u}^*(t_f), t_f) + \frac{\partial h}{\partial t} (\underline{x}^*(t_f), t_f) + \underline{p}^{*T}(t_f) \big[\underline{a}(\underline{x}^*(t_f), \underline{u}^*(t_f), t_f \big] \Big] \delta t_f = 0 \tag{17}$$

where we have used the fact that $\dot{\underline{x}}^*(t_f) = a(\underline{x}^*(t_f), \underline{u}^*(t_f), t_f)$.

Equations (14), (15), (16) are the necessary conditions for optimality and consist of 2n first order differential equations (i.e; n state equations and n costate quations) and m algebraic relations (for the control (equation (16)) which need to be satisfied over the optimisation period $[t_0, t_f]$. To solve these equations, we require 2n boundary conditions. n of these are given by the initial conditions on the state i.e. $\underline{x}(t_0) = \underline{x}_0$ and an additional n or (n+1) relationships depending on whether t_f is specified, are given by equation (17).

To write the necessary conditions for optimality in a more compact form, define the function H called the Hamiltonian as

$$H(\underline{x}(t), \underline{u}(t), \underline{p}(t), t) = g(\underline{x}(t), \underline{u}(t),t) + \underline{p}^T \left[\underline{a}(\underline{x}(t), \underline{u}(t),t)\right].$$

Then the necessary conditions become

$$\left.\begin{aligned} \dot{\underline{x}}^*(t) &= \frac{\partial H}{\partial \underline{p}} (\underline{x}^*(t), \underline{u}^*(t), \underline{p}^*(t), t) \\ \dot{\underline{p}}^*(t) &= -\frac{\partial H}{\partial \underline{x}} (\underline{x}^*,t), \underline{u}^*(t), \underline{p}^*(t),t) \\ \underline{0} &= \frac{\partial H}{\partial \underline{u}} (\underline{x}^*(t), \underline{u}^*(t), \underline{p}^*(t), t) \end{aligned}\right\} \quad \forall t \in \left[t_0, t_f\right] \tag{18}$$

and

$$\left[\frac{\partial h}{\partial \underline{x}} (\underline{x}^*(t_f),t_f) - \underline{p}^*(t_f) \right]^T \delta \underline{x}_f + \Big[H(\underline{x}^*(t_f, \underline{u}^*(t_f), \underline{p}^*(t_f), t_f) + \frac{\partial h}{\partial t} (\underline{x}^*(t_f), t_f)\Big] \delta t_f = 0 \tag{19}$$

2.2. Boundary conditions

In the techniques used in this book, basically two kinds of boundary conditions arise. In all our treatment, t_f is fixed, but $x(t_f)$ is free. In that case from equation (19), $\delta t_f = 0$ whilst $\delta \underline{x}_f$ is arbitrary so that we obtain the n boundary conditions

$$\frac{\partial h}{\partial x} (\underline{x}^*(t_f)) - \underline{p}^*(t_f) = \underline{0} \tag{20}$$

Often, in our cost function, h is zero so that from equation (20), $\underline{p}^*(t_f)=\underline{0}$ (21)

2.3. Two point boundary value problems

We saw above that the necessary conditions for optimality for our dynamic optimisation problem yielded a non-linear two point boundary value problem. Such non-linear two point boundary value problems are very difficult to solve analitically and we have, in practice, to resort to numerical techniques. Now, if the boundary conditions were all known at t_0 or at t_f, we could have numerically integrated the differential equations formed by substituting the control from equation (16) into the state equation (14) and the costate equation (15) to obtain $\underline{x}^*(t)$, $\underline{p}^*(t)$, $t \in [t_0, t_f]$. In that case we could have found the optimal control $\underline{u}^*$ by substituting for $\underline{x}^*(t)$, $\underline{p}^*(t)$ in equation (16). Now if the two point boundary value problem had been linear, as we see later on, we could have converted it to a single point boundary value problem by using the principle of superposition. However, solution by direct integration of non-linear two point boundary value problems is not feasible and we have to resort to iterative techniques.

A number of iterative techniques exist for the solution of non-linear two-point boundary value problems. In all these techniques, an initial guess is used to obtain the solution to a problem in which one or more of the five necessary conditions (the state equations, the costate equations,the control relationship, the initial conditions and the final conditions) is not satisfied. This solution is then used to improve the initial guess such that the next solution comes closer to satisfying the necessary conditions for optimality. Eventually, all the necessary conditions are satisfied to a prespecified degree of accuracy.

In the main text, the only technique for solving two point boundary value problems that we use is the quasilinearisation approach. Next we describe the quasi-linearisation approach.

2.4. Quasilinearisation approach

The basis of the quasi-linearisation approach to the solution of non-linear two point boundary value problems is tolinearise and solve instead a series of linear two point boundary value problems. Linear two point boundary value problems can be solved non-iteratively.

We begin the development of the quasilinearisation method by assuming that the control relationship (16) has been solved i.e. we have obtained from $\partial H/\partial \underline{u} = \underline{0}$ the control $\underline{u}(t)$ as a function of $\underline{x}(t)$ and $\underline{p}(t)$ and that we have substituted this into the state equation (14) and costate equation (15) to obtain

$$\dot{\underline{x}}(t) = \underline{a}\,(\underline{x}(t),\ \underline{p}(t),\ t) \tag{22}$$

$$\dot{\underline{p}}(t) = -\frac{\partial H}{\partial \underline{x}}\,(\underline{x}(t),\ \underline{p}(t),\ t) \tag{23}$$

Equations (22) and (23) are called the reduced equations. The boundary conditions are $\underline{x}(t_0) = \underline{x}_0$ and $\underline{p}\,(t_f) = \underline{p}_f$, were $\underline{p}_f$ is an n x 1 vector of constants, t_f is specified whilst $\underline{x}\,(t_f)$ is free.

Let us assume that an initial guess $\underline{x}^{(i)}(t)$, $\underline{p}^{(i)}(t)$ is available of the state and costate trajectories over the optimisation interval. We can use this guess to linearise the state-costate equations (22) and (23) about these trajectories by expanding (22), (23) in a Taylor series about these trajectory and truncating this series at order one. This leads to the following new linearised trajectories for $\underline{x}^i$ and $\underline{p}^i$ i.e.

$$\begin{aligned}\dot{\underline{x}}^{i+1}(t) &= \underline{a}(\underline{x}^{(i)}(t),\ \underline{p}^{(i)}(t),t) + \left[\frac{\partial \underline{a}^T}{\partial \underline{x}}\ (\underline{x}^{(i)}(t),\ \underline{p}^{(i)}(t),t)\right]^T \\ &\left[\underline{x}^{i+1}(t) - \underline{x}^i(t)\right] + \left[\frac{\partial \underline{a}^T}{\partial \underline{p}}(\underline{x}^i(t),\ \underline{p}^i(t),\ t)\right]^T\left[\underline{p}^{i+1}(t) - \underline{p}^i(t)\right]\end{aligned} \tag{24}$$

$$\begin{aligned}\underline{p}^{i+1}(t) &= -\frac{\partial H}{\partial \underline{x}}\ (\underline{x}^{(i)}(t),\ \underline{p}^{(i)}(t),\ t) \\ &= -\frac{\partial}{\partial x}\ (\frac{\partial H}{\partial \underline{x}})^T(\underline{x}^{(i)}(t),\ \underline{p}^{(i)}(t),t)\Big]^T\left[\underline{x}^{(i+1)}(t) - \underline{x}^{(i)}(t)\right] \\ &\frac{\partial}{\partial \underline{p}}(\frac{\partial H}{\partial \underline{x}})^T(\underline{x}^{(i)}(t),\underline{p}^{(i)}(t),t)\Big]^T\left[\underline{p}^{i+1}(t) - \underline{p}^i(t)\right]\end{aligned} \tag{25}$$

where the ijth element of the above matrices is given by

$$\left[\frac{\partial \underline{a}}{\partial \underline{x}}\right]_{ij} = \frac{\partial a_i}{\partial x_j}\ ;\ \left[\frac{\partial \underline{a}}{\partial \underline{p}}\right]_{ij} = \frac{\partial a_i}{\partial p_j}$$

$$\left[\frac{\partial^2 H}{\partial \underline{x}^2}\right]_{ij} = \frac{\partial^2 H}{\partial x_i \partial x_j}\ ;\ \left[\frac{\partial^2 H}{\partial \underline{x}\partial \underline{p}}\right]_{ij} = \frac{\partial^2 H}{\partial x_i \partial p_j}$$

Now let us rewrite equations (24), (25) as

$$\dot{\underline{x}}^{i+1}(t) = f_{11}(t)\ \underline{x}^{i+1}(t) + f_{12}(t)\ \underline{p}^{i+1}(t) + \underline{d}_1(t) \tag{26}$$

$$\underline{p}^{i+1} = f_{21}(t)\,\underline{x}^{i+1}(t) + f_{22}(t)\,\underline{p}^{i+1}(t) + \underline{d}_2(t) \tag{27}$$

or in partitioned form :

$$\begin{bmatrix} \dot{\underline{x}}^{i+1}(t) \\ \dot{\underline{p}}^{i+1}(t) \end{bmatrix} \begin{bmatrix} f_{11}(t) & f_{12}(t) \\ f_{21}(t) & f_{22}(t) \end{bmatrix} \begin{bmatrix} \underline{x}^{i+1}(t) \\ \underline{p}^{i+1}(t) \end{bmatrix} + \begin{bmatrix} \underline{d}_1(t) \\ \underline{d}_2(t) \end{bmatrix}$$

$$= F(t) \begin{bmatrix} \underline{x}^{i+1}(t) \\ \underline{p}^{i+1}(t) \end{bmatrix} + \begin{bmatrix} \underline{d}_1(t) \\ \underline{d}_2(t) \end{bmatrix} \tag{28}$$

where $f_{11}(t) = \left(\frac{\partial \underline{a}}{\partial \underline{x}}\right)^{T\,T}$; $f_{12}(t) = \left(\frac{\partial \underline{a}}{\partial \underline{p}}\right)^{T\,T}$; $f_{21}(t) = -\left[\frac{\partial}{\partial x}\left(\frac{\partial H}{\partial \underline{x}}\right)^T\right]^T$; $f_{22}(t) = -\left[\frac{\partial}{\partial p}\left(\frac{\partial H}{\partial \underline{x}}\right)^T\right]^T$

$$\underline{d}_1(t) = -f_{11}(t)\,\underline{x}(t) - f_{12}(t)\,\underline{p}(t) + \underline{a}$$

$$d_2(t) = -f_{21}(t)\,x(t) - f_{22}(t)\,p(t) - \frac{\partial H}{\partial x}$$

These functions are evaluated at $\underline{x}^{(i)}(t)$, $\underline{p}^{(i)}(t)$ and are hence known functions of time.

We use an initial guess $\underline{x}^{(0)}(t)$, $\underline{p}^{(0)}(t)$, $t \in [t_0, t_f]$ to evaluate these known functions of time at the beginning of the first iteration. Next, in order to solve equation (28), we generate n solutions to the 2n homogeneous differential equations by numerical integration.

$$\begin{aligned} \dot{\underline{x}}^{(i+1)}(t) &= A_{11}(t)\,\underline{x}^{(i+1)}(t) + A_{12}(t)\,\underline{p}^{i+1}(t) \\ \dot{\underline{p}}^{(i+1)}(t) &= A_{21}(t)\,\underline{x}^{(i+1)}(t) + A_{22}(t)\,\underline{p}^{i+1}(t) \end{aligned} \tag{29}$$

Let us denote these solutions at the ith iteration by $\underline{x}^{h1}, \underline{p}^{h1}, \underline{x}^{h2}, \underline{p}^{h2}, \ldots \underline{x}^{hn}, \underline{p}^{hn}$. The above integration is performed using the boundary conditions

$$\begin{aligned} &\underline{x}^{h1}(t_0) = \underline{0}\ ,\ \underline{p}^{h1}(t_0) = [1 \quad 0 \quad 0 \ \ldots\ldots\ 0]^T \\ &\underline{x}^{h2}(t_0) = \underline{0}\ ,\ \underline{p}^{h2}(t_0) = [0 \quad 1 \quad 0 \ \ldots\ldots\ 0]^T \\ &\cdot \\ &\cdot \\ &\underline{x}^{hn}(t_0) = \underline{0}\ ,\ \underline{p}^{hn}(t_0) = [0 \quad 0 \ \ldots\ldots\ldots 0 \quad 1]^T \end{aligned} \tag{30}$$

Next, we generate a particular solution by integrating equation (28) from t_0 to t_f using the boundary conditions $\underline{x}(t_0) = \underline{x}_0$, $\underline{p}(t_0) = \underline{0}$. Then from the principle of superposition, the complete solution of equation (28) is

$$\begin{aligned} \underline{x}^{i+1}(t) &= c_1\underline{x}^{h1}(t) + c_2\,\underline{x}^{h2}(t) + \ldots + c_n\underline{x}^{hn}(t) + \underline{x}^{p}(t) \\ \underline{p}^{i+1}(t) &= c_1\underline{p}^{h1}(t) + c_2\underline{x}^{h2}(t) + \ldots + x_n\underline{p}^{hn}(t) + \underline{p}^{p}(t) \end{aligned} \tag{31}$$

where $\underline{x}^p(t)$, $\underline{p}^p(t)$ are the particular solutions obtained above and $c_1, c_2 \ldots c_n$ are constant which ensure that $\underline{p}^{i+1}(t_f) = \underline{p}_f$. To evaluate these constants , write

$$\underline{p}_f = \left[\underline{p}^{h1}(t_f) \,\vdots\, \underline{p}^{h2}(t_f) \,\vdots\, \ldots\ldots \,\vdots\, \underline{p}^{Hn}(t_f)\right] \underline{c} + \underline{p}^{P}(t_f) \tag{32}$$

where the only unknown quantity is $\underline{c}$. Solving for $\underline{c}$ yields

$$\underline{c} = \left[\underline{p}^{h1}(t_f) \,\vdots\, \underline{p}^{h2}(t_f) \,\vdots\, \ldots \,\vdots\, \underline{p}^{hn}(t_f)\right]^{-1} \left[\underline{p}_f - \underline{p}^{P}(t_f)\right] \tag{33}$$

Substituting this $\underline{c}$ in equations (30), (31) gives the (i+1)th trajectory and completes one iteration of the quasilinearisation method. The (i+1)th trajectory can be used to begin another iteration if desired.

In deriving equation (33) we assumed that the final costate $\underline{p}(t_f)$ is a given constant. If

$$\underline{p}(t_f) = \frac{\partial h}{\partial \underline{x}} \left(\underline{x}(t_f)\right)$$

then it is easy to show that

$$\underline{c} = \Big[\underline{p}^{h1}(t_f) - \frac{\partial^2 h}{\partial \underline{x}^2}(\underline{x}^{(i)} t_f)\, \underline{x}^{h1}(t_f) \,\vdots\, \underline{p}^{h1}(t_f) - \frac{\partial^2 h}{\partial \underline{x}^2}(\underline{x}^{(i)}(t_f))\, \underline{x}^{h2}(t_f) \,\vdots\, \ldots \,\vdots\, \underline{p}^{hn}(t_f) - \frac{\partial^2 h}{\partial \underline{x}^2}(\underline{x}^{(i)}(t_f))\underline{x}^{hn}(t_f)\Big]^{-1}$$
$$\Big[\frac{\partial h}{\partial \underline{x}}(\underline{x}^{(i)}(t_f)) - \frac{\partial^2 h}{\partial \underline{x}^2}(\underline{x}^{(i)}(t_f))\, \underline{x}^{(i)}(t_f) + \frac{\partial^2 h}{\partial \underline{x}^2}(\underline{x}^{(i)}(t_f))\, \underline{x}^{P}(t_f) - \underline{p}^{P}(t_f)\Big] \tag{34}$$

Thus to summarise, the algorithm is :

Step 1 : Form the reduced state-costate equations by solving $\frac{\partial H}{\partial \underline{u}} = \underline{0}$ for $\underline{u}(t)$ in terms of $\underline{x}(t)$, $\underline{p}(t)$, t and substituting in the state-costate equations (which now contain only $\underline{x}(t)$, $\underline{p}(t)$, t .

Step 2 : Form the linearised reduced differential equations in terms of $\underline{x}^{(i)}(t)$, $\underline{p}^{(i)}(t)$, t by using equations (26), (27).

Step 3 : Guess an initial trajectory $\underline{x}^{(0)}(t)$, $\underline{p}^{(0)}(t)$, $t \in [t_0, t_f]$ and let the iteration index i be zero.

Step 4 : Evaluate the matrices f_{11}, f_{12}, f_{21}, f_{22}, $\underline{d}_1$, $\underline{d}_2$ of equation (28) on the trajectory $\underline{x}^{(i)}$, $\underline{p}^{(i)}$.

Step 5 : Integrate numerically the homogeneous differential equations (29) from t_0 to t_f using the n sets of initial conditions given in equation (30). Compute a particular solution to equation (28) by numerical integration from t_0 to t_f using the initial conditions $\underline{x}^P(t_0) = \underline{x}_0$, $\underline{p}^P(t_0) = \underline{0}$. All this can be done by performing a single integration of n(2n) + 2n = 2n (n+1) differential equations. Store the values of the appropriate variables at $t = t_f$.

Step 6 : Use the values found in step 5 to compute $\underline{c}$ from equation (33) or (34) (depending on the particular boundary values on $\underline{p}$ in the problem).

Step 7 : Use $\underline{c}$ found in step 6 and equations(31) to obtain the $(i+1)^{th}$ trajectory

Step 8 : Compare the ith and $(i+1)^{th}$ trajectories by calculating the norm

$$\left\| \begin{bmatrix} \underline{x}^{(i+1)} \\ \underline{p}^{(i+1)} \end{bmatrix} - \begin{bmatrix} \underline{x}^{(i)} \\ \underline{p}^{(i)} \end{bmatrix} \right\| = \sum_{j=1}^{n} \Big\{ \max_t \left| x_j^{(i+1)}(t) - x_j^{(i)}(t) \right| + \max_t \left| p_j^{(i+1)}(t) - p_j^{(i)}(t) \right| \Big\}$$

Test if $\left\| \begin{bmatrix} \underline{x}^{i+1} \\ \underline{p}^{i+1} \end{bmatrix} - \begin{bmatrix} \underline{x}^{i} \\ \underline{p}^{i} \end{bmatrix} \right\| \leq \gamma$

where γ is a small prechosen constant. If the above inequality is satisfied, go to step 9. Else return to step 4 using the trajectory $\underline{x}^{i+1}$, $\underline{p}^{i+1}$ in the place of $\underline{x}^{i}$, $\underline{p}^{i}$.

Step 9 : Integrate the original non-linear reduced state and costate equations with the given split boundary conditions. Compare the results of this integration with the final trajectory $\underline{x}^{(i+1)}$, $\underline{p}^{(i+1)}$ using a suitable norm, and also with the specified split boundary conditions. This comparison should verify that the sequence of solutions to the linearised differential equations has converged to the solution of the original non-linear differential equations. Using the $\underline{x}$, $\underline{p}$, the optimal control can be calculated.

Note that the steps 1 through 3 are performed off-line by the user whilst the steps 4 through 9 are performed on a computer.

3. APPLICATION TO LINEAR-QUADRATIC PROBLEMS [55]

The difficulty in solving the optimal control problem arises mainly from the fact that for the general non-linear case, minimising the Hamiltonian leads to a problem of solving a set of 2n simultaneous non-linear differential equations in $\underline{x}$ and $\underline{p}$ with split boundary conditions. As we have seen, these equations can not be directly integrated to yield the optimal control and we have to resort to an iterative approach to ensure that eventually the trajectories of $\underline{x}$ and $\underline{p}$ obtained satisfy not only the governing differential equations but also the split boundary conditions on $\underline{x}$ and $\underline{p}$. We have discussed above the quasilinearisation method. Other possible ways in which these can be solved numerically, are described fully by Sage [55] . Here we describe an important special case where the two point boundary value problem, which arises on the application of the Maximum principle is linear. This two point boundary value problem can be solved by a non-iterative method. The special case, called the linear servomechanism case, arises when the functional to be minimised is a quadratic function of the states and controls and the dynamic constraints are linear, i.e. it is desired to minimise

$$J = \frac{1}{2} \|\underline{\eta}(t_f)-\underline{z}(t_f)\|^2_S + \frac{1}{2} \int_{t_0}^{t_f} (\|\underline{\eta}(t)-\underline{z}(t)\|^2_{Q(t)} + \|\underline{u}(t)\|^2_{R(t)}) \tag{35}$$

subject to
$$\dot{\underline{x}}(t) = A(t)\,\underline{x}(t) + B(t)\,\underline{u}(t) + \underline{w}(t) \tag{36}$$

$$\underline{x}(t_0) = \underline{x}_0 \tag{37}$$

$$\underline{z}(t) = C(t)\,\underline{x}(t) \tag{38}$$

Q is assumed to be a positive semidefinite matrix and R is assumed to be positive definite.

The Hamiltonian for this system can be written as

$$H(\underline{x},\underline{u},\underline{p},t) = \frac{1}{2}\|\underline{\eta}(t) - C(t)^T\underline{x}(t)\|^2_Q + \frac{1}{2}\|\underline{u}(t)\|^2_R + \underline{p}^T\left[\underline{Ax}+\underline{Bu}+\underline{w}\right] \tag{39}$$

Using the Maximum principle, $\frac{\partial H}{\partial \underline{u}} = \underline{0}$ or,

$$\underline{u} = - R^{-1} B^T \underline{p} \tag{40}$$

and
$$\frac{\partial H}{\partial \underline{x}} = -\dot{\underline{p}} = +C^T Q\left[C\underline{x} - \underline{\eta}\right] + A^T \underline{p} \tag{41}$$

with
$$\underline{p}(t_f) = C^T(t_f)\, S\left[C(t_f)\,\underline{x}(t_f) - \underline{\eta}(t_f)\right] \tag{42}$$

Let us assume a solution of the two point boundary value problem to be

$$\underline{p}(t) = P(t)\,\underline{x}(t) - \underline{\xi}(t) \tag{43}$$

Then by fairly obvious manipulations, it is easy to show that the optimal control $\underline{u}$ is given by

$$\underline{u}(t) = -R^{-1}(t)\,B^T(t)\left[P(t)\,\underline{x}(t) - \underline{\xi}(t)\right] \tag{44}$$

where P and $\underline{\xi}$ are the solutions of the following single point boundary value problems :

$$\dot{P} = -PA - A^T P + PBR^{-1} B^T P - C^T QC \tag{45}$$

with
$$P(t_f) = C^T(t_f)\, SC\,(t_f) \tag{46}$$

and
$$\dot{\underline{\xi}} = -\left[A - BR^{-1} B^T P\right]\underline{\xi} + P\underline{w} - C^T Q\,\underline{\eta} \tag{47}$$

with
$$\underline{\xi}(t_f) = C^T(t_f)\, S\,\underline{\eta}(t_f). \tag{48}$$

4. DYNAMIC PROGRAMMING

Finally we describe the powerful technique of dynamic programming for solving functional optimisation problems. The underlying idea behind the approach is Bellman's principle of optimality which states that :

> "An optimal policy has the property that whatever the initial state and decision are, the remaining decisions must constitute an optimal policy with regard to the state resulting from the first decision"

Let us see how we can apply this principle to the dynamic optimisation problem that we have been considering. For convenience, let us rewrite this problem as :

$$\text{Min } J = \int_{t_0}^{t_f} g(\underline{x}(t), \underline{u}(t), t)\, dt \tag{49}$$

subject to
$$\dot{\underline{x}}(t) = \underline{a}\,(\underline{x}(t), \underline{u}(t), t) \tag{50}$$
$$\underline{x}(0) = \underline{x}_0$$

where $\underline{u}(t) \in U$ where U is possibly infinite or semi-infinite closed interval. The admissible input set U may depend on $\underline{x}(t)$ and t. t_f is assumed fixed and $\underline{x}(t_f)$ is free. Suppose that we have calculated $\hat{\underline{u}}(t)$ as the optimal control and $\hat{\underline{x}}(t)$ as the resulting state trajectory. The cost function is then a function of the initial state, $\underline{x}(t_0)$ and initial time, t_0 only. Let us write this minimal cost as

$$V(\underline{x}_0, t_0) = J\,(\hat{\underline{x}}, \hat{\underline{u}}) = \int_{t_0}^{t_f} g(\hat{\underline{x}}\,(t), \hat{\underline{u}}(t), t)\, dt$$

$V(\underline{x}_0, t_0)$ is a function only of $\underline{x}_0$ and t_0 since $\hat{\underline{x}}(t)$ and $\hat{\underline{u}}(t)$ are the known optimal values $\forall t \in [t_0, t_f]$.

Consider a time Δt between t_0 and t_f and rewrite the cost function in equation (49) as

$$V(\underline{x}_0,t_0) = \int_{t_0}^{t_0+\Delta t} g(\hat{\underline{x}}, \hat{\underline{u}},t)\, dt + \int_{t_0+\Delta t}^{t_f} g(\hat{\underline{x}},\hat{\underline{u}},t)\, dt = J_1(\hat{\underline{x}},\hat{\underline{u}}) + J_2(\hat{\underline{x}},\hat{\underline{u}}) \tag{51}$$

If g is assumed smooth over the interval $t_0 \leqslant t \leqslant t_0 + \Delta t$ and Δt is sufficiently small, we may write J_1 above as

$$J_1 = \Delta t\, g\left[\hat{\underline{x}}(t_0 + \alpha \Delta t)\, ,\, \hat{\underline{u}}(t_0 + \alpha \Delta t),\, t_0 + \alpha \Delta t\right] \quad 0 < \alpha < 1 \tag{52}$$

The second part of the cost function is

$$V_2 = V\left[\hat{\underline{x}}(t_0 + \Delta t), t_0 + \Delta t\right] = \int_{t_0+\Delta t}^{t_f} g(\hat{\underline{x}}(t),\, \hat{\underline{u}}(t),t)\, dt \tag{53}$$

This is because of the principle of optimality stated in the beginning of this section which implies that any part of an optimal trajectory is an optimal trajectory.

Let us now write the cost function along the optimal trajectory as

$$V(\underline{x}_0,t_0) = \Delta t g \left[\hat{\underline{x}}(t_0 + \alpha\Delta t),\, \hat{\underline{u}}(t_0 + \alpha\Delta t),\, t_0 + \alpha\Delta t\right] + V\left[\hat{\underline{x}}(t_0 + \Delta t),\, t_0 + \Delta t\right] \tag{54}$$

By expanding the last term in this equation in a Taylor's series about $\Delta t = 0$, we have

$$V(\underline{x}_0,t_0) = \Delta t\, g\left[\hat{\underline{x}}(t_0+\alpha \Delta t),\, \hat{\underline{u}}(t_0+\alpha \Delta t),\, t_0 + \alpha \Delta t\right] + V(\underline{x}_0,\, t_0) + \left[\frac{\partial V(\underline{x}_0,\, t_0)}{\partial t_0}\right] \Delta t + \left[\frac{\partial V(\underline{x}_0,t_0)}{\partial \underline{x}_0}\right]^T \dot{\underline{x}}_0\, \Delta t + \ldots \tag{55}$$

On taking the limit as Δt approaches zero and recalling the dynamic constraint (50), we obtain the well known Hamilton Jacobi equation

$$\frac{\partial V(\underline{x}_0,t_0)}{\partial t_0} + g\left[\hat{\underline{x}}(t_0),\, \hat{\underline{u}}(t_0),\, t_0\right] + \left[\frac{\partial V(\underline{x}_0,t_0)}{\partial \underline{x}_0}\right]^T \underline{a}(\hat{x}(t_0),\, \hat{\underline{u}}(t_0),\, t_0) = 0 \tag{56}$$

In this expression we define

$$\underline{p}\,(t_0) = \frac{\partial V(\underline{x}_0,t_0)}{\partial \underline{x}_0} \tag{57}$$

we may then rewrite the Hamilton-Jacobi equation, after dropping the subscript "0" for convenience as

$$\frac{\partial V(\underline{x},t)}{\partial t} + H\,(\hat{\underline{x}},\, \hat{\underline{u}},\, \underline{p},\, t) = 0 \tag{58}$$

It should be noted that the Hamiltonian H in equation (58) is the Hamiltonian evaluated (at time t_0) for the optimal control $\hat{\underline{u}}(t)$ since it has been assumed that g was evaluated about the optimal control and state.

If we had used the cost function of equation (2) i.e.

$$J = h\,(\underline{x}(t_f),\ t_f) + \int_{t_0}^{t_f} g(\underline{x}(t),\ \underline{u}(t),\ t)\ dt \tag{59}$$

we would have obtained the same Hamilton-Jacobi equation except that in this case the initial condition (at the terminal time) would have been

$$V\left[\underline{x}(t_f),\ t_f\right] = h\,(\underline{x}\,(t_f),\ t_f) \tag{60}$$

4.1. Remarks

1. The Hamilton-Jacobi equation cannot be easily solved in general. However, when it can $\underline{u}(t)$ is determined as a function of $\underline{x}(t)$, i.e. we find a closed loop control.

2. The method can incorporate inequality constraints easily.

3. The solution obtained is the globally optimal solution.

APPENDIX 2

LAGRANGE DUALITY

Consider the problem (Problem I)

$$\underset{\underline{x} \in X}{\text{Minimise}} \quad f(\underline{x}) \text{ subjet to } \underline{g}(\underline{x}) \leqslant \underline{0}$$

where $\underline{g}(x) = (g_1(x), \ldots g_m(t))^T$, f and each g_i are real valued functions defined on $X \subseteq R^n$. It is assumed that X is a non-empty convex set on which all functions are convex.

The dual of problem I w.r.t. the $\underline{g}$ constraints is :

(Problem II)

$$\underset{\underline{u} \geqslant \underline{0}}{\text{Maximise}} \quad \left[\underset{\underline{x} \in X}{\text{infimum}} \left[f(\underline{x}) + \underline{u}^T \underline{g}(\underline{x})\right]\right]$$

where $\underline{u}$ is an m vector of dual variables. Note that the maximand of Problem II is a concave function of $\underline{u}$ alone (even in the absence of convexity assumptions) since it is a pointwise infimum of a collection (indexed by $\underline{x}$) of functions linear in $\underline{u}$.

Before stating the duality results, it is necessary to define certain quantities.

Definition 1:

The optimal value of problem I is the infimum of $f(\underline{x})$ subject to $\underline{x} \in X$ and $\underline{g}(\underline{x}) \leqslant \underline{0}$. The optimal value of problem II is the supremum of its maximand subject to $\underline{u} \geqslant \underline{0}$.

Definition 2 :

A pair $(\underline{x}, \underline{u})$ is said to satisfy the optimality conditions for problem I if

(i) $\underline{x}$ minimises $f + \underline{u}^T \underline{g}$ over X

(ii) $\underline{u}^T \underline{g}(\underline{x}) = \underline{0}$

(iii) $\underline{u} \geqslant \underline{0}$

(iv) $\underline{g}(\underline{x}) \leqslant \underline{0}$

Definition 3 :

The perturbation function $v(\underline{y})$ associated with problem I is defined on R^m as

$$v(\underline{y}) = \underset{\underline{x} \in X}{\text{infimum}} \; f(\underline{x}) \quad \text{subject to } \underline{g}(\underline{x}) \leqslant \underline{y}$$

where $\underline{y}$ is called the perturbation vector.

Definition 4 :

Let $\underline{y}$ be a point at which v is finite. An m vector $\underline{\bar{\gamma}}$ is said to be a subgradient of v at $\underline{y}$ if

$$v(\underline{y}) \geq v(\underline{\bar{y}}) + \underline{\bar{\gamma}}^T (\underline{y} - \underline{\bar{y}}) \quad \text{for all } \underline{y} .$$

Definition 5 :

Problem I is said to be stable if v $(\underline{0})$ is finite and there exists a scaler M > 0 such that

$$\frac{v(\underline{0}) - v(\underline{y})}{\| \underline{y} \|} \leq M \quad \text{for all } \underline{y} \neq 0$$

Definition 6 :

A vector u is said to be essentially infeasible in problem II if it yields a value of $-\infty$ for the maximand of problem II. If every $\underline{u} \geq 0$ is essentially infeasible in II then problem II itself is said to be essentially infeasible. If problem II is not essentially infeasible, it is said to be essentially feasible.

Having defined some useful quantities and concepts, we are now in a position to state the main duality results. We do this by stating a number of theorems. For proofs of these theorems, the reader is referred to the excellent paper of Geoffrion [35] .

THEOREM 1 (optimality)

Assume that problem I has an optimal solution. Then an optimal multiplier vector exists if and only if $(-\underline{u})$ is a subgradient of v at $\underline{y} = \underline{0}$.

THEOREM 2 (Weak Duality)

If $\bar{x}$ is feasible in problem I and $\bar{u}$ is feasible in problem II, then the objective function of problem I evaluated at $\bar{x}$ is not less than the objective function of problem II evaluated at $\bar{u}$

i.e. $\quad \text{Infimum} \left\{ f(\underline{x}) + \underline{u}^T \underline{g}(\underline{x}) \,\middle|\, \underline{x} \in X \right\} \leq f(\underline{\bar{x}}) + \underline{\bar{u}}^T \underline{g}(\underline{x}) \leq f(\underline{\bar{x}})$

THEOREM 3 (Strong Duality)

If problem I is stable then

(a) problem II has an optimal solution

(b) the optimal values of problems I and II are equal

(c) $\underline{u}^*$ is an optimal solution of problem II if and only if $-\underline{u}^*$ is a subgradient of v at $\underline{y} = \underline{0}$

(d) every optimal solution $\underline{u}^*$ of problem II characterises the set of all optimal solutions (if any) of problem I as the minimisers of f $+(\underline{u}^*)^T$ $\underline{g}$ over X which also satisfy the feasibility condition $\underline{g}(\underline{x}) \leq \underline{0}$ and the complementary slackness condition $(\underline{u}^*)^T \underline{g}(\underline{x}) = \underline{0}$.

Remarks

Theorem 3 is obviously a very powerful result since

(1) all optimal solution of problem I can be found from any single solution of problem II ;

(2) (b) above ensures that there is no DUALITY GAP between the optimal values of problems I and II ;

(3) (c) above gives us the connection between the set of optimal solutions of problem II and the perturbation function, i.e. if problem I has an optimal solution as well as the property of stability, then, using Theorem 1, the optimal solution set of problem II is the set of optimal multiplier vectors for problem I. It can be shown [35] that this result also holds under a slightly weaker assumption than

stability, i.e. when v(0) is finite and the optimal values of problems I and II are equal.

The above results can easily be extended to the case of discrete dynamical systems by considering such systems to be collections of the type of problem I at each point in time.

Hanson [80] has shown that the results can be extended to the continuous time optimisation problem. We next give a simplified version of these results due to Simon and Stubberud [79].

The primal problem germane to this discussion can be formulated as follows :

Find $\underline{u}(t) \in E^m$ which minimises $\nu(\underline{x}_0, \underline{u}(t))$;

where $$\nu(\underline{x}_0, \underline{u}(t)) = g_1(\underline{x}(T)) + \int_{t_0}^{T} \ell(\underline{x}, \underline{u}, t)\, dt \tag{1}$$

T and t_0 are fixed, and $\underline{x} \in E^n$ satisfies

$$\dot{\underline{x}}(t) = f(\underline{x}, \underline{u}, t) \qquad \underline{x}(t_0) = x_0 \tag{2}$$

It is assumed that g_1, ℓ, f are continuous and doubly differentiable functions of $\underline{x}(t)$, $\underline{u}(t)$ and that g_1, ℓ are nonnegative definite functions of $\underline{x}$, $\underline{u}$. This formulation applies to the fixed-time regulator and final-value control problems. The primarily desired characteristics of the dual problem are that it be a maximisation problem whose extremal curves and optimal cost functional coincide with those of the primal problem and that existence of the solution of one of the problems implies existence of the solution to the other. The appropriate dual problem to (1-2) can thus be derived as follows.

The Lagrangian of the primal problem is defined as

$$L(\underline{x}, \dot{\underline{x}}, \underline{u}, \underline{\lambda}, t) = \ell(\underline{x}, \underline{u}, t) + \underline{\lambda}^T [\dot{\underline{x}} - f(\underline{x}, \underline{u}, t)] \tag{3}$$

It is well-known that the extremal K of the primal problem, defined by $\tilde{\underline{x}}(t)$, $\tilde{\underline{u}}(t)$ necessarily satisfies the Euler-Lagrange equations (Ref. [81]).

$$L_{\underline{x}}(\underline{x}, \dot{\underline{x}}, \underline{u}, \underline{\lambda}, t) = (d/dt)\, L_{\dot{\underline{x}}}(\underline{x}, \dot{\underline{x}}, \underline{u}, \underline{\lambda}, t) \tag{4}$$

$$(d/dt)\, L_{\underline{u}}(\underline{x}, \dot{\underline{x}}, \underline{u}, \underline{\lambda}, t) = \underline{0} \tag{5}$$

or

$$\ell_{\underline{x}}(\underline{x}, \underline{u}, t) - \underline{\lambda}^T f_{\underline{x}}(\underline{x}, \underline{u}, t) = \dot{\underline{\lambda}}^T \tag{6}$$

$$\ell_{\underline{u}}(\underline{x}, \underline{u}, t) - \underline{\lambda}^T f_{\underline{u}}(\underline{x}, \underline{u}, t) = \text{Const.} \tag{7}$$

The transversality condition for the fixed-time problem then guarantees that

$$\underline{\lambda}(T) = -g^T_{1\underline{x}}(\underline{x}(T)) \tag{8}$$

$$\ell_{\underline{u}}(\underline{x}, \underline{u}, t) = \underline{\lambda}^T f_{\underline{u}}(\underline{x}, \underline{u}, t) \tag{9}$$

on the extremal K. The assumption is made at this point that Eq. (9) can be solved for the optimal control $\underline{u} = \tilde{\underline{u}}(\underline{x}, \underline{\lambda}, t)$.

Now, consider the following problem : Find $\underline{x}(t) = \hat{\underline{x}}(t)$ giving $\max_{\underline{x}(t)} \omega(\underline{x}(t))$, where

$$\omega(\underline{x}(t)) \equiv g_0^*(\underline{\lambda}(t_0), \underline{x}(t_0)) + g_1^*(\underline{\lambda}(T)) + \int_{t_0}^{T} \ell^*(\underline{\lambda}, \underline{x}, t)\, dt \tag{10}$$

$$g_0^{*}(\underline{\lambda}(t_0), \underline{x}(t_0)) \equiv -\underline{\lambda}^T(t_0)\,\underline{x}(t_0),$$

$$g_1^{*}(\underline{\lambda}(t), \underline{x}(t)) \equiv g_1(\underline{x}(T)) + \underline{\lambda}^T(T)\,\underline{x}(T),$$

and

$$\ell^{*}(\underline{\lambda},\underline{x},t) \equiv \ell(\underline{x},\underline{\tilde{u}}(\underline{x},\underline{\lambda},t),t) - (d/dt)\left[\underline{\lambda}^T(t)\,\underline{x}(t)\right] \tag{11}$$

subject to the differential equation constraint (6) which can be written as

$$\dot{\underline{\lambda}} = f^{*}(\underline{\lambda},\underline{x},t), \tag{12}$$

$$f^{*}(\underline{\lambda},\underline{x},t) \equiv \ell_{\underline{x}}^{T}(\underline{x},\underline{\tilde{u}}(\underline{x},\underline{\lambda},t),t) - f_{\underline{x}}^{T}(\underline{x},\underline{\tilde{u}}(\underline{x},\underline{\lambda},t),t)\,\underline{\lambda}. \tag{13}$$

If the extremal of this problem provides the desired maximisation, then (10) and (12) define the dual problem. The dual Lagrangian, with $-\underline{q}(t)$ as the Lagrange multiplier, is thus

$$L^{*}(\underline{\lambda},\dot{\underline{\lambda}},\underline{x},\underline{q},t) = \ell^{*}(\underline{\lambda},\underline{x},t) - \underline{q}^T\left[\dot{\underline{\lambda}} - f^{*}(\underline{\lambda},\underline{x},t)\right] \tag{14}$$

The corresponding Euler-Lagrange equations are

$$L_{\underline{\lambda}}^{*}(\underline{\lambda},\dot{\underline{\lambda}},\underline{x},\underline{q},t) = (d/dt)\,L_{\dot{\underline{\lambda}}}^{*}(\underline{\lambda},\dot{\underline{\lambda}},\underline{x},\underline{q},t) \tag{15}$$

$$L_{\underline{x}}^{*}(\underline{\lambda},\dot{\underline{\lambda}},\underline{x},\underline{q},t) = \underline{0} \tag{16}$$

or

$$-\ell_{\underline{\lambda}}^{*}(\underline{\lambda},\underline{x},t) - \underline{q}^T f_{\underline{\lambda}}^{*}(\underline{\lambda},\underline{x},t) = \dot{\underline{q}}^T, \tag{17}$$

$$-\ell_{\underline{x}}^{*}(\underline{\lambda},\underline{x},t) = q^T f_{\underline{x}}^{*}(\underline{\lambda},\underline{x},t) \tag{18}$$

From Eqs. (11, 12) ℓ^{*} can be written as

$$\ell^{*}(\underline{\lambda},\underline{x},t) = \ell(\underline{x},\underline{u},t) - \underline{\lambda}^T f(\underline{x},\underline{\tilde{u}},t) - \underline{x}^T f^{*}(\underline{\lambda},\underline{x},t) \tag{19}$$

Thus Eq. (17) becomes

$$\dot{\underline{q}}^T = f^T(\underline{x},\underline{\tilde{u}},t) - (\underline{q}-\underline{x})^T f_{\underline{\lambda}}^{*}(\underline{\lambda},\underline{x},t) + \left[\ell_{\underline{u}}(\underline{x},\underline{\tilde{u}},t) - \underline{\lambda}^T f_u(\underline{x},\underline{u},t)\right] \underline{\tilde{u}}_{\underline{\lambda}}(\underline{x},\underline{\lambda},t). \tag{20}$$

Using Eqs. (2) and (9)

$$(d/dt)\,(\underline{q}-\underline{x})^T = -(\underline{q}-\underline{x})^T f_{\underline{\lambda}}^{*}(\underline{\lambda},\underline{x},t) \tag{21}$$

The transversality condition for this problem guarantees that

$$\underline{q}(T) = g_{1\underline{\lambda}}^{*}(\underline{\lambda}(T), \underline{x}(T)) \tag{22}$$

or

$$\underline{q}(T) = \underline{x}(T) \tag{23}$$

implying that the optimal state $\underline{x} = \hat{x}(\underline{q},t)$ satisfies

$$\underline{x}(t) = \underline{q}(t) \tag{24}$$

or the state of the primal problem is the multiplier for the dual problem and vice versa.

It is apparent that the extremals of the primal problem (1-2) and those of the problem (10-12) coincide. Moreover, by the definitions of ν and ω,

$$\nu(\underline{\bar{u}}(t)) = \omega(\underline{\hat{x}}(t)). \tag{26}$$

Thus, (10-12) is the desired dual problem. It is noted that the natural conditions of one problem are the constraints of the other. Further, it can be easily shown that the primal problem can be derived as the dual of problem (10-12).

The discussion in Pearson's [61] paper is much more involved although it is more general since he includes hard inequality constraints on the states and controls as well. There is one more point to note which is that the dual functional $[\omega(\underline{x}(t))]$ is concave without any convexity requirements on the primal functional $[\nu(\underline{\bar{u}}(t))]$.

This is a particularly useful property since the dual functional has as a result only one extremum and this extremum is of course easy to find numerically as discussed in Chapter II.

APPENDIX 3

CONVERGENCE STUDY OF THE ALGORITHM IN CHAPTER 3 SECTION 4

1. PROOF OF THEOREM (1)

To facilitate the proof let us put

$$\underline{X} = \underline{x} - \hat{\underline{x}}$$

$$\underline{U} = \underline{u} - \hat{\underline{u}}$$

and $F : \underline{X}, \underline{U} \to \underline{f}(\underline{X} + \hat{\underline{x}}, \underline{U} + \hat{u})$

Thus the necessary condition of optimality can be written in the form:

$$\underline{U} = -R^{*-1}B^T\underline{\Lambda} + R^{*-1}H\underline{U}^0 - R^{*-1}\underline{\boldsymbol{\beta}} \quad (1)$$

$$\dot{\underline{X}} = A\underline{X} + BR^{*-1}\left[-B^T\Lambda + H\underline{U}^0 \underline{\boldsymbol{\beta}}\right] + \underline{\mathfrak{D}}(\underline{X}^0, \underline{U}^0, t) \quad (2)$$

with $\underline{X}(0) = \underline{0}$

where $\mathfrak{D}(\underline{X}^0, \underline{U}^0, t) = \underline{F}(\underline{X}^0, \underline{U}^0, t) - A\underline{X}^0 - B\underline{U}^0 \quad (3)$

$$\dot{\underline{\Lambda}} = -A^T\underline{\Lambda} - Q\underline{X} - \underline{\Pi} \quad (4)$$

with $\underline{\Lambda}(T) = S\underline{X}(T) + S_2\underline{X}^0(T)$

$$\underline{X}^0 = \underline{X} \quad (5)$$

$$\underline{U}^0 = \underline{U} \quad (6)$$

$$\underline{\Pi} = Q_2\underline{X}^0 + \left[\frac{\partial \underline{F}^T}{\partial \underline{X}^0} - A^T\right]\underline{\Lambda} \quad (7)$$

$$\boldsymbol{\beta} = (R_2 + H)\underline{U}^0 - H\left[-R^{*-1}B^T\underline{\Lambda} + R^{*-1}H\underline{U}^0 - R^{*-1}\boldsymbol{\beta}\right] + \left[\frac{\partial \underline{F}^T}{\partial \underline{U}^0} - B^T\right]\underline{\Lambda} \quad (8)$$

Assuming that we are at the kth iteration, by using equation (2) and (4) we have:

$$\begin{bmatrix} \dot{\underline{X}}^k \\ \dot{\underline{\Lambda}}^k \end{bmatrix} = \begin{bmatrix} A & -BR^{*-1}B^T \\ -Q & A^T \end{bmatrix}\begin{bmatrix} \underline{X}^k \\ \underline{\Lambda}^k \end{bmatrix} + \begin{bmatrix} -A & 0 & BR^{*-1}H-B & -BR^{*-1} \\ 0 & -I & 0 & 0 \end{bmatrix}\underline{\ell}^k + \begin{bmatrix} \underline{F}^k \\ \underline{0} \end{bmatrix} \quad (9)$$

where $\underline{\ell}^{k^T} = \left[\underline{X}^{0k^T}, \underline{\Pi}^{k^T}, \underline{U}^{0k^T}, \boldsymbol{\beta}^{k^T}\right]$

The solution of equation (9) gives:

$$\begin{bmatrix} \underline{X}^k(t) \\ \underline{\Lambda}^k(t) \end{bmatrix} = \phi(t,0) \begin{bmatrix} \underline{X}^k(0) \\ \underline{\Lambda}^k(0) \end{bmatrix} + \int_0^t \phi(t,\tau)\mathfrak{F}\ell^k(\tau)d\tau + \int_0^t \phi(t,\tau) \begin{bmatrix} \underline{F}^k(\tau) \\ \underline{0} \end{bmatrix} d\tau \tag{10}$$

where $\phi = \begin{bmatrix} \phi_{11} & \phi_{12} \\ \phi_{21} & \phi_{22} \end{bmatrix}$ is the transition matrix relative to the vector $\left[\underline{X}^{k^T}(t), \underline{\Lambda}^{k^T}(t)\right]$ and $\mathfrak{F}$ is the coefficient matrix of $\underline{\ell}^k(t)$ in equation (9).

By using the transversality conditions: $\underline{\Lambda}^k(T) = S\underline{X}^k(T) + S_2\underline{X}^{0k}(T)$; $\underline{X}(0) = \underline{0}$; the initial value of the adjoint vector $\underline{\Lambda}^k(0)$ can be written as:

$$\underline{\Lambda}^k(0) = -\phi_{22}^{-1}(T,0)\{-S\underline{X}^k(T) - S_2\underline{X}^{0k}(T) + \int_0^t [\phi_{21}(T,\tau) \vdots \phi_{22}(T,\tau)]\mathfrak{F}\underline{\ell}^k(\tau)d\tau + \int_0^t \phi_{21}(T,\tau)F^k(\tau)d\tau \tag{11}$$

$$\therefore \begin{bmatrix} \underline{X}^k(t) \\ \underline{\Lambda}^k(t) \end{bmatrix} = \psi_1(t,T,0)\underline{X}^k(T) + \psi_2(t,T,0)\underline{X}^{0k}(T) + \int_0^T \psi_3(t,T,\tau)\mathfrak{F}\,\underline{\ell}^k(\tau)d\tau + \int_0^T \psi_4(t,T,\tau) \begin{bmatrix} \underline{F}^k(\tau) \\ \hline \underline{0} \end{bmatrix} d\tau \tag{12}$$

where:

$$\psi_1(t,T,0) = \begin{bmatrix} \phi_{12}(t,0) \\ \hline \phi_{22}(t,0) \end{bmatrix} \phi_{22}^{-1}(T,0)S \tag{13}$$

$$\psi_2(t,T,0) = \begin{bmatrix} \phi_{12}(t,0) \\ \hline \phi_{22}(t,0) \end{bmatrix} \phi_{22}^{-1}(T,0)S_2 \tag{14}$$

$$\psi_3(t,T,\tau) = \phi(t,\tau) - \begin{bmatrix} \phi_{12}(t,0) \\ \hline \phi_{22}(t,0) \end{bmatrix} \phi_{22}^{-1}(T,0)[\phi_{21}(T,\tau) \vdots \phi_{22}(T,\tau)] \tag{15}$$

$$\psi_4(t,T,\tau) = \phi(t,\tau) - \begin{bmatrix} \phi_{12}(t,0) \\ \phi_{22}(t,0) \end{bmatrix} \phi_{22}^{-1}(T,0)[\phi_{21}(T,\tau) \quad 0] \tag{16}$$

$$\underline{U}^{0k+1} = -R^{*-1}B^T\underline{\Lambda}^k + R^{*-1}H\underline{U}^{0k} - R^{*-1}\mathfrak{B}^k \tag{17}$$

$$\underline{\mathfrak{B}}^{k+1} = (H + R_2 - HR^{*-1}H)\underline{U}^{0k} + HR^{*-1}\underline{\mathfrak{B}}^k + p^k\underline{\Lambda}^k \tag{18}$$

where:

$$p^k = \left[HR^{*-1}B^T - B^T + \left.\frac{\partial \underline{F}^T}{\partial \underline{U}^0}\right|_{\substack{X^0=X^{0k} \\ \underline{U}^0=\underline{U}^{0k}}} \right]$$

$$\underline{\Pi}^{k+1} = Q_2\underline{X}^{0k} + C^k\underline{\Lambda}^k \tag{19}$$

$$C^k = -A^T + \left.\frac{\partial \underline{F}^T}{\partial \underline{X}^0}\right|_{\substack{\underline{X}^0=\underline{X}^{0k} \\ \underline{U}^0=\underline{U}^{0k}}}$$

Hence, one gets:

$$\begin{bmatrix} \underline{X}^{0k+1} \\ \underline{\Pi}^{k+1} \\ \underline{U}^{0k+1} \\ \underline{\mathfrak{P}}^{k+1} \end{bmatrix} = \begin{bmatrix} 0 & 0 & 0 & 0 \\ Q_2 & 0 & 0 & 0 \\ 0 & 0 & R^{*-1}H & -R^{*-1} \\ 0 & 0 & H+R_2-HR^{*-1}H & HR^{*-1} \end{bmatrix} \underline{\ell}^k + \begin{bmatrix} I & 0 \\ 0 & C^k \\ 0 & -R^{*-1}B^T \\ 0 & p^k \end{bmatrix} \begin{bmatrix} \underline{X}^k \\ \underline{\Lambda}^k \end{bmatrix} \tag{20}$$

$$\text{i.e.} \quad \underline{\ell}^{k+1} = \Gamma \underline{\ell}^k + E^k \begin{bmatrix} \underline{X}^k \\ \underline{\Lambda}^k \end{bmatrix} \tag{21}$$

where:

$$\Gamma = \begin{bmatrix} 0 & 0 & 0 & 0 \\ Q_2 & 0 & 0 & 0 \\ 0 & 0 & R^{*-1}H & R^{*-1} \\ 0 & 0 & H+R_2-HR^{*-1}H & HR^{*-1} \end{bmatrix} ; \quad E^k = \begin{bmatrix} I & 0 \\ 0 & C^k \\ 0 & -R^{*-1}B^T \\ 0 & p^k \end{bmatrix}$$

Substituting from equation (12) in (21) we get:

$$\underline{\ell}^{k+1}(t) = \Gamma \underline{\ell}^k(t) + E^k\psi_1(t,T,0)\underline{X}^k(T) + E^k\psi_2(t,T,0)\underline{X}^{0k}(T) + \int_0^T E^k\psi_3(t,T,\tau)\,\mathfrak{F}\,\underline{\ell}^k(\tau)d\tau + \int_0^T E^k\psi_4(t,T,\tau)\begin{bmatrix} \underline{F}^k(\tau) \\ \underline{0} \end{bmatrix} d\tau \tag{22}$$

let us define the length of the vector $\underline{\ell}^k(t)$ by $\left[\sup_t ||\ell^k(t)||\right]$; then:

$$\left[\sup_t ||\underline{\ell}^{k+1}(t)||\right] \leq \mu_1 \left[\sup_t ||\underline{\ell}^k(t)||\right] + \left[\sup_{t,T} ||E^k\psi_1\underline{X}^k(\tau)||\right] + \left[\sup_{t,T} ||E^k\psi_2\underline{X}^{0k}(T)||\right] + \int_0^T \left[\sup_{t,} ||E^k\psi_3\mathfrak{F}\right] \left[\sup_\tau ||\underline{\ell}^k(\tau)||\right] d\tau + \int_0^T \left[\sup_{t,\tau} ||E^k\psi_4||\right] \left[\sup_\tau ||\underline{F}^k(\tau)||\right] d\tau \tag{23}$$

where:

$$\mu_1 = \sup\{||Q_2|| \; ||\Gamma_2||\}; \quad \Gamma_2 = \begin{bmatrix} R^{*-1}H & R^{*-1} \\ H+R_2-HR^{*-1}H & HR^{*-1} \end{bmatrix}$$

let:

$$\psi_1(t,T,0) = \begin{bmatrix} \psi_{11}(t,T,0) \\ ------ \\ \psi_{12}(t,T,0) \end{bmatrix} ; \quad \psi_2(t,T,0) = \begin{bmatrix} \psi_{21}(t,T,0) \\ ------ \\ \psi_{22}(t,T,0) \end{bmatrix}$$

$$\psi_3(t,T,\ ) = \begin{bmatrix} \psi_{31}(t,T,\ ) \\ ------ \\ \psi_{32}(t,T,\ ) \end{bmatrix} ; \quad \gamma(T,0) = \left[I - \psi_1(T,0) \right]$$

Thus, from equation (12) we get:

$$\underline{X}^k(T) = \psi_{11}(T,0)\underline{X}^k(T) + \psi_{21}(T,0)\underline{X}^{0k}(T) + \int_0^T \psi_{31}(T,\tau)\mathfrak{F}\,\underline{\ell}^k(\tau)d\tau + \int_0^T \psi_{41}(T,\tau) \begin{bmatrix} \underline{F}^k(t) \\ --- \\ \underline{0} \end{bmatrix} \tau \tag{24}$$

$$\underline{X}^k(T) = \gamma^{-1}(T,0)\psi_{21}(T,0)\underline{X}^{0k}(\tau) + \int_0^T \gamma^{-1}(T,0)\psi_{31}(T,\ )\mathfrak{F}\,\underline{\ell}^k(\tau)d\tau + \int_0^T \gamma^{-1}(T,0)\psi_{41}(T,\tau) \begin{bmatrix} \underline{F}^k(\tau) \\ --- \\ \underline{0} \end{bmatrix} d\tau$$

$$E^k\psi_1\underline{X}^k(T) = E^k\psi_1\gamma^{-1}(T,0)\psi_{21}(T,0)\underline{X}^{0k}(T) + \int_0^T E^k\psi_1\gamma^{-1}(T,0)\psi_{31}(T,\tau) \times \underline{\ell}^k(\tau)d\tau + \int_0^T E^k\psi_1\gamma^{-1}(T,0)\psi_{41}(T,\tau) \begin{bmatrix} \underline{F}^k(\tau) \\ --- \\ \underline{0} \end{bmatrix} d\tau \tag{25}$$

$$\left[\sup_{t,T} ||\underline{X}^k(T)||\right] \leq \left[\sup_{t,T} ||E^k\psi_1\gamma^{-1}(T,0)\psi_{21}(T,0)\underline{X}^{0k}(T)||\right] + \int_0^T \left[\sup_{t,\tau} ||E^k\psi_1\gamma^{-1}(T,0)\psi_{31}(T,\tau\mathfrak{F})||\right] \left[\sup_t ||\underline{\ell}^k(t)||\right] d\tau + \int_0^T \left[\sup_{t,\tau} ||E^k\psi_1\gamma^{-1}(T,0)\psi_4(T,\tau)||\right] \left[\sup_\tau ||\underline{F}^k(\tau)||\right] d\tau \tag{26}$$

let ξ_i^k ; $i = 1,2$, such that

$$\left[\sup_{t,T} ||E^k\psi_1\gamma^{-1}(T,0)\psi_{21}(T,0)\underline{X}^{0k}(T)||\right] \leq \xi_1^k\, T \left[\sup_t ||\underline{\ell}^k(t)||\right] \tag{27}$$

$$\left[\sup_{t,} ||E^k\psi_1\gamma^{-1}(T,0)\psi_{31}(T,\tau\mathfrak{F}||\right] \leq \xi_2^k \tag{28}$$

Since $\underline{F}^k(T)$ is a function of $\underline{X}^{k-1}$, $\underline{U}^{k-1}$ and a bounded function of $\underline{X}$ and $\underline{U}$;

in addition since $\underline{F}(\underline{X},\underline{U}) \to 0$ if $\underline{X},\underline{U} \to 0$. Thus, there exists a bound for $[\sup||\underline{F}^k(t)||]$. Let:

$$\left[\sup_{t,\tau}||E^k\psi_1\gamma^{-1}(T,0)\psi_4(T,\tau)||\right]\left[\sup_{\tau}||\underline{F}^k(\tau)||\right] \leq \xi_3^k\left[\sup||\underline{\ell}^k(t)||\right] \tag{29}$$

Therefore, we have:

$$\left[\sup_{t,T}||\underline{X}^k(T)||\right] \leq \left[\xi_1^k + \xi_2^k + \xi_3^k\right] T\left[\sup_t||\underline{\ell}^k(t)||\right]$$
$$\leq \mu_2^k\, T\left[\sup_t||\underline{\ell}^k(t)||\right] \tag{30}$$

OR: $$\mu_2^k = \xi_1^k + \xi_2^k + \xi_3^k \tag{31}$$

Also, let:

$$\left[\sup_{t,T}||E^k\psi_2\underline{X}^{0k}(T)||\right] \tag{32}$$

$$\left[\sup_{t,\tau}||E^k\psi_3\mathcal{F}||\right] \leq \mu_4^k \tag{33}$$

and as in equation (29) let us put:

$$\left[\sup_{t,\tau}||E^k\psi_4||\right]\left[\sup_{\tau}||\underline{F}^k(\tau)\right] \leq \mu_5^k\left[\sup_t||\underline{\ell}^k(t)||\right] \tag{34}$$

hence:

$$\left[\sup_t||\underline{\ell}^{k+1}(t)||\right] \leq \left[\mu_1 + \mu_2^kT + \mu_3^kT + \mu_5^kT\right]\left[\sup_t||\underline{\ell}^k(t)||\right] \tag{35}$$

However, since $\underline{F}(\underline{X},\underline{U})$; $\dfrac{\partial\underline{F}^T}{\partial\underline{X}}$; $\dfrac{\partial\underline{F}^{T^t}}{\partial\underline{U}}$ are bounded functions of $\underline{X}$ and $\underline{U}$, the maxima of μ_i, $i = 2$ and 5 are bounded. Thus let us choose τ as:

$$\mu_1 + \left[\sum_{i=2}^{5}\mu_{i_{max}}\right]\tau = 1 \tag{36}$$

$$\tau = \frac{1-\mu_1}{\sum_{i=2}^{5}\mu_{i_{max}}} \tag{37}$$

Such a Γ exists since $\mu_1 < 1$ and independent of the initial choice of $\underline{\ell}^1(t)$.

Then for $T \in [0,\tau[$ and $t \in [0,T]$

$$\left[\sup_t\{\{\underline{\ell}^{k+1}(t)||\right] \leq \alpha\left[\sup_t||\underline{\ell}^k(t)||\right] \tag{38}$$

where $0 \leq \alpha < 1$ since $T \in [0,\tau[$ and the sequence converges to zero as $k \to \infty$.

2. PROOF OF THEOREM (2)

Consider equation (30). For $k = 1$ if $\underline{\ell}^1(t)$ is chosen in the neighbourhood of the optimal solution, then using the hypotheses (b) and (c) in Theorem (2); μ_i^1, $i = 2,\ldots 5$ are finite variables. Hence choosing T_1 such that:

$$T_1 < \Gamma \qquad \Gamma = \frac{1 - \mu_1}{\sum_{i=2}^{5} \mu_i^1} \tag{39}$$

$$\therefore \qquad \left[\sup_t ||\underline{\ell}^2(t)||\right] \leq \alpha_1 \left[\sup_t ||\underline{\ell}^1(t)||\right] \; ; \quad 0 \leq \alpha_1 < 1 \tag{40}$$

Since equation (40) is satisfied, then μ_i^2, $i = 2$ to 5 are finite. Choosing:

$$T_2 < \Gamma_2 \; ; \quad \tau_2 = \frac{1 - \mu_1}{\sum_{i=2}^{5} \mu_i^2} \tag{41}$$

$$\left[\sup_t ||\underline{\ell}^3(t)||\right] \leq \alpha_2 \left[\sup_t ||\underline{\ell}^2(t)||\right] \; ; \quad 0 \leq \alpha_2 < 1 \tag{42}$$

In general, at the kth iteration, choose T_k such that:

$$T_k < \tau_k \; ; \quad \tau_k = \frac{1 - \mu_1}{\sum_{i=2}^{5} \mu_i^k} \tag{43}$$

$$\left[\sup_t ||\underline{\ell}^{k+1}(t)||\right] \leq \alpha_k \left[\sup_t ||\underline{\ell}^k(t)||\right] \; ; \quad 0 \leq \alpha_k < 1 \tag{44}$$

Since at each iteration equation (44) is satisfied, then such $T_k > 0$, $\{k = 1,2,\ldots,\infty\}$ exists. Let

$$T = \inf_k \{T_k \; ; \; k = 1,2,\ldots,\infty\} \tag{45}$$

Thus, for an optimization horizon T and $t \in [0,T]$ the algorithm converges to the optimal solution.

Remark:

If one chooses the matrices A and B as functions of $\underline{X}^0,\underline{U}^0$ then the matrices ψ_i, $i = 1$ to 4 and the transition matrix ϕ depend on the iteration and the matrices P^k and C^k will be defined as follows:

$$P^k = HR^{*-1}B^{k^T} + \frac{\partial \underline{Z}^{k^T}}{\partial \underline{U}^{0k}} - \frac{\partial \underline{Z}_1^{k^T}}{\partial \underline{U}^{0k}} + \frac{\partial \underline{Y}^{k^T}}{\partial \underline{U}^{0k}} - \frac{\partial \underline{Y}_1^{k^T}}{\partial \underline{U}^{0k}} + \frac{\partial \underline{F}^{k^T}}{\partial \underline{U}^{0k}} \tag{46}$$

$$C^k = \frac{\partial \underline{Z}^{k^T}}{\partial \underline{X}^{0k}} - \frac{\partial \underline{Z}_1^{k^T}}{\partial \underline{X}^{0k}} + \frac{\partial \underline{Y}^{k^T}}{\partial \underline{X}^{0k}} - \frac{\partial \underline{Y}_1^{k^T}}{\partial \underline{X}^{0k}} + \frac{\partial \underline{F}^{k^T}}{\partial \underline{X}^{0k}} \tag{47}$$

where:

$$\underline{Z}^k = A(\underline{X}^{0k},\underline{U}^{0k},t)\underline{X}^k \tag{48}$$

$$\underline{Z}_1^k = A(\underline{X}^{ok},U^{0k},t)\underline{X}^{0k} \tag{49}$$

$$\underline{Y}^k = B(\underline{X}^{0k},U^{0k},t)\underline{U}^k \tag{50}$$

$$\underline{Y}_1^k = B(\underline{X}^{0k},\underline{U}^{0k},t)\underline{U}^{0k} \tag{51}$$

APPENDIX 4

CONVERGENCE STUDY OF THE ALGORITHM
BASED ON THE PREDICTION OF THE ADJOINT VECTOR IN CHAPTER 3 SECTION 6

1. PROOF OF THEOREM (1):

To facilitate the demonstration of the proof, let us do the following

$$\underline{X} = \underline{x} - \underline{\hat{x}}$$

$$\underline{U} = \underline{u} - \underline{\hat{u}}$$

and let $\underline{F} : \underline{X}, \underline{U} \rightarrow \underline{f}(X + \underline{\hat{x}}, \underline{U} + \underline{\hat{u}})$

Thus, the optimality conditions can be written as follows:

$$\underline{U} = -R^{-1}B^T\underline{\Lambda} - R^{-1}\underline{\mathfrak{B}} \quad (1)$$

$$\dot{\underline{X}} = A\underline{X} + BR^{-1}\left[-B^T\underline{\Lambda} - \underline{\mathfrak{B}}\right] + \mathfrak{D}(\underline{X}^0, U^0, t) \quad (2)$$

with $\underline{X}(0) = \underline{0}$

$$\mathfrak{D}(\underline{X}^0, \underline{U}^0, t) = \underline{F}(X, U, t) - A\underline{X}^0 - B\underline{U}^0 \quad (3)$$

$$\dot{\underline{\Lambda}} = -A^T\Lambda - QX - \underline{\Pi} ; \quad \Lambda(T) = S_2\underline{X}^0(T) + S\,\underline{X}(T) \quad (4)$$

$$\Pi = Q_2\underline{X}^0 + \left[\frac{\partial \underline{F}^T}{\partial x}\Bigg|_{\substack{\underline{X} = X^0 \\ \underline{U} = U^0}} - A^T\right]\underline{\Lambda} \quad (5)$$

$$\underline{X}^0 = \underline{X} \quad (6)$$

$$\underline{U}^0 = \underline{U} \quad (7)$$

$$\underline{\mathfrak{B}} = R_2\underline{U}^0 + \left[\frac{\partial \underline{F}^T}{\partial \underline{U}}\Bigg|_{\substack{\underline{X} = \underline{X}^0 \\ \underline{U} = \underline{U}^0}} - B^T\right]\underline{\Lambda} \quad (8)$$

Assuming that we are at the kth iteration, using equation (2) we get:

$$\underline{X}^k(t) = \int_0^t \phi(t,\tau)\,\mathfrak{F}\,\underline{\ell}^k(\tau)d\tau + \int_0^t \phi\,(t,\tau)F^k(\tau)d\tau \quad (9)$$

where
$$\frac{d\phi}{dt} = A\phi$$
$$\mathfrak{F} = \left[-B \;\vdots\; -BR^{-1} \;\vdots\; -A \;\vdots\; -BR^{-1}B^T\right]$$
$$\underline{\ell}^{kT}(t) = \left[\underline{U}^{OkT}, \underline{\beta}^{kT}, \underline{X}^{Ok}, \underline{\Lambda}^{k}\right]$$
$$\underline{F}^k(\tau) = \underline{F}(\underline{X}^{Ok}, \underline{U}^{Ok}, \tau)$$

Thus, from equation (4) one gets:

$$\underline{\Lambda}^{k+1} = \phi'(t,T)S_2X_2^{Ok}(T) + \phi'(t,T)S\,\underline{X}^k(T) + \int_t^T \phi'(\tau,t)Q\underline{X}^k(\tau)d\tau$$
$$+ \int_t^T \phi'(\tau,t)Q_2\underline{X}^{Ok}(\tau)d\tau + \int_t^T \phi'(\tau,t)\left.\frac{\partial \underline{F}^T}{\partial X}\right|_{\substack{\underline{X}=\underline{X}^{Ok}\\ \underline{U}=\underline{U}^{Ok}}} \underline{\Lambda}^k(\tau)d\tau$$
$$- \int_t^T \phi'(\tau,t)A^T\Lambda^k(\tau)d\tau \tag{10}$$

where $\phi'(t,\tau)$ is the adjoint operator of A.

Using equation (9) we have:

$$\underline{\Lambda}^{k+1}(t) = \phi'(t,T)S_2\underline{X}_2^{Ok}(T) + \int_0^T \psi_1(t,T,\tau)\ell^k(\tau)d\tau$$
$$+ \int_0^T \psi_2(t,T,\tau)F^k(\tau)d\tau + \int_0^T\int_0^\tau \psi_3(t,\tau,\nu)\ell^k(\nu)d\nu d\tau$$
$$\int_0^T\int_0^\tau \psi_4(t,\tau,\nu)\underline{F}^k(\nu)d\nu d\tau + \int_0^T \psi_5(t,\tau)\ell^k(\tau)d\tau \tag{11}$$

where
$$\psi_1(t,T,\tau) = \phi'(t,T)S\phi(T,\tau)$$
$$\psi_2(t,T,\tau) = \phi'(t,T)S\phi(T,\tau)$$
$$\psi_3(t,\tau,\nu) = \phi'(\tau,t)Q\phi(\tau,\nu)$$
$$\psi_4(t,\tau,\nu) = \phi'(\tau,t)Q\phi(\tau,\nu)$$
$$\psi_5^k(t,\tau) = \phi'(\tau,t)\left[0 \;\vdots\; 0 \;\vdots\; Q_2 \;\vdots\; \left.\frac{\partial \underline{F}^T}{\partial \underline{X}}\right|_{\substack{\underline{X}=\underline{X}^{Ok}\\ \underline{U}=\underline{U}^{Ok}}} \;\; -A^T\right]$$

Also, we have:

$$\underline{U}^{0k+1} = \underline{U}^{k}$$

$$= -R^{-1}B^T\underline{\Lambda}^k - R^{-1}\ k \quad (12)$$

$$\underline{\beta}^{k+1} = R_2\underline{U}^{0k} + P^k\underline{\Lambda}^{k+1} \quad (13)$$

where $$P^k = \begin{bmatrix} \left.\dfrac{\partial \underline{F}^T}{\partial \underline{U}}\right|_{\substack{\underline{U}=\underline{U}^0 \\ \underline{X}=\underline{X}^0}} & -B^T \end{bmatrix}$$

$$\underline{X}^{0k+1} = \underline{X}^k \quad (14)$$

From equation (9), (11), (12) to (14) we obtain:

$$\underline{\ell}^{k+1}(t) = G\,\underline{\ell}^k(t) + \underline{E}^k(t) \quad (15)$$

where $$G = \begin{bmatrix} 0 & R^{-1} & 0 & -R^{-1}B^T \\ R_2 & 0 & 0 & 0 \\ 0 & 0 & 0 & 0 \\ 0 & 0 & 0 & 0 \end{bmatrix} \; ; \quad \underline{E}^{k^T} = \left[\underline{E}_1^{k^T}, \underline{E}_2^{k^T}, \underline{E}_3^{k^T}, \underline{E}_4^{k^T}\right]$$

$$\underline{E}_1^k = \underline{0} \quad (16)$$

$$\underline{E}_2^k = P^k\,\{\phi'(t,T)S_2\underline{X}^{0k}(T) + \int_0^T \psi_1(t,T,\tau)\underline{\ell}^k(\tau)d\tau + \int_0^T \psi_2(t,T,\tau)F^k(\tau)d\tau$$

$$+ \int_0^T\int_0^\tau \psi_3(t,\tau,\nu)\underline{\ell}^k(\nu)d\nu d\tau + \int_0^T\int_0^\tau \psi_4(t,\tau,\nu)\underline{F}^k(\nu)d\nu d\tau$$

$$+ \int_0^T \psi_5^k(t,\tau)\underline{\ell}^k(\tau)d\tau\} \quad (17)$$

$$\underline{E}_3^k = \int_0^T \phi(t,\tau)\,\mathfrak{J}\,\underline{\ell}^k(\tau)d\tau + \int_0^T \phi(t,\tau)\underline{F}^k(\tau)d\tau \quad (18)$$

$$\underline{E}_4^k = \phi'(T,t)S_2X^{0k}(T) + \int_0^T \psi_1(t,T,\tau)\underline{\ell}^k(\tau)d\tau + \int_0^T \psi_2(t,T,\tau)F^k(\tau)d\tau$$

$$+ \int_0^T\int_0^T \psi_3(t,\tau,\nu)\underline{\ell}^k(\nu)\,d\nu d\tau + \int_0^T\int_0^\tau \psi_4(t,\tau,\nu)\underline{F}^k(\nu)d\nu d\tau$$

$$+ \int_0^T \psi_5^k(t,\tau)\underline{\ell}^k(\tau)d\tau \tag{19}$$

let: $\Gamma = \left[R^{-1} \;\vdots\; -R^{-1}B^T \right]$

$\mu_1 = \sup \left| \,||\Gamma||, ||R_2||\, \right|$

$\mu_2^k = \left[\sup_t ||P^k||\right]$

$\mu_3 = \left[\sup_{t,\tau,T} ||\psi(t,T,\tau)||\right]$

$\mu_4 = \left[\sup_{t,\tau,\nu} ||\psi_3(t,\tau,\nu)||\right]$

$\mu_5^k = \left[\sup_{t,\tau} ||\psi_5^k(t,\tau)||\right]$

$\mu_6 = \left[\sup_{t,\tau} ||\phi\;(t,\tau)\,\mathfrak{F}||\right]$

and let us choose the numbers μ_7^k, μ_8^k μ_9^k μ_{10}^k such that:

$$\left[\sup_{t,T} ||\phi'(T,t)S_2\underline{X}^{0k}(T)||\right] \leq \mu_7^k T \left[\sup_t ||\underline{\ell}^k(t)||\right]$$

$$\left[\sup_{t,\tau,T} ||\psi_2(t,\tau,T)\underline{F}^k(\tau)||\right] \leq \mu_8^k \left[\sup_t ||\underline{\ell}^k(t)||\right]$$

$$\left[\sup_{t,\tau,\nu} ||\psi_4(t,\tau,\nu)\underline{F}^k(\nu)||\right] \leq \mu_9^k \left[\sup_t ||\underline{\ell}^k(t)||\right]$$

$$\left[\sup_{\tau} ||\phi(t,\tau)\underline{F}^k(\tau)||\right] \leq \mu_{10}^k \left[\sup_t ||\underline{\ell}^k(t)||\right]$$

Then, by taking the norm of equation (15) we get:

$$\left[\sup||\underline{\ell}^{k+1}(t)||\right] \leqslant \{\mu_1 + (1+\mu_2^k)\left[\mu_7^k T + \mu_3 T + \mu_8^k T + \mu_4 \frac{T^2}{2}\right.$$

$$\left. + \mu_9^k \frac{T^2}{2} + \mu_5 T\right] + \mu_6 T + \mu_{10}^k T \} \quad \left[\sup_t ||\underline{\ell}^k(t)||\right] \tag{20}$$

Under the assumption that $\underline{f}(\underline{x},\underline{u}t)$, $\left[\frac{\partial \underline{f}^T}{\partial \underline{x}}\right]$, $\left[\frac{\partial \underline{f}^T}{\partial \underline{u}}\right]$ are bounded functions of $\underline{x},\underline{u}$ which implies that:

$$\underline{F}(X,U,t), \left[\frac{\partial \underline{F}^T}{\partial \underline{X}}\right], \left[\frac{\partial \underline{F}^T}{\partial \underline{U}}\right]$$

are also bounded functions of $\underline{X}$ and $\underline{U}$, then the numbers μ_2^k,μ_5^k,μ_i^k i=7 to 10 are independent of the initialisation. (We note that if A,B are chosen such that:

$$A_i = \frac{\partial \underline{F}_i^T}{\partial \underline{X}_i^{Ok}}, \quad B_i = \left[\frac{\partial \underline{F}_i^T}{\partial \underline{U}_i^{Ok}}\right]$$

μ_i ; i=2 to 10 have also maximum finite values.)

Choosing T_1 such that:

$$\mu_1 + \left[(1+\mu_{2_{max}})(\mu_{7_{max}} + \mu_3 + \mu_{8_{max}} + \mu_{5_{max}}) + \mu_6 + \mu_{10_{max}}\right] T_1$$

$$+ \left[(1+\mu_{2_{max}})(0.5\mu_4 + 0.5\mu_{9_{max}})\right] T_1^2 = 1$$

or $$aT_1^2 + bT_1 + C = 0 \tag{21}$$

where $a = (1+\mu_{2_{max}})(0.5\mu_4 + 0.5\mu_{9_{max}}$

$b = (1+\mu_{2_{max}})(\mu_{7_{max}} + \mu_3 + \mu_8 + \mu_{5_{max}} + \mu_6 + \mu_{10_{max}}$

$c = \mu_1 - 1$

$$T_1 = \frac{-b + \sqrt{b^2 - 4ac}}{2a}$$

Therefore for $T_1 > 0$, C must be -ive, i.e. $\mu_1 < 1$

Thus, by choosing $T \varepsilon [0, T_1 |$ and for $t \varepsilon [0,T]$, the algorithm converges to the optimal solution since for each iteration the condition

$$\left[\sup_t ||\underline{\ell}^{k+1}(t)||\right] \leqslant \alpha \left[\sup_t ||\underline{\ell}^{k}(t)||\right] \quad ; 0 \leqslant \alpha < 1 \tag{22}$$

is satisfied.

One can see easily from equation (5) that if $\underline{X}^0 \to \underline{0}$, $\underline{A} \to \underline{0}$ then $\underline{\Pi} \to \underline{0}$

PROOF OF THEOREM (2):

Assuming that k=1 and choosing τ_1^1 such that:

$$\tau_1^1 \ \varepsilon \ \left[0, T_1^1\right[\quad \text{where } T_1^1 = \frac{-b_1 + \sqrt{b_1^2 - 4a_1c_1}}{2a_1}$$

This value of T_1^1 exists since:

a) $\mu_1 < 1$

b) $\underline{\ell}^1(t)$ is chosen in the neighbourhood of the optimal and hence $\mu_i < \infty$ (i = 2 to 10 ; i ≠ 6) from the hypothesis (a) and (b) of the theorem.

Therefore, for an optimization horizon τ_1^1 :

$$\left[\sup_t ||\underline{\ell}^{2}(t)||\right] \leqslant \alpha \quad \left[\sup_t ||\underline{\ell}^{1}(t)||\right] ; 0 \leqslant \alpha_1 < 1 \tag{23}$$

Since (23) is satisfied, then the values of μ_i^2(i=2 to 10, i≠6) are still finite ;choosing

$$\tau_1^2 \ \varepsilon \ \left|0, T_1^2\right| \quad \text{where } T_1^2 = \frac{-b_2 + \sqrt{b^2 - 4a_2c_2}}{2a_2}$$

Thus for this value of τ_1^2 we have:

$$\left[\sup_t ||\underline{\ell}^3(t)||\right] \leqslant \alpha_2 \left[\sup_t ||\underline{\ell}^2(t)||\right]; \; 0 \leqslant \alpha_2 < 1 \qquad (24)$$

In general, at the kth iteration, one chooses

$\tau_1^k \; \varepsilon \left[0, \Gamma_1^k\right[$ with $T_1^k = \dfrac{-b_k + \sqrt{b_k^2 - 4a_k c_k}}{2a_k}$. Then

$$\left[\sup_t ||\underline{\ell}^k(t)||\right] \leqslant \alpha_k \left[\sup_t ||\underline{\ell}^k(t)||\right] \; ; \; 0 \leqslant \alpha < 1 \qquad (25)$$

Since for each iteration we choose τ_1^k satisfying the inequality (25), then at the next iteration $\tau_1^{k+1} > 0$ and $\tau = \inf_k \{T_k \; ; \; k=1,2,\ldots\infty\} > 0$ exists. Thus, for an optimization horizon $T \leqslant \tau$, the algorithm converges to the optimal solution.

R E F E R E N C E S

1. Cole, J.D. and Sage, A.P. "Multi-person decision analysis in large-scale hierarchical systems - team decision theory", International Journal of Control, Vol. 22, 1, p. 1-28, 1975.

2 Lasdon, L.S. "Optimisation theory for large systems". MacMillan, New York, 1970.

3 Varaiya, P. "Decomposition of large systems" in "Systems Theory", Zadeh, L. and Polak, P. (editors), McGraw-Hill, 1969.

4 Bellman, R. "Dynamic Programming", Princeton University Press, 1957.

5 Pontryagin, L.S., Boltyanski, V.G., Gamrelidze, R.V. and Mischenko, E.F. "Mathematical theory of optimal processes". English translation, Wiley, New York, 1962.

6 Mesarovic, M.D., Macko, D. and Takahara, Y. "Theory of hierarchical multi-level systems", Academic Press, New York, 1970.

7 Pearson J.D., "Dynamic decomposition techniques", in "Optimisation methods for large scale systems", D.A. Wismer (editor) McGraw-Hill, 1971.

8 Smith, N.J. and Sage, A.P. "An introduction to hierarchical systems theory" Computers and Electrical Engineering, vol. 1, p. 55-71, 1973.

9 Titli, A. "Contribution à l'étude des structures de commande hiérarchisées en vue de l'optimisation des processus complexes", Thèse d'Etat, n° 495, Toulouse, France, 1972.

10 Tamura, H. "Decentralised optimisation for distributed-lag models of discrete systems",Automatica, vol. 11, 6, p. 593-602, 1975.

11 Tamura, H. "A discrete dynamic model with distributed transport delays and its hierarchical optimisation to preserve stream quality", IEEE Trans. Syst. Man and Cybernetics, vol.SMC 4, p. 424-429, 1974.

12 Takahara, Y. "A multi-level structure for a class of dynamical optimisation problems", M.S.Thesis, Case Western Reserve University, Cleveland, USA, 1965.

13 Singh, M.G.,"Some applications of hierarchical control for dynamical systems" University of Cambridge, Ph.D.Thesis, 1973.

14 Singh, M.G., Drew, S. and Coales, J.F. "A comparison of practical hierarchical control methods for interconnected dynamical systems", Automatica, vol.11, 4, p. 331-350, 1975.

15 Singh, M.G. "Practical methods for the control and state estimation of large interconnected dynamical systems", Revue Française d'Automatique, Informatique et Recherche Opérationnelle, J3, p. 5-45, 1974.

16 Singh, M.G. "Hierarchical strategies for the on-line control of urban road traffic signals", Proc.IFIP Symposium on Optimisation Techniques, Rome, May 1973 (Springer Verlag, 1974).

17 Singh, M.G. and Tamura, H. "Modelling and hierarchical optimisation for oversaturated urban road traffic networks", International Journal of Control vol. 20, p. 913-934, 1974.

18 Singh, M.G. and Hassan M. "A comparison of two hierarchical optimisation methods" International Journal of Systems Science, vol. 7, 6, 603-611, 1976.

19 Singh, M.G., Titli, A.,and Galy, J. "A method for improving the efficiency of the Goal Coordination method for large dynamical systems with state variable coupling", Computers and Electrical Engineering, vol. 2, 4, p. 339-346, 1976.

20 Titli, A., Galy, J. and Singh, M.G. "Méthodes de décomposition-coordination en calcul des variations et couplage par variables des états", Revue Française d'Automatique, Informatique et Recherche Opérationnelle, J4, December 1975.

21 Singh, M.G. "A new algorithm for the on-line control of large interconnected systems with fast dynamics", International Journal of Control, vol. 21, 4, pp. 587-597, 1975.

22 Singh, M.G., Hassan, M. and Calvet , J.L. "Hierarchical optimisation of non-linear systems with application to a synchronous machine", International Journal of Systems Science , vol. 7, 9, 1041-1051, 1976.

23 Singh, M.G. and Galy, J. "A note on the convergence of infeasible dynamical hierarchical controllers", International Journal of Systems Science, vol. 6, 8, pp. 701-711, 1975.

24 Hassan, M. and Singh, M.G. "A hierarchical model follower for certain non-linear systems", International Journal of Systems Science, vol. 7, 7, 727-730, 1976.

25 Hassan, M. and Singh, M.G. "The hierarchical control of a synchronous machine using a model follower", Automatica, March 1977.

26 Singh, M.G. and Hassan, M. "A closed loop hierarchical solution for the continuous time river pollution control problem", Automatica, vol. 12, May 1976.

27 Singh, M.G. and Titli, A. "Closed loop hierarchical control for non-linear systems using quasi-linearisation", Proc. 6th IFAC World Congress, Boston 1975. Also Automatica, vol. 11, pp. 541-546, 1975.

28 Singh, M.G. and Titli, A. "Hierarchical feedback control for large dynamical systems", International Journal of Systems Science, 8, 1, 31-47, 1977.

29 Singh, M.G. "A feedback solution for the large scale infinite stage discrete time regulator and servo-mechanism problems", Computers and Electrical Engineering, vol. 3, 93-99, 1976.

30 Cheneveaux, B. "Contribution à l'optimisation hiérarchisée des systèmes dynamiques", Doctor Engineer Thesis, n°4, Nantes, France, 1972.

31 Cohen G., Benveniste, A. and Bernhard, P. "Commande hiérarchisée avec coordination en ligne d'un système dynamique", Revue Française d'Automatique, Informatique et Recherche Opérationnelle, J4, pp. 77-101, 1972.

32 Singh, M.G. and Coales, J.F. "A heuristic approach to the hierarchical control of multivariable serially connected dynamical systems", International Journal of Control, vol. 21, 4, pp. 575-585, 1975.

33 Eaglen, C.J., Singh, M.G. and Coales, J.F. "A hierarchical strategy for the temperature control of a hot steel roughing process", Automatica, vol. 9, 2 pp. 209-222, 1973.

34 Tamura, H., "Decomposition techniques in large scale systems with applications", Systems and Control, vol. 17, 6, 1973 (in Japanese).

35 Geoffrion, A.M. "Duality in non-linear programming", SIAM Review, vol. 13, 1, pp. 1-37, 1971.

36 Fallside, F. and Perry, P. "Hierarchical optimisation of a water supply network", Proc. IEE vol. 122, 2, pp. 202-208, 1975.

37 Cohen, G., Benveniste, A. and Bernhard, P. "Coordination algorithms for optimal control problems Part I", Report N° A/57, Centre d'Automatique, Ecole des Mines, Paris 1974.

38 Varaiya, P. "A decomposition technique for non-linear programming", Dept. of Electrical Engineering, University of California, Berkeley, Unpublished Report, 1969.

39 Noton, A.R.M. "Variational methods in control engineering", Pergamon Press, Oxford, 1965.

40 Webster, F.V. and Cobb, B.M. "Traffic signals", Road Research Technical Paper 56, Her Majesty's Stationary Office, 1966.

41 Beck, M.B. "The application of control and systems theory to problems of river pollution", University of Cambridge, Ph.D. Thesis, 1974.

42 Singh, M.G. "River pollution control", International Journal of Systems Science, vol. 6, pp. 9-21, 1975.

43 Young, P., Beck, M.B. and Singh, M.G. "The modelling and control of pollution in a river system ", Proc. IFAC Symposium on Water Resource Systems, Haifa, 1973.

44 Bauman, E.J. "Multi-level optimisation techniques with application to trajectory decomposition", Advances in Control Systems, 6, pp. 160-222, 1968.

45 Whittle, P. "Optimisation under constraints", Wiley - Interscience, London, 1971.

46 Mukhopadhayay, B.K. and Malik, O.P. "Optimal control of synchronous machine excitation by quasi-linearisation", Proc. IEE, vol. 119, 1, pp. 91-98, 1972.

47 Hassan, M. and Singh, M.G. "Optimisation of non-linear systems using a new two-level method", Automatica, vol. 12, 359-363, 1976.

48 Calvet, J.L. "Optimisation par calcul hiérarchisée et coordination en ligne des systèmes dynamiques de grande dimension", Doctor of Control Eng., Thesis n° 1824, Toulouse, France 1976.

49 Singh, M.G., Hassan, M. and Titli, A. "Multi-level control of interconnected dynamical systems using the prediction principle", IEEE Trans. Syst. Man and Cyb., vol. SMC 6, 233-239, 1976.

50 Kendric, D.A., Rao, H.S. and Wells, C.H. "Optimal operation of a system of waste treatment facilities", Proc. IEEE Symposium on Adaptive Processes, Austin, Texas, 1970.

51 Javdan, R. "Extension of dual coordination to a class of non-linear systems", International Journal of Control, Dec. 1976.

52 Simmons, M. "The decentralised profit maximisation of interconnected production systems", Cambridge University Engineering Department Report CUED/F Control/TR101, 1975.

53 Arafeh, S. and Sage, A.P. "Multi-level discrete time system identification in large scale systems", International Journal of Systems Science, vol. 5, 8, pp. 753-791, 1974.

54 Arafeh, S. and Sage, A.P. "Hierarchical system identification of states and parameters in interconnected power systems", International Journal of Systems Science, vol.5, 9, pp. 817-846, 1974.

55 Sage, A.P. "Optimum systems control", Prentice Hall Inc., 1968.

56 McGill, R. and Kenneth, "A convergence theorem on the iterative solution of non-linear two point boundary value systems",Proc XIV Int. Astronautical Congress, Paris, 1963.

57 Gibson, J.A. and Lowinger, J.F. "A predictive Min-H method to improve convergence to optimal solutions", International Journal of Control, vol. 19, 3, pp. 575-592, 1974.

58 Sew Hoy, W. and Gibson, J.A. "An extension of the predictive min H method to multivariable control", International Journal of Control, vol. 21, 5, pp. 353-373, 1975.

59 Bryson, A.E. and Ho, Y. "Applied optimal control", Blaisdell, New York, 1969.

60 Fuller, A.T. "Optimal non-linear control of systems with pure delays", International Journal of Control, vol. 8, 2, pp. 155-169, 1968.

61 Pearson, J.D. "Reciprocity and duality in control programming problems", Systems Research Center Report (no number given), Case Western Reserve University, Cleveland, Ohio, 1965.

62 Drew, S. "Hierarchical control methods with applications to managerial problems", University of Cambridge , Ph.D. Thesis, 1975

63 Aoki, M. "Control of large scale dynamic systems by aggregation" IEEE Trans. on Auto. Control, vol. AC-13, 3, pp. 246-253, 1968.

64 Kokotovic, P.V.and Sannuti, P. "Singular perturbation methods for reducing the model order in optimal design", IEEE Trans. Auto. Control, vol. AC-13, 4, pp. 377-384, 1968.

65 Kokotovic, P.V. "Feedback design of large linear systems", in J.B. Cruz Jr. (editor) "Feedback systems", McGraw-Hill, New York, 1972.

66 Desoer , C.A. and Shensa, M. "Networks with very small and very large parasitics", Report ERL-M 276, Electronics Research Laboratory, University of California at Berkeley, 1970.

67 Wang, F. "Suboptimisation of decentralised control systems", University of Minnesota, Ph.D. thesis, 1972.

68 Milne, R.D. "The analysis of weakly coupled dynamic systems", International Journal of Control, vol. 2, 2, pp. 171-199, 1965.

69 Kleinman, D.L. and Athens, M. "The design of suboptimal linear time-varying systems", IEEE Trans. on Auto. Control, vol. AC 13, 2, pp. 150-159, 1968.

70 Eaglen, C.J. "Hybrid and digital simulation techniques developed for control system and plant performance studies for a hot strip rolling mill", University of Cambridge, Ph.D. thesis, 1971.

71 Kalman, R.E. "New methods and results in linear prediction and filtering theory", Technical Report n° 61-1, R.I.A.S., 1961.

72 Joseph, P.D. and Tou, J.T. "On linear control theory", Trans. AIEE (Appl. and Industry) vol. 80, pp. 193-196, 1961.

73 Cox, H. "On the estimation of state variables and parameters for noisy dynamical systems", IEEE Trans. on Auto. Control, vol. AC 7, pp. 5-12, 1964.

74 Shah, M.M. "Suboptimal filtering theory for interacting control systems", Ph.D. thesis, University of Cambridge 1971.

75 Singh, M.G. "Multi-level state estimation " International Journal of Systems Science, vol. 6, pp. 533-555, 1975.

76 Singh, M.G. "A decentralised filter for certain time-lag systems", Chapter 17 in D.J. Bell's "Recent Mathematical Developments in Control", Academic Press, 1973.

77 Chong, C.Y. and Athens, M. "On the periodic coordination of linear stochastic systems", Proc. 6th IFAC World Congress, Boston, 1975.

78 Noton, A.R.M. "A two-level form of the Kalman filter", IEEE Trans. on Auto. Control, vol. AC 16, 2, pp. 128-132,1971.

79 Simon, K.W. and Stubberud, A.R. "Duality of linear estimation and control" Journal of Optimisation Theory and Applications, vol. 6, 1, pp. 55-67, 1970.

80 Hanson, M.A. "Bounds of functionally convex optimal control problems",Journal of Applied Mathematical Analysis and Applications, vol. 8, 1, 1964.

81 Bliss, G.A. "Lectures on the calculus of variations", University of Chicago Press, 1946.

82 Fan, L.T. and Wang, C.S. "The discrete maximum principle" John Wiley and Sons, New York, 1964.

83 Hassan, M. and Singh, M.G. "A two level costate prediction algorithm for non-linear systems", Automatica 1977 (to appear).

84 Singh, M.G. and Hassan, M. "Hierarchical optimisation of non-linear dynamical systems with non separable cost functions". Automatica (to appear)

85 Singh, M.G. and Hassan, M. "A two level prediction algorithm for non-linear systems", Automatica, Janv. 1977.

86 Meditch, J. "Stochastic optimal linear estimation and control", McGraw-Hill, 1969.

87 Kirk, D. "Optimal control theory " Prentice Hall, 1970.

88 Galy, J. "Optimisation dynamique par quasilinearisation et commande hierarchisée", Thèse de specialite number 1495, Toulouse 1973

89 Falb, P.L. and De Jong, J.L. "Some successive approximisation methods in control and oscillation theory", Academic Press, New York, 1969

90 Kelly H.J. "Method of gradients" in "optimisation techniques with application to aerospace systems", G. Leitmann (editor), Academic Press, New York, 1962

91 Bellman, R.E. and Kalaba, R. "Quasilinearisation and non-linear boundary value problems" in "Modern analytical and computational methods in Science and Mathematics", Elsevier, New York, 1965

92 Geoffrion, A.M. "Elements of large scale mathematical programming parts I and II", Management Science, vol. 16,11, 1970

93 Singh, M., Hassan, M. and Calvet, J.L. "Simplifying the control of certain non-linear systems using hierarchical optimization", Computers and Electrical Engineering, vol. 3, 215-225, 1976

94 Hassan, M.F. "Optimisation et commande hierarchisée des systemes dynamiques interconnectes", Thèse d'état (Sciences) number 814, Toulouse, 1978

95 Wismer, D. (editor) "Optimisation methods for large scale systems with applications", McGraw Hill, New York, 1971

96 Singh, M.G. and Titli, A. "Systems : Decomposition, Optimisation and Control", Pergamon Press, Oxford, 1978

97 Mahmoud, M.S., Vogt, N. and Mickle, M. "Multi-level control and optimisation using generalised gradients", Int. J. Control, 25, 4, 525-543, 1977

98 Hassan, M.F., Hurteau, R., Singh, M.G. and Titli, A. "A three-level costate prediction algorithm for continuous dynamical systems", Automatica, 1978

99 Jamshidi, M. "Optimal control of non-linear power systems by an imbedding method", Automatica, vol. 11, 633-636, 1975

100 Javdan, M. "On the use of Lagrange duality in multi-level optimal control", Proc. IFAC LSSTA Symposium, Udine, 1976

101 Hassan, M., Hurteau, R., Singh, M. and Titli, A. "A new three-level algorithm for river pollution control", Proc. IFAC Symposium on Systems Approaches to Development, Cairo, 1977

102 Hassan, M. and Singh, M.G. "Hierarchical successive approximation algorithms for non-linear systems : parts I and II", Control Systems Centre Reports, 465, 466, UMIST, 1979

103 Hassan, M., Salut, G., Singh, M.G. and Titli, A. "A decentralised computational algorithm for the global Kalman filter", IEEE Trans. AC-23, 2, 262-268, 1978

104 Luenburger, D. "Optimisation by vector space methods", New York, Wiley, 1969

105 Darwish, M. and J. Fantin, "Application of Lyapunov methods to large power systems using decomposition and aggregation techniques", Int. J. Control, 1978

106 Witsenhausen, S. "A counter example in stochastic optimal control", SIAM J. of Control, 6, 1, 1968

107 Mahmoud, M., Hassan, M. and Singh, M.G. "A new hierarchical approach to the joint problem of systems identification and optimisation", LSS,1, 1980

108 Wismer, D., Perrine, R. and Haimes, Y. "Modelling and identification of aquifer systems of high dimension", Water Resources Research

109 Haimes, Y. and Wismer, D. "Integrated systems identification and optimisation via quasilinearisation", JOTA, 8, 2, 100-109, 1971

110 Haimes, Y. "Decompositions and multi-level techniques for water quality control", Water Resources Research, 8, 3, 779-784, June, 1972

111 Haimes, Y. and Wismer, D. "A computational approach to the combined problem of optimisation and parameter identification", Automatica, 6,1, 77-86, 1980

112 Geoffrion, A.M. "Solving bicriterion mathematical programs", Operations Research, 15, 1, 39-54, 1967

113 Singh, M.G. and Titli, A. (editors) "Handbook of large scale systems engineering applications", North-Holland, 1977